Democracy and Civil Society in a Global Era

Democracy and Civil Society in a Global Era addresses institutional and societal barriers to building a more active and engaged citizenry. It examines the challenges to fostering a culture of peace and non-violence, to the lessening of fear and insecurity, and to leading more dignified lives in regions as diverse as the Indian subcontinent, Malaysia, Indonesia, Turkey, Iran, China, the Middle East, Nigeria, and the EU, with a focus on the commonality and universality of the obstacles faced by regions around the globe.

Presenting a dynamic combination of theory and field research, this book demonstrates how social movements can introduce and strengthen equality, inclusion, accountability, and the free flow of information—and how these elements, in turn, contribute to the acculturation of freedom and social justice in both the developed and developing worlds. Rather than another vague exploration of ideas and processes, this is a book about action, and will be required reading for policymakers, think tanks, and development practitioners.

Scott Nicholas Romaniuk is a Ph.D. Candidate in International Studies at the University of Trento and Affiliate Researcher at the Bruno Kessler Foundation, Italy.

Marguerite Marlin is a Ph.D. Candidate in Comparative Public Policy, at McMaster University in Hamilton, Canada.

PUBLIC ADMINISTRATION AND PUBLIC POLICY
A Comprehensive Publication Program

EDITOR-IN-CHIEF

DAVID H. ROSENBLOOM
Distinguished Professor of Public Administration
American University, Washington, DC

Founding Editor

JACK RABIN

RECENTLY PUBLISHED BOOKS

Democracy and Civil Society in a Global Era, Scott Nicholas Romaniuk and Marguerite Marlin

Development and the Politics of Human Rights, Scott Nicholas Romaniuk and Marguerite Marlin

Public Administration and Policy in the Caribbean, Indianna D. Minto-Coy and Evan Berman

The Economic Survival of America's Isolated Small Towns, Gerald L. Gordon

Public Administration and Policy in the Caribbean, Indianna D. Minto-Coy and Evan Berman

Sustainable Development and Human Security in Africa: Governance as the Missing Link, Louis A. Picard, Terry F. Buss, Taylor B. Seybolt, and Macrina C. Lelei

Information and Communication Technologies in Public Administration: Innovations from Developed Countries, Christopher G. Reddick and Leonidas Anthopoulos

Creating Public Value in Practice: Advancing the Common Good in a Multi-Sector, Shared-Power, No-One-Wholly-in-Charge World, edited by John M. Bryson, Barbara C. Crosby, and Laura Bloomberg

Digital Divides: The New Challenges and Opportunities of e-Inclusion, Kim Andreasson

Living Legends and Full Agency: Implications of Repealing the Combat Exclusion Policy, G.L.A. Harris

Politics of Preference: India, United States, and South Africa, Krishna K. Tummala

Crisis and Emergency Management: Theory and Practice, Second Edition, Ali Farazmand

Labor Relations in the Public Sector, Fifth Edition, Richard C. Kearney and Patrice M. Mareschal

Democracy and Public Administration in Pakistan, Amna Imam and Eazaz A. Dar

The Economic Viability of Micropolitan America, Gerald L. Gordon

Personnel Management in Government: Politics and Process, Seventh Edition, Katherine C. Naff, Norma M. Riccucci, and Siegrun Fox Freyss

Public Administration in South Asia: India, Bangladesh, and Pakistan, edited by Meghna Sabharwal and Evan M. Berman

Making Multilevel Public Management Work: Stories of Success and Failure from Europe and North America, edited by Denita Cepiku, David K. Jesuit, and Ian Roberge

There is a vast and burgeoning literature on "democracy" and "modernity" and their links to "civilized values", and this project became even more urgent after the events of 9/11. Much of this work presents only a partial, inevitably western-centric view. This latest volume adopts a broader, global perspective. Bringing together some of the leading theorists in the field of democracy studies, the book explores less familiar approaches; in the process, it raises and seeks to answer highly pertinent questions. An impressive and refreshing addition to the field, it is likely to appeal to researchers, students and those with a need to know what can be done differently.

Maria Holt, University of Westminster, UK

This book is a must-read for anyone interested in understanding the complex socio-economic and political matrix in a Global Era. The collection of works is representative of truly transnational issues. Immigration and human trafficking, democratization for peace and security, active citizenship, role of civil society, political corruption, and ethnic diversity are some of the many issues addressed in the book. Readers will be enthralled by the richness of the collection of articles and case studies.

Hasnat Dewan, Fulbright scholar and award-winning professor
of Economics, Thompson Rivers University, Canada

Democracy and Civil Society in a Global Era

Edited by
Scott Nicholas Romaniuk
and Marguerite Marlin

 Routledge
Taylor & Francis Group

NEW YORK AND LONDON

First published 2016
by Routledge
711 Third Avenue, New York, NY 10017

and by Routledge
2 Park Square, Milton Park, Abingdon, Oxon OX14 4RN

Routledge is an imprint of the Taylor & Francis Group, an informa business

Library of Congress Cataloging in Publication Data
Names: Romaniuk, Scott Nicholas, editor. | Marlin, Marguerite, editor.
Title: Democracy and civil society in a global era/edited by Scott Nicholas
Romaniuk and Marguerite Marlin.
Description: New York: Routledge, 2016. | Includes bibliographical references
and index.
Identifiers: LCCN 2015040280| ISBN 9781498707039 (hardback: alk. paper)
| ISBN 9781315630366 (ebook)
Subjects: LCSH: Democracy—Case studies. | Civil society—Case studies |
Globalization—Political aspects—Case studies. | World politics—1989—
Case studies.
Classification: LCC JC423 .D397827 2016 | DDC 321.8—dc23
LC record available at http://lccn.loc.gov/2015040280

ISBN: 978-1-4987-0703-9 (hbk)
ISBN: 978-1-315-63036-6 (ebk)

Typeset in Goudy and Optima
by Florence Production Ltd, Stoodleigh, Devon, UK

Printed and bound in the United States of America by Publishers Graphics,
LLC on sustainably sourced paper.

Contents

Illustrations

Figures

Tables

Notes on Editors

Scott Nicholas Romaniuk is a Ph.D. Candidate in International Studies at the University of Trento, School of International Studies. He holds an MRes in Political Research from the University of Aberdeen, School Politics and International Relations, a BA in History, and German Language and Literature from the University of Alberta, and a Certificate in Terrorism Studies from the University of St. Andrews, Handa Centre for the Study of Terrorism and Political Violence (CSTPV). He is a recipient of the Fondazione Bruno Kessler (FBK) PhD grant focused on "International Politics and Conflict Resolution," and is a Junior Affiliate of the Canadian Network for Research on Terrorism, Security, and Society (TSAS). His research focuses on asymmetric warfare, counterterrorism, international security, and foreign policy. He is a native speaker of English and is proficient in German and French. Email: scott.romaniuk@unitn.it.

Marguerite Marlin is a Ph.D. Candidate in Political Science (Comparative Public Policy) at McMaster University in Hamilton. She specializes in comparative legislatures, non-governmental influence on public policy, and Arctic affairs. She previously completed an MA in European, Russian, and Eurasian Studies at Carleton University in Ottawa and continues to provide analysis on Canadian–Russian relations and Ukrainian constitutional reform at speaking engagements associated with the Canadian International Council and others. She was a Young Researcher at the Northern Research Forum's Open Assembly in 2014 and has had written works featured in a variety of academic and non-academic publications. Email: margueritemarlin@gmail.com.

Notes on Contributors

Kudus Adebayo is a graduate student at the Department of Sociology, University of Ibadan in Ibadan, Nigeria. He holds a BA in Philosophy and an MSc degree in Sociology from the same university and was in 2014 a short-term scholar at Brown International Advance Research Institutes (BIARI), Watson Institute for International Development, Brown University, RI, United States. A recipient of the prestigious Postgraduate School Scholarship of University of Ibadan, his ongoing dissertation focuses on the dispersal and formation of Nigerian trade diaspora in Guangzhou, China. Kudus has conducted research and published works on unequal globalization, social protest, migration, and livelihood. Email: kudus_adebayo @biari.brown.edu/oluwatoyinkudus@gmail.com.

Sayed Javed Ahmad is Chief Executive Officer (CEO) of the Bangladesh Rating Agency Limited (BDRAL) in Dhaka, Bangladesh, and has a Master of Public Affairs (MPA) in Governance and Public Policy (GPP) from the Civil Service College at the University of Dhaka in Bangladesh. He also has a Master of Business Administration (MBA) in Digital Technology Management (DTM) from Royal Roads University in Victoria, Canada, and was Assistant Professor and Head of the Department of Computer Science and Information Technology (CSIT) at Southern University Bangladesh from 2005 to 2007.

Dr. Abhilash Babu is Assistant Professor at the Department of Rural Management in the School for Management studies at Babasaheb Bhimrao Ambedkar Central University in Lucknow, India. He received his MPhil and Ph.D. from the Centre for Studies in Science Policy of Jawaharlal Nehru University (JNU) New Delhi, India. He has also published a number of articles on water rights and community participation in national and international journals, and his research interest includes water governance, participatory development, and policy studies.

Barbara Buraczynska is a Ph.D. candidate at the Politics Department at the University of Sheffield, where she has also been awarded her MA (Hons) in Politics and Research Methods and BA (Hons) in International Relations and Politics. Her current research focuses on the relationship between foreign military conflict and power centralization within the state, with a special focus on developing a theory of how various forms of authoritarian regimes respond to military crises. Other areas of interest include humanitarian intervention, just war theory, international security, political psychology, and animal rights theory. Her primary research is quantitative in nature, using tools such as event history analysis and structural equations modeling. In 2012, Barbara was awarded an Economic and Social Research Council scholarship for the course of her postgraduate studies.

Eugenio Dacrema is a Ph.D. Student at the University of Trento. His research focuses on the history of economic relations between the European Union and North African countries, analyzing the socioeconomic effects sparked by such relations in Egypt and Tunisia. He is also involved in research programs of various organizations analyzing Islamic fundamentalism from a socioeconomic perspective. In addition to his research activities, he periodically writes for several Italian national newspapers such as *Corriere della Sera*, *Il Foglio*, *Limes*, *Formiche*, and *Linkiesta*. Furthermore, he writes and edits a blog focused on the Mediterranean region of the Italian think tank ISPI.

Dr. Caroline Fielder is a Lecturer in Chinese Studies at the University of Leeds, UK. A specialist in researching the interface between religion and the development of contemporary Chinese society (particularly through the development of religiously inspired social service organizations), she has previously spent three years working for a Chinese nonprofit organization on education programs in northern Jiangxi province, and eight years working as Director of China Desk for CTBI—the national ecumenical council of Britain and Ireland.

Munafrizal Manan is a Lecturer at the University of Al-Azhar Indonesia, Jakarta. He obtained a Master of Political Science from Gadjah Mada University, Indonesia; a Master of International Politics from the University of Melbourne, Australia; and a Master of Law in International Law of Human Rights and Criminal Justice from Utrecht University, the Netherlands. He has published four books on Indonesian politics and law, as well as various articles on Indonesian newspapers and magazines. His articles and book reviews have appeared in *Journal of Politics and Law*, *Bulletin of Indonesian Economic Studies*, *Asian Journal of Comparative Law*, *Multiversa: Journal of International Studies*, and *Jurnal Ilmiah Hubungan Internasional*. Email: munafrizal2003@yahoo.com.

Benoît Masset is a European Governance master's student at Luxembourg University. He has a bachelor's degree in European Studies from Maastricht University (Netherlands). His research interests span the fields of European and international affairs, and human rights and Southeast Asia (ASEAN). He specializes in Mediterranean European states and has participated in exchange programs at Salamanca University (Spain) and the Università degli studi di Trento (Italy). He is a native speaker of French and is proficient in English, Spanish, and Italian.

Sorin Mitrea is a Ph.D. Candidate in Comparative Public Policy in the Department of Political Science at McMaster University and a member of the Austerity Research Group (ARG). His research focuses on the intersection of political economy, labor market policy, social construction, and their effect on understandings of politics and political participation in advanced industrial states. The author would like to acknowledge research support from SSHRC Canada. Email: mitreasi@mcmaster.ca.

Dr. Muhammad Mushtaq is the Head of the Department of Political Science and International Relations at the University of Gujrat in Punjab, Pakistan. He is a specialist in comparative politics, elections, public opinion and voting behavior, federalism, and inter-governmental relations, and has had a number of scholarly publications on these topics. He holds a Ph.D. in Political Science from Bahauddin Zakariya University in Multan, Pakistan.

Emeka Thaddues Njoku is a Ph.D. Candidate in the Department of Political Science, University of Ibadan, Nigeria. His research foci include terrorism, counterterrorism, civil society, and development studies. He is a fellow of the Social Science Research Council (SSRC) in New York and the Institut de Recherche français en Afrique (IFRA) in Ibadan, Nigeria. He is an Academic Advisor in the Department of Political Science, University of Ibadan Distance Learning Centre, Ibadan, Nigeria, and a Contributing Analyst for Wikistrat Crowdsourced Consulting, Washington, DC, USA. Email: emeka.njoku.thaddues@gmail.com/njoku.emeka@dlc.ui.edu.ng.

Sarah Shoker is a Doctoral Candidate at McMaster University. She has previously published work on why civilians joins militant organizations, with a special focus on the Tamil Tigers of Tamil Eelam. Her current research focuses on the gendered foundations of counter-insurgency efforts in the Middle East and South Asia. Email: sarah.shoker@gmail.com.

Dr. Manasi Singh is Assistant Professor at the Centre for Security Studies, School of International Studies, Central University of Gujarat, India. She holds a master's degree in International Relations and an MPhil and Ph.D. in European Studies from Jawaharlal Nehru University, New Delhi. She was a Visiting Research Fellow at ULB, Brussels, Freie University, Berlin, and University of Bonn, and has presented papers at international conferences held at the Indira Gandhi Institute of Development Research, Mumbai, and the Centre for Comparative European Union Studies, IIT Madras. She has also worked in the media and development sectors and was briefly associated with the UN Millennium Campaign. Her research interests include EU external relations, international and regional organizations, global governance, India's foreign policy, security, and development.

Dr. Yannis (Ioannis) Stivachtis is Associate Professor of International Studies at Virginia Tech in Blacksburg, VA, the Director of the International Studies Program, and the Chair of the English School Section at the International Studies Association (ISA). He is also the Director of the Social Sciences Research Division and Head of the Politics and International Affairs Research Unit at ATINER and Senior International Security Analyst at RIEAS. He is editor of the *Athens Journal of Social Sciences* and co-editor of the *Critical European Studies* book series.

Minkyu Sung is Assistant Professor of Rhetoric of Inquiry in Division of General Studies at Ulsan National Institute of Science and Technology, South Korea. He earned his Ph.D. in Communication Studies from the University of Iowa, USA. His work has been published in journals including *Inter-Asia Cultural Studies*, *Citizenship Studies*, *Korean Journal of Rhetoric*, *Acta Koreana*, and *Asian Social Science*. He is the coauthor of *Books Talk about Television* (Seoul: Culture Look, 2013). He served as Principal Investigator of two National Research Foundation of Korea projects: "Rhetoric of Science in Korea" (2010–2011) and "Multiculturalism and

Public Culture in Korea" (2013–2014). He was awarded New Scholar of the Year 2013 in the Korean Association of Journalism and Communication Studies. Email: minkyusung @unist.ac.kr.

Georgiana Turculet is currently a Ph.D. candidate at Central European University. Within the field of Political Science, she specializes in the subfield of Political Theory. She is especially interested in exploring issues concerning migration and the rights of migrants from a normative perspective, and attempts to bridge the gap between the realm of philosophers with those of migration scholars and policymakers. She focuses on migration, citizenship, and democracy, particularly the moral and political issues raised by the movement of people across state borders. Former awards and visiting fellowships include her affiliation with New York University, Koc University, and Columbia University.

Joshua K. Wasylciw has a JD from the University of Calgary's Department of Political Science, and is the recipient of many academic awards and commendations—including the Governor General's Academic Award of Excellence. He has written on Russian politics, military and strategic studies, maritime travel and exploration, gender and war, and genocide in war.

Mark S. Williams is a University College Professor in the Department of Political Studies at Vancouver Island University. His research examines the political culture of democracy in the Republic of Indonesia, as well as the international political economy of the Asia-Pacific.

Preface: Social Movements in a Global Era

Scott Nicholas Romaniuk and Marguerite Marlin

> Democracy as the majority of us experience it is arguably an empty ritual. The NSW Electoral Office once produced some wonderful advertising that came out to alert people to the importance of registering to vote, plus the satisfaction of voting in a forthcoming state election. In it, a happy voter wakes up in the morning and thinks, "Oh, goody, today's the day I get to vote, how, when, where? Isn't it exciting?" But what is particularly significant is the final caption that says "end of story." And that probably sums up democracy for us: we're allocated a certain number of votes, and that's all we get to spend in our lifetime, and sometimes you have that feeling that you're actually craving something a little more than putting a cross on a ballot paper and pretending that it's meaningful.
>
> (Carson 2003)

This quotation is entwined with the ongoing literature on democracy and civil society as movements in and for a contemporary and global era. Rather than portraying a situation of perfect uniformity, harmony, and promise, they capture part of the scope of autonomy and self-determination in the world today; they represent the range of constraint and limitation equally present across a deceptively and seemingly united globe.

There can be little doubt that national and international forces have driven liberty and self-determination across much of the world. More often than not, societies in the contemporary international system have witnessed instances in which government has completely out-stroked the means with which it can suppress and repress peoples that underlie the very substance of the states and communities that they govern. The very obvious result of this reality has been a complete overhaul of state systems and governing elements. Too often, however, the process of reforming state systems and systems of public participation has resulted in widespread instability and insecurity to the point that various forms of conflict and outright war have emerged.

On the one hand, this book provides an analysis of the current state of affairs for democracy and civil society in various contexts across the globe, and provides helpful frameworks to understand how challenges to the furthering of either in a meaningful way can be addressed. Themes addressed in this vein include governmentality, constitutional democracy, democratization of information, political parties, and micro-ethnicity in urbanization policies—each employing case studies of a developing nation context to exemplify the authors' points. On the other hand, this is also a book about action rather than mere ideas and processes. It demonstrates how social movements can introduce and strengthen equality, inclusion, accountability, and the free flow of information. These elements, in turn, can contribute to the acculturation of freedom and social justice, in the developed world just as much as in the developing world. The United States (US) is one such attention-winning case in which the fundamental quality of democracy has been called into question. Further across the global map, "democracy" has been likened to malaria, whereby semi-developed states have been suffering from as opposed to prospering from the concept and practice. In many parts of the world, functioning democracy and a vibrant civil society are not products of externalities or factors originating beyond the region in which these forces are active and growing. These phenomena are the inevitable outcome of multilevel interaction between civic awareness and civic participation.

It might seem intuitive to expect that the elements and invisible technologies presented and discussed at length in this book are fated, particularly given many centuries of trial and error in Western democratic states. Similarly, looking beyond Western borders, one might consider that the advent of democracy and civil society was bound to blossom and flourish if only because these phenomena have come about elsewhere. That is, the concepts and practices are bound to prevail in one state or community simply because they prosper in those elsewhere. The contributions that comprise this volume, however, paint a different portrait. Not only do they demonstrate that the misguided intuition about the inevitability of these elements is remiss; they contribute to the emerging literature on the breadth of opposition movements to factors that build a mutual understanding of relations within and among divided states, societies, and institutions.

This volume is composed of 18 chapters with foci on democracy as practice and experimentation and civil society's role in upholding a myriad of principles fundamental to freedom. The use of case studies is a common feature for many chapters in this volume, and the geographic diversity of the contexts studied by the authors in the following pages serves to present a globally comprehensive array of perspectives, character, and understanding.

Reference

Carson, L. (2003) "Building Sustainable Democracies," Active Democracy: Citizen Participation in Decision-Making, available at: www.activedemocracy.net/articles/building_sustainable_democracies.pdf (accessed March 11, 2015).

DEMOCRACY

1

Chapter 1

Constitutional Democracy for Divided Societies*

Munafrizal Manan

International attention to democracy, both theoretical and practical, has been increasing significantly since the "third wave" of democratization began in 1974 (Huntington 1991). According to Samuel Huntington (1991), from the 1970s to 1990s, more countries moved toward democracy, resulting in the emergence of an optimistic view about the future of democracy—including the much-appraised perspectives and movements centering on the concept of liberal democracy. For Francis Fukuyama, this dynamic reveals that the victory of liberal democracy over its ideological rivals—authoritarianism and totalitarianism—represents "the end of history" (Fukuyama 1992: xi).

Since Fukuyama composed his work on the ending of struggles between two rival systems, an increase in fundamentalist religion and the ascendance of the developed world into "a paroxysm of ideological violence" (Fukuyama 1989: 114), democracy has grown in popularity and has even come to be an influential factor in international relations. Apart from the emerging current of democracy in the contemporary world, upholding the ideals of democracy in the modern state is no easy task, particularly as many societies in the global era remain, or are becoming further divided in terms of race, ethnicity, religion, language, culture, and gender.

Rather than making a positive impact on societies overall, democratic movements actually give rise to or potentially stimulate tensions and social stratification, and even alight horizontal conflicts among societies with variegated backgrounds. Snyder (2000) shows that the early phase of democratization triggered nationalistic conflicts in some countries, and provides a solid reason for the failure of democracy and democratic institutions in pluralistic societies. Moreover, democracies also tend to fail in states with weak capacity; this has been the case in many third-wave democracies (Dominguez and Jones 2007: 7; Tilly 2007: 15–21).

As a result of the inherent challenges and obstacles that surface in the face of democratization in the modern age, one cannot rule out the possibility that a different brand of democracy is more suitable for divided societies. Scholars in the field of political science have debated the issue, with some attempting to present a remedy for issues that bedevil divided society in the context of budding democracy. This chapter presents the single and straightforward argument that constitutional democracy is best suited for divided societies. It begins by discussing the suitability of several types of democracy for divided societies, and follows with an examination of constitutional democracy in the Indonesian context.

Democracy and Its Many Forms

Scholars in the recent and distant past have introduced many forms of democracy and democratic practice, indicating that there are many views on this inclusionary form of government and governance (see Held 1987; Heywood 1997). Electoral democracy emphasizes the importance of the right of universal suffrage in which one person can cast a single vote. Electoral democracy defines democracy merely as voting in elections in order to choose public officers to represent a wide array of public interests (Schumpeter 1987). In this regard, electoral democracy has a close relation with representative democracy. The problem with these democracies is that they are inclined to benefit the majority and neglect the minority. In such democracies, the will of the majority must be obeyed (Mueller 1997: 84).

There is the general understanding that if competition is solely based on the number of votes, then the minority will ultimately lose. Subsequently, it can be concluded that these kinds of democracies do not provide divided societies with adequate playing fields for democratic growth or practice. For this reason, it is argued that electoral democracy combined with other forms of democracy present an ideal model for societies characterized by intense social, cultural, political, and economic stratification. Arend Lijphart (1977) offers what he terms consociational democracy for divided societies, and sketches a range of favorable conditions for consociational democracy. He and other scholars pay a great deal of attention to the importance of a constitution as the pivotal pillar in the overall democratic machine (Horowitz 2000; Issacharoff 2004; Lijphart 2004; Reynolds 2005).

Deliberative democracy is another type suitable for a plural society. Theorists of deliberative democracy argue that the democratic process should include open spheres for public involvement in policymaking that relate to public interest or the so-called "common good" (Chambers 2003). Deliberative democracy is useful to prevent the domination of the majority group in the democratic process while simultaneously providing an opportunity to minority or marginalized groups to voice their interests in all walks of society. Deliberative democracy is a remedy to reconcile the clash between democracy and rights, as well as between the majority will and individual rights of those belonging to underrepresented peoples and their communities (Chambers 2003: 311). Some theorists of deliberative democracy stress the importance of the rule of law and constitutional rights (Chambers 2003: 309–311); however, less attention has been paid to the relationship between deliberative democracy and the constitution as a critical coupling in the successful democratic process. Although deliberative democracy and constitutional democracy seem to be similar ideas, the main focus of deliberative democracy is not on the constitution, but rather on how peoples retain equal opportunity in within the democratic process.

There can be little doubt that democracy is a complicated practice; as such, it is somewhat difficult to claim that one type of democracy operates or meets the needs of a state's citizens better than any other type of government. In practice, it is common to apply a mixed type of democracy to states with a variegated population base. However, a well-functioning democracy within the framework of a divided society requires the existence and legal establishment of a constitution. Constitutional democracy is necessary for divided societies as it regulates and guarantees the enforceability of democracy for a divided society. Any type of democracy may be referred to as constitutional democracy so long as it is supported by a constitution. Constitutional democracy thus might well be seen as an octopus, with other types of democracy as its tentacles; this form of democracy is often considered *primus inter pares* among other types.

Constitutional Democracy

Although in literal terms constitutional democracy may be accepted as the combination of constitutionalism and democracy, it is important to gain a deeper understanding of what both constitutionalism and democracy truly are. One source explains that the first use of the word "constitutionalism" was made in 1832 (Gordon 1999: 5). According to Jon Elster, constitutionalism pertains to "limits on majority decisions, more specifically, to limits that are in some sense self-imposed" (Elster 1988: 2). Scott Gordon argues that the notion of constitutionalism refers to the coercive power of the state being constrained (Gordon 1999: 5). For Gordon, "the problem of controlling the power to coerce" is the most important aspect of constitutionalism (Gordon 1999: 7). Meanwhile, the origin of the term "democracy" is the Greek language, and consists of two words: those of (1) *demos* (the people) and (2) *kratos* (rule or authority) (Gordon 1999: 60). One of the simplest and most popular definitions of democracy was introduced by Abraham Lincoln, who argued that democracy is a government from the people, by the people, and for the people.

According to Charles Tilly, "a regime is democratic to the degree that political relations between the state and its citizens feature broad, equal, protected and mutually binding consultation" (Tilly 2007: 13–14). In discussing constitutional democracy, some scholars argue that there exists tension between democracy (democrats) and constitutionalism (constitutionalists). Such a tension has appeared as early as the eighteenth century (Holmes 1988: 198). One of the historical debates centering on constitutionalism and democracy occurred between Thomas Jefferson and James Madison (Sunstein 1988: 327).

Democracy facilitates a political competition by which a decision is made based on majority power. By contrast, constitutionalism limits majority rule, which potentially leads to majority tyranny. Moreover, to use Walter Murphy's words, "whereas democratic theory turns to moral relativism, constitutionalism turns to moral realism" (Murphy 1993: 6). Therefore, those who believe that there is tension between the two argue that "constitutional democracy is a marriage of opposites, an oxymoron" (Holmes 1988: 197). However, other scholars rebut such a view; Cass Sunstein presents the argument that there is no inherent tension between the two poles of democracy and constitutionalism (Sunstein 1988). Similarly, Jon Elster also believes that constitutional constraints on democracy represent the means of strengthening democracy (Elster 1988: 9). Stephen Holmes comes to the same view, asserting that the two are "mutually supportive," and thus argues that the tension between the two is a myth of modern political thought (Holmes 1988: 197). Both of these views should not be overly contrasted or their differences over-exaggerated (Murphy 1993).

Constitutional democracy attempts to compensate for the weaknesses of constitutionalism and democracy by combining them. Dennis Mueller argues that the possession of a constitution by all democracies indicates that there is a close relation between constitutionalism and democracy (Mueller 1997).[1] Although constitutional democracy is able to overcome potential conflicts in divided societies, it is important to note that what is meant by constitutional democracy here is not only based on the existence of a constitution, but also on the idea that a constitution regulates and guarantees the balance of majority and minority relationship.[2] This is needed to prevent the potential tension and conflict in divided societies. Thus, while the existence of a constitution is a necessary condition, it is not a sufficient condition unless it is not intended to enforce the harmony and stability of divided societies.

Constitutional democracy is more effective in enforcing the stability and harmony in divided societies as compared to other forms of democracy given that constitution is a supreme law. As the fundamental and the highest law, the constitution is the heart of power. A constitution is very important for all parties in divided societies because it is a social contract that stipulates the rules of the game politically (Mueller 1996). Furthermore, as Walter Murphy contends, constitutional democracy has the tendency to "accept the centrality of human dignity" (Murphy 1993: 6), which is very useful for divided societies. In short, constitutional democracy implies that democracy should be based on constitutional legitimacy; conversely, the constitution should be one entrenched in the ideals and values of democracy and democratic practice.

Constitutional democracy is a global phenomenon. A large number of countries having applied a combination of democracy theory and constitutionalism to their national systems (Murphy 1993); indeed, most countries around the world that employ so-called democratic systems should essentially be labeled as constitutional democracies (Murphy 1993). While a positive constitutional design affects the enforceability of constitutional democracy overall, a democratic constitution is needed to provide the framework of a sound relationship between societies in the future. Drafters of constitutions should, therefore, consider the plurality of the society for which that specific constitution is designed. Most importantly, the many interests and perspectives that exist within divided societies should be taken into consideration when drafting a constitution; the inclusion of both majorities and minorities should exist (Dominguez and Jones 2007: 7).

A constitution is a crucial aspect of enforcing and stabilizing democracy in its early stages. The process of transition to democracy should be followed by the (re)construction of a democratic constitution. The (re)construction of a democratic constitution is a starting point to democracy; this is a reason why almost all new democratic states consider constitutional amendment a top priority for building, maintaining, and strengthening democratic growth. The undemocratic constitution inherited from an authoritarian regime is replaced by a democratic constitution.

An effort to anticipate potential conflict in a divided society should also inform the constitution of the state in question. However, the building of a constitution in transitional democracies is not an easy task to accomplish given that all parties have to agree to achieve constitutional settlements, which requires constitutional negotiation among them. In spite of all good intentions by conflicting sides within a divided society, constitutional negotiation can lead to a deadlock (constitutional crisis) if each party only focuses on their own interests —particularly if there are adversarial interests between the majority and minority. To be clear, it is difficult to reconcile the need for constitutional constraints on the majority and the desire of the majority to become dominant. It is also difficult to balance the empowerment of majorities and the safeguarding of representation and participation of minorities in democratic governance. The experience of the democratization process in Eastern and Central Europe as well as in Africa have shown that the most important challenge for deeply divided societies is to strike a proper balance between unity and diversity (Simeon and Turgeon 2007); this is commonly related to the relationships between the majority and minority, as previously stressed.

The failure to reconcile the tension between the majority and minority potentially leads to what Richard Simeon and Luc Turgeon refer to as the insecure majority, a condition in which the majority "represses or dominates the minority," and insecure minority, a condition in which the minority "rebels or secedes" (Simeon and Turgeon 2007: 82). Conversely, the success of reconciling the tension between the majority and minority guarantees the consolidation of democracy. This is why, as Simeon and Turgeon argue, "making a constitution, especially in divided societies, warrants careful statecraft" (Simeon and Turgeon 2007: 93). If a common consensus for a constitution has been reached, then the prospect of a harmonized society can be realized—since people have a common platform that binds them legally, politically, and socially. Based on this, the abuse of a common platform will invariably be judged as unconstitutional.

The Case of Indonesia

The following sections of this chapter present an examination of the Indonesian case. Even as constitutional democracy has played a key role in the making and preservation of the Republic of Indonesia, coping with horizontal conflicts among divided societies is still a contentious and conflicting point. On the one hand, it describes the portrait of the Republic of Indonesia as a multicultural country. On the other, it highlights the historical context in which constitutional consensus has played an important role in Indonesian history. This further reveals that the current constitution is now still far from the ideal hoped for.

A Multicultural Country

Indonesia is a vast equatorial archipelago of approximately 17,000 islands extending roughly 5,150 kilometers from east to west. With an estimated population of approximately 220 million people, Indonesia is the fourth largest country in the world as well as the most populous Muslim country, with roughly 90 percent of its population being of Muslim identity. Adrian Vickers observes that Indonesia's surface area (joined by the ocean surrounding it) is as wide as the United States or Europe (Vickers 2005). Historically, the territorial boundaries of Indonesia are based on the islands that had been colonized by the Netherlands (see Brown 2004).

In a political development context, following the fall of the authoritarian power of President Suharto on May 21, 1998, Indonesia is currently considered the third largest democratic country in the world following the United States and India. In this context, it should be noted that Indonesian politics has been fragmented by a number of ideologies or political streams in both political and historical terms (Feith and Castles 1970; Bourchier and Hadiz 2003), which further serves as a means of representing the essential diversity of Indonesian culture. To be sure, ideological conflicts have been a challenge to the prospect of Indonesian democracy. As Bourchier and Hadiz (2003: 2) note, "[c]onflict over ideology has been a feature of political life in Indonesia since the early days of the nationalist movement." Such a conflict occurred during the 1950s, when strong competition between those who wanted "to reform society along Islamic or communist lines" and "who wanted to follow the example of a Western Democracy" occurred (Dijk 1990: 102).

In dealing with the plurality of culture, Indonesia is an eminent multicultural country in which there are at least 300 ethnic groups and 200 different languages across its many islands and regions (Geertz 1967, cited in Dijk 1990). Each of these ethnic groups is in possession of its own cultural life—including music, theater, the visual arts, and poetry and literature (Vickers 2005: 2). Various reverent movements in Indonesia consist of major religions that include Islam, Catholicism, Protestantism, Hinduism, and Buddhism, as well as a swathe of other spiritual faiths and religious sects. All of these should be taken into consideration when measuring the cultural richness of Indonesia. However, like other multicultural states in the contemporary world, this degree of diversity can serve as a great source of tension and conflict. According to Vickers, "[t]his diversity and depth of Indonesian culture is a product of openness to new ideas and practice" (Vickers 2005: 2). Similarly, Dennis Lombard (1996) has revealed that Indonesian cultures had been influenced by India, China, Western states, and Islamic civilizations. Such a view has also been expressed by historians J.D. Legge (1977) and M.C. Ricklefs (1993). Indonesia, indeed, is a country that is open to other cultural influences as well.

Constitutional Consensus and Horizontal Conflicts

As a multicultural country, the diversity of ethnic groups has been a crucial issue and greatly contentious point. J.D. Legge has noted that "one of Indonesia's major problems in the modern world is that of merely preserving the unity of the nation" (Legge 1977: 3). There can be little doubt that it is difficult to unite the people of Indonesia in a nation-state, as well as to accommodate their many values, ideologies, and interests that sometimes sharply oppose each other. In the words of Vickers, "[Indonesia] has struggled to balance the interests of different groups and maintain coherence against both the pressure of its own diversity and tensions created by international politics" (Vickers 2005: 3).

Indeed, how to reconcile the big (the majority) and the small (the minority) ethnic groups so that they can live side by side peacefully and equally is an enduring question in Indonesian history and contemporary society. Such an issue emerged at an early state when Indonesia as a mere conceptual state was being discussed during the 1940s. It was, therefore, an extraordinary achievement that the founders were able to persuade and unite peoples with different backgrounds in order to create an, to use the phrase of Benedict Anderson (1983), "imagined community" known as the Republic of Indonesia. At least two factors have contributed to the achievement of a unified Indonesia. In the first place, the similar feeling among Indonesian people that the Dutch colonialist was a common enemy for them is a powerful and compelling force. Such a sentiment, which was raised frequently by nationalists during the Independence Revolution, had united people against the Dutch colonialists in an overwhelming way.

In the second place, the Indonesian language (Bahasa Indonesia) plays an important role in unifying Indonesian peoples utilizing different languages in their everyday lives. It is also critical to note that the Indonesian language was and is not taken from the largest number of speakers, such as Javanese, but was adopted from the Malay language, which was used by minority peoples located on the Riau islands. Malay was the *lingua franca* at that time and, unlike Javanese, an egalitarian language that was relatively easy to learn and accept by other ethnic groups. The use of Malay as a national language is a way of avoiding the dominance of major culture in Indonesia. Malay has been accepted as national language and its status has been incorporated into the 1945 Constitution of the Republic of Indonesia. It is reaffirmed later in the Second Amendment in 2000.

Bahasa Indonesia has been a constitutional consensus for Indonesian people. Looking back in time, it can be argued that the constitutional consensus has played a very important role in the making of a nation-state, namely the Republic of Indonesia. Following the drafting of the Independence Proclamation by Sukarno and Mohammad Hatta on August 17, 1945— marking the establishment of the Republic of Indonesia—the founders discussed the Constitution for the new Republic. They nearly failed to achieve a consensus as a result of a disagreement over Indonesia's national ideology. Some strongly defended Islam as the national ideology, while others endorsed the *Pancasila* (the Five State Principles), which consist of the belief in one supreme God, just and civilized humanity, national unity, democracy led by wisdom and prudence through consultation and representation, and social justice. In such a constitutional crisis, the prospect of the new republic was under serious threat, as "regions where Christian or Hindus formed the majority of the population would refuse to join the Republic" (Dijk 1990: 107).

Constitutional consensus was eventually achieved and, as a result, Indonesia did not become an Islamic state even though 90 percent of the population is Muslim. Moreover, other religious minorities were not made to feel like second-class citizens (Cribb and Brown 1995: 38). The constitutional consensus, in this case, was a remedy to Indonesia as a society that is heavily divided. It is useful to note that the proponents of an Islamic state continue to struggle tirelessly in order to achieve their vision. They have been urging a constitutional amendment or to re-apply the Jakarta Charter, "which would have obliged the state to impose Islamic law on all its Muslim citizens" (Cribb and Brown 1995: 38). The Jakarta Charter has been considered the justification of an Islamic state for Indonesia. There were two instances of momentum within Indonesian history after the Independence Revolution in which the proponents of an Islamic state strove to reach their vision. First, in the second half of the 1950s, the Constituent Assembly members implemented the process of drafting a permanent constitution to replace the 1950 provisional constitution (Legge 1977: 155).

These members could not reach constitutional consensus of national ideology as it had occurred in the early years of the new republic. As a result, there was the deadlock of constitution making, demonstrating that the national unity was under serious threat. To cope with this, President Sukarno (who was supported by the Indonesian military and moderate Muslims) dissolved the Constituent Assembly and promulgated a return to the 1945 Constitution that had been adopted by the new republic after its Independence Proclamation. This was done through the presidential decree on July 5, 1959, which brought Indonesia into Sukarno's "Guided Democracy" after that date. Even though the presidential decree was an unconstitutional decision (Legge 1977: 156; Nasution 1992; Ricklefs 1993: 266), in fact it is widely admitted that it was an acceptable solution to escape the constitutional impasse and prevent national disunity. In the second place, proponents of an Islamic state had also echoed their vision when constitutional amendments were taking place from 1999 to 2002. However, it was only voiced by a few people, and not supported by the vast majority of Indonesians— or even by Muslims; consequently, they failed again.

Even today, there are many who think that Indonesia should be an Islamic state given that the majority of the population is Muslim. Nevertheless, it seems that the majority agree with the *Pancasila* ideology compared to other ideologies, as it is generally believed that the *Pancasila* is able to facilitate unity amid diversity referred to as *Bhinneka Tunggal Ika* in Indonesian language. The *Pancasila* represents, essentially, the middle ground in accommodating all Indonesian peoples of varied and diverse cultures. Generally speaking, most Indonesians in the present day believe that such a constitutional consensus is final and, therefore, no further opportunities exist to alter this document. It is widely held that the 1945 Constitution is necessary to preserve national unity, although the 1945 Constitution was not a truly democratic constitution until it was amended from 1999 to 2002. As a consequence, the opponents of the *Pancasila* have become alienated, and they are deemed unconstitutional given that they reject the constitutional consensus. However, this is not to say that the constitutional consensus is the panacea and therefore able to stop horizontal conflicts; these remain potential as well as actual conflicts even today, although a constitutional consensus has been reached.

Many horizontal conflicts that were triggered by religious, ethnic, economic, and political factors have occurred—indicating that such issues are still highly contentious and pose a great challenge to the government. In historical terms, each ethnic group has coexisted in peaceful terms for some time. Sociologically, there has been a general acculturation of tolerance and respect of difference and diversity. As a result of this, Indonesia has fostered a rather positive reputation for being a very tolerant country, especially given its somewhat negatively perceived cultural and political bases. Nonetheless, the violent conflict that had suddenly erupted in some regions in the years following the fall of President Suharto produced a shockwave across the entire country and even further afield. Suharto banned any discussion of sectarian issues—called SARA, an acronym for *suku*, *agama*, *ras*, and *antargolongan* (ethnic group, religion, race, and inter-group relations)—in the media during his time in power, which lasted for more than three decades. Gerry van Klinken's study illustrates the communal violence that occurred in several places across Indonesia between 1997 and 2002; these are West and Central Kalimantan, Central Sulawesi, Maluku/Ambon, and North Maluku (Klinken 2007).

Similarly, the study of Chris Wilson focuses on the bloody religious conflict between Christians and Muslims in North Maluku from 1999 until 2000 (Wilson 2008). These instances provide evidence that horizontal conflict is still a dangerous force in a multicultural country such as Indonesia. However, it is difficult to conclude that all horizontal conflict was triggered by cultural differences exclusively. In some cases, horizontal conflict has been triggered by competition for resources, particularly competition related to economic and political issues, among societies. Undoubtedly, such competition has likely brought them into further conflict. In some cases, primordial and religious sentiments are exploited to cover such motives. Indeed, primordial and religious sentiments are likely to be effective ways to mobilize solidarity *en masse*.

Horizontal conflict, after all, reveals the paradox of Indonesia insofar as they have been occurring when the democratic process is present, and people experience a greater degree of liberty and equalities than previously—which they have been guaranteed by the 1945 Constitution and laws. Furthermore, the guarantee of constitutional rights has been extended in both quantity and quality after amendments of the 1945 Constitution (1999–2002). Establishment of the new state body—namely, the Constitutional Court of the Republic of Indonesia in 2003—allowed many to defend their constitutional rights before the court. In short, there is no reason for horizontal conflict to flare up under such constructive conditions. Indeed, the constitutional consensus "is not conceived as a binding instrument" (Hassall and Saunders 2002: 3).

In the context of the constitutional consensus, the living constitution still embodies a critical struggle in Indonesia. The Constitution is inherently "good" in theory, but remains very poor in practice. Moreover, the level of constitutional awareness in Indonesia tends to be limited to Indonesia's societal elite. As in the period of constitutional democracy between December 1949 and March 1957 in which "[m]ost members of the political elite had some sort of commitment to symbols connected with constitutional democracy" (Feith 1962: xi)—although they had faced challenges to applying it in reality—today's elite also have the same commitment to constitutional democracy. Unfortunately, such a commitment has not been disseminated widely to Indonesia's general population. This indicates that, in the words of Hassall and Saunders (2002: 241), "'[t]he language of the law' is not that of 'the people.'"

Conclusion

This chapter has presented an argument for the importance of considering constitutional democracy for divided societies. Seen from its status as the supreme law, a constitution represents a very positive and useful vantage point for fostering a relationship of mutual understanding among divided societies. However, it is not an easy task to reach a constitutional consensus in regions that have been torn apart by or are characterized by intense social, political, cultural, and economic stratification.

This chapter has also examined how constitutional democracy has been applied, as well as how constitutional consensus has been achieved in Indonesia. Indonesia is a relevant country to see the application of constitutional democracy within the context of divided and strained societies. Such a multicultural reality can have both positive and negative impacts. In positive terms, a country of multicultural reality is a state comprised of a rich and diverse body of culture(s). In negative terms, a multicultural base in any society represents a potential source for horizontal, and possibly violent, conflict.

In terms of making and preserving the Republic of Indonesia, people might come to a constitutional consensus. In this context, and to use Dijk's words, "Indonesia remain[s] an unbreakable political entity" and "has forged a remarkably strong unity from the diversity of separate ethnic groups" (Dijk 1990: 106, 125). To a great extent, bringing constitutional consensus into social relationships among divided societies is a difficult task due to the fact that horizontal conflict that exploits religious and primordial sentiments still appears throughout Indonesian society. To a lesser extent, constitutional democracy for divided societies has been functioning well in the case of Indonesia, even though this form and practice of government and governance requires more time to become established before it can be celebrated.

Notes

* This chapter is a revised version of the author's published article: Munafrizal, M. (March 2010) "Constitutional Democracy for Divided Societies: The Indonesian Case," *Journal of Politics and Law*, 3(1): 125–132.

1. By saying "all democracies have constitutions," it does not mean that Mueller denies that there are democratic countries that do not have a written constitution; for example, Great Britain.

Mueller means to stress that a written constitution is "an essential feature of constitutional democracy" (Mueller 1997: 65, 85).

2. Although I agree with Dennis C. Mueller that a written constitution is important in constitutional democracy (Mueller 1996: 43; 1997: 85), I tend to argue that it does not matter whether a country has a written or unwritten constitution, as long as there are regulations and guarantees for harmony and stability in a divided society. For the context of this chapter, I agree with Scott Gordon, who argues that "constitutionalism has little to do with the existence of a written constitution" (Gordon 1999: 5).

References

1945 Constitution of the Republic of Indonesia and the Act Number 24 of 2003 on the Constitutional Court of the Republic of Indonesia (2003) Jakarta: Secretariat General of the Constitutional Court of the Republic of Indonesia.

Anderson, B. (1983) *Imagined Communities: Reflections on the Origins and Spread of Nationalism*, London: Verso.

Bourchier, D. and Hadiz, V.R. (2003) *Indonesian Politics and Society: A Reader*, London: Routledge Curzon.

Brown, C. (2004) *A Short History of Indonesia: The Unlikely Nation?* Crows Nest: Allen & Unwin.

Chambers, S. (2003) "Deliberative Democratic Theory," *Annual Review of Political Science*, 6: 307–326.

Cribb, R. and Brown, C. (1995) *Modern Indonesia: A History since 1945*, London: Longman.

Dijk, K. van (1900) "The Indonesian State: Unity in Diversity," in S.K. Mitra (Ed.), *The Post-Colonial State in Asia: Dialectics of Politics and Culture*, Hemel Hempstead: Harvester Wheatsheaf.

Dominguez, J.I. and Jones, A. (2007) "Building and Sustaining a Contemporary Democratic State," in J.I Dominguez and A. Jones (Eds.), *The Construction of Democracy: Lessons from Practice and Research*, Baltimore, MD: Johns Hopkins University Press.

Elster, J. (1988) "Introduction," in J. Elster and R. Slagstad (Eds.), *Constitutionalism and Democracy: Studies in Rationality and Social Change*, Cambridge: Cambridge University Press.

Feith, H. (1962) *The Decline of Constitutional Democracy in Indonesia*, Ithaca, NY: Cornell University Press.

Feith, H. and Castles, L. (1970) *Indonesian Political Thinking 1945–1965*, Ithaca, NY: Cornell University Press.

Fukuyama, F. (1989) "The End of History?" in G. O'Tuathail, S. Dalby, and P. Routledge (Eds.), *The Geopolitics Reader*, London and New York: Routledge, pp. 114–124.

Fukuyama, F. (1992) *The End of History and the Last Man*, London: Hamish Hamilton.

Gordon, S. (1999) *Controlling the State: Constitutionalism from Ancient Athens to Today*, Cambridge, MA: Harvard University Press.

Hassall, G. and Saunders, C. (2002) *Asia-Pacific Constitutional Systems*, Cambridge: Cambridge University Press.

Held, D. (1987) *Models of Democracy*, Stanford, CA: Stanford University Press.

Heywood, A. (1997) *Politics*, London: Macmillan Press.

Holmes, S. (1988) "Precommitment and the Paradox of Democracy," in J. Elster and R. Slagstad (Eds.), *Constitutionalism and Democracy: Studies in Rationality and Social Change*, Cambridge: Cambridge University Press.

Horowitz, D. (2000) "Constitutional Design: An Oxymoron," in I. Shapiro and S. Macedo (Eds.), *Designing Democratic Institutions*, New York: New York University Press.

Huntington, S.P. (1991) *The Third Wave: Democratization in the Late Twentieth Century*, Norman, OK: University of Oklahoma Press.

Issacharoff, S. (2004) "Constitutionalizing Democracy in Fractured Societies," *Journal of International Affairs*, 58(1): 73–93.

Klinken, G. van (2007) *Communal Violence and Democratization in Indonesia: Small Town Wars*, London: Routledge.

Legge, J.D. (1977) *Indonesia* (2nd ed.), Sydney: Prentice-Hall of Australia.

Lijphart, A. (1977) *Democracy in Plural Societies: A Comparative Exploration*, New Haven, CT: Yale University Press.

Lijphart, A. (2004) "Constitutional Design for Divided Societies," *Journal of Democracy*, 15(2): 96–109.

Lombard, D. (1996) *Nusa Jawa Silang Budaya*, Jakarta: Gramedia Pustaka Utama.

Mueller, D.C. (1996) *Constitutional Democracy*, Oxford: Oxford University Press.

Mueller, D.C. (1997) "Constitutional Democracy: An Interpretation," in A. Breton et al. (Eds.), *Understanding Democracy: Economic and Political Perspectives*, Cambridge: Cambridge University Press.

Murphy, W.F. (1993) "Constitutions, Constitutionalism, and Democracy," in D. Greenberg, S.N. Katz, S.C. Wheatley. and M.B. Oliviero (Eds.), *Constitutionalism and Democracy: Transition in the Contemporary World: The American Council of Learned Societies Comparative Constitutionalism Papers*, Oxford: Oxford University Press.

Nasution, A.B. (1992) *The Aspiration for Constitutional Government in Indonesia: A Socio-Legal Study of the Indonesian Konstituante 1956–1959*, Jakarta: Pustaka Sinar Harapan.

Reynolds, A. (2005) "Constitutional Medicine," *Journal of Democracy*, 16(1): 54–68.

Ricklefs, M.C. (1993) *A History of Modern Indonesia Since C. 1300* (2nd ed.), Basingstoke: Macmillan Press.

Schumpeter, J.A. (1987) *Capitalism, Socialism and Democracy*, London: Unwin Paperbacks.

Simeon, R. and Turgeon, L. (2007) "Constitutional Design and the Construction of Democracy," in J.I. Dominguez and A. Jones (Eds.), *The Construction of Democracy: Lessons from Practice and Research*, Baltimore, MD: Johns Hopkins University Press.

Snyder, J. (2000) *From Voting to Violence: Democratization and Nationalist Conflict*, New York: Norton.

Sunstein, C.R. (1988) "Constitutions and Democracies: An Epilogue," in J. Elster and R. Slagstad (Eds.), *Constitutionalism and Democracy: Studies in Rationality and Social Change*, Cambridge: Cambridge University Press.

Tilly, C. (2007) *Democracy*, Cambridge: Cambridge University Press.

Vickers, A. (2005) *A History of Modern Indonesia*, Cambridge: Cambridge University Press.

Wilson, C. (2008) *Ethno-Religious Violence in Indonesia: From Soil to God*, London: Routledge.

Chapter 2

Democracy Promotion as a Security Strategy: The Case of the European Union

Yannis A. Stivachtis

In *Common Sense*, Thomas Paine (1776: 95) suggested that republics (democracies) tended to be peaceful and that peace among states results from the democratic tendency to negotiate "mistakes" rather than resort to war. In *Perpetual Peace*, Immanuel Kant (1795: 100) made a similar claim. Although the two theorists took fundamentally opposite positions on the issue of intervention as a means to democratize third countries, their claims over the peaceful nature of democratic regimes and their positive impact on international security have constituted the basis of the "democratic peace theory" (Doyle 1997), which has exercised considerable influence over security studies.

On April 2, 1917, President Woodrow Wilson declared before the US Congress that making the world safe for democracy should serve as the guiding principle of US policy. Almost a century later, democracy has emerged as the predominant form of political governance within the Westphalian international system. This development has been strengthened by the emergence of an international norm that considers the promotion of democracy to be an accepted and necessary component of international behavior.

In a historic June 2000 meeting in Warsaw (which was coordinated by the Clinton Administration), foreign ministers and other representatives from 106 countries gathered to discuss their common interest in advancing an "international community of democracies." The resulting Warsaw Declaration committed its signatories to a wide range of pro-democracy actions, ranging from the preservation and strengthening of democratic practices to the actual promotion of such practices in countries where they were absent. Since then, several US officials have repeatedly urged the significance of democratization, while the establishment of democracy has been used as a justification for regime change in third countries.

The United States is not the only international actor that has made democracy promotion a policy priority; many international organizations, including the EU, have adopted similar policies. For example, the widespread acceptance of democracy promotion as an international norm is clearly demonstrated by the activities of the United Nations, which promotes democracy through its norm-creating ability. UN organs have promulgated a considerable body of international law that expresses the cardinal principles and values of democracy—especially through human rights treaties. The UN also actively promotes democratic principles and institutions internationally by encouraging a culture of democracy in newly emerging state societies via the holding of referendums and the monitoring and verifying of national elections. As a result, international law has undergone a gradual transformation in favor of recognizing democracy as an "entitlement" to be both defended and promoted.

Democratization and human rights are also central to the requirements of "political" or "democratic conditionality" reflected in the policies of international organizations such as the IMF, WTO, NATO, and the European Union. All these organizations, by making democracy a precondition for membership or assistance, provide a powerful incentive for aspiring members or assistance-seekers to rethink their domestic political arrangements.

The purpose of this chapter is twofold: first, to provide a historical account of the development of democracy promotion as an international norm; second, to discuss democracy promotion as a European Union (EU) strategy to address security threats. In doing so, the chapter is divided into three sections. In the first section, the chapter will discuss the development of democracy promotion as an international norm. The second part will examine the EU's conceptualization of security and how democracy promotion fits into the Union's strategy to address its security concerns. The last section will focus on the instrument of conditionality and how it is used to promote democracy.

Europe and Democracy Promotion: A Historical Perspective

Although as an end in itself democracy may be a good thing, historical analysis shows that the project of democracy promotion has been hegemonic and European in nature. Specifically, the origins of this project can be traced back to the time that ideological and political events in Europe began having a significant impact on the idea of civilization and on what it really means for a state to be "civilized." According to Norbert Elias (1978), the idea of civilization in modern international politics began with the efforts of the Europeans to relate the concept to the way in which the modern state should function. Thus, for the rest of the world to be "civilized," states outside Europe should be modeled on the European archetype of the state and should perform functions similar to those of the European states. Evolving historical conditions in Europe gave rise to competing political claims as to the principles on which the modern state should be based, with conservatism being succeeded by liberalism and absolute monarchies being succeeded by enlightened monarchies and parliamentary democracies.

During the eighteenth century, the non-European world played a decisive role in the evolution of European identity and in the maintenance of order among European states. As the sense of the specifically European character of the society of states increased, so did the sense of its cultural differentiation from what existed beyond itself. International society was by then regarded as a privileged association of states having visible expression in international institutions such as international law, diplomacy, and the balance of power, but also in the way that the domestic politics of these states were conducted (Bull and Watson

1984; Watson 1992). Nineteenth-century international lawyers perpetuated the cultural duality between Europeans and non-Europeans, and between "civilized" and "non-civilized" peoples; states belonging to either category were accorded different stages of legal recognition. Thus, political communities that could not satisfy the necessary criteria to be sovereign states could not, by the same token, be members of international society.

Eventually, there was established a "standard of civilization" that reflected the norms of European civilization and included such elements as the guarantee of basic rights (to life, dignity, and property, to freedom of travel, commerce, and religion) and the maintenance of a domestic system of courts, legal codes, and published laws guaranteeing justice for all (Gong 1984). Non-European states wishing to join European international society had to accommodate themselves to this standard, whatever the cost to their own societies.

Gradually, democracy came to be viewed as a product of the development of the capitalist state and its spread as an imperative for the spread of the capitalist system. For example, one of the main functions of the nineteenth-century "standard of civilization" was to protect capitalist operations in foreign territories. The price of admission to European international society included acceptance of the economic and commercial practices associated with liberalism and capitalism. Thus, the "standard of civilization" came to be seen, in part, as a tool to export capitalism and protect its operations in foreign lands.

Eventually, most of the peoples outside the European community of states subscribed to the vocabulary of political symbols that had been composed in the West, adopted forms of government that Europeans and Americans had devised, and acknowledged the validity of the tenets of international interaction long associated with the European society of states. They thus came to see both their present and their future in terms of Western aspirations and achievements. This widespread diffusion of the Western legacy had the undeniable effect of providing the modern society of states with a unifying structure.

However, it was the end of the First World War and the subsequent Wilsonian campaign to spread democracy around the world that more than anything else made the Western democratic state the highest stage of "civilized" statehood. In addition, democracy and democracy promotion became political strategies aiming at "civilizing" international affairs, improving international security, and creating a liberal world order.

In the interwar years, democracy and democratic statehood became the flag and symbol of the liberal states in their fight against the totalitarian regimes in Europe and elsewhere. In other words, the historical distinction between "civilized" and "barbarous" humanity was transformed into a division of the world between democratic and totalitarian states.

The experiences in democracy and constitutional thought and practice that had accumulated in the history of Western states provided the basis for the establishment of global institutions such as the League of Nations and the United Nations. According to Adda Bozeman (1960: 518):

> The complex framework of international organizations that spans the world today may thus be viewed as the logical culmination of the political history of the West. As a non-territorial power structure, embodying ideas of unity and peace for which generations have contended with varying success, it recalls traditions set by the great medieval concerts [of powers]. As an international extension of the modern democratic state, it incorporates the values that have governed European and American societies in recent centuries.

It took the impact of the Second World War and of the emerging US hegemony that favoured democratic constitutions (partly because of its growing Cold War anti-communism) to kick-start the process of the second wave of democratization. Post-1945, the struggle between communism and the "free world" became another way of distinguishing between the "civilized" West and the tyrannical and "barbarous" East. While democracy was equated with "civilized" regimes in this imaging, authoritarianism and authoritarian democracy also served as useful political alternatives wherever the spread of communism posed threats to Western and particularly US interests.

The fall of the Soviet Union and the break-up of the Eastern bloc was a major boost to the third wave of democratization (Muravchik 1992). The result of the downfall of these authoritarian regimes has been the introduction of either liberal democracy or partial democracy. The Soviet collapse caused scholars such as Francis Fukuyama (1992) to declare the triumph of democratic liberalism and the end of history. Politicians and international institutions did not lag behind in hailing a new democratic dawn. President George Bush senior called for a new world order based on democratic states, while President Boris Yeltsin was quick to reciprocate by declaring that Russia should become a democracy in order to join the "community of civilized nations." The G7 group of industrialized countries made the promotion of democracy a major feature of its blueprint for a twenty-first-century peace.

The collapse of the Soviet Union and the decline of communist ideology were also viewed as the triumph of civilization over totalitarianism. Consequently, the democratization of the "barbarians" became an accepted and necessary component of international behavior. Peace, stability, and predictability in international relations could be achieved only through the democratization of the non-democratic "other." Therefore, despite the major changes that have occurred, new "standards of civilisation" that had emerged through the original term acquired a negative connotation (Donnelly 1998; Fidler 2001). The contemporary "standard of civilisation" is reflected in the principle of political or democratic conditionality advocated by major international organizations such as NATO, WTO, IMF, and the European Union (Bowden and Seabrooke 2006; Stivachtis 2008, 2010). Membership of or assistance from these organizations can be obtained only if the candidate states undertake measures to democratize themselves (Stivachtis 2007).

As in the world of the nineteenth century, democracy promotion today has two significant implications for international politics: first, states that seek to promote democracy abroad create and maintain, consciously or unconsciously, a paternalistic relationship with those that are to be democratized, determining when and how they will achieve democratization; second, democratic conditionality has helped to create new hierarchies in international society, placing the Western states in a privileged position vis-à-vis non-Western countries.

An important outcome of the global spread of democracy in the post-Cold War era is that scholars and politicians alike are increasingly prone to speak of democracy as a "universal value" (Bowden 2009). For example, "democratic peace theory"—the argument that democracies do not wage war against one another, that wars are primarily waged by non-democratic states, either with each other or with democracies—has become one of the most prominent liberal approaches to the academic study of international relations, with important consequences for political practice (Doyle 1997). As a result, debates within both the academic and policymaking worlds have gradually shifted from a Cold War focus on whether democracy constitutes the best form of government to whether and to what extent state and non-state actors should be actively involved in democracy promotion efforts abroad.

A critical aspect of these discussions is our evolving understanding of the relative importance of domestic versus international factors in promoting the spread of democracy. The common denominator of the internal and external approaches to democratization is the Kantian and Wilsonian belief that democracy is central to the creation of a peaceful and prosperous international system. Although key elements of the democratic peace theory have recently been challenged, there still exists a strong belief that the world will be more peaceful if it is inhabited by democratic states.

The emergence of what is essentially a global consensus in favor of democracy promotion has prompted a debate among its proponents as to what forms of intervention should constitute part of the global arsenal in seeking democracy's spread. A range of interventionist tools has been employed in the name of democracy, such as diplomacy, foreign aid, political conditionality, economic sanctions, covert intervention, paramilitary intervention, and military intervention. Questions have been raised as to whether certain tools are both proper and effective in securing democratic norms. In this context, political/democratic conditionality and foreign aid appear to enjoy widespread support—especially in the policymaking establishments of the Western democracies—as a useful "middle road" between diplomacy and military action; a dichotomy that reflects the original differentiation between Paine and Kant. A noteworthy example is the EU's requirement that aspiring countries must attain a certain level of democratic standards before being considered for membership.

The European Union's Conceptualization of Peace and Security

There is a general consensus that the EU plays an ever-increasing role in world affairs (Elgstrom and Smith 2006; Stivachtis 2007; Orbie 2008). Nowhere is the increasing important role of the EU—as a single international actor—in world affairs better reflected than in the European Foreign and Security Policy (EFSP). During the past few years, EFSP has continued its steady development and the EU has gained additional status as an international political player (Kirchner and Sperling 2007). The use of these instruments is guided by the ambitious objectives set out in the European Security Strategy (ESS) that was adopted in December 2003. Despite the criticism it has received and the calls for its revision (Leonard and Gowan 2004; Andersson et al. 2011; Lundin 2012), for the first time the ESS established principles and set clear objectives for advancing the EU's security interests based on the EU's core values. The ESS represents a comprehensive approach to the EU's security. The *Report on the Implementation of the European Security Strategy* that was presented in December 2008 did not seek to replace the ESS, but to reinforce it (European Commission 2008: 1). It provided the EU decision-makers with an opportunity to examine how the EU fared in practice, and what could be done to improve its implementation. Nevertheless, in doing so, it highlighted and emphasized security issues that had not received adequate attention in the 2003 document.

Examining the ESS, one can easily observe that the EU has taken a comprehensive approach to security where "the internal and external aspects of security are indissolubly linked" (European Commission 2003: 2). According to this security approach, threats operate in the military, political, economic, societal, and environmental sectors. In addition, due to the interdependence of the security sectors, threats operating in one sector may give rise to threats in other sectors. As a result, economic failure and poverty, hunger and malnutrition, diseases and pandemics are all seen as being linked and leading to political problems and violent conflict (European Commission 2003: 2). Therefore, security is regarded as a pre-condition of development (European Commission 2003: 2). Conflict not only destroys infrastructure (including social infrastructure), but it also encourages criminality, deters investment and makes normal economic activity impossible. As the ESS and the 2005 Consensus on Development have acknowledged, there cannot be sustainable development without peace and security, and without development and poverty eradication there will be no sustainable peace. In other words, if security is addressed in a comprehensive way, comprehensive EU policies are needed to address security threats effectively. In this process, the promotion of democracy and the establishment of strong democratic states are considered as fundamental. For example, attention is drawn to the fact that the European Neighborhood Policy (ENP) is unequivocally directed at promoting the EU's values "as a means to spread stability, security and prosperity in the southern and eastern neighbourhoods . . . and to strengthen the EU's contribution to the solution of regional conflicts" (Tocci 2007: 7).

Indeed, the study of the EU's security strategy reveals that the creation of stable states is considered as a prerequisite for international peace and stability. At the same time, domestic stability is associated with the establishment of democratic regimes. Consequently, democratization and democracy promotion can been seen as strategies that the EU seeks to employ in order to achieve international peace and security (Stivachtis and Georgakis 2013).

The democracy–security nexus has been clearly established in the 2003 European Security Strategy document, which identifies bad governance, state failure, corruption, and organized crime as major security threats (Stivachtis et al. 2013). According to the European Commission (2003: 4), "Bad governance—corruption, abuse of power, weak institutions and lack of accountability—and civil conflict corrode States from within . . . Collapse of the state can be associated with obvious threats, such as organised crime or terrorism." Consequently, state failure is viewed as an alarming phenomenon that undermines global governance and adds to regional instability. Also, bad governance—reflected in corruption, abuse of power, weak or collapsed institutions, and lack of accountability—and civil conflict lead to state failure, which is regarded as a key threat to the EU's security (European Commission 2003: 4). Therefore, spreading good governance, supporting social and political reform, dealing with corruption and abuse of power, establishing the rule of law, and protecting human rights are viewed by the EU as the best means for increasing European security.

Another key threat to European security is organized crime, which can have links with terrorism (and, in extreme cases, can come to dominate the state). This internal threat to state security, according to the European Security Strategy, has an important external dimension: cross-border trafficking in drugs, women, illegal migrants, and weapons accounts for a large part of the activities of criminal gangs. As it is stated in the ESS document, organized crime:

> can have links with terrorism. Such criminal activities are often associated with weak or failing states. Revenues from drugs have fuelled the weakening of state structures in several drug-producing countries. Revenues from trade in gemstones, timber and small arms, fuel conflict in other parts of the world. All these activities undermine both the rule of law and social order itself. In extreme cases, organised crime can come to dominate the state.
>
> (European Commission 2003: 5)

The 2008 Report acknowledges that progress in fighting organized crime has been slow and incomplete, and highlights the necessity to improve the way in which the EU brings together the internal and external dimensions of organized crime (European Commission 2008: 4). According to the 2008 Report, better coordination, transparency, and flexibility are needed across different agencies, at national and European level.

The European Security Strategy also highlights the security–development nexus by stating that security is "a precondition of development. Conflict not only destroys infrastructure, including social infrastructure; it also encourages criminality, deters investment and makes normal economic activity impossible. A number of countries and regions are caught in a cycle of conflict, insecurity and poverty" (European Commission 2003: 2). Human rights and good governance are also seen as fundamental parts of the equation (European Commission 2008: 2). In other words, democratization—as linked to human rights and good governance—becomes the main instrument to achieve development and peace.

To address these threats, the European Security Strategy calls the EU Member States to "think globally and to act locally" (European Commission 2003: 6). In practice, restoring good government to the Balkans, fostering democracy and enabling the authorities there to tackle organized crime has been seen as one of the most effective ways of dealing with organized crime (European Commission 2003: 6), while building security in its neighborhood has been a priority for the European Union (European Commission 2003: 7). Since democracy is linked to peace and security, it has been in the EU's interest that countries on its borders are well-governed. Neighboring states that are engaged in violent conflict, weak states where organized crime flourishes, dysfunctional societies, or exploding population growth on its borders all pose problems for the European Union. Therefore, the integration of acceding states has been viewed as increasing the EU's security. Consequently, the main EU task has been to promote a ring of well-governed countries to the east of the EU and on the borders of the Mediterranean.

The European Union's Strategic Objectives

Taking into account the threats mentioned above, building security in the EU's neighborhood and promoting an international order based on democracy and effective multilateralism constitute two of the EU's fundamental strategic objectives, with democracy promotion serving as an essential tool to achieve them (European Commission 2003: 7).

The integration of acceding states has brought the EU closer to troubled areas. Therefore, the main task has been the promotion of a ring of well-governed countries to the east of the EU and on the borders of the Mediterranean, with whom the EU enjoys cooperative relations. Consequently, the EU has sought to extend the benefits of economic and political cooperation to its eastern neighbors while tackling political problems there. For example, the EU has taken a stronger and more active interest in the problems of the Southern Caucasus, while the resolution of the Arab–Israeli conflict has been a strategic priority for Europe. The EU's interests in the Mediterranean area—which continues to undergo serious problems of economic stagnation, social unrest, and unresolved conflicts—continue to require a close engagement with Mediterranean partners through economic, security, and cultural cooperation in the framework of the Barcelona Process.

According to the ESS, "in a world of global threats, global markets and global media" EU's security and prosperity "increasingly depend on an effective multilateral system"

(European Commission 2003: 9). Therefore, the development of well-functioning international institutions and a rule-based international order are identified as fundamental EU objectives. In this context, the EU is committed to upholding and developing international law and work within the framework of the UN Charter. Moreover, it is considered in the EU's interest that global and regional international organizations, regimes, and treaties are effective in confronting threats to international peace and security. Because regional organizations strengthen global governance, for the EU the strength and effectiveness of NATO, the OSCE, and the Council of Europe has a particular significance (Forsberg and Herd 2006; Bishop and Lembke 2008; Gheciu 2008). Other regional organizations such as ASEAN, MERCOSUR, and the African Union are also seen as making important contributions to international peace and stability (Söderbaum and Stålgren 2010). What is important to note is that ideas pertaining to democracy and democracy promotion are central to the rhetoric and practices of all these international organizations.

The ESS notes that "the quality of international society depends on the quality of the governments that are its foundation" (European Commission 2003: 10). As a result, the best protection for the EU's security is a world of well-governed democratic states. Trade and development policies are seen as powerful tools for promoting democratic reforms in third states. Contributing to better governance through assistance programs, conditionality and targeted trade measures have consequently become important features in EU's external policy (European Commission 2003: 10).

Having examined how and why the EU sees the establishment of democracy as essential for the attainment of peace and development, the remaining portion of this chapter will discuss how the policy of conditionality and the programs and measures associated with it contribute toward the democratization of states that wish to establish and maintain close relations with the European Union.

EU Conditionality

Among notions of international influences on democratization, "conditionality" represents a deliberate effort to determine the outcome of the process through external pressure (Whitehead 1996; Pridham 2000; Schimmelfennig et al. 2006). This is achieved by specifying conditions or even preconditions for support, involving either promise of material aid or political opportunities. A special version is "democratic conditionality," which emphasizes respect for and the furtherance of democratic rules, procedures, and values. While other international organizations make such conditionality demands, it is the EU that has elaborated an extensive policy of "democratic conditionality." The latter has considerable leverage, because the prize for compliance on the part of applicant states is full EU membership and often financial and development assistance.

Because the EU began as an economic organization, the definition of the economic conditions that prospective member states or third countries should fulfill was in place from the very beginning. It was the end of the Soviet Union, the collapse of communism in Eastern Europe, and the subsequent request of Eastern and Central European countries for EU membership that made "economic" and "political conditionality" a central feature of EU enlargement (Kliewer and Stivachtis 2007: 146). The increasing role of the EU in world affairs also made "economic" and "political conditionality" a central feature of the EU's external policy.

The formulation of "political conditions" (which have been an essential feature of the EEC enlargement since the 1960s) has undergone considerable evolution over time, to include substantive democratic requirements. Initially, it was the European Parliament (EP) that took the initiative to issue a report on the necessary political and institutional conditions for membership and association status of the EEC. The report stated clearly that "only states which guarantee on their territories truly democratic practices and respect for fundamental rights and freedoms can become members of the Community" (cited in Pridham 2005: 30). Subsequent developments related to the relations between the EEC and the authoritarian states in Southern Europe (Greece, Spain, and Portugal) proved essential in assisting the definition of "political conditionality."

The formulation of "political conditionality" became a more central and proactive part of the overall enlargement process, influenced partly by concern over special problems relating to post-communist politics (Pridham 2002b: 205–206). Specifically, since the end of the Cold War in 1989 the EU (then EEC) made assistance and institutional ties—first informally and later formally—conditional on the fulfillment of democratic and human rights standards. In January 1989, the European Parliament demanded that "reference to human rights should figure" in the Trade and Cooperation Agreements the EEC was beginning to negotiate with the Central and Eastern European countries (CEECs), and should be mentioned specifically in the negotiating mandates given to the Commission. In April 1989, the European Council made resumption of the negotiations with Romania conditional upon the country's compliance with its human rights commitments in the CSCE framework. In November of the same year, the Paris European Summit established that "initiatives aimed at the countries of Eastern Europe as a whole are applicable only to those which re-establish freedom and democracy" (cited in Schimmelfennig et al. 2006: 30). In May 1992, the European Council underscored that "respect for democratic principles and human rights . . . as well as the principles of a market economy, constitute essential elements of cooperation and association agreements between the Community and its CSCE partners" (cited in Schimmelfennig et al. 2006: 30). Henceforth, the EU added a clause to the agreements that stipulated a suspension of the agreements if partner countries failed to comply with these principles. In November of the same year, the European Council approved guidelines for PHARE, the EEC's main program of assistance to the CEECs, which made aid conditional upon the state of advance of the reforms in each of the beneficiary countries. In July 1993, the new regulations of the aid program for the former Soviet republics (TACIS) strengthened conditionality to coincide with the degree of progress toward reform in the beneficiary nation (Schimmelfennig et al. 2006: 31).

At its Copenhagen Summit in June 1993, the European Council established the "stability of institutions guaranteeing democracy, the rule of law, human rights and respect for and protection of minorities" as the *sin qua non* for accession to the European Union. The Copenhagen political conditions have been elaborated on in the European Commission's (EC) Opinion of 1997 and from 1998 in the regular annual reports on candidate countries. The political conditions have been tied in with EU's programs of financial assistance, the accession partnerships, and the whole pre-accession strategy (Papadimitriou and Phinnemore 2004; Knill and Lenschow 2005).

EU Conditionality and Candidate States

Before the EU acknowledges an applicant state as a member, the applicant state's behavior must be modified to fit within liberal norms. Conditionality of acceptance uses a reward system to entice applicant states to adopt EU norms. The European Commission relies upon five "levers" of conditionality: (1) access to negotiations and further stages in the accession process; (2) provision of legislative and institutional templates; (3) aid and technical assistance; (4) policy advice and twinning projects; and (5) monitoring, demarches, and public criticism (Grabbe 1998, 1999, 2006: 261).

If the EU conditions are not met, the EU has three reinforcement strategies available for use: reinforcement by reward, reinforcement by punishment, and reinforcement by support (Schimmelfennig and Sedelmeir 2005a: 108; 2005b). Reinforcement strategies differ from persuasion in two fundamental ways: first, reinforcement polices are exercised in an asymmetrical power structure where incentives and disincentives are used to entice applicants to adopt desired norms; and second, reinforcement polices look to modify state behavior over time (Schimmelfennig et al. 2003: 498). The substance of the reinforcement strategies involves two components: material incentives and social reinforcement (Schimmelfennig 2005a: 109). Material incentives involve tangible rewards, including (but not limited to) financial assistance, market access, technology experience, and participation in decision. Social reinforcement refers to "sociopsychological" rewards such as international recognition and public praise (Schimmelfennig 2005a: 109).

The EU's potential for impacting democratization in candidate states varies between three broad stages: first, pre-negotiations (when the Copenhagen criteria have to be satisfied before negotiations commence); second, actual negotiations (when political conditions as updated are monitored regularly); and third, once membership begins when the EU's direct leverage over new entrants begins to weaken, but at the same time the indirect effects of European integration in helping to consolidate democracy increase through the very intensification of networking that goes with membership (Pridham 2002a: 957). Although the deeper effects of integration most likely occur through the embedding of new democracies within the EU itself, the most decisive stages for direct effects remain the pre-negotiation and accession negotiation stages. During the first phase, negotiations may be blocked by a country's failure to satisfy the political conditions; during the second phase, negotiations may be interrupted or terminated if a negotiating country reverses its fulfillment of the political conditions, or chooses seriously to violate any one of them.

EU Conditionality and the Democratization and the EU's Neighborhood

The European Neighbourhood Policy (ENP) is a valuable tool for increasing democratization and security in the states surrounding the EU borders in the sense that in order to obtain the benefits of the ENP or be a signatory to bilateral agreements with the EU, states must show commitment to the respect of human rights, political freedoms, and democratization. Even though candidacy may not be a short-term goal for some of these states, the EU nevertheless emphasizes the importance of building communication and shared values related to issues such as security, democracy, human rights, political freedom, environmental protection, and trade liberalization.

In 2001, the Commission laid out a set of policies that characterize the overall approach to democratization in external countries and recommended: the promotion of consistent policies among states; a proactive approach, focusing on political dialogue and assistance; and the adoption of a strategic approach, focusing on the implementation of specific projects (Commission Communication 2001). According to the European Commission, there were many areas and situations that required attention in the aspect of assessing democratization and the protection of human rights (Commission Communication 2003). Following the Communication from the European Commission to the Council and the European Parliament (European Commission 2003), the ENP was developed in 2004 with the objective of strengthening the prosperity, stability, and security of the EU and its neighboring states.

The ENP framework proposed to 16 of the EU's closest neighbors is manly a bilateral policy between the EU and each partner country. However, it is complemented by regional and multilateral cooperation initiatives such as the Eastern Partnership (launched in Prague in May 2009), the Union for the Mediterranean (the Euro-Mediterranean Partnership, formerly known as the Barcelona Process, relaunched in Paris in July 2008), and the Black Sea Synergy (launched in Kiev in February 2008) (Mocanu 2010).

In the ENP framework, the EU uses financial and diplomatic means to ensure that there is a move toward democratization in third states. In 2010–2011, the EU reviewed the ENP and put a strong focus on the promotion of deep and sustainable democracy, accompanied by inclusive economic development (European Commission 2011). Within the ENP, the EU offers its neighbors a privileged relationship, building upon a mutual commitment to common values (democracy and human rights, rule of law, good governance, market economy principles, and sustainable development). The ENP builds upon the legal agreements in place between the EU and the partner in question with Partnership and Cooperation Agreements (PCA) or Association Agreements (AA). Implementation of the ENP is jointly promoted and monitored through the committees and subcommittees established in the frame of these agreements. The European External Action Service and the European Commission publish each year the ENP Progress Reports. The assessments contained in the Progress Reports form the basis for EU policy toward each ENP partner (Schimmelfennig 2005b).

Central to the ENP are the bilateral "Action Plans" between the EU and each ENP partner. These set out an agenda of political and economic reforms with short- and medium-term priorities of three to five years. ENP Action Plans reflect each partner's needs and capacities, as well as their and the EU's interests. Under the ENP Action Plans, the EU works together with its partners to develop democratic, socially equitable, and inclusive societies. Because civil society plays an important role in contributing to democracy and good governance building in partner countries, the EU supports organizations via the Civil Society Facility. Moreover, the EU offers its neighbors economic integration, improved circulation of people across borders, financial assistance, and technical cooperation toward approximation with EU standards. The European Commission provides financial support in grant form to partners; the European Investment Bank and the European Bank for Reconstruction and Development complement this support through loans.

Countries determinedly embarking on political reforms are offered, in addition to the incentives available to other partners, elements of market access: economic integration and development (DCFTAs), mobility of people (mobility partnerships), and a greater share of the EU financial support. In this context, the Commission decided to set up specific programs both for the Eastern (EAPIC) and Southern (SPRING) neighbors that will allocate extra financial support only to those neighbors taking clear and concrete steps on political reforms.

While the EU includes the language of democratization in agreements made with third states, there are no clear, concrete political ramifications for third states that do not further pursue democratization. Economic incentives and positive conditionality—such as the financial aid given to particular programs or organizations in third parties—is a popular way for the EU to influence democratization measures. However, their effectiveness should be critically examined as there may be concerns that the involvement with the EU in the Mediterranean can inadvertently support authoritarian regimes (Gillespie and Whitehead 2002: 198). Despite the criticism it has received (Sasse 2008), the ENP has served as a valuable tool for increasing democratization and security in the states surrounding the borders of the European Union. At the same time, despite its integrative potential, the analysis of case studies in various policy sectors has revealed that the network governance provided by the ENP is not void of hegemonic traits (Tzifakis 2007; Lavenex 2008).

EU Conditionality and the Democratization of the ACP Countries

The origins of the EU's development policy date back to 1957, when the European Economic Community (EEC) was created and its relations with the sub-Africa, the Caribbean, and the Pacific states (ACP) were established. Following the decolonization process, a new approach was needed to regulate the relations between the European states and the new independent states. The Yaoundé Conventions grounded the relations on a legal basis and provided the fertile ground for the enhancement of the partnership between the EEC and these states. Later, the Lomé Conventions sought to provide a broader and enhanced relation between the partners. Lomé IV (1990–2000) became the first development agreement to incorporate a human rights clause as a "fundamental part of cooperation." An updated clause confirmed human rights as an "essential element of cooperation," signifying that any violation could lead to partial or total suspension of development aid by the EU after prior consultation of other ACP nations and the abusing party (Holland 2002; Youngs 2003).

When the Cotonou Agreement was established in 2000, it introduced a new approach to EU-ACP relations while preserving the fundamental instruments of the partnership from the Lomé Conventions—including conditionality clauses on human rights (European Commission 2010a). With the Cotonou Agreement, the EU changed its role from a sole aid provider to an international actor that would monitor on a regular basis the application of the political conditionality principles by its ACP partners (Marsh and Mackenstein 2005; Bretherton and Volger 2006). Thus, EU development assistance became a motive for these developing countries to reform their policies and practices associated with democracy, the rule of law, social justice, and respect for human rights.

The European Commission contends that stability and security are some of the most important factors for long-term engagement with third states. Thus, by focusing on "good governance": in some of the most politically unstable regions, the EU seeks to address "the root causes of conflict and insecurity" (European Commission 2010b: 2). Established by the European Parliament in 1994, the European Initiative for Democracy and Human Rights (EIDHR) focuses precisely on the issue of democratization and the promotion on human rights in third countries (Commission Communication 2003). This primarily takes place through funding activities of nongovernmental and international organizations. In 2003, the annual sum for the worldwide projects amounted to €100 million—making the organization the world's largest aid donor (Commission Communication 2012: 1).

According to the 2012 Annual Report by EUROPEAID, the need to deliver aid cannot be removed from democratization efforts, or the further pursuit of human rights regimes (Commission Communication 2012: 1). For example, the report places particular emphasis on the EU's relationship with Central Asian states, where it is "seen as a close political ally and trusted partner on whom they can rely on [*sic*] in the challenging transition process on which they have embarked" (Commission Communication 2012: 5). Similarly, the EU–Latin America/Caribbean (LAC) Madrid summit in May 2010 outlined greater political relations with Central and South American countries. Even in Southeast Asia, the EU works toward strengthening bilateral partnerships with countries to increase the promotion of democratization in the region, in the hopes of securing other regions in order to secure EU's interests (Commission Communication 2012: 6).

Although it has received considerable criticism (Holland 2002), EU development policy has served as a valuable tool for increasing democratization in the developing and less developed world. On the other hand, it has been acknowledged that the degree of acceptance and implementation of the EU political conditions is subject to two constraints: first, the financial, political and social constraints facing the countries in question; second, the lack of significant economic and financial benefits that these states could extract from the EU even if they introduce the changes requested (Marsh and Mackenstein 2005). In other words, as in the case of the ENP states, the governments of the developing and less developed states are confronted by a basic question: why should they introduce any social, political, and economic changes that would probably meet popular resistance if the costs of doing so are higher than the benefits they could gain? In addition, there is a difference between the formal introduction of institutional changes, on the one hand, and their implementation and enforcement, on the other—as historical, societal, economic, and political conditions in the countries at hand would only allow the democratization process to produce concrete results in the medium and long run. Last, but not least, the EU approach to ACP countries is not void of hegemonic traits (Hurt 2003; Sepos 2013).

Conclusion

The purpose of this chapter was twofold: first, to provide a historical account of the development of democracy promotion as an international norm; and second, to discuss democracy promotion as a European Union (EU) strategy to address security threats.

Since the end of the Cold War, the EU has acted as the stage of a large-scale project of international socialization (Flockhart 2005) with democracy promotion lying at the heart of this process. When communism collapsed and the Soviet Union ceased to exist, European organizations proclaimed liberal democracy as the standard of legitimacy for the "new Europe." Among European organizations, the EU assumed the task of inducting the ex-communist Central and Eastern European countries to this standard, and devised several programs and institutional arrangements to assist and advance their democratic transformation. Among those programs and institutional arrangements, conditionality has played a major role in the socialization and democratization of candidate countries.

However, it was not only within candidate states that the strategy of democratization was deployed. ENP and ACP countries have also become subject to the prioritization of democracy and human rights. Thus, it is not simply about making the space *within* the EU democratic. Rather, the EU sees the promotion of democracy in regions across the globe as an issue that is relevant not just to the regions involved, but also to European security. The language of security in EU documents is directly linked to the stability of democratic regimes throughout the world. Consequently, foreign aid and development assistance have been used as mechanisms for increasing the likelihood of states developing democratic practices.

The pressures of international anarchy in conjunction with power and interdependence asymmetries (Engelbrekt 2002) and the subsequent need of ENP and ACP states to maintain close relations with the EU in order to achieve their national goals and objectives enables the Union to define certain expectations and impose certain standards of behavior on the former. Therefore, EU pressures aimed at altering attitudes and policies have been equally applicable to all states irrespective of whether or not they seek EU membership. At the same time, despite their integrative potential, the study of the ENP- and ACP-related frameworks reveal that the network governance provided is characterized by its hegemonic traits.

All this begs the question of how successful the EU has been in achieving its political and strategic objectives; the answer depends on the degree of the EU's commitment. In other words, the governments of the ENP and ACP states are confronted by a dilemma: why should they introduce any social, political, and economic changes that would result in social upheaval and loss of popularity and legitimacy if the costs of doing so are higher than the benefits they could gain? In addition, there is a difference between the formal introduction of institutional changes and their enforcement, which means that laws, rules, regulations, and policies may be formally introduced to satisfy EU conditions but may not be implemented in practice.

References

Andersson, J.J., Brattberg, E., Häggqvist, M. and Ojanen, H. (2011) *The European Security Strategy: Reinvigorate, Revise or Reinvent?* UI Occasional Papers, Swedish Institute of International Affairs.

Bishop, S. and Lembke, J. (2008) *EU Enlargement and the Transatlantic Alliance: A Security Relationship in Flux*, Boulder, CO: Lynne Rienner.

Bowden, B. (2009) *The Empire of Civilization*, Chicago, IL: Chicago University Press.

Bowden, B. and Seabrook, L. (2006) *Global Standards of Market Civilization*, London: Routledge.

Bozeman, A. (1960) *Politics and Culture in International History*, Princeton, NJ: Princeton University Press.

Bretherton, C. and Volger, J. (2006) *The European Union as a Global Actor* (2nd ed.), London: Routledge.

Bull, H. and Watson, A. (Eds.) (1984) *The Expansion of International Society*, Oxford: Clarendon Press.

Commission Communication (2001) *The European Union's Role in Promoting Human Rights and Democratisation in Third Countries*, COM(2001) 252 final, May 8.

Commission Communication (2003) *Wider Europe—Neighbourhood: A New Framework for Relations with Our Eastern and Southern Neighbours*, COM(2003) 104 final, March 11.

Commission Communication (2004) *European Neighbourhood Policy*, COM(2004) 373 final, May 12.

Commission Communication (2012) *Annual Report 2012 on the European Union's Development and External Assistance Policies and their Implementation in 2011*, COM(2012) 444 final, August 6.

Donnelly, J. (1998) "Human Rights: A New Standard of Civilization?" *International Affairs*, 74(1): 1–24.

Doyle, M. (1997) *Ways of War*, London: Norton.

Elgstrom, O. and Smith, M. (2006) *The European Union's Roles in International Politics*, London: Routledge.

Elias, N. (1978) *The Civilizing Process*, New York: Urizen Books.

Engelbrekt, K. (2002) "Multiple Asymmetries: The European Union's Neo-Byzantine Approach to Eastern Enlargement," *International Politics*, 39(1): 37–51.

European Commission (2003) *European Security Strategy: A Secure Europe in a Better World*, Brussels, December 12, available at: www.consilium.europa.eu/uedocs/cmsUpload/78367.pdf (accessed September 7, 2012).

European Commission (2008) *Report on the Implementation of the European Security Strategy: Providing Security in a Changing World*, Brussels, December 11, available at: www.consilium.europa.eu/ueDocs/cms_Data/docs/pressdata/EN/reports/104630.pdf (accessed September 7, 2012).

European Commission (2010a) *European Instrument for Democracy and Human Rights (EIDHR)*, Strategy Paper 2007–2010, April 1.

European Commission (2010b) *European Instrument for Democracy and Human Rights (EIDHR)*, Strategy Paper 2011–2013, April 21.

European Commission (2011) *A New Response to a Changing Neighbourhood: A Review of European Neighbourhood Policy*, Joint Communication by the High Representative of the Union for Foreign Affairs and Security Policy and the European Commission, Brussels, 25 May 2011, available at: http://eeas.europa.eu/enp/pdf/pdf/com_11_303_en.pdf (accessed December 14, 2015).

European Commission (2012a) *EU Awarded the Nobel Peace Prize*, available at: http://ec.europa.eu/languages/news/20121012-eu-nobel-peace-prize_en.htm (accessed December 8, 2012).

European Commission (2012b) *Joint Statement of José Manuel Barroso, President of the European Commission, and Herman Van Rompuy, President of the European Council on the Award of the 2012 Nobel Peace Prize to the EU*, available at: http://europa.eu/rapid/press-release_MEMO-12-779_en.htm#PR_metaPressRelease_bottom (accessed December 8, 2012).

Fidler, D. (2001) "The Return of the Standard of Civilization," *Journal of International Law*, 2001(1): 137–157.

Flockhart, T. (Ed.) (2005) *Socializing Democratic Norms*, Basingstoke: Palgrave.

Forsberg, T. and Herd, G.P. (2006) *Divided West: European Security and the Transatlantic Relationship*, London: Chatham House.

Fukuyama, F. (1992) *The End of History and the Last Man*, London: Hamish Hamilton.

Gheciu, A. (2008) *Securing Civilization: The EU, NATO and the OSCE in the Post-9/11 World*, Oxford: Oxford University Press.

Gillespie, R. and Whitehead, L. (2002) "European Democracy Promotion in North Africa: Limits and Prospects," *Democratization*, 9(1): 192–206.

Gong, G. (1984) *The Standard of Civilization in International Society*, Oxford: Clarendon Press.

Grabbe, H. (1998) *Enlarging Europe Eastward*, London: Cassell.

Grabbe, H. (1999) *A Partnership for Accession? The Implications of EU Conditionality for the Central and Eastern European Applicants*, Florence: EUI.

Grabbe, H. (2006) *The EU's Transformative Power: Europeanization through Conditionality in Central and Eastern Europe*, Basingstoke: Palgrave.

Holland, M. (2002) *The European Union and the Third World*, Basingstoke: Palgrave.

Hurt, S. (2003) "Cooperation and Coercion? The Cotonou Agreement between the European Union and ACP States and the End of the Lome Convention," *Third World Quarterly*, 24: 161–176.

Kant, I. ([1795] 1991) "Perpetual Peace," in H. Reiss (Ed.), *Kant's Political Writings*, Cambridge: Cambridge University Press, pp. 93–130.

Kirchner, E. and Sperling, J. (2007) *EU Security Governance*, Manchester: Manchester University Press.

Kliewer, B. and Stivachtis, Y.A. (2007) "Democratizing and Socializing Candidate States: The Case of EU Conditionality," in Y.A. Stivachtis (Ed.), *The State of European Integration*, Aldershot: Ashgate, pp. 143–160.

Knill, C. and Lenschow, A. (2005) "Compliance, Competition and Communication: Different Approaches to European Governance and Their Impact on National Institutions," *Journal of Common Market Studies*, 43(3): 583–606.

Lavenex, S. (2008) "A Governance Perspective on the European Neighborhood Policy: Integraiton Beyond Conditionality?" *Journal of European Public Policy*, 15(6): 938–955.

Leonard, M. and Gowan, R. (2004) *Global Europe: Implementing the European Security Strategy*, Brussels: The British Council.

Lundin, L-E. (2012) *From European Security Strategy to a European Global Strategy*, UI Occasional Papers, Swedish Institute of International Affairs.

Marsh, S. and Mackenstein, H. (2005) *International Relations of the European Union*, London: Pearson Longman.

Mocanu, O. (2010) "Brief Overview on the Conditionality in the European Neighbourhood Policy," *Romanian Journal of European Affairs*, 10(4): 42–49.

Muravchik, J. (1992) *Exporting Democracy*, Washington, DC: AEI Press.

Orbie, J. (Ed.) (2008) *Europe's Global Role: External Policies of the European Union*, Aldershot: Ashgate.

Paine, T. ([1776] 1986) *Common Sense*, London: Penguin Books.

Papadimitriou, D. and Phinnemore, D. (2004) "Europeanisation, Conditionality and Domestic Change," *Journal of Common Market Studies*, 42(3): 619–639.

Pridham, G. (2000) *The Dynamics of Democratisation: A Comparative Approach*, London: Continuum.

Pridham, G. (2002a) "EU Enlargement and Consolidation Democracy in Post-Communist States: Formality and Reality," *Journal of Common Market Studies*, 40(3): 953–973.

Pridham, G. (2002b) "The European Union's Democratic Conditionality and Domestic Politics in Slovakia," *Europe-Asia Studies*, 54(2): 203–227.

Pridham, G. (2005) *Designing Democracy: EU Enlargement and Regime Change in Post-Communist Europe*, New York: Palgave.

Sasse, G. (2008) "The European Neighbourhood Policy: Conditionality Revisited for the EU's Eastern Neighbours," *Europe-Asia Studies*, 60(2): 295–316.

Schimmelfennig, F. (2005a) "The EU: Promoting Liberal Democracy Through Membership Conditionality," in T. Flockhart (Ed.), *Socializing Democratic Norms*, Basingstoke: Palgrave, pp. 106–126.

Schimmelfennig, F. (2005b) *European Neighborhood Policy: Political Conditionality and Its Impact on Democracy in Non-Candidate Neighbouring Countries*, paper presented at the 9th EUSA Biennial Conference, Austin, Texas, March 31–April 2, Austin, Texas.

Schimmelfennig, F. and Sedelmeir, U. (2005a) *The Politics of European Union Enlargement*, London: Routledge.

Schimmelfennig, F. and Sedelmeir, U. (Eds.) (2005b) *The Europeanization of Central and Eastern Europe*, Ithaca, NY: Cornell University Press.

Schimmelfennig, F., Engert, S., and Knobel, H. (2003) "Costs, Commitment and Compliance: The Impact of EU Democratic Conditionality on Latvia, Slovakia and Turkey," *Journal of Common Market Studies*, 41(3): 495–518.

Schimmelfennig, F., Engert, S., and Knobel, H. (2006) *International Socialization in Europe: European Organizations, Political Conditionality and Democratic Change*, Basingstoke: Palgrave.

Sepos, A. (2013) "Imperial Power Europe? The EU's Relations with the ACP Countries," *Journal of Political Power*, 6(2): 261–287.

Söderbaum, F. and Stålgren, P. (Eds.) (2010) *The European Union and the Global South*, Aldershot: Ashgate.

Stivachtis, Y. (2007) "The EU as an International Actor," in Y.A. Stivachtis (Ed.), *The State of European Integration*, Aldershot: Ashgate, pp. 41–58.

Stivachtis, Y. (2008) "The Standard of Civilization in Contemporary International Society: The Case of the European Union," *Contemporary Politics*, 14(1): 71–90.

Stivachtis, Y. (2010) "Civilizing the Post-Soviet/Socialist Space," *Perspectives: Review of International Affairs*, 18(2): 5–32.

Stivachtis, Y. and Georgakis, S. (2013) "Democratization as a Peace Strategy," in M. Stephenson Jr., Y.A. Stivachtis, and L. Zanotti (Eds.), *The European Union and Peacebuilding*, Special Issue, *Review of European Studies* 5(3): 95–104.

Stivachtis, Y., Price, C., and Habegger, M. (2013) "The European Union as a Peace Actor," in M. Stephenson Jr., Y.A. Stivachtis, and L. Zanotti (Eds.), *The European Union and Peacebuilding*, Special Issue, *Review of European Studies* 5(3): 4–17.

Tocci, N. (2007) *The EU and Conflict Resolution: Promoting Peace in the Backyard*, London: Routledge.

Tzifakis, N. (2007) "EU's Region-Building and Boundary-Drawing Policies: The European Approach to the Southern Mediterranean and the Western Balkans," *Journal of Southern Europe and the Balkans*, 9(1): 47–64.

Watson, A. (1992) *The Evolution of International Society*, London: Routledge.

Whitehead, L. (Ed.) (1996) *The International Dimensions of Democratization*, Oxford: Oxford University Press.

Youngs, R. (2003) "European Approaches to Democracy Assistance: Learning the Right Lessons?" *Third World Quarterly*, 24(1): 127–138.

Chapter 3

The EU's Democracy Promotion in Its "Neighborhood": Renegotiating the Post-Arab Spring Framework

Manasi Singh

Democracy promotion tied to development aid was one of the main strategic objectives of the Western powers during the Cold War. Democracy has also become a salient feature of European Union (EU) external governance and figures as a resonant theme in its key policy documents—Lisbon Treaty, Copenhagen Criteria for EU membership, European Security Strategy (ESS), European Development Policy, and the European Neighbourhood Policy (ENP).[1] The EU projects democracy as a positive form of governance to fight poverty and encourage development, and subsequently to build peace and stability. Thus, there is a clear causal link between development and new conceptualizations of security by the EU (Peters [personal communication] 2011). The global interconnectedness and its concomitant negative policy externalizations have led the EU to collaborate with its neighborhood in pursuit of constructive policy solutions (Filtenborg et al. 2002: 389). The changed security landscape in the aftermath of the September 11 terrorist attacks, the ensuing war in Iraq in 2003, and the big bang enlargement[2] of the EU in 2004 and 2007 further reinforced the normative foundations for exporting democracy.

In such a context, the EU's narrative of democracy promotion serves as an extremely powerful rationale for its political, economic, and security interests in this so-called neighborhood, and is often presented as a response to the changing realities in a variety of different contexts throughout the many countries that comprise it. However, the reality is more complex than what EU discursive practices imply (Hinnebusch 2006). As Bicchi (2009: 75) notes, "the daily practices of promotion of democracy have been more modest than EU discourse on democracy." Despite its philanthropic essence, much of the EU's international aid is caught up in geopolitics and so is the ENP, which is primarily driven by the EU's security interests related to migration, energy, and combating terrorism. The ESS of 2003 calls for promoting a "ring of well-governed countries" around the EU—a sentiment echoed by the ENP that refers to "shared interests," which ultimately boil down to the EU's interests (Zaiotti 2007). Malmvig (2006) aptly refers to this as a built-in tension between liberal discourse and cooperative security discourse; a dilemma between offering friendship, and building fences. The EU's lack of commitment to softening the Schengen borders reinforces the idea that its neighbors are a potential security threat.

Until 2011, stability was the preferred choice in the Mediterranean region at the expense of democracy—at least in practice. The stability–democracy promotion dilemma was resolved in favor of a stable autocracy over a fragile democracy, creating a tension between stability and legitimacy (Börzel, personal communication, April 19, 2011). As post-Arab Spring the Mediterranean region remains volatile, the logical question is how the EU might export its democratic model to a region that is gradually turning into a laboratory of ideas and discourses—challenging the EU's normative and ideational project. The political transitions and their outcomes are unpredictable. A democratic model ushered in the aftermath of popular uprisings and the growing popularity of Islamist groups may not be to the liking of the EU. Moreover, with the US keeping a close eye on the region, a point of scrutiny can be whether the EU and US efforts to promote democracy are in tandem. The goal of democracy promotion as a critical component of the EU's foreign, security, and development policies needs further assessment given that the new external challenges in Eastern Europe, West Asia, and Africa often see less consensus-building among the EU 28.

The chapter attempts to build an immanent critique of the EU's discourse on democracy promotion and its image as a force for good in light of the Union's misplaced perception of the neighborhood region. The ENP having been in operation for more than a decade stands at a crossroads. The chapter argues that the normative aspirations of the EU in expanding the "zone of prosperity, stability and security" beyond the EU's borders have not translated into success. In fact, it is the unintended consequences of the EU's misconceived and ill-informed policies that have made its neighborhood more politically fragmented and unstable. By holding up democracy as an unquestionable value and an end in itself, the EU takes for granted that democracy and political reform is external to the region, and thus can be successfully exported. The first section of the chapter contextualizes and analyzes the ENP framework under which the EU attempts to promote democracy in its backyard. The second section argues that the EU's democracy promotion is nothing but an exercise in *real-politik*, where interests take precedence over norms and values. The third section examines the EU's response to the pro-democracy social movements unleashed by the Arab Spring in 2011, and the fourth concludes with the argument that instead of following an outdated prescription, the EU needs to come out of its paradoxical thinking and reflect upon alternative values and factor in the changing realities to develop a more meaningful engagement with its neighborhood.

Contextualizing the ENP Framework: Norm Promotion vs. Security Management

To some extent, the focus in EU foreign policy shifted from human rights to broad political reform only after September 11, 2001. The rationale for this was that democracy promotion policies must be better articulated and structured in order to achieve long-term goals. The EU's engagement with its near abroad represents one of the most critical areas of its foreign and security policy, which will also have implications for its future evolution and capability as a global actor (Dannreuther 2004). As the events unfold in Ukraine and Syria and the EU grapples with a changed political landscape in its neighborhood, it needs to prioritize and sharpen the focus of its foreign and security policy toward the countries and regions along its borders. It was to resolve the dilemma on its never-ending enlargement that the EU devised the ENP. The timing of this policy was also crucial in view of the accession of 10 countries in 2004, which along with them brought several frozen conflicts, migration problems, and other related security issues closer to Europe's borders. To address these issues, the ENP offers the countries in the EU's eastern and southern neighborhood many benefits (such as financial assistance, technical support, and access to markets) except membership. These benefits are conditional upon ENP countries fulfilling their commitments to strengthen the rule of law, democracy, and respect for human rights; promoting market-oriented economic reforms; and cooperating on key foreign policy objectives such as counterterrorism and nonproliferation of weapons of mass destruction. As they make progress on these fronts, the EU is to deepen its partnership and offer more rewards.

The interrelated logics of stabilization (associated with the need for secured and properly managed EU borders) and that of democracy promotion and reform (to reduce the socioeconomic gap for the EU's outer frontiers) inform the ENP objectives. The former stems from the need for an increased cooperation in fighting against transborder threats, a high-priority agenda for the EU and its citizens. The latter reflects the enlarged Union's ambition to enhance its normative and strategic engagement in wider Europe. However, such a pursuit is a tightrope walk for the EU fraught with dilemmas and challenges. It has been argued that the EU's policy toward the neighborhood is about pursuing a double strategy: the identification of the EU as a normative power, on the one hand, and, on the other, the pursuit of political and economic interests. The challenge is how to synchronize two interrelated yet conflicting logics.

The Lisbon Treaty states that in international affairs, the EU would seek to promote the values on which the Union is founded, including democracy, human rights, fundamental freedoms, and the rule of law (European Commission 2007). Leveraging its normative power, the EU strives to build a secure and peaceful Europe by promoting norms of democracy, rule of law, and using the multilateral framework for dispute settlement. Acting as a "force for good," these very norms, values, and *acquis* that define the EU are also projected upon the neighborhood in order to provide a sense of orientation and purpose to third states (Scott and Liikanen 2011). As Lippert states, "the ENP reflected an ordering principle for structuring the neighbourhood in accordance with principles, values and procedures on which the EU is based and for which it enters into international relations" (Lippert 2008: 6). However, the problem lies in installing its own value framework of top-down Europeanization in a setting with little or no previous experience of democratic rule (Shapovalova and Youngs 2012). The ENP and its carrot of a privileged partnership attempts to extend "the idea of Europe," not conceptualized in the cartographic sense per se but an idea understood in terms of having a European identity (Møller 2005). The rationale of the partnership approach enshrined in ENP before 2011 was that the EU is an inherently civilian power that does not seek to impose its values, but rather seeks to persuade and attract its neighbors. The EU aims to be a pole of attraction by serving as a reference point for EU partners to emulate (Tulmets 2007: 205). The paradox of this rationale is that the "outside" view of democracy and reform seems to be in conflict with the "inside" view.

According to the Commission's strategy paper on ENP, "the level of the EU's ambition in developing links with each partner through the ENP will take into account the extent to which these values are effectively shared" (European Commission 2004: 13). This was essentially "a softly phrased reference to conditionality: the more the country conforms to EU values, the closer it can co-operate with the EU" (Kelley 2006: 30). This security-driven EU rhetoric, as distinct from the original discourse on "increasing the neighbours' prosperity, stability and security" necessitated a parallel shift in the methodology of the ENP. Conditionality serves in this context as a promising tool of the EU to promote democracy. For it to work, it has to offer attractive incentives such as trade liberalization and financial assistance. It has to be credible in terms of having clearly defined and measurable criteria and evaluation mechanism(s); it must have low adoption costs; there must be a lack of alternatives for the target country to gain the desired incentive; and it should not adversely affect the interests of important stakeholders in the target country (Schimmelfennig and Sedelmeier 2006). In addition to the qualifications attached to conditionality, there are other complex issues, including the linkages between political demands and economic incentives, the ability of the EU and its member states to coordinate and deliver such incentives, and the need to devise tailor-made policies toward individual countries. It also calls for questioning the very assumption regarding the EU's legitimacy in using conditionality in any country. The application of this criteria, therefore, has made ENP a less attractive option for the neighbourhood countries as the EU faces increasing contestation of the very values it seeks to promote via ENP framework. The Arab revolutions have put forth competing narratives of democracy and reform. The "brand EU" faces rivalry from other actors in the region who are offering normative and strategic alternatives. The next section sets the tone for this discussion.

Democracy Promotion via ENP: Nothing but *Realpolitik*

The absolute priority that democracy promotion has been assigned in US and EU foreign policies post-9/11 stems from linking terrorism to backwardness (Aliboni 2005). Democracy promotion and the correction of failed states is the underlying theme of the ESS, the first of its kind adopted in 2003. The ESS calls for an all-encompassing approach to prevent security spillover, which means building a conducive international environment consisting of the democratic states with good-quality control systems. Building on Manners' (2002) conception of normative power, the EU aims to create an international identity by promoting its values through its interaction and socialization with other actors (Diez 2005). Socialization implies that the EU engages its neighborhood countries through multiple institutional contacts and joint activities, thereby facilitating a successful transformation. Lavenex and Schimmelfennig (2011) explain EU democracy promotion through three models viz. linkage, leverage, and governance. Linkage refers to the bottom-up support for enabling and empowering societal, nongovernmental actors to work for democracy. Leverage constitutes a top-down strategy of democracy promotion where the EU targets third-country governments with the aim of inducing them toward democratic reforms. This inducement is done through conditionality. However, all this is not sufficient to foster a democratic culture and civil society. It is the ENP's governance model of democracy promotion that guides principles and practices in the conduct of public policy—such as transparency, accountability, and participation.

However, the EU's actual policy postures toward its neighborhood contradict this self-conception. It is argued that an "interests and values" approach is better suited to explain political outcomes in EU external relations (Pace 2006). The civilian and normative power that the EU claims itself to be is in no way different from the pursuits of realist foreign policy and security interests by other states. The ENP's aim to create a "ring of friends" along the EU's periphery is a friendship not founded on equal footing or benevolence. Such celebrated norms and values as the EU's USP are not meant to be exported out of a philanthropic zeal; rather, these "exports" have a price drawn up and decided in Brussels. The ENP is a foreign policy instrument and its democracy promotion agenda is thus squarely political.[3] Concerns such as the dependence on the Mediterranean energy resources and the need to secure partners to avoid derailment of the West Asian peace process constrain the EU to use sanctions against violators. As T. Risse (personal communication, April 19, 2011) suggests, it is unclear whether the EU supports democracy as a normative goal or for its own security. Successful norm transfer is assumed to have taken place whenever EU regulations become enshrined in national legislation of third countries (Van Hüllen 2011). The ENP is tasked with developing a policy that "stabilises the neighbourhood and draws it into a virtual circle of development and democracy without offering the prospect of accession" (Balfour and Rotta 2005: 8). This poses a perennial dilemma before the EU of reconciling the conflicting objectives of securing the neighborhood and managing the neighbors' accession aspirations. The very legitimacy of a policy needs to be questioned, which seeks to offer "all but institutions." Although the ENP has made promoting democracy and human rights a priority, the EU's response raises doubts about the depth of its commitment on this front. The EU's unwillingness to extend official membership perspectives further dampens the incentives for democratic reforms among countries such as Ukraine (Emerson and Youngs 2009). "Incidents like manipulation of the Tunisian elections, the imprisonment of democracy activists in Egypt, a restrictive law on political parties in Morocco, an amnesty for the perpetrators of human rights abuses in Algeria have exposed the gap between EU's rhetoric and actual action" (Cameron and Balfour 2006: 10). The EU finds itself caught between the need to promote good governance—considered as a long-term solution to many economic, social, and demographic security threats—and the simultaneously realist-driven interest of preserving the political stability of many authoritarian regimes out of strategic and geopolitical calculations. This implies that *realpolitik* plays a prominent role in the EU's formulation and implementation of democracy promotion policies.

The EU, however, needs to develop a more nuanced understanding of the current challenges to democracy promotion. Each country is a *sui generis* case where the "backlash" (though having a similar form and nature) has its roots in different structural factors unique to that country, its geopolitical and historical context. The goal and the accompanying process of democracy promotion must be informed by the characteristics of the local political culture and societal identity, especially when the target audience has never really lived the experience of a democracy. The cultural and ideological fault lines that have emerged after the popular protests are making it difficult to reach any agreement on goals and the means of achieving them. Experiments in Afghanistan and Iraq have given rise to competing visions of democracy and delegitimization of the neoliberal and Western conception. The EU must factor in the changing realities of international politics while designing strategies to facilitate deepening of democracy. It must be receptive to the new discourse rather than promoting certain social and cultural constructions that perpetuate institutions and practices.

The role of internal factors such as the country's domestic structures also needs to be thoroughly examined while assessing the EU's success or failure in democracy promotion (Youngs 2009). The challenge of fostering civil society and pluralism remains a key hurdle in countries where state authorities resist the status quo. When the EU negotiates its Action Plans[4] with ENP countries, there is always an apprehension on the other side with regard to proposals such as reforming the security sector or establishing a genuinely independent judiciary. However, the policies designed to promote democracy and human rights have to be primarily addressed to citizens and civil society. These policies must enable local actors to promote their own democratic reform strategies. They must help set in motion the essential political and institutional conditions for people in the neighborhood to be able to engage in free debates and make decisions freely.

The EU faces several challenges in its goal of democracy promotion in the neighborhood. The Union's eastern member states are constrained by their relations with Russia in making any attempt to develop strong EU policies aimed at democratic stability in the region. Concerns such as securing energy supplies, historical ties, and Russia's importance as a regional and global player influence the decision-making of the EU's eastern member states. Russia's policies and actions in the region can impede the effectiveness of EU democracy promotion in the eastern neighborhood, coupled with the Union's unwillingness to offer any prospect of accession. This is further compounded by the region's legacy of ethnic conflict, extreme political polarization, and severe weaknesses in governance capacity. Whereas in the south, the fear of radical elements taking part in the government formation through democratic elections, cooperation in migration control, containment of the conflict in West Asia, and relations with the energy exporting countries have blocked any attempt to promote a degree of political pluralism in the region. To add to the conundrum, lack of agreement among member states on each issue results in piecemeal policies that falter on implementation. Thus, the democracy promotion via the existing ENP framework compounds the problem of coordinating EU foreign policy. The use of conditionality as one of the main instruments for advancing democracy has often been influenced by the member states' strategic interests in the region/country. In such a scenario, convergence among member states over the conditionality principle is difficult to achieve. It also constrains the EU institutions engaged in monitoring partner countries' performance in complying with democratic values. The consensus-building exercise leads to a lengthy, nontransparent bargaining process and adoption of a "lowest common denominator" to minimize divergence among member states.

The ENP finds itself dealing with countries following very different political trajectories post-Arab Spring. The EU has focused much of its attention on Tunisia and Egypt—which show existence of an expanding civil society and a middle class (Joseph 2010). The EU's lack of enthusiasm in the cases of Libya and Syria can be attributed to precarious and uncertain situations in these countries, which even led the EU to support the idea of military intervention in Libya. As Lehne (2014: 4) points out, "there is hardly any other external policy of the EU with a larger gap between its stated objectives and the actual outcome." This becomes clear as we discuss the EU's response to the Arab Spring in the next section.

Revised ENP Post-Arab Spring: Old Wine in a New Bottle?

The EU's disjointed response to the Arab Spring highlighted problems with its own policies and the divisions that existed among the member states. A weak response could be attributed to an influx of migrants and refugees, concerns related to energy security, rise of radical Islam, and wide disagreements among member states on how to react to Arab uprisings. The uprisings challenged the assumption that political stability in North Africa and West Asia is vital to contain security risks such as terrorism and immigration. As Tocci (2011: 10) states: "the revolts in the Arab world demonstrated the weakness of EU policy towards the region, through its lopsided emphasis on economic cooperation and migration management at the expense of sustainable development." The Arab Spring exposed the EU's lack of clarity over short-term and long-term goals (i.e. whether to favor stability over the status quo; K. Böttger, personal communication, April 18, 2011). Indeed, the EU had increasingly ignored the underlying fragility of the regimes such as Egypt and Tunisia it cooperated with, mistakenly equating their short-term stability with deeper and long-term sustainability, while pursuing its commercial and strategic interests. The EU's response formulated as a revised ENP and announcement of many other new measures to reorient its neighborhood policy merit a carefully assessment. For example, it remains to be seen whether this revised policy has incorporated lessons from the past or if it is still guided by security and strategic considerations; what path the EU treads when efforts at norm promotion come in conflict with the need to safeguard its own interests; and to what extent this can undermine an authentic EU role in building deep democracy in the region.

Post-Arab Spring, the EU adopted a revised ENP with special emphasis on support to civil society—as well as committing itself to deep democracy based on free and fair elections, freedom of association, expression and assembly, institution-building, good governance, rule of law, checks and balances, the fight against corruption, effective law enforcement, and security sector reform. The document reads, "the EU is ready to support the democratic and constitutional reform processes both to encourage foreign and domestic economic investment and to demonstrate to people a visible change in their lives" (European Commission 2011a: 5). Hence, the linking the constitutional and democratic reforms to market concerns suggests the underlying economic rationale to the whole approach. The sharper, more strategic vision was elaborated in the ENP Communication—which called for creating space for a "greater political role of non-states actors," and a "partnership with societies" and recognized the mutual benefit for the EU and civil society in building a relationship beyond funding (European Commission 2011b). To support political actors striving for democratic change in their countries (especially political parties and non-registered NGOs or trade unions and other social partners), the Commission proposed a European Endowment for Democracy (EED) in 2011 that was established in 2012. This new independent grant was meant to support local actors, including political movements, journalists, and non-registered NGOs, that are not financed under other EU aid instruments—with initial although not exclusive focus on the EU neighborhood. A Polish initiative to support pro-democracy activists and organizations in Eastern Europe, the EED was conceptualized to share lessons learnt by post-communist members of the EU during their transitions, with the countries facing pro-democracy protest movements. It was argued that "CEECs had important comparative advantages in democracy support in the region because they were not colonial powers (unlike other EU member states)" (Giusti and Fassi 2014: 119).

This is a significant departure for the EU, which until now—and unlike the US—has not funded partisan groups. Availability of quick and flexible funding under the EED makes it more user-friendly for civil society organizations. The EED is also making forays into Russia to bring about a plurality of debate, especially in the Russian-language media space. The killing of Russian liberal politician Boris Nemtsov in February 2015 has given the EED a newfound logic to expand its geographical scope beyond the EU's eastern neighborhood. The EED claims not to export but foster democracy, although a key challenge remains as to how successfully it coordinates the work of Western-funded professional civil society and grassroots pro-democracy initiatives driven by endogenous factors (Shapovalova and Youngs 2012). As to whether this support will be sustained in the long term or remain ad hoc, the EED is innovative in being more flexible, less formal, and widening its target constituencies to engage with a host of actors working to support democracy. This also includes support not just for countries who are consolidating democracy, but also to those who are still in a transition phase. However, the absence of support for the EED from several EU member states once again highlights the lack of norm convergence with regard to democracy promotion. Another vital question that needs to be answered is whether initiatives such as the EED will do something different or simply replicate existing tools such as the European Instrument for Democracy and Human Rights and Governance Facility. As more funds become available, it is all the more necessary to differentiate between the various instruments used for democracy promotion. In order to facilitate complementarity of the existing and new instruments, a clear division of labor needs to be highlighted.

Launched in response to the criticisms for its failure to transform the neighborhood, the revised approach anchored in instruments such as the EED and Civil Society Facility seems to have still not recognized the nature of existing challenges entrenched in the politics of the region (Morillas and Eduard 2012). The fact that the EU is reorienting its priorities and moving away from the stabilization paradigm (prevalent so far in the approach to the southern neighborhood) to support democratization and the process of civil society evolution in the region merits a positive assessment. However, it is not just the question of political and civil rights, but also social and economic rights (as highlighted by the revolutions) that need to be adequately addressed in EU policies and programmes designed for the neighbourhood (Huber 2013). For a vibrant civil society to emerge in the region, it is important to encourage a plurality of actors. There seems much agreement among EU officials, academics, and grassroots organizations that the EU democratic model remains ambiguous. On the one hand, the European Consensus on Development makes reference to issues such as the "management of migration flows" and a "climate conducive to private investment as vital to democratic governance." On the other hand, the deep democracy mentioned in the revised ENP document does not make any such connection (Wetzel and Orbie 2012). This indeed makes a case for lack of clarity within the EU on what it actually means when the EU wants to promote or build democracy as part of its foreign policy. While there are a range of available instruments and initiatives such as election observation missions and various other funding bodies that support democracy-related activities, the substance of the EU's democracy promotion remains vague. Kurki (2013) argues that inconsistencies characterizing the EU's views on democracy have created a situation of conceptual fuzziness. Whether the revised rationale for policy reflects a paradigm shift remains to be seen.

Taking stock after four years of a revised ENP in place, the EU launched a joint consultation paper meant to trigger a debate with member states and other stakeholders on how to revive the ENP on March 4, 2015. In wake of recent developments altering the political landscape of the EU, the paper calls for "a need to understand better the different aspirations, values and interests of our partners" (European Commission 2015). As the EU struggles to find innovative strategies to overcome protracted problems across its borders, this document intends to steer the neighborhood policy in a new direction. With the Islamic State spreading its tentacles in the Mediterranean and unleashing brutal violence, the EU and its ideational project of promoting liberal democracy has more to worry about. The revised ENP—which emphasizes a "more for more" approach in terms of greater incentives (money, markets, and mobility) to realign policies with EU values—has largely proved ineffectual.

In the absence of a clearly conceptualized linkage between democracy promotion, political reform, human rights, and socioeconomic development, there stands a risk of EU policies backfiring when it comes to their implementation. A flexible interpretation of what all can be included under the name of democracy promotion will serve the EU no good and may be detrimental not only for its long-term interests, but also for its perception in the outside world. Struggling to speak in a coherent voice as a foreign policy actor, it is even more imperative for the EU to enunciate a transparent definition of its stated objective of democracy promotion and to have a clear sense of allocating funds for the same. Given the diverse constituencies of interests and perceptions that shape the EU, there will never be one model or approach to democracy. In fact, having a flexible approach that gives scope to accommodate plural voices would be advantageous. However, such an approach should not disguise ambiguity.

The EU should be more explicit about the intended goals of different policies and critically assess compatibility with objectives of democracy promotion. The latter can neither be an umbrella framework nor an underlying theme of EU policy on development, human rights, etc. because in that case, it will add to what can be called "policy incoherence." The EU also needs to be careful while linking goals such as socioeconomic development and governance with democracy promotion. A techno-bureaucratic methodology is of little help when the each country has different set of incentives and priorities. A revised strategy alone would not result in the necessary changes, as the Mediterranean region features substantial complexity and democracy remains an essentially contested concept.

Conclusion

The EU as a post-Westphalian actor has a wide array of policy choices in its diplomatic arsenal. It certainly can enhance its competence to use non-security tools to contribute toward improving peace and security in the neighboring areas. Certainly, its diplomatic strategy is based more on policy-specific considerations and cost–benefit calculations than on ideological proclamations. The "brand EU" is waning in popularity in today's global environment, and the model of democracy and the associated cosmopolitan values that it propagates is increasingly being questioned and re-examined. In fact, for many, the EU's response to the eurozone crisis was also non-democratic. To get past this crisis of confidence and convert the challenge posed by the Arab Spring into an opportunity, the EU must reinvent its narrative toward the region and prepare to hear new voices and involve a host of other interlocutors that have emerged on the scene. In a region witnessing rapid transitions, the EU and the US are not the only "maze runners." The role of external actors such as Russia and China and regional organizations such as the GCC, the Arab League, and the African Union is also crucial for any collaborative approach to succeed. Until the deeper and long-standing problems of engagement with the region are addressed, any change in the form of revised or repackaged initiatives will be of a cosmetic nature and limited scope.

A genuine commitment toward the cause of fostering democracy in transition countries would require much greater political will on the part of the EU. This would mean not just articulating grand strategies from Brussels, but reaching to deeper layers of society and involving diverse stakeholders at the local level, and not merely political groups, Western donors, and foreign NGOs. What can enhance the EU's credibility and legitimate its norm exportation is reference to interdependence, identification of common interests and concerns as enunciated by the protests in the Arab world. The consistent projection of the EU as a quintessential model of democracy requires reinvestigation. The EU in order to improve its nature of engagement—not only with its neighborhood, but also with world at large—urgently needs to understand and recognize other perceptions and viewpoints that are enriching the discourse on democracy. A monolithic conception of democracy seen from the European lens blurs the actual picture on the ground, which is a mosaic of cultural traditions and colonial legacy. While taking stock of the intended or unintended consequences of its policies toward the region, it is crucial for the EU to do away with subjectivities.

Acknowledgments

The author would like to thank the Centre for European Studies at Jawaharlal Nehru University, New Delhi, for providing the field visit grant to pursue her doctoral research. The interviews conducted during March–April 2011 in Brussels and Berlin helped in writing this chapter.

Notes

1. The ENP framework includes 16 countries in the EU's eastern and southern neighborhood viz. Algeria, Armenia, Azerbaijan, Belarus, Egypt, Georgia, Israel, Jordan, Lebanon, Libya, Moldova, Morocco, Palestine, Syria, Tunisia, and Ukraine.
2. In May 2004, the EU 15 expanded to the EU 25 with the accession of Estonia, Latvia, Lithuania, Poland, the Czech Republic, Hungary, Slovakia, Slovenia, Cyprus, and Malta. The addition of eight Central and Eastern European countries brought a striking Eastern dimension to EU foreign policy, with the aim of anchoring stability and democracy and steering economic dynamism in Europe.
3. One can understand this statement in the context of the EU's milieu and possession goals (Wolfers 1962). Tocci (2006) applies this concept in the context of ENP, whereby milieu goals aim at transforming the environment by promoting peace, democracy, human rights, and sustainable development in the neighborhood. Possession goals refer to strategic interests such as commercial relations, migration and border management, or energy security. The distinction between the two often gets blurred; in pursuit of its milieu goals, the EU is often seen as protecting its possession goals.
4. Action Plans are similar in outline, but the content is specific to each country. They include: political dialogue, economic and social cooperation, trade-related issues, market and regulatory reform, cooperation in justice and home affairs, sectoral issues such as transport, energy, information society, environment, research and development, human dimensions including people-to-people contacts, civil society, education, and public health.

References

Aliboni, R. (2005) "The Geopolitical Implications of the European Neighbourhood Policy," *European Foreign Affairs Review*, 10(1): 1–16.

Balfour, R. and Rotta, A. (2005) "Beyond Enlargement: The European Neighbourhood Policy and Its Tools," *The International Spectator*, 40(1): 7–20.

Bicchi, F. (2009) "Democracy Assistance in the Mediterranean: An Overview," *Mediterranean Politics*, 14(1): 61–78.

Cameron, F. and Balfour, R. (2006) "The European Neighbourhood Policy as a Conflict Prevention Tool," *EPC Issue Paper*, 47, Brussels: EPC.

Dannreuther, R. (Ed.) (2004) *European Union Foreign and Security Policy: Towards a Neighbourhood Strategy*, London: Routledge.

Diez, T. (2005) "Constructing the Self and Changing Others: Reconsidering 'Normative Power Europe'," *Millennium: Journal of International Studies*, 33(3): 613–636.

Emerson, C. and Youngs, R. (Eds.) (2009) *Democracy's Plight in the European Neighbourhood*, Brussels: CEPS.

European Commission (2004) *European Neighbourhood Policy Strategy Paper*, available at: http://eur-lex. europa.eu/legal-content/EN/TXT/PDF/?uri=CELEX:52004DC0373&from=EN (accessed December 11, 2015).

European Commission (2007) *Treaty of Lisbon Amending the Treaty on European Union and the Treaty Establishing the European Community*, available at: http://eur-lex.europa.eu/legal-content/EN/TXT/ PDF/?uri=OJ:C:2007:306:FULL&from=EN (accessed December 11, 2015).

European Commission (2011a) *A Partnership for Democracy and Shared Prosperity with the Southern Mediterranean*, available at: http://eur-lex.europa.eu/legal-content/EN/TXT/PDF/?uri=CELEX: 52011DC0200&from=EN (accessed December 11, 2015).

European Commission (2011b) *A New Response to a Changing Neighbourhood*, available at: http://eur-lex.europa.eu/legal-content/EN/TXT/PDF/?uri=CELEX:52011DC0303&from=EN (accessed December 11, 2015).

European Commission (2015) *Towards a New European Neighbourhood Policy*, available at: http://ec. europa.eu/enlargement/neighbourhood/consultation/consultation.pdf (accessed December 11, 2015).

Filtenborg, M.S., Gänzle, S., and Johansson, E. (2002) "An Alternative Theoretical Approach to EU Foreign Policy: 'Network Governance' and the Case of the Northern Dimension," *Cooperation and Conflict*, 37(4): 387–407.

Giusti, S. and Fassi, E. (2014) "The European Endowment for Democracy and Democracy Promotion in the EU Neighbourhood," *The International Spectator: Italian Journal of International Affairs*, 49(4): 112–129.

Hinnebusch, R. (2006) "Authoritarian Persistence, Democratization Theory and the Middle East: An Overview and Critique," *Democratization*, 13(3): 373–395.

Huber, D. (2013) "US and EU Human Rights and Democracy Promotion since the Arab Spring: Rethinking Its Content, Targets and Instruments," *The International Spectator: Italian Journal of International Affairs*, 48(3): 98–112.

Joseph, J. (2010) "The Limits of Governmentality: Social Theory and the International," *European Journal of International Relations*, 16(2): 223–246.

Kelley, J. (2006) "New Wine in Old Wineskins: Promoting Political Reforms through the New European Neighbourhood Policy," *Journal of Common Market Studies*, 44: 29–55.

Kurki, M. (2013) *Democratic Futures: Revisioning Democracy Promotion and Democratization*, London: Routledge.

Lavenex, S. and Schimmelfennig, F. (2011) "Democracy Promotion in the EU's Neighbourhood: From Leverage to Governance?" *Democratization*, 18(4): 885–909.

Lehne, S. (2014) *Time to Reset the European Neighbourhood Policy*, Brussels: Carnegie Europe.

Lippert, B. (2008) "European Neighbourhood Policy: Many Reservations—Some Progress—Uncertain Prospects," *International Policy Analysis*, Berlin: Friedrich-Ebert Stiftung, pp. 1–16.

Malmvig, H. (2006) "Caught between Cooperation and Democratization: The Barcelona Process and the EU's Double-Discursive Approach," *Journal of International Relations and Development*, 9: 343–370.

Manners, I. (2002) "Normative Power Europe: A Contradiction in Terms?" *Journal of Common Market Studies*, 40(2): 235–258.

Møller, B. (2005) "The EU as a Security Actor: Security by Being and Security by Doing," DIIS Report, Copenhagen: Danish Institute of International Studies (DIIS).

Morillas, P. and Eduard, S.L. (2012) "The EU and the Arab Spring, One Year After: A View from the North," *EuroMeSCo Brief*, 39: 1–4.

Pace, M. (2006) *The Politics of Regional Identity: Meddling with the Mediterranean*, London: Routledge.

Schimmelfennig, F. and Sedelmeier, U. (2006) *The Europeanization of Central and Eastern Europe*, Ithaca, NY: Cornell University Press.

Scott, J.W. and Liikanen, I. (2011) "Civil Society and 'Neighbourhood': Europeanization through Cross-Border Cooperation." in J.W. Scott and I. Liikanen (Eds.), *European Neighbourhood through Civil Society Network?* New York: Routledge, pp. 1–16.

Shapovalova, N. and Youngs, R. (2012) "EU Democracy Promotion in the Eastern Neighbourhood: A Turn to Civil Society?" *FRIDE Working Paper*, 115, Madrid: FRIDE.

Tocci, N. (2006) "Can the EU Promote Democracy and Human Rights through the ENP? The Case for Refocusing on the Rule of Law," in M. Cremona and W. Sadurski (Eds.), *The European Neighbourhood Policy: A Framework for Modernisation?* EUI Law Working Papers, 2007/21, Florence: EUI.

Tocci, N. (2011) "State (Un)sustainability in the Southern Mediterranean and Scenarios to 2030: The EU's Response," *MEDPRO Policy Paper*, Brussels: CEPS.

Tulmets, E. (2007) "Can the Discourse on 'Soft Power' Help the EU to Bridge Its Capability-Expectations Gap?" *European Political Economy Review*, 7: 195–226.

Van Hüllen, V. (2011) "Europeanisation through Cooperation? EU Democracy Promotion in Morocco and Tunisia," *West European Politics*, 35(1): 117–134.

Wetzel, A. and Orbie, J. (2012) "The EU's Promotion of External Democracy: In Search of the Plot," *CEPS Policy Brief*, 8: 1–6.

Wolfers, A. (1962) *Discord and Collaboration: Essays on International Politics*, Baltimore, MD: Johns Hopkins Press.

Youngs, R. (2009) "Democracy Promotion as External Governance?" *Journal of European Public Policy*, 16(6): 895–915.

Zaiotti, R. (2007) "Of Friends and Fences: Europe's Neighbourhood Policy and the 'Gated Community Syndrome'," *Journal of European Integration*, 29(2): 143–162.

Chapter 4

States of Depoliticization: The Trans-Pacific Partnership and the Political Economy of Discretion

Sorin Mitrea

Accelerating changes in the nature and scope of democracy and authority in Western democracies have among many other things given appreciable weight to the proclamation by Jose Saramago that governments in the West are but the "political facades of economic power" (Saramago, cited in Swyngedouw 2011: 370). A fruitful site to examine the dynamics of the bounds that the global economic system places on democracy is Canada's approach to rules-based mechanisms of investment and trade agreements such as the Trans-Pacific Partnership (TPP).[1] These investment and trade agreements (under the general rubric of "foreign investment protection agreements" or FIPAs) are considered "new constitutionalist" insofar as they insulate international capital from domestic policy changes, enforced by international arbitration, or "investor state dispute settlement" (ISDS). This case illustrates how the political discretion of parts of the state (i.e. the executive) promulgate globalization, actively working to depoliticize policy areas so as to facilitate accumulation. The TPP negotiations—like many FIPAs before it—have been conducted in secrecy, with only select members of the Conservative government and certain lobbyists having access to the negotiations or text. Meanwhile, opposition critics, parliament, and the public are excluded from analyzing these stipulations (LeBreton 2012; Kelsey 2013). Rather than simply "shifting" authority from public to private, the TPP constructs a state of exception wherein certain policy areas are insulated from democratic accountability and political discretion, effectively bifurcating politics into private and public realms and constitutionalizing a rising private authority to which government (public authority) is beholden. The path dependency of liberal and new constitutionalism, how the latter is predicated on the former, and their effect on democratic politics are all examined herein. The TPP negotiations evince how political discretion (facilitated by liberal constitutionalism) is used to depoliticize the process by which the rights of capital would supersede the rights of citizens.

The following sections outline the theoretical underpinnings of constitutionalism, authority, trade and investment agreements, and depoliticization. First, depoliticization describes the ways in which politics are removed from an artifact or process (Burnham 2000). Depoliticization can be social (e.g. apolitical populaces) or institutional (undermining the state's ability to act with discretion in various areas) (Burnham 2000: 21; Kenis and Mathijs 2014). Depoliticization can also be "hard" or "soft" wherein the former refers to explicit legal preclusion from an action(s) while the latter refers to less direct deterrents. Finally, political discretion refers to the ability of state-based elected officials to enact legislation where they have authority (Savoie 1999: 651).

The expansion of capitalism is contingent on the state to be enacted and sustained, such that the depoliticization resulting from the rules-based mechanism of a domestic (liberal) constitution is duplicated by the state and capital to form a new constitutionalism (Burnham 2000). This connection is substantial insofar as the logic of supra-political binding mechanisms is normalized and entrenched in liberal democratic states, constructing a path-dependent precedent.

Constitutionalism

Constitutionalism operates as a rules-based mechanism that is intentionally situated beyond normal (i.e. legislative) political engagement (Ward 2005: 719). Rules-based mechanisms work to preclude discretionary or deliberative politics by subjecting a realm(s) of social or political action to a (relatively) static framework so as to limit and shape the possibilities of action (Burnham 2000: 21). A liberal constitution is only amendable "by an extraordinary supra-legislative process," provides the legal and procedural framework for representative institutions (i.e. separation of powers), and outlines and enforces civil rights, liberties, and checks and balances (Warren 1989: 511; Ward 2005: 719). Although constitutionalism constructs and delineates the political realm and can offer protections for the individual, it is inherently depoliticizing insofar as it limits the political possibilities of the state and its citizens and dissuades deliberative democratic politics by being a relative absolute (a rules-based mechanism above politics) legitimated by a higher absolute (e.g. "natural rights," liberal universality, etc.) (Honig 1991: 108).

Transnational organizations and powerful economies operate together to form a "new constitutionalism," which is an extension of the counter-discretionary movement of neoliberalism (Bousfield 2013: 403). Bretton Woods, and later the World Trade Organization (WTO), sought to depoliticize transnational liberalism by insulating trade, fiscal, monetary (via central bank independence), and investment policies from political (government discretion) and democratic (parliament and public) manipulation (Schneiderman 2005: 847; Bousfield 2013: 403). In this way, the interest of private authority (capital) are upheld over the democratic rights of citizens *within* states, constitutionalizing (securing) accumulation by dispossessing public authority (government) of discretion and the demos of their ability to hold government accountable (public accountability) (Gill 1995: 412). New constitutionalist arrangements hold government accountable to private authority through various surveillance mechanisms, such as global creditors, international arbitration (ISDS), and organizations such as the WTO (Gill 1995: 412). The rules and institutions of new constitutionalist arrangements amount to a strategy of "pre-commitment" that binds future generations to the normative institutional forms of neoliberalism, constraining the possibilities for political practice, minimizing redistributive functions for the vulnerable, and maximizing policing functions to ensure the smooth operation of the market (Schneiderman 2005: 847).

Whereas the accountability of government (public authority) to the demos was constitutionally defined and discretionary (i.e. to what degree parliament is consulted in treaty-making), new constitutionalism depoliticizes certain policy areas completely by insulating them from both public accountability and political discretion. The TPP negotiations also illustrate how the state seeks out and uses its discretion to depoliticize its own binding (i.e. conducting negotiations in secret).

The Politics of Authority

Public authority is defined here as the supremacy of the government of any state over the people, resources, and all other authorities (save for and outlined by its constitution, where applicable) (Axtmann 2004: 259). The authority of the state is internally contingent, resting on its accountability ("responsiveness") to the collective legitimation of the demos (via voting) as expressed through the constitutionally outlined electoral process (Smith 1995: 22; Axtmann 2004: 259). Conversely, private authority is defined as the deference, respect, or accountability toward markets and capital (Porter 2005: 21, 2011: 176). Private authority is evinced in the ways markets and firms create pressures to adopt global standards (i.e. those found in FIPAs) on the grounds that they will produce efficiencies, make a state "attractive" to transnational capital in an era of global competition, or more intuitively that these standards "make business sense" (Porter 2005: 21; Bearce and Bondanella 2007: 708; Best 2010: 197; Babb 2013).

Public authority has become increasingly dependent on, part of, and beholden to private authority—particularly since the mid-1970s, when states began relying on a complex set of robust and autonomous transnational regulatory arrangements that accompanied the liberalization of trade and capital flows (Best 2010: 194; Porter 2011: 175; Babb 2013). The shift toward private authority does not mean that public authority is "dissolved"; rather, it is consensually deferential to the former insofar as governments choose to adopt and implement new constitutionalist arrangements, adhere to private regulatory regimes, and engage in hybrid programs (Porter 2005: 22). Private authority can be coercive: with regards to new constitutionalist arrangements such as FIPAs, public authority is formally bound by ISDS, which can award hundreds of millions for capital if states violate FIPAs provisions (Poulsen and Aisbett 2013: 273). Informally, violations damage the credibility of a state in the eyes of transnational capital and other states by "betraying" the confidence of investors (Poulsen and Aisbett 2013: 273). In this way, FIPAs only increase investment if the signing government exhibits consistent "good behaviour" (paralleling the function of credit rating agencies) (Gill 1995: 412; Poulsen and Aisbett 2013: 273). As such, public authority has become accountable to private authority with FIPAs, while its accountability to the public is mitigated (Cheng 2005: 466).

International Trade and Investment Agreements

International trade and investment agreements are new constitutionalist mechanisms that govern how states regulate foreign-owned assets and the flow of goods and services (CCIC n.d.: 1). In terms of common provisions, FIPAs empower investors: (1) with protections from present or future policy changes that could affect their activities, particularly expropriation;[2] and (2) ensuring investors are treated comparably to domestic capital and exempting them from performance requirements or capital controls (e.g. local inputs, employment of marginalized groups) (CCIC n.d.: 2). FIPAs protect investors and exporters by allowing them to leapfrog domestic courts and sue governments in international (based on commercial) arbitration (ISDS), a process that lacks transparency (the hearings are not open and case-related documents are not disclosed publicly in some cases), has diplomatic, political, and legal costs (benefitting wealthier states that can afford it), and in which arbitrators have no tenure and can work non-judicially (often advising corporations) (Cheng 2005: 466; CCIC n.d.: 3). Further, loans and other support are often tied to compliance to FIPAs and ISDS resolutions (Cheng 2005: 466).

ISDS are heard in a policy venue sympathetic to liberal market interpretations, such that rulings do not hinge on economic, social, or environmental implications for states or populations (Pritchard 2005: 796). Governments are also limited in their understanding of FIPAs and ISDS processes (and investor lobbies aim to keep it this way), often contracting out to private law firms that may have conflicts of interest (Cheng 2005: 466; Van Harten 2005: 618). If governments refuse to comply with an arbitral award or do not take part in proceedings, an investor can confiscate their property in most places in the world (Poulsen and Aisbett 2013: 273). New constitutionalist agreements insulate trade and investment liberalization from public authority (government) and accountability (parliament, the public), stabilizing and systematizing accumulation and holding public authority accountable to transnational capital (and to a lesser degree, major capital exporting states) (Pritchard 2005: 776; Van Harten 2005: 618; Tienhaara 2011: 185).

Despite the asymmetrical power and authority afforded to private actors and the increasing global protests[3] of FIPAs, governments continue to adopt them for several reasons (Gill 1995: 403; Pritchard 2005: 797; Poulsen and Aisbett 2013: 301). States and publics often support FIPAs, echoing dominant neoclassical arguments that barriers to investment and trade obstruct "vast gains" and "higher levels of . . . market access," which are good economic necessities (Poulsen and Aisbett 2013: 274; McKenna 2014; Trew 2014). As of 2012, 55 percent of Canadians believed the TPP would be good for the economy, while only 29 percent disagreed (*Canadian Business* 2012). Similarly, criticism in parliament of the TPP's binding mechanisms, policies, and lack of transparency have been met with dogmatic recitations that FIPAs are important for the middle class, for growing exports, businesses, and jobs (Keddy 2012; LeBreton 2012; Garneau 2014). This view is complicated by NAFTA's effects on Canada (discussed below) and in light of existing and growing trade deficits such that the gains from the TPP will be negligible for the Canadian economy (Davies 2012; Trew 2014). There is also support for depoliticized trade, seen by some parliamentarians as "a good way to do business" (Gerald 2012).

Another argument is the need to protect "investor rights" so as to be competitive in acquiring capital flows for growth, providing the ideological legitimation for the material coercive mechanisms of FIPAs (Gill 1995; Bearce and Bondanella 2007: 708; Fairbrother

2010: 319). This competitive drive pushes governments to join and conclude talks quickly so that other states do not secure preferable trade and investment terms (Freeland 2014). States join or remain within these coercive organizations and agreements at times because it is still more advantageous than being outside of the system altogether (Bearce and Bondanella 2007: 708). Even with hundreds of millions awarded in key areas of public provision via ISDS, many states continue to sign onto these agreements; Canada, which has lost tremendously through ISDS mechanisms—losing $17.3 million to ExxonMobil and Murphy Oil in March 2015 because Newfoundland mandated that they invest a percentage of their revenues into research and training, violating NAFTA's Chapter 11 performance requirements clause—continues to pursue FIPAs (Tienhaara 2011: 194; Poulsen and Aisbett 2013: 273; Whittington 2015).

Historical Trajectory

The discursive and ideological rise of neoliberalism can be traced as a political, cultural, and economic process by which market logics—which were compatible with the tenets of liberal constitutionalism (in individualization and self-interest)—came to dominate the state (Pierre 1995: 55–56; Savoie 1999). Examples include market criteria for allocating public resources, the entrance of market ideology into public administration, and a shift away from collective/public solutions to social problems (Pierre 1995: 56–57).

The State and Neoliberalism

An explicit reification of the above is the "competition state," wherein the pressures of globalizing capitalism change how states and domestic politics are organized to reconstruct the state via top-down liberalization (driven by new constitutionalist agreements such as FIPAs and international organizations) toward: (1) organizing policy and administration around efficiency, flexibility, coordination, and multilevel governance (Cerny 2006: 1); and (2) shifting from protecting people (progressive redistribution) to protecting the market (regulation), which is global and integrated (necessitating competition for investment/capital) (Cerny 2006: 5). This is certainly not to say that the state is powerless in an era of global capital; rather, state apparatuses work concertedly to facilitate these changes (Burnham 2000: 21).

The TPP, and other FIPAs, may be more accurately termed "managed trade" agreements, which undermine local production, have asymmetrical provisions (continuing various protections for the global north—e.g. agriculture and intellectual property rights—at the expense of the global south), continue a trend of upward redistribution within states, and drive a "race to the regulatory bottom" (Gill 1995: 414; Schneiderman 2005: 823). Since the initial intensification of this phenomenon in the 1970s, governments have been caught between the increasing mobility of transnational capital, crises, and the globalization of finance, circumscribing their ability to raise operating finance and competing to attract investment (e.g. via major tax restructuring to reduce marginal rates on capital and high-income earners so as to gain the faith of investors) (Gill 1995: 412). New constitutionalism stabilizes accumulation, shifting the industrial welfare state to the competition state in parallel with the rise of international legal sovereignty (the mutual recognition of state, other entities, and their authority) and challenges to state sovereignty, undermining public accountability (McBride 2003: 254; Axtmann 2004: 274).

Liberal Constitutionalism in Canada

Liberal constitutionalism entrenches liberal tenets (particularly individualism and judicialization) codified and elevated beyond the realm of democratic politics (Collins 2009: 284). Further, in being "the supreme law," all policies and laws must be crafted with respect to constitutional provisions[4] because it is a site of authority above political intervention, to which governments have ceded discretion so as to become and remain legitimate and accountable to their people (McBride 2003: 253). New constitutionalism builds on the depoliticizing precedent of liberal constitutionalism in acting as a site of (private) authority above political intervention, to which governments have ceded authority so as to be legitimate and accountable to capital (McBride 2003: 253).

The depoliticization of liberal constitutionalism is evident in Canada through constitutional supremacy, wherein the Charter ultimately subordinates the institutions it creates (i.e. the legislative branch) to "procedural and substantive constitutional rules" (Choudhry 2003: 380).[5] This is related to the perceived impartiality of liberalism and liberal constitutionalism, such that the depoliticizing framework and effects of this institution *are a legitimate* way of organizing society and politics that "individuals cognitively rely on to frame their orientations toward the political world" (Warren 1989: 511; Evans 2003: 21).

Further, the Supreme Court's legal liberalism has been used to promote market values, valorizing market relations of free individuals and contending that freedom is obstructed by the state, not by disparities in wealth or concentrations of private power (Jackman 2005: 72; Schneiderman 2005: 846). The Charter has been used by the Supreme Court to legitimate governments that have pursued regressive policies such as privatization, program cuts, weakening progressive tax regimes, and to condition Canadians to accept these precarious trends (Petter 2005: 128). While judicial activism has helped vulnerable groups (occasionally softening the negative rights bias of the Charter), it is thoroughly contingent on financial resources now that the Court Challenges program has ended, remaining a viable option for the affluent minority (Petter 2009: 26). The formalism of liberal constitutionalism precludes a substantive realization of the protections it sets out. For example, while protections of private property (not explicitly included in the Canadian Charter) apply to all, they disadvantage those who do not "own productive resources" (Warren 1989: 512). The Canadian Charter does not have specific social rights clauses, but rights to property and secured accumulation are the backbone of new constitutionalism (Warren 1989: 512; Gill 1995).

Liberal constitutionalism provides a socially legible politico-legal precedent for new constitutionalism (as a rules-based mechanism above "normal"—i.e. parliamentary—politics), similar to the latter in depoliticization and enforcement via resource-contingent courts amenable to market values (*Supreme Court of Canada vs. ISDS*; Evans 2003: 21; Pritchard 2005: 796; Hirschl 2008: 113). Although the Canadian Charter exhibits legal liberalism, it does not prevent public authority from expanding public accountability by including parliament and the public in more decision-making (indeed, it may be a site through which resistance to capital can be articulated). Conversely, new constitutionalism insulates policy areas from public accountability *and* political discretion so as to secure accumulation.

New Constitutionalism's Discipline: The North American Free Trade Agreement

The North American Free Trade Agreement (NAFTA) is an example of new constitutionalism evinced in FIPAs, and understanding its disciplinary and depoliticizing effects provides insights into the possibilities of the TPP. NAFTA's investment rules operate constitutionally insofar as they are difficult to amend, utilize binding enforcement mechanisms, and often draw from the language of domestic constitutions (Schneiderman 2008: 69). NAFTA rules limit expropriation and complicate anything that has a similar affect to it (Schneiderman 2008: 69). Fear of arbitration induces "policy chill" wherein governments avoid particular policy orientations, such as when New Brunswick abandoned a public auto insurance regime idea in 2003 (Schneiderman 2008: 70). NAFTA's broad scope of compensable takings could "catch all varieties of legitimate, regulatory initiatives" (Schneiderman 2008: 71). As of January 2015, Canada has been the target of over 70 percent of all NAFTA ISDS claims since 2005 (damages over $172 million), and faces nine active claims in which "government measures . . . allegedly interfere with the *expected* profitability of foreign investments" (Sinclair 2015: 34, emphasis added).

The material effects of NAFTA on the Canadian economy were substantial: employment fell by 12 per cent[6] while labor productivity rose by 15 percent (Trefler 2004: 31). The already strong staples (resources) sectors of the Canadian economy grew while the weaker (e.g. manufacturing) sectors shrank (Watkins 1997: 35). However, increasing productivity often led to overall increasing precarity as less efficient producers were thinned out, resulting in higher unemployment (Trefler 2004: 37). Because plant closures are geo-economic (ownership often determines which plants are closed, and subsidiaries often come first), unemployment increases, and because the profits from increased productivity are concentrated upward, aggregate welfare is undermined by FIPAs (Watkins 1997: 35; Trefler 2004: 38). Quantitative analyses illustrate that FIPAs are a politico-economic transformation written by and for dominant capital, increasing capital returns, regressive wage–profit redistributions, deepening concentration, and stabilizing accumulation (Brennan 2013: 715, 743).

NAFTA's rules-based framework created a state of exception wherein policy areas that could threaten accumulation were insulated from political discretion and public accountability (parliament and the public) (Schneiderman 2008: 70). Thus, the established depoliticization (as a rules-based mechanism above democratic politics) of liberal constitutionalism is compounded by FIPA's bifurcation of politics into private and public. The adoption of NAFTA (and CUFTA before it) heralded the move from the activist to the competition state, wherein economic success and social concerns (e.g. the environment, labor conditions, social policy, etc.) can only be articulated within a circumscribed and depoliticized policy regime that may be facilitative of markets, but which cannot undermine accumulation (Schneiderman 2005: 848).

New Constitutionalism Refined: The Trans-Pacific Partnership

The Trans-Pacific Partnership has been under negotiation since 2010 and is a mega-regional economic agreement between Pacific economies (notably excluding China) with binding legal mechanisms meant to be a "blueprint for the future" (Palamar and Jardine 2012: 255). Canada's participation in the agreement undermines the state's ability to protect its industries (i.e. dairy) or citizens (i.e. from environmental externalities of foreign industries) according to national law (Palamar and Jardine 2012: 255). Further, by joining the negotiations after they began, Canada cannot veto chapters that have been agreed upon thus far, including intellectual property rights (IPR) provisions (LeBreton 2012). The real impact of the TPP will likely not be in substantial trade liberalization, as existing multi- and bilateral agreements have already achieved that to the political capacity of most states involved (e.g. protectionism in Canadian and the US dairy sectors are entrenched), but rather in further reducing the scope of political discretion to constrain capital (Rude and An 2013: 404).

The TPP is most palpably a disciplinary mechanism, emblematic of the tenets of new constitutionalism with the goal of determining the bounds of states' domestic policy and regulatory regimes to insulate and stabilize accumulation from democratic manipulation (Kelsey 2013: 237). There are several distinct features of the TPP: (1) a "seamless" regulatory regime for cross-border flows of goods, capital, data, and elite personnel and commercial activities (similar to the existing regime in the EU); (2) "targeting" the orientation, processes, and substance of states' domestic policy and regulatory powers; (3) eliding domestic policy and regulatory contexts so as to achieve harmonization; (4) an increase in institutionalized surveillance and reporting mechanisms in addition to coherence around existing FIPA norms; and (5) establishing the TPP as a "living agreement" to which other Asia-Pacific states will accede without the opportunity to negotiate its framework (Kelsey 2013: 242).

The scope of the TPP is also unprecedented, intensifying and harmonizing regulatory regimes more than previous agreements and applying to all levels of government and nongovernmental entities (Kelsey 2013: 242). Most of the chapters deal with regulatory and policy limitations—such as intellectual property rights, trade facilitation, and investment protections—with explicit criteria for decision-making (Kelsey 2013: 242). For example, the chapters assume a minimalist regulatory approach, requiring states to provide evidence of the need for regulation, include industry in regulation, and to enact "diverse disclosure, notification, consultation, and enforcement mechanisms" (Kelsey 2013: 243).[7] Relatedly, two novel areas in the TPP are chapters on regulatory harmonization and transparency (Kelsey 2013: 246). The TPP institutionalizes "best practices" of domestic policy and regulation (as those already established and followed by the US) oriented around minimal intervention and pro-market frameworks (Kelsey 2013: 246). These practices have an "enforceable obligation on governments" to cohere with the "best practices," including regulatory impact assessments (RIAs) (Kelsey 2003: 247).[8]

The Trans-Pacific Partnership extends new constitutionalism's protection of capital interests with its focus on policy convergence and integration, making it a special kind of constitution: while liberal constitutions often have provisions for vulnerable groups, the TPP builds on the former's rules-based precedent and the competition state to create a constitution for a privileged group—international capital. Any policies or regulatory activities that could limit accumulation now or in the future are constrained by the TPP's new constitutionalist tenets, and industry voice is privileged (in having actual authority) over public voice. Even under NAFTA, which is less ambitious than the TPP, Chapter 11 dispute settlement clauses were used to protect corporate profits regardless of social, environmental, or even local economic costs (Schneiderman 2008: 66).

The Contingency of Discretion

The various examples of discipline illustrated above are contingent on political discretion to be enacted: states have to acquiesce to be bound (CCIC n.d.: 4). When political actors are bound by domestic constitutions, they are bound by a rules-based mechanisms whose ultimate guarantor is the will of the polity (potentially articulated through referendum or revolution) that elected them, making the depoliticization of domestic constitutions *internally contingent*. New constitutionalism's guarantor is an international body of economic actors, and so the depoliticization it levels onto states is *externally contingent*.

In the case of the TPP, depoliticization and political discretion are mutually informed. The depoliticization of new constitutionalist mechanisms was discussed previously: the scope of domestic political authority to enact policies or regulation that is contrary to the institutionalized interests of capital is constrained by severe economic penalties (Kelsey 2013).

However, the depoliticized process of negotiating the TPP is constitutional (Crown prerogative powers enabling the executive to sign treaties) *and* discretionary: although individual Members of Parliament (MPs) serve as trustees of their constituencies and their political (party) choices, and so have strong independence, executive centralization,[9] leader dominance,[10] and executive federalism[11] are *discretionary choices* that limit representatives' ability to hold government accountable, thereby depoliticizing the negotiation of new constitutionalist agreements that will undermine public accountability and political discretion (Resnick 1990: 97; Docherty 2005).

The use of political discretion to depoliticize the implementation of new constitutionalism in keeping the TPP away from parliament undermines perhaps the most democratic form of political accountability (Kelsey 2013: 240). Public outcry is contained by political discretion because it has undermined FIPAs before: the Free Trade Area of the Americas (FTAA) negotiations collapsed shortly after the negotiating text went public (Trew 2014). Democratic accountability asserting itself to check public authority has been carefully avoided: even as recently as July 2014, TPP talks were moved in the last minute to avoid protest (Tencer 2014). As was the case in the Senate, there has been debate about the lack of debate in the House, but no substantive discussion on or access to the TPP chapters (LeBreton 2012). Since Canada joined the negotiations (informally since 2010, formally since 2012), executive political discretion has prevented an official text from reaching parliament (including the opposition member responsible for trade policy), the media, or the public, while lobbyists have been given privileged access (Brown 2013; Ravignat 2014). Executive centralization was on display in 2012 when Prime Minister Harper sent his chief of staff to a TPP negotiation instead of the Minister of Trade, again, behind closed doors (Davies 2012). There is little concrete information on what concessions Canada may have made to join the TPP negotiations or since joining (LeBreton 2012).

Although the federal government brought in civil society groups in foreign policy in the 1990s to balance out industry interests, they did not have veto points or significant influence, but did create an appearance of "community involvement," which bypassed parliament (Capling and Nossal 2003: 851). Unsurprisingly, civil society meetings on FIPAs had little discernable impact in Canada as the considerations were technical (e.g. the type and intensity of tariff removals) rather than political (e.g. environment and employment implications), benefiting industry interests that were already involved (Capling and Nossal 2003: 851; Moini 2011: 149). Critical groups are more often excluded from FIPA discussions: a recent panel of advisors put together by the Minister of Trade to go to the TPP negotiations did not include any representatives of organized labour, environmental groups, human rights groups, or supply management, illustrating the discretion of the executive in deciding which interests or groups to include (Davies 2012; Skogstad 2012: 173). However, even when parliaments are involved and provide an institutionalized means for parliamentarians and civil society to express their concerns about the internationalization of policy, the lack of substantive authority (i.e. in veto points) undermines their ability to hold executives accountable (Capling and Nossal 2003: 851).

Similarly, because the federal government can sign, but not implement FIPAs in provincial jurisdictions, provinces (via executive federalism) have been included in FIPA discussions (Lazar 2006: 32; Cameron 2006: 70). However, federalism is compromised by new constitutionalist arrangements, as the federal government acquires new supervisory roles (rooted in centralized finance and trade apparatuses) in areas of provincial jurisdiction to ensure compliance (necessitated by NAFTA's article 105 and the WTO) (Savoie 1999: 651; McBride 2003: 257). Similarly, NAFTA's Chapter 11 on investment protection intrudes on provincial regulatory capacity (e.g. barring performance requirements, technology transfers, domestic content purchasing requirements, etc., as illustrated by the $17.3 million 2015 ExxonMobile decision), and the courts have upheld the constitutionality of federal authorities enacting legislation compelling provinces to pay damages resulting from Chapter 11 violations (McBride 2003: 259).

This does not mean that political discretion is exhausted; rather, it can only be used in areas outside the purview of accumulation or to its benefit. For example, the Canadian government has recently blocked NAFTA's environmental "watchdog," whose interventions are already rare, from investigating Alberta tar sands leakages into ponds (Environmental Defence 2015).

Treaty Tabling in Canada

Significantly, among the centralized powers is the ability of Canadian Prime Ministers (channeling the powers of the Crown) to freely negotiate and conclude trade deals: NAFTA was negotiated by Chretien (Liberal) while CETA and the TPP have been negotiated exclusively by the Harper (Conservative) executive (illustrating a party convergence around FIPAs; Savoie 1999: 651; Ravignat 2014).

From 1926 to 1966, the federal government tabled all important treaties to be approved by parliament before ratification; by 1974, tabling in parliament became discretionary (Harrington 2006: 136). Further, since (then titled) External Affairs is no longer required by statute to report annually to parliament about its activities (1909–1995, no explanation for why this function was repealed), parliament and the public are no longer kept well informed of the treaty-making process (Harrington 2006: 140). Beginning in January 2008, the Harper minority government began tabling already signed international treaties in the House of Commons for 21 days after signature and before ratification (Danesi 2014: 189). This has come in response to parliament's (and therefore the public's) formal absence from a role of treaty negotiation, analysis, and debate in supranational laws that permeate jurisdictions, depoliticize even executive power, and have direct effects on citizens (Danesi 2014: 189). However, this amounts to another legitimating mechanism insofar as parliament, let alone the public, has no institutionalized checks on the executive to delay or prevent the signing of a treaty (Danesi 2014: 190).

Post-signing tabling is less effective than pre-signing transparency because it does not provide the time for parliament or the public to scrutinize (and possibly mobilize against) these agreements (Danesi 2014: 205). Worse still, pre-signing, the government exercises total discretion as to whether and how much information to release to parliament or the public (Harrington 2006: 141). An example of this was the Canada–China Investment Treaty, which was passed by executive order with no hearings before trade committees, no opportunities for parliamentary examination, and no vote in the House of Commons (May 2014). The pause between signing (adoption of the final treaty text) and ratification is designed to allow states to incorporate treaty obligations into domestic law and gauge public opinion, but with executive centralization (particularly with majority governments), this can also be a discretionary exercise (Harrington 2006: 124). Treaty tabling practices in Canada illustrate the discretion of the executive in making itself, provincial governments, and the demos accountable to capital's private authority.

Private Authority and Bifurcated Politics

The discretionary limitations to public accountability of government are the institutional foundations of post-democracy, but these are exacerbated by new constitutionalism. If a demos is a collection of persons in a state for whom "a given set of transactions *affects to such an extent that the consequences need to be cared for*" (the "affected principle"), then democracy is only substantial if the vulnerable and affected have a voice (Dewey, cited in Scholte 2008: 308, emphasis added). Parliament is an already limited site of public accountability even before the rise of new constitutionalism, as constitutionally enabled political discretion has limited public scrutiny and debate via party discipline, executive centralization, and executive federalism. Public authority (government) can only be held accountable when members of the public decide—collectively, equally, non-coercively, transparently, and responsibly—the policies that shape their common life and joint destinies (Scholte 2008: 310).

The rise of new constitutionalism sees private authority bifurcate politics into private and public realms. In the private realm, capital utilizes the affected principle (for profits and expropriation) in ISDS in line with their constitutionalized rights, demanding government accountability, thereby securing accumulation. Any policy area that could interfere with accumulation is removed (depoliticized) from public politics—government discretion and public accountability (parliament and the demos). Although both liberal and new constitutionalism represent depoliticized authority, the former entrenched liberal democratic politics while the latter constitutionalizes post-democracy. With liberal constitutions, individual rights and the rules of the polity are depoliticized (raised above democratic politics), guarded by courts, and protect people from the coercive power of the state. A liberal constitution is accountable to and legitimated by the demos (can be changed by revolution or amendment), making depoliticization internally contingent. Conversely, with new constitutionalism, capital rights and the rules of accumulation are depoliticized, guarded by courts, and protect capital from public authority and accountability (the demos). New constitutionalism is accountable to and legitimated by (change can result in capital flight, asset repossession, and loss of credibility without amendment mechanisms) its own rules, making depoliticization externally contingent.

New constitutionalism creates a state of exception wherein the public's affected principle is suspended by isolating policy areas from public authority (government) and accountability (parliament and the public): the environmental, social, and economic externalities of capital accumulation, which absolutely affect the public, are isolated from public accountability and even from political discretion. On the other hand, private authority's affected principle is overarching: any policy measure or government action that undermines accumulation is potentially open to scrutiny. In this way, FIPAs such as the TPP constitutionalize post-democracy such that states discretionarily abandon their accountability to the public so as to attract capital (including austerity, privatization, tax cuts, and executive centralization), actively seeking out depoliticization (Crouch 2004). Public authority does not "shift" to private authority; instead, it is beholden to it via the bifurcation of politics: governments still make laws and hold elections, but they are now "constitutionally" accountable to private authority. The insulation of policy areas from political discretion and democratic input ("private politics") translates political issues into technical questions on the most efficient pursuit of a priori policy aims (Kioupkiolis 2014: 145).

Policy chill, NAFTA's material and political consequences and precedent, and the TPP's new regulatory regime drive this state of exception. Another example is the Harper government's abandonment of supply management in its current form, as parliamentary debates revealed that the government plans to compensate[12] the dairy, poultry, and egg farming industries if they suffer loses as a result of FIPAs (Bernier 2014). This sustains the state of exception wherein capital is insulated from political interference in accumulation, and so the government will essentially subsidize local industries to sustain accumulation brought in by FIPAs.

Discussion

New constitutionalism's state of exception and bifurcation of politics hastens post-democratic trends, increasing the use of participatory and consultative rhetoric as a legitimating mechanism, such that democracy has become a performance of the state. This has led to "consensual democracy," wherein negotiation for optimal shares of objective gains is preferred over conflict (i.e. protest, labor strikes, etc.), as evinced in the selective inclusion of civil society groups in FIPA negotiations: everyone is framed as a partner in an apparently open deliberation in an attempt to undermine dissent and silence critical voices (Kenis and Mathijs 2014: 150). In this way, the (public) authority of government to make regulations to protect public well-being are reinterpreted as barriers to investment and trade, such that citizen voice and government authority are restricted to enhance the voice of capital (private authority) (Cheng 2005: 466).

The intensification of depoliticized authority via new constitutionalism operates at the intersection of political economy and democratic politics and is contingent on political discretion to enact, suggesting the need to conceptualize political structures of accumulation (PSAs).[13] The concept of a PSA is used to describe the complex role of the state as a driver, guarantor, and cushion of globalization, at once facilitating and mitigating its realization. Similarly, the constitutionalization of accumulation evidenced in the TPP may signal the rise of a supra-political economy, insofar as the consequences of accumulation are increasingly isolated from public authority and accountability.

It should be clear that the TPP and FIPAs no longer focus exclusively on trade; rather, they work to constitutionalize accumulation by dispossessing public authority of discretion and the demos of accountability, breaking the cycle that legitimates the state. While the institutional limitations on public accountability in Westminster democracies are constitutionally established, the exclusion of parliament and the public from policy and treaty-making processes are a matter of political discretion (Harrington 2006). Conversely, the state of exception created by new constitutionalism and its bifurcation of politics constitutionalizes the depoliticization above in policy areas that affect accumulation: even if current executive trends reversed, and public authority voluntarily gave more substantive power (i.e. veto points) to parliament or the public, already ratified FIPAs cannot be abdicated without incurring substantial direct (via ISDS) and indirect (the "credibility" ascribed to the state by international capital) costs (Cheng 2005: 465; Harrington 2006: 135; Danesi 2014: 190). While the Westphalian state was defined by consolidating authority, we are witnessing a return to multiple authorities, politics, and constitutionalisms (Axtmann 2004: 256).

Notes

1. The TPP is a multilateral trade and investment agreement under negotiation by pacific economies and is chosen as a case study because it is unprecedented in its scope and ambition (Kelsey 2013: 237). NAFTA is chosen as a comparison because it is an earlier agreement that Canada subjected itself to.
2. Ranging from nationalization to "creeping expropriation" (measures that cumulatively amount to expropriation, although tempered by the Methanax case with NAFTA), regulatory expropriation (measures that so impact on an investment interest that they are equivalent to a taking), and partial expropriations (measures that take only part of an investment interest) (Schneiderman 2005: 847).
3. It is beyond the scope of this chapter to discuss resistances. Rather, the focus is on the shifts in authority and accountability resulting from new constitutionalism.
4. Leading to a heightened role for lawyers and legal discourse and decreasing discretion for politicians and the public, as with new constitutionalism (Choudhry 2003; Petter 2009).
5. See the work of Choudhry (2003) and Petter (2005, 2009).
6. Even when measuring the Gini coefficient since CUFTA's 1989 signing, when unemployment returned to pre-CUFTA levels by 2000, Gini did not shrink, illustrating the entrenched inequality brought on by FIPAs (Brennan 2013: 724).
7. Canada has not expressed resistance to the investor–state dispute settlement mechanisms in the TPP despite its intensification and normalization of those processes evinced in existing FIPAs (as illustrated earlier) (Kelsey 2013: 243).
8. RIA measures are implemented so that states must justify why they are pursuing a policy/regulation, whether the goals of a policy/regulation could be achieved voluntarily, what the net impact would be for every alternative, and to make decisions "on the best reasonably obtainable scientific, technical, economic, and other information" (247). (Un)surprisingly, there is no mention of social or environmental information in the above mechanism (Kelsey 2013: 247).
9. Instrumentalizing prerogative powers to control committee, senate, judicial, and senior public servant appointments, the ability to sign treaties, increasing control of cabinet and the House via the PMO and PCO, and the ability to subject debate via prorogation (Smith 1995: 12, 20; Savoie 1999: 635; Aucoin et al. 2011).
10. Party discipline, and the centralization of candidate selection and promotion, in addition to information overload, limit MPs' ability to scrutinize the government (Savoie 1999: 657; Docherty 2005; Bittner and Kopp 2013).
11. Closed meetings of first ministers that are non-transparent and never reach legislatures, making it all the more difficult for citizens' concerns to be represented over new constitutionalist arrangements (McBride 2003: 258; Cameron 2006: 70; Lazar 2006: 32; Skogstad 2012).
12. Something that they already failed to do with Newfoundland (Bailey 2015).
13. Social structures of accumulation refer to the "ensemble of economic, political, and ideological institutions which serve to reproduce capitalist relations of production" (McBride 2010: 20).

References

Aucoin, P., Jarvis, M.D., and Turnbull, L. (2011) *Democratizing the Constitution: Reforming Responsible Government*, Toronto: Emond Montgomery.

Axtmann, R. (2004) "The State of the State: The Model of the Modern State and Its Contemporary Transformation," *International Political Science Review*, 25(3): 259–279.

Babb, S. (2013) "The Washington Consensus as Transnational Policy Paradigm: Its Origins, Trajectory, and Likely Successor," *Review of International Political Economy*, 20(2): 268–297.

Bailey, S. (2015) "Newfoundland Suspends Participation in All Trade Agreements," *Huffington Post*, January 19, available at: www.huffingtonpost.ca/2015/01/19/newfoundland-free-trade-agreements_n_6501006.html (accessed February 3, 2015).

Bearce, D.H. and Bondanella, S. (2007) "Intergovernmental Organizations, Socialization, and Member-State Interest Convergence," *International Organization*, 61: 703–733.

Bernier, M. (2014) "International Trade," Canada, Parliament, House of Commons, *Edited Hansard* 147(137), 41st Parliament, 2nd session, November 3.

Best, J. (2010) "Bringing Power Back In: The IMF's Constructivist Strategy in Critical Perspective," in R. Abdelal, M. Blyth, and C. Parsons (Eds.), *Constructing the International Economy*, Ithaca, NY: Cornell University Press, pp. 194–210.

Bittner, A. and Kopp, R. (Eds.) (2013) *Parties, Elections, and the Future of Canadian Politics*, Vancouver: UBC Press.

Bousfield, D. (2013) "Canadian Foreign Policy in an Era of New Constitutionalism," *American Review of Canadian Studies*, 43(3): 394–412.

Brennan, J. (2013) "The Power Underpinnings, and Some Distributional Consequences, of Trade and Investment Liberalisation in Canada," *New Political Economy*, 18(5): 715–747.

Brown, J. (2013) "Why Are the Conservatives Keeping Trans-Pacific Partnership Negotiations Secret?" *Maclean's*, August 28, available at: www2.macleans.ca/2013/08/28/why-is-the-trans-pacific-partnership-such-a-secret/ (accessed February 5, 2015).

Burnham, P. (2000) "Globalization, Depoliticization, and 'Modern' Economic Management," in W. Bonefeld and K. Psychopedis (Eds.), *The Politics of Change: Globalization, Ideology and Critique*, Basingstoke: Palgrave, pp. 9–27.

Cameron, B. (2006) "Social Reproduction and Canadian Federalism," in K. Bezanson and M. Luxton (Eds.), *Social Reproduction: Feminist Political Economy Challenges Neo-Liberalism*, Montreal: McGill-Queen's University Press, pp. 45–74.

Canadian Business (2012) "TPP Poll: We Want Our Free-Trade Cake, *Canadian Business*, July 31, available at: www.canadianbusiness.com/business-strategy/tpp-poll-we-want-our-free-trade-cake/ (accessed February 3, 2015).

Capling, A. and Nossal, K.R. (2003) "Parliament and the Democratization of Foreign Policy: The Case of Australia's Joint Standing Committee on Treaties," *Canadian Journal of Political Science*, 36(4): 835–855.

CCIC (n.d.) *Bilateral Investment Treaties: A Canadian Primer*, available at: www.ccic.ca/_files/en/what_we_do/trade_2010-04_investmt_treaties_primer_e.pdf (accessed February 3, 2015).

Cerny, P. (2006) "Political Globalization and the Competition State," in R. Stubbs and G. Underhill (Eds.), *Political Economy and the Changing Global Order*, Oxford: Oxford University Press, pp. 376–386.

Cheng, T-H. (2005) "Power, Authority and International Investment Law," *American University International Law Review*, 20(465): 466–503.

Choudhry, S. (2003) "Judicial Power and the Charter: Canada and the Paradox of Liberal Constitutionalism (Review)," *I.CON*, 1(2): 379–403.

Collins, R. (2009) "Constitutionalism as Liberal-Juridical Consciousness: Echoes from International Law's Past," *Leiden Journal of International Law*, 22: 251–287.

Crouch, C. (2004) *Post-Democracy*, Cambridge: Polity Press.

Danesi, S.L. (2014) "Tabling and Waiting: A Preliminary Assessment of Canada's Treaty-Tabling Policy," *Canadian Foreign Policy Journal*, 20(2): 189–208.

Davies, D. (2012) "International Trade," Canada, Parliament, House of Commons, *Edited Hansard* 146(180), 41st Parliament, 1st session, November 19.

Docherty, D.C. (2005) *Legislatures*, Vancouver: UBC Press.

Environmental Defence (2015) "Statement by Environmental Defence's Dale Marshall on Canada Blocking NAFTA's Environmental Watchdog from Investigating Leaking Toxic Tailings Ponds," *Environmental Defence*, January 28, available at: http://environmentaldefence.ca/articles/statement-environmental-defence%E2%80%99s-dale-marshall-canada-blocking-nafta%E2%80%99s-environmental-watch (accessed February 8, 2015).

Evans, M. (2003) "Public Reason as Liberal Myth: Impartialist Liberalism, Judicial Review and the Cult of the Constitution," *Journal of Transatlantic Studies*, 1(1): 8–25.

Fairbrother, M. (2010) "Trade Policymaking in the Real World: Elites' Conflicting Worldviews and North American Integration," *Review of International Political Economy*, 17(2): 319–347.

Freeland, C. (2014) "Canada-Korea Economic Growth and Prosperity Act, C-41," Canada, Parliament, House of Commons, *Edited Hansard* 147(115), 41st Parliament, 2nd session, September 24.

Garneau, M. (2014) "Canada-Korea Economic Growth and Prosperity Act, C-41," Canada, Parliament, House of Commons, *Edited Hansard* 147(132), 41st Parliament, 2nd session, October 27.

Gerald, K. (2012) "International Trade," Canada, Parliament, House of Commons, *Edited Hansard* 146(180), 41st Parliament, 1st session, November 19.

Gill, S. (1995) "Globalisation, Market Civilisation, and Disciplinary Neoliberalism," *Millennium: Journal of International Studies*, 24(3): 399–423.

Harrington, J. (2006) "Scrutiny and Approval: The Role for Westminster-Style Parliaments in Treaty-Making," *International and Comparative Law Quarterly*, 55: 121–160.

Hirschl, R. (2008) "The Judicialization of Mega-Politics and the Rise of Political Courts," *Annual Review of Political Science*, 11: 93–118.

Honig, B. (1991) "Declarations of Independence: Arendt and Derrida on the Problem of Founding a Republic," *American Political Science Review*, 85(1): 84–113.

Jackman, M. (2005) "Misdiagnosis or Cure? Charter Review of the Health Care System," in Colleen M. Flood (Ed.), *Just Medicare: What's In, What's Out, How We Decide*, Toronto: University of Toronto Press (Scholarly Publishing Division), pp. 58–79.

Keddy, G. (2012) "International Trade," Canada, Parliament, House of Commons, *Edited Hansard* 146(142), 41st Parliament, 1st session, June 18.

Kelsey, J. (2013) "The Trans-Pacific Partnership Agreement: A Gold-Plated Gift to the Global Tobacco Industry?" *American Journal of Law & Medicine*, 39: 237–264.

Kenis, A. and Mathijs, E. (2014) "Climate Change and Post-Politics: Repoliticizing the Present by Imagining the Future," *Geoforum*, 52: 148–156.

Kioupkiolis, A. (2014) "Towards a Regime of Post-Political Biopower? Dispatches from Greece, 2010–2012," *Theory, Culture & Society*, 31(1): 143–158.

Lazar, H. (2006) "The Intergovernmental Dimensions of the Social Union: A Sectoral Analysis," *Canadian Public Administration*, 49(1): 23–45.

LeBreton, M. (2012) "International Trade: Trans-Pacific Partnership," *Debates of the Senate of Canada*, 98: 148.

May, E. (2014) "Canada-Korea Economic Growth and Prosperity Act, C-41," Canada, Parliament, House of Commons, *Edited Hansard* 147(115), 41st Parliament, 2nd session, September 24.

McBride, S. (2003) "Quiet Constitutionalism in Canada: The International Political Economy of Domestic Institutional Change," *Canadian Journal of Political Science*, 36(2): 251–274.

McBride, S. (2010) "The New Constitutionalism: International and Private Rule in the New Global Order," in S. McBride and G. Teeple (Eds.), *Relations of Global Power: Neoliberal Order and Disorder*, Toronto: University of Toronto Press, pp. 19–40.

McKenna, B. (2014) "In Protecting Agriculture, We Sacrifice Other Trade Gains," *The Globe and Mail*, January 27, p. B1.

Moini, G. (2011) "How Participation Has Become a Hegemonic Discursive Resource: Towards an Interpretivist Research Agenda," *Critical Policy Studies*, 5(2): 149–168.

Palamare, S. and Jardine, E. (2012) "Does Canada Need a New Asia Policy?" *Canadian Foreign Policy Journal*, 18(3): 251–263.

Petter, A. (2005) "Wealthcare: The Politics of the 'Charter' Revisited," in C. Flood, K. Roach, and L. Sossin (Eds.), *Access to Care, Access to Justice: The Legal Debate Over Private Health Insurance in Canada*, Toronto: University of Toronto Press, pp. 116–138.

Petter, A. (2009) "Legalise This: The Chartering of Canadian Politics," in J. Kelly and C. Manfredi (Eds.), *Legislative Activism and Parliamentary Bills of Rights: Institutional Lessons for Canada*, Vancouver: UBC Press, pp. 33–49.

Pierre, J. (1995) "The Marketization of the State: Citizens, Consumers, and the Emergence of the Public Market," in G. Peters and D. Savoie (Eds.), *Governance in a Changing Environment*, Montreal: McGill-Queen's University Press, pp. 55–82.

Porter, T. (2005) "Private Authority, Technical Authority, and the Globalisation of Accounting Standards," *Business and Politics*, 7(3): 1–30.

Porter, T. (2011) "Public and Private Authority in the Transnational Response to the 2008 Financial Crisis," *Policy and Society*, 30: 175–184.

Poulsen, L.N. and Aisbett, E. (2013) "When the Claim Hits: Bilateral Investment Treaties and Bounded Rational Learning," *World Politics*, 65(2): 273–313.

Pritchard, B. (2005) "How the Rule of the Market Rules the Law: The Political Economy of WTO Dispute Settlement as Evidenced in the US-Lamb Meat Decision," *Review of International Political Economy*, 12(5): 776–803.

Ravignat, M. (2014) "Routine Proceedings," Canada, Parliament, House of Commons, *Edited Hansard* 147(143), 41st Parliament, 2nd session, November 18.

Resnick, P. (1990) *The Masks of Proteus: Canadian Reflections on the State*, Montreal: McGill-Queen's University Press.

Rude, J. and An, H. (2013) "Trans-Pacific Partnership: Implications for the Canadian Industrial Dairy Sector," *Canadian Public Policy*, 39(3): 393–410.

Savoie, D. (1999) "The Rise of Court Government in Canada," *Canadian Journal of Political Science*, 32: 635–664.

Schneiderman, D. (2005) "Banging Constitutional Bibles: Observing Constitutional Culture in Transition," *University of Toronto Law Journal*, 55(3): 833–852.

Schneiderman, D. (2008) *Constitutionalizing Economic Globalization*, Cambridge: Cambridge University Press.

Scholte, J.A. (2008) "Reconstructing Contemporary Democracy," *Indiana Journal of Global Legal Studies*, 15(1): 305–350.

Sinclair, S. (2015) *NAFTA Chapter 11 Investor-State Disputes*, Toronto: Canadian Centre for Policy Alternatives.

Skogstad, G. (2012) "International Trade Policy and Canadian Federalism: A Constructive Tension?" in H. Bakvis and G. Skogstad (Eds.), *Canadian Federalism: Performance, Effectiveness, and Legitimacy*, Don Mills: Oxford University Press, pp. 157–177.

Smith, D.E. (1995) *The Invisible Crown*, Toronto: University of Toronto Press.

Swyngedouw, E. (2011) "Interrogating Post-Democratization: Reclaiming Egalitarian Political Spaces," *Political Geography*, 30: 370–380.

Tencer, D. (2014) "TPP Talks' Last-Minute Venue Shift Marks 'A New Low in Transparency'," *Huffington Post*, July 27, available at: www.huffingtonpost.ca/2014/07/07/tpp-talks-ottawa-vancouver_n_5564683.html (accessed February 5, 2015).

Tienhaara, K. (2011) "Once BITten, Twice Shy? The Uncertain Future of 'Shared Sovereignty' in Investment Treaty Arbitration," *Policy and Society*, 30: 185–196.

Trefler, D. (2004) "The Long and Short of the Canada-US Free Trade Agreement," *The American Economic Review*, 94(4): 1–40.

Trew, S. (2014) "We're Pushing the Democracy (Not Panic) Button on Trans-Pacific Partnership," *The Council of Canadians*, January 24, available at: http://canadians.org/blog/we%E2%80%99re-pushing-democracy-not-panic-button-trans-pacific-partnership (accessed February 10, 2015).

Van Harten, G. (2005) "Private Authority and Transnational Governance: The Contours of the International System of Investor Protection," *Review of International Political Economy*, 12(4): 600–623.

Ward, L. (2005) "Locke on Executive Power and Liberal Constitutionalism," *Canadian Journal of Political Science*, 38(3): 719–744.

Warren, M. (1989) "Liberal Constitutionalism as Ideology: Marx and Habermas," *Political Theory*, 17(4): 511–534.

Watkins, M. (1997) "Canadian Capitalism in Transition," in W. Clement (Ed.), *Understanding Canada*, Montreal: McGill-Queens University Press, pp. 19–37.

Whittington, L. (2015) "Oil Giants Win $17M from Ottawa under NAFTA," The Star, March 13, available at: www.thestar.com/news/canada/2015/03/13/oil-giants-win-17m-from-ottawa-under-nafta.html (accessed March 14, 2015).

Chapter 5

The Public Sphere and Practice of Democracy in Nigeria: The Context and Contribution of the Nigerian Diaspora

Kudus Oluwatoyin Adebayo and Emeka Thaddues Njoku

In this chapter, the context and contribution of the Nigerian diaspora in the transformation of Nigeria's public sphere is examined. Relying mainly on secondary materials, the chapter contends that Nigeria's public sphere has taken a transnational turn. The "public sphere," as articulated by Jürgen Habermas, has inspired critical debates on democratic theory in the social and political sciences since it was proposed in 1962. Although Habermas' vision of an ideal deliberative social space was criticized on many fronts, its relevance continues to endure. Several factors may account for this, ranging from the theoretical depth of the idea itself to its multidisciplinary applicability. In the context of this chapter, however, the value of the public sphere as a social and political idea lies in its recognition of civil society as a core constituent element of practicing democracies.

In Fraser's (1990: 57) interpretation, the public sphere "designates a theater in modern societies in which political participation is enacted through the medium of talk. It is the space in which citizens deliberate about their common affairs, hence, an institutionalized arena of discursive interaction." As key participants in the discursive realm, civil society shapes public discourse and produces public opinion through rational communicative exchanges. While the public sphere represents the sociopolitical organization for articulation of autonomous views directed at influencing political institutions, civil society is the organized expression of these views (Castells 2008). Civil society bridges the gap between the state and the society by expanding avenues for rational discussions and improving the quality of public debates.

By partaking in "public talk," civil society helps bring the state and citizens more closely together to engage over diverse ideas and conflicting interests; this relationship, notes Castells (2008), is the cornerstone of democracy.

While confusion persists on what sort of social groupings actually constitute civil society—a confusion that has now been complicated by the ascendance of the idea of global civil society, occasioned by prevailing contexts of deterritorialization, boundary disappearance and realities of unbounded "-scapes" and social spaces (Schiller et al. 1992; Appadurai 1996; Bartelson 2006)—certain groups may reasonably be considered as one, including transnational diaspora communities. In fact, evidence supporting "diaspora as civil society" dots existing literature on transnational diaspora hometown associations and self-helps in host societies (Mercer et al. 2008; Heath 2009), and in studies exploring diaspora–homeland development practices (Sørensen 2007; Judge and Plaen 2011; Plaza and Ratha 2011). Although most of the civil society engagements of transnational diaspora communities are clustered around remittances and social assistance issues, political engagement has also become important among diaspora populations. In developing democracies across Africa, politically oriented civic engagement has assumed greater importance due to the advent of the Internet and growing accessibility to—and adoption of—information technologies. Through the use of social media platforms and by participating actively in online discussions, a growing number of the African diaspora population are joining the ranks of "netizens" or "digital diasporas" in order to shape the public spheres of their home countries (Brinkerhoff 2009; Everett 2009; see Bernal 2005, 2006 for detailed study of the Eritrean diaspora).

By first describing the contribution of the Nigerian diaspora in Nigeria's democratization process and then analyzing their recent online homeland-oriented political discourses and practices, we bring into focus the participation of foreign-based Nigerians in enshrining democracy and in shaping the practice of democratic ideals in Africa's most populous country.

Diaspora and Democratization in Nigeria

During the colonial and postcolonial historical epochs, the African diaspora made significant contributions to the attainment of statehood and state-building in many African countries. From the early eighteenth to the nineteenth century, Africans were either forced out of their homeland through the slave trade or were compelled due to the quest for educational or employment opportunities in the Western world (Adi 2000). Interestingly, this coerced and consensual congregation of Africans in a new setting created a unique form of political consciousness—particularly on issues that related to their homeland (Papastergiadis 2000). Similarly, Van der Veer (1995: 5) states that "the marginal position of the migrant and the special qualities of group formation among exiles seem in general to play a significant role in the formulation of a nationalist discourse." The African diaspora of the eighteenth and nineteenth centuries was credited for its immense contributions to the establishment of pan-Africanist ideologies, established in response to racism and the quest for the decolonization of African states (Adi 2000; Blake 2005). Moreover, in the twentieth century, the writings of James Africanus Beale Horton and Edward Blyden expedited the idea of West African nationalism—an idea that attracted West African intellectuals (Langley 1973: 37). By the 1920s, the increased cognizance of a West African nationalism aided the formation of three major organizations in Ghana, Nigeria, and the United Kingdom: namely, the National

Congress of British West Africa (NCBWA), formed in 1920; the Nigerian Progress Union (NPU), created in 1924; and the West African Student Union, established in 1925. These organizations became the major vehicles for the idea of West African nationalism. Moreover, among its contemporaries, WASU grew to become a formidable force not only in the political socialization of young Africans in the UK, but a major anti-colonial force (Olusanya 1982: 19). According to Adi (2000: 75–76), WASU championed the concept of West African nationalism by nurturing "a healthy nationalist sentiment throughout West Africa." The struggle of these groups paid off in the 1960s, as many African states became independent politically.

Furthermore, the postcolonial era saw another wave of African diaspora, many of whom were forced into self-exile by despotic governments. Akyeampong (2000: 204) stresses that the emergence of military rule in the 1960s, economic crisis, stymied expectations, and civil wars contributed to the destabilization of a newly independent African nation and consequently led to "new waves of political and economic refugees" that migrated to the West. Hence, a new form of African diaspora was established. Mohan and Zack-Williams (2002: 231) best captured this when they stated that:

> A related element of political activity in diaspora is around democratisation and human rights. As some states have entered progressive legitimacy crises they have tended to clamp down on political dissent, which can escalate into violence and murder. In turn this sets up waves of out-migration either as people flee the potential risk of persecution or leave as formal political refugees. While far from perfect, their diasporic location may permit them the political space to lobby against repressive regimes; a space which is flatly denied to them at home ... Indeed, one could argue further that given the geographical and political closeness of the diaspora to the centres of global decision-making in London, Paris, New York and Washington it should be better placed to lobby for changes in development policy towards the continent.

As with most other African countries, the debacle that characterized the postcolonial states in the 1960s to the 1980s—consisting of such institutional and policy failures as those that accompanied the implementation of the Structural Adjustment Programme (SAP), the socio-economic underdevelopment or disparity, and augmentation of dictatorial administrations —facilitated the mass departure of consummate Nigerians to the developed world. Remarkably, this period also saw the emergence of a vibrant civil society that advocated for democratic governance, accountability, transparency, and respect for the principle of rule of law in Nigeria. Aiyede (2003) contends that the general dissatisfaction by the people in the processes of governance provided a fecund site for civil society organizations to strive. Hence, such groups as the Committee for the Defence of Human Rights (CDHR), Transition Monitoring Group (TMG), civil liberties organizations (CLO), Campaign for Democracy (CD), etc. surfaced and came up with creative strategies to resist despotic and corrupt administrations.

Similarly, the diaspora groups were equally involved in the struggle for democratic consolidation in Nigeria. This was more evident in the aftermath of the annulled June 12, 1993, presidential elections. This period saw the birth of diaspora groups such as the National Democratic Coalition (NADECO), National Liberation Council of Nigeria (NALICON), the United Democratic Front of Nigeria (UDF), and Radio Kudirat, a short radio program pioneered by Wole Soyinka to criticize the government. According to Shettima (1999), within this period there were no fewer than 100 Nigerian pro-democracy groups in the US, UK, and Canada. According to Kperogi (2011: 112), these organizations were "a central and symbolic locus of political mobilization in the long and arduous struggle to dislodge totalitarian military regimes in Nigeria in the 1990s."

Civil Society, Internet, and Diasporic Public Sphere

To the extent that it contributes toward the discursive environment known as the public sphere, civil society continues to be critical to the both the development and survival of democracy. Civil society promotes the practice of democracy as a system of collective discussion, exchange, and action, and facilitates the process through which the public refine expectations and make demands on the state (Diamond 1994, cited in Aiyede 2003; Fraser 2007). It has been observed that much of the literature tends to focus on civil society within a particular society. This, note Hall and Trentmann (2005), has benefits of depth but risks a loss of perspective on the changing overall contours of the civil society debate. In this regard, Fraser (2007) argues that current mobilizations of public opinion rarely terminate at the borders of states, with implications that manifestations of civil society have multiplied and transnationalized. Castells (2008) identified at least four modes of civil society formations: the first is local civil society that defend local or sectoral interests (i.e. grassroots organizations); the second is nongovernmental organizations with global or international frame of reference in both actions and goals (i.e. the so-called "global civil society"); third are social movements aiming to control process of globalization that build networks of action and organization to induce global social movements for global justice (i.e. the Zapatistas); and fourth are movements of public opinion that operate within a diversified media system and employ Internet and wireless communications as organizing tools and means for debate, dialogue, and collective decision-making (i.e. networked mobilizers against the Iraq war).

On the ground that the last three manifestations of civil society are underlain by similar globalizing processes, the question of whether Castells' (2008) typifications constitute meaningfully distinguishable categorization can be raised. Nonetheless, Castells was right to make this distinction between global–local focus/orientated actions of civil society. Both in form and action, diasporic civil society straddles local and global spaces. Through identification with the homeland, diasporas (wherever dispersed) often direct their civic engagements toward home countries and invest in homeland politics by drawing upon globalizing structures that blur the lines between here and there. An extrapolative undertaking that regroups Castells' typifications into two broad (local and global) forms will conceive diaspora civil society as a "third way." Because of their multi-spatial dispersion, diaspora civil society are globally situated (Safran 1991; Cohen 1997), although participation in the public sphere is mostly locally oriented—tending primarily toward the homeland.

While residing abroad, strong attachment to—and interest in—homeland publics, politics, and wider public sphere constitute motivations for engagement (Gillespie 1998). The Internet has been a critical part of diasporic civil service participation in homeland politics. Political participation is a core research theme in recent studies on the Internet and online behaviors. In studying online politics, DiMaggio et al. (2001) observe that the literature has developed from the stages of unjustifiable euphoria and unjustified skepticism to the gradual realization that the Internet does possess unique and politically significant properties. As a growing substructure within an established system of political communication, the Internet accentuates the sprawling character of the public sphere as it permits rational political deliberation while also offering alternative space for challenging established power (Dahlgren 2005). The argument has been made that the Internet can promote the practice of deliberative democracy as it "will enhance the quality of political discussion and the viability, meaningfulness, and diversity of the public sphere by lowering the access barrier to meaningful public speech" (DiMaggio et al. 2001: 321). Also, the transnational public sphere established using the Internet transcends and sets itself apart from the Habermasian public sphere, because it accommodates diverse identities and multiple participatory cultures (Dahlgren 2005).

The attraction of diaspora civil society to the Internet cannot be divorced from the possibilities it holds for the development of an alternative public sphere. More than anything else, the Internet has helped in overcoming the boundaries of time and space and provides the infrastructure necessary for deliberation and discussion among special interest groups, ad hoc pressure groups, or cyber protesters (Grbeša 2003). Bernal (2005) especially emphasized that diaspora and cyberspace are linked because of shared images of "displacement" and the feeling of "community" it engenders—be they real or imagined. Elsewhere, the same author showed that diasporas appropriate the Internet to set up "a transnational public sphere where they produce and debate narratives of history, culture, democracy and identity" (Bernal 2006: 162). Describing how Eritrean diaspora appropriate the Internet, Bernal (2006) explains how the Internet-facilitated, transnational pathway is used to mobilize demonstrators, raise funds for war, debate the content and formation of constitution, and also influence the government of Eritrea. Thus, in accordance with the precepts of the Habermasian public sphere, Eritreans online construct a national space within cyberspace for the purpose of circulating views about homeland politics.

It is worth noting that the structure of the Internet accommodates varied forms of public spheres. In light of the fact that Habermas' public sphere failed to recognize non-liberal, non-bourgeois, competing public spheres (Fraser 1990), Dahlgren (2005) identifies at least five sectors of Net-based public spheres. First, there is the *version of e-government* in which government representatives interact with citizens employing top-down tactics. Second, there is the *advocacy/activist domain* where organizations frame issues using generally shared perceptions, values, and goals for the purposes of political intervention. Third, the Internet-based public sphere can take the form of *civic forums* wherein citizens exchange views and deliberate issues of mutual interest. The civic forum is considered the paradigmatic version of public sphere on the Internet. The *pre-political or parapolitical domain* is the fourth of Dahlgren's Net-based public spheres. Here, the main topics discussed revolve around commonly shared social and cultural issues, although political issues are sometimes interwoven in the discussions. The final sector identified is the *journalism domain*, which is constituted by major news organizations—from online/offline news media to Web news crowding sites and blogs. Dahlgren (2005) was quick to note that the journalistic domain is a core element of the public sphere on the Internet. Suffice it to note that while the different sectors of the Net-based public sphere may be conceptually distinguishable, it is possible for most (or even all) the domains to blend into one another or manifest conterminously through the activities of a single diaspora civil society. Much of this will be substantiated in the next section through the analysis of practices of Nigerian diaspora civil society.

Nigeria's Declining Public Sphere: Diaspora to the Rescue?

The participation of civil society in the public sphere is critical to the practice and survival of democracies. Civil society intersects with the development of a vibrant democracy by providing clarity across positions and facilitating the processes of deliberation that will over time entrench what Guidry and Sawyer (2003) called "contentious pluralism" in the societal political architecture. Yet, civil society may not necessarily succeed at sustaining "contentious pluralism" once established.

As shown in the previous section, civil society contributed immensely to Nigeria's democratization in the years following the economic collapse and political repression of the 1980s. After the handover of power to civilians by the military on May 1999, locally based civil society has since been set on a path of decline. This has negatively impacted the quality of deliberation in the public sphere (Kperogi 2011). The development of a full-fledged diaspora civil society can be traced to this context of decline, with grave implications for the transnationalization of the public sphere. Indeed, as Castells (2008) observed, the crisis of the national public sphere makes the emergence of an international public sphere particularly relevant. In a recent assessment, Kperogi (2011) argues that Nigerian online diaspora media emerged from the ashes of a dying media tradition that hitherto succeeded in pressing for the demilitarization of the government of Nigeria. For pro-democracy NGOs and other civil society organizations, the percolation of militaristic tendencies across all segments of society affected their constitution and modes of operation (Aiyede 2003), thus preventing them from making meaningful contributions to the public sphere.

Although homeland political engagement appropriating the Internet took off in the 1990s, the participation of Nigerian diasporic civil society in the national public sphere began much earlier—spanning colonial and postcolonial periods. With the Internet, however, the cyberspace provided an avenue for Nigerian diasporic civil society to establish a transnational public sphere with which deliberation over matters of national interests was carried out. From the 1990s, Nigerians in the United States assembled in cyberspace using multiple Web platforms (Bastian 1999) and reconstructed imaginations of the homeland and identities. In the period between the annulled elections in 1993 up until 1999, democracy and other matters of political significance were discussed vigorously in chat rooms. Their online activities throughout the 1990s helped lay the foundation for what was to come (Adebayo 2014).

Before narrowing to a single case, it is fruitful to point out that the Internet-based practices of Nigerian diaspora civil society contributing to the emergence of transnational public sphere have different manifestations. It has manifested in terms of mobilizing or organizing transnationally to protest against the state, as occurred during the 2012 fuel subsidy protest. In response to the government's decision to remove subsidies from petroleum products in January 2012, Nigerian diaspora communities organized protests in cities across Europe and America and recorded images and videos that were later circulated on popular social media sites (Adebayo 2014; Akanle et al. 2014). While it lasted, protest spaces were littered with placards that communicated diaspora preferences while diasporic public performances were used to express solidarity with citizens at home. Another recent instance of diaspora-initiated mobilization was the worldwide protest that trailed the kidnapping of over 250 schoolgirls in Chibok Town by Boko Haram in April 2014. Armed with a simple Twitter hashtag #bringbackourgirls inscribed on cardboard sheets, the Nigerian diaspora successfully staged one of the most massive social media mobilization efforts of recent times, attracting solidarity from political leaders around the world—including the US—as well as high-profile visits to Nigeria from figures such as the Nobel Laureate and Malala Yousafzai. Meanwhile, diaspora civil society could also manifest itself in terms of monitoring the activities of Nigerian public figures or government activities in places of settlement, and ensuring that discoveries are circulated as appropriate. A good example of this was when the US-based diaspora obtained and made public evidence of fraudulent accumulations by members of the Nigerian political class in the United States (Kperogi 2011).

In the paragraphs that follow, we focus on an online media to discuss a transnational public sphere in which Nigerian diasporic civil society are active participants. The case discussed revolves around www.saharareporters.com (hereafter Sahara Reporters/Sahara), an online news media organization that was established by New York-based Nigerian political activist Omoleye Sowore. It is one of the most visited Nigeria-focused news media online (see Table 5.1). The character of this transnational public sphere reflects the motivation and attitude of its founder, who in the early 1990s mobilized students and organized several protests against the military regimes and their "anti-people" policies (Oyedoyin 2003; Kperogi 2011). From a journalistic point of view, the website is a brand of citizen's journalism where "everyday people" supply news contents, report misdoings, and assist in verifying controversial news materials (the so-called "citizen verifiers" and "citizen editors" (Egbunike 2011). One study found that issues that get reported often become topical issues in the local news media scene as well (Kperogi 2011).

As a transnational public sphere for rational deliberation over matters of national significance, Sahara Reporters has been more than a news medium. On the "About Us" section of the website, it is written that:

> Sahara Reporters is an online community of international reporters and social advocates dedicated to bringing you commentaries, features, news reports from a Nigerian-African perspective. A unique organization, founded in the spirit of Article 19 of the Universal Declaration of Human Rights, comprising of ordinary people with an overriding commitment to seeking the truth and publishing it without fear or favor. Because its core members are unapologetic practitioners of advocacy journalism, Sahara Reporters also serves as an umbrella outlet for objective reporting of verifiable and accurate news and untainted social commentaries for anyone wishing to exercise their freedom of speech in the public interest and common good.
>
> (Sahara Reporters 2015)

The statement of purpose is clear enough. The owners intend to make a public sphere out of Sahara Reporters, and with choice of phrases such as "practitioners of advocacy," "untainted social commentaries," "exercise of freedom of speech," and "public interest and common good," the website accommodates multiple Net-based public sphere domains at the same time. Although operating from the US, the politics discussed are mainly about Nigeria and of Nigerian political personalities. Also, while most of its opinion writers are based in the US, mostly connected to the academic/intelligentsia class, most of those participating in the sphere are based in Nigeria.

From Table 5.2, it will be noticed that the audience of Sahara is very similar to other Nigerian online news media. This suggests that the primary target of Sahara are co-citizens in the homeland. While geographically dispersed, the Net-based transnational public sphere

Table 5.1 Most Visited Nigeria-Focused Online News Sites, March 20, 2015

Online Media	Country Ranking of Site	Ranking by News Content	Base of Operation	Nature of News Publishing
Punch www.punchng.com	#19	#1	Nigeria	Online/offline
Vanguard www.vanguardngr.com	#26	#2	Nigeria	Online/offline
Sahara Reporters www. saharareporters.com	**#48**	**#3**	**United States**	**Online**
Premium Times www. premiumtimesng.com	#61	#4	Nigeria	Online
Thisday www.thisdaylive.com	#82	#5	Nigeria	Online/offline

Note: The news content ranking is based on the main focus of the online media in question. Blogs, foreign news websites, marketing and shopping sites, and information crowding and sports websites—many of which ranked higher on the most visited sites list—are not included here. Sites in the top sites lists are ordered by their one-month Alexa traffic rank. The one-month rank is calculated using a combination of average daily visitors and page views over the past month. The site with the highest combination of visitors and page views is ranked #1.

Source: www.alexa.com

Table 5.2 Locations of Top Visitors to Nigeria-Focused Online News Media

Online Media	Top Five Locations of Visitors				
Punch www.punchng.com	Nigeria (85.4%)	US (2.4%)	South Africa (2.1%)	UK (1.9%)	India (1.6%)
Vanguard www.vanguardngr.com	Nigeria (76%)	UK (4.1%)	US (3.5%)	India (2.9%)	South Africa (2.6%)
Sahara Reporters www. saharareporters.com	Nigeria (75%)	UK (4.7%)	South Africa (4.2%)	US (4.1%)	Finland (2.8%)
Premium Times www. premiumtimesng.com	Nigeria (81.4%)	South Africa (4.7%)	UK (3.4%)	US (3.3%)	Finland (2.9%)
Thisday www.thisdaylive.com	Nigeria (76.4%)	US (4.1%)	South Africa (3.5%)	UK (3.3%)	India (2.2%)

Source: www.alexa.com

helps the Nigerian diaspora to remain connected to the homeland while also giving allowance for them to offer viewpoints that differ sharply from those prevailing in national public sphere. By seeking to clarify complex sociopolitical issues, opinion writers transcend government propaganda and lay bare matters that ordinary citizens may consider too confusing. With the hyper-interactive nature of the website, visitors find it easy to comment, reanalyze, and interpret issues as they wish. Discussing what the organization was doing to mentor the next generation of activist writers, Sowore's position revealed a fact that underlines the character of Sahara as a quintessential public sphere:

> What we experience on the website is a dynamic interaction of different thought processes, a clashing and mixing of ideas, where you publish a report and people come forward to dissect, redirect and make additions and sometimes provide better ideas than the original report. Sometimes you watch a story develop and through this participatory infusion of ideas, it grows a life of its own. I am seeing better writers and reporters on the site every day, making measured comment. The real mentors are the readers and commentators, they are my mentors. It is not the other way round.
>
> (Egbunike 2011)

On Sahara, opinion articles of fewer than 1,000 words often generate over 100 comments from both regular visitors and new users. Articles and associated raw documents are mostly archived and commentary sections are never closed, making it possible for participants to explore and reflect over the contours of issues for long periods of time. This means that issues are/can be revisited and reviewed in a continuous manner. The capacity of record-keeping appears to further distinguish the Net-based transnational public sphere from a Habermasian public sphere in which deliberations are at best "fleeting." In other words, the Net-based public sphere that diaspora civil society create consist of durable spaces, and rather than merely arriving at some aggregated "public opinion," there is room to both achieve aggregation and compartmentalization—compartmentalization meaning that we will be able to say "this is what most of them think," as distinct from "this group said A rather than B, with B being the opinion of that other group."

No doubt, the activities of Sahara and other Nigerian diasporic civil society groups have widened the space for democracy to take root in Nigeria. In the face of a declining national public sphere, the Nigerian diaspora stepped in and continued to question the government and have been deliberating over matters of social and political significance. From the goals of the organization and the viewpoints it supports, the Sahara Reporters' transnational public sphere possesses the features of advocacy/activist, civic forums, and journalistic domains (as conceived by Dahlgren 2005). The website not only informs its mostly Nigeria-based audience, but also provides an avenue through which Nigerians at home and abroad discuss government actions/inactions and mobilize for change.

Conclusion: Diaspora Civil Society, Transnational Public Sphere, and Democracy

The practices of diaspora civil society connect geographically dispersed nodes through a transnational public sphere, and the Internet has been a great enabler of this process. In the era of globalization, the transnational expansion of deliberative space has implications for the practice of democracy. As Fraser (2007) observes, the notion of a transnational public sphere may be indispensable to those interested in reconstructing democratic theory in the current "postnational constellation"—in which boundaries among nations are disappearing. Members of the diaspora form opinion over important matters and subject the views to citizens' critical scrutiny, with the view to either modify, reject, or supply alternative perspective through reasoned arguments. In social settings where the national public sphere is in crisis—perhaps due to takeover of local media by powerful individuals as in the case of Nigeria (Kperogi 2011)—the transnational public sphere offers an alternative outlet for continued expression of free speech, opinion formation, and citizens' participation.

While acknowledging that the transnational public sphere could promote democracy, Dahlgren (2005) warns us that it can also have destabilizing consequences. Taking a clue from Fraser's (1990: 67) concern about counter-publics, the structure of and practices within transnational public sphere can be antidemocratic in character, having in mind that "even those with democratic and egalitarian intentions are not always above practicing their own modes of informal exclusion and marginalization." For one, a transnational public sphere that is based on Internet infrastructure basically marginalizes those without access (thus excluding people with alternative, and perhaps superior, arguments). Similar criticism was leveled against the Habermasian public sphere. What is more, the discussion of the transnational public sphere presented here ignores the inherently diverse/fragmented nature of diaspora (Akinrinade and Ogen 2011), which can lead to the formation of fragmented "public opinion" instead of a truly balanced position. The interest of diverse participants and the power differentials among those deliberating in a transnational public sphere will also stifle equitable democratic expression and undermine the possibility of arriving at representative outcomes. Nevertheless, diaspora civil society holds great promise for the reconstruction of democratic theory in the postmodern world.

References

Adebayo, K. (2014) "Occupy-Nigeria Movement, Organised Labour Unions and Oil-Subsidy Struggle: An Analysis of Processes in Media(ted) 'Revolution' and Its Demise" (Nijerya'yi İşgal Et Hareketi İşçi Sendikaları ve Petrol Sübvansiyon Mücadele: Medya Devrim/Medyatikleşen Devrim ve Devrimin Sönümlenme Sürecine Dair Bir Analiz ölümü), in B. Çoban (Ed.), *Social Media R/evolution*, Istanbul: Su Publisher, pp. 77–96.

Adi, H. (2000) "Pan-Africanism and West African Nationalism in Britain," *African Studies Review*, 43(1): 69–82.

Aiyede, E.R. (2003) "The Dynamics of Civil Society and the Democratization Process in Nigeria," *Canadian Journal of African Studies*, 37(1): 1–27.

Akanle, O., Adebayo, K., and Olorunlana, A. (2014) "Fuel Subsidy in Nigeria: Contexts of Governance and Social Protest," *International Journal of Sociology and Social Policy*, 34(1/2): 88–106.

Akinrinade, S. and Ogen, O. (2011) "Historicising the Nigerian Diaspora: Nigerian Migrants and Homeland Relations," *Turkish Journal of Politics*, 2(2): 71–85.

Akyeampong, E. (2000) "Africans in the Diaspora: The Diaspora and Africa," *African Affairs*, 99(395) (Centenary Issue: A Hundred Years of Africa): 183–215.

Appadurai, A. (1996) *Modernity at Large: Cultural Dimensions of Globalization* (Vol. 1), Minneapolis, MN: University of Minnesota Press.

Bartelson, J. (2006) "Making Sense of Global Civil Society," *European Journal of International Relations*, 12(3): 371–395.

Bastian, M.L. (1999) "Nationalism in a Virtual Space: Immigrant Nigerians on the Internet," *West Africa Review*, 1(1), available at: www.icaap.org/iuicode?101.1.1.2 (accessed December 14, 2015).

Bernal, V. (2005) "Eritrea On-Line: Diaspora, Cyberspace, and the Public Sphere," *American Ethnologist*, 32(4): 660–675.

Bernal, V. (2006) "Diaspora, Cyberspace and Political Imagination: The Eritrean Diaspora Online," *Global Networks*, 6(2): 161–179.

Blake, C. (2005) "An African Nationalist Ideology Framed in Diaspora and the Development Quagmire: Any Hope for a Renaissance?" *Journal of Black Studies*, 35(5): 573–596.

Brinkerhoff, J.M. (2009) *Digital Diasporas: Identity and Transnational Engagement*, Cambridge: Cambridge University Press.

Castells, M. (2008) "The New Public Sphere: Global Civil Society, Communication Networks, and Global Governance." *Annals of the American Academy of Political and Social Science*, 616: 78–93.

Cohen, R. (1997) *Global Diasporas: An Introduction*, London: UCL Press.

Dahlgren, P. (2005) "The Internet, Public Spheres, and Political Communication: Dispersion and Deliberation," *Political Communication*, 22: 147–162.

DiMaggio, L., Hargittai, E., Neuman, W.R., and Robinson, J.P. (2001) "Social Implications of the Internet," *Annual Review of Sociology*, 27: 307–336.

Egbunike, N. (2011) "Nigeria: SaharaReporters: Africa's Wikileaks," *Global Voices*, May 12, available at: http://globalvoicesonline.org/2011/05/12/nigeria-saharareporters-africas-wikileaks/ (accessed March 20, 2015).

Everett, A. (2009) *Digital Diaspora: A Race for Cyberspace*, New York: SUNY Press.

Fraser, N. (1990) "Rethinking the Public Sphere: A Contribution to the Critique of Actually Existing Democracy," *Social Text*, 25/26: 56–80.

Fraser, N. (2007) "Transnationalizing the Public Sphere on the Legitimacy and Efficacy of Public Opinion in a Post-Westphalian World," *Theory, Culture & Society*, 24(4): 7–30.

Gillespie, M.B. (1998) "Media, Minority Youth and the Public Sphere," *Zeitschrift für Erziehungswissenschaft*, 1(1): 73–87.

Grbeša, M. (2003) "Why if at All Is the Public Sphere a Useful Concept?" *Politička Misao*, 40(5): 110–121.

Guidry, J.A. and Sawyer, M.Q. (2003) "Contentious Pluralism: The Public Sphere and Democracy," *Perspectives on Politics*, 1(2): 273–289.

Hall, J.A. and Trentmann, F. (2005) "Contests over Civil Society: Introductory Perspectives," in J.A. Hall and F. Trentmann (Eds.), *Civil Society: A Reader in History, Theory and Global Politics*, New York: Palgrave Macmillan, pp. 1–25.

Heath, C. (2009) *Diasporas: Doing Development or Part of Development: A Study of Two Sierra Leonean Diaspora Organisations in London*, Strategic Policy Impact and Research Unit, London: Overseas Development Institute.

Judge, R. and Plaen, R.D. (2011) *"Courting the Diaspora": Emerging Roles of Diaspora Groups in the International Development Industry*, International NGO Training and Research Center (INTRAC), available at: www.intrac.org/data/files/resources/707/Briefing-Paper-27-Courting-the-Diaspora.pdf (accessed March 12, 2015).

Kperogi, F.A. (2011) *Webs of Resistance: The Citizen Online Journalism of the Nigerian Digital Diaspora*, Department of Communication, Georgia State University, available at: http://scholarworks.gsu.edu/communication_diss/27 (accessed March 20, 2015).

Langley, J.A. (1973) *Pan-Africanism and Nationalism in West Africa 1900–45: A Study in Ideology and Social Classes*, Oxford: Oxford University Press.

Mercer, C., Page, B., and Evans, M. (2008) *Development and the African Diaspora: Place and the Politics of Home*, London: Evans Zed Books.

Mohan, G. and Zack-Williams, A.B. (2002) "Globalisation from Below: Conceptualising the Role of the African Diasporas in Africa's Development," *Review of African Political Economy*, 29(92): 211–236.

Olusanya, G.O. (1982) *The West African Students' Union and the Politics of Decolonisation, 1925–1958*, Ibadan: Daystar.

Oyedoyin, T. (2003) "Omoyele Sowore: The 10 Year Old Boy Who Became an Activist," *Nigeria World*, February 17, available at: http://nigeriaworld.com/feature/publication/oyedoyin/2003/021703p.html (accessed March 20, 2015).

Papastergiadis, N. (2000) *The Turbulence of Migration Globalization, Deterritorialization and Hybridity*, Cambridge: Polity Press.

Plaza, S. and Ratha, D. (Eds.) (2011) *Diaspora for Development in Africa*, Washington, DC: The International Bank for Reconstruction and Development/The World Bank.

Safran, W. (1991) "Diasporas in Modern Societies: Myths of Homeland and Return," *Diaspora*, 1(1): 89–99.

Sahara Reporters (2015) "About Us," *Sahara Reporters*, available at: http://saharareporters.com/about (accessed March 18, 2015).

Schiller, N.G., Basch, L., and Blanc-Szanton, C. (1992) "Transnationalism: A New Framework for Understanding Migration," in N.G. Schiller, L. Basch, and C. Blanc-Szanton (Eds.), *Annals of the New York Academy of Science* (Vol. 645), New York: The New York Academy of Science, pp. 1–24.

Shettima, K.A. (1999) "Nigerian Pro-Democracy Movements in the Diaspora," paper presented at the ISA Conference, Washington, DC, February.

Sørensen, N.N. (Ed.) (2007) *Living Across Worlds: Diaspora, Development and Transnational Engagement*, Geneva: International Migration Organisation.

Van der Veer, P. (1995) "Introduction: The Diasporic Imagination," in P. Van der Veer (Ed.), *Nation and Migration: The Politics of Space in the South Asian Diaspora*, Philadelphia, PA: University of Pennsylvania Press, pp. 1–16.

Chapter 6

Immigration and Democratic States' Borders: A Normative Map of Migration Theories

Georgiana Turculet

This chapter concerns transnational migration;[1] specifically, the rights of migrants and the rights of states to unilaterally set their border policies. According to United Nations estimates, there are 214 million international migrants worldwide and 44 million forcibly displaced people, while another 50 million people are living and working abroad with irregular status. The proliferation of terms to describe the varieties of migrancy—permanent resident, guest worker, illegal alien, refugee, displaced person, asylum seeker—is itself indicative of the scale of the phenomenon. Each term denotes a different type of experience and a different relationship to the new society—which has inevitable implications for democratic politics and the meaning of citizenship (Bellamy 2008). Plainly stated, the global migration phenomenon seems to "challenge" states' borders as we understand them today, while states try unsuccessfully to "resist" this expanding phenomenon by erecting new fences and walls and manning borders with more guards.

While current liberal democratic states enact a *porous* regime of immigration policies (that is, states are increasingly inhabited by citizens, migrants, refugees, and so on), some theorists advocate a world of open borders, while others support the full sovereignty of states in matters of immigration. Generally, open border views try to "weaken" the right of the state to restrict immigration with *justice*-based arguments, whereas closed border theories uphold the *legitimacy* of the right of the state to restrict immigration. While each position offers important insights to the debate, my interest starts with acknowledging that a more nuanced reflection on how morality imposes limits on the right of states to exclude is still needed. While the current debate is far from being settled, upholding legitimacy and justice as normative concerns implies two other normative important concerns, *democracy* and *cosmopolitanism*, both advanced by the theory of porous borders .

Open Borders

A fundamental assumption of democratic thought that stands at the basis of citizenship in Western liberal democracies is the principle of national sovereignty (Pevnick 2011). When it comes to contemporary transnational migration (usually, from the Third World to wealthy, Western democracies), the right to exclude migrants is inherent in national sovereignty and considered by most theorists to be essential for any political community. Every state has the legal and moral right to act on this right in its own national interest,[2] even if that means denying entry to peaceful migrants. States may choose to be generous in admitting immigrants, but they are under no obligation to do so.[3]

In his extensive work on *The Case for Open Borders*, Joseph Carens directly challenges the conventional, "liberal-statist" view (which I call "closed border theory"[4] view) on migration that upholds the legitimacy of closed national borders. According to Carens, borders should generally be open and people should normally be free to leave their country of origin and settle in another country, and then have the same rights and obligations as the citizens of the state to which they have moved. While Carens' argument in favor of open borders has been extensively criticized for being unrealistic and utopian—and for undermining the fundamental principles of the Western democratic political tradition, especially that of state sovereignty and democratic self-determination—there are merits to his argument.

First, Carens should be credited for drawing theoretical attention to the previously taken-for-granted issue of national borders. He challenges our tendency to assume the legitimacy of denying entry to foreigners and forces us to engage normatively with the rights of migrants, the lack of which would constitute an isolation of theoretical concerns from the empirical world.[5] This draws our attention to the fact that migration is mostly a *need*-driven social phenomenon, which triggers justice-based claims.

Second, Carens' argument illuminates the deeply rooted conflict between the demands of universalism[6] and particularism through the lens of the migration ethics. Drawing particularly upon Kantian cosmopolitanism and Rawlsian liberalism, Carens uses core democratic assumptions that shape contemporary political theory on the state and democracy, yet challenges the conventional view of migration that is based on these assumptions.

In criticizing the conventional view justifying the restriction of immigration, Carens considers Western democracies to be the modern equivalent of feudal privilege—an inherited status that greatly enhances one's life chances. Like feudal birthright privileges, those born in a particular state or to parents who are citizens of a given state are more entitled to the benefits of citizenship than those born elsewhere or born of alien parents. Thus, birthplace and parentage are considered natural contingencies that are arbitrary and irrelevant from a moral point of view. Carens extends therefore a basic right to freedom of movement from one city to another within the same country or from one social class to another, to one country to another. Being born in an African country in today's society and being impeded by migration regulations to join a wealthier country is the equivalent of being destined, Carens would argue, to remain in the same social class. In condemning the closed borders thesis of Michael Walzer (1983)—his main communitarian interlocutor, which assumes that political space is the same as the ethical and cultural space—Carens takes a cosmopolitan position based upon Kantian universalism. Morally, the cosmopolitan tradition is committed to viewing each individual as an equal unit of moral respect and concern; legally, cosmopolitanism views each individual as a legal person and grants protection of their human rights by virtue of their moral personality and not based on national membership or any other status.

Carens emphasizes in his open borders view the Rawlsian "original position" (Rawls 1999) to justify his argument, even though Rawls explicitly assumes a closed political system in which questions about immigration could not arise. Echoing Rawls, Carens argues that people in the original position would choose two principles: the first principle would guarantee equal liberty to all, and the second—the "difference principle"—would permit social and economic inequalities as long as they were to the advantage of the least well-off and attached to positions open to all under fair conditions of equal opportunity. According to Carens, these principles are satisfied when individuals are free to pursue the best opportunities wherever they are in the world, regardless of their place of birth. In this respect, Carens' argument is in line with Robert Nozick's (1974) libertarian theory in which the state of nature justifies the creation of a minimal state whose sole task is to protect people within a given territory against violations of their natural rights, including rights to property and to enter in voluntary exchanges. According to this view, the individual should not be impeded in pursuing his or her their life goals. Therefore, a significant amount of freedom—including freedom to migrate to the land in which life plans are fulfilled—is desirable.

Closed borders

Carens' basic argument is correct in assuming that moral equality cannot stop at the border; however, this does not explain why citizenship is as arbitrary as ethnicity or race. Although citizenship arises in such a manner that individuals cannot be blamed or credited for it (thus appearing morally *arbitrary*), the border is not *irrelevant* insofar as it marks the morally relevant relationship between its citizens. Furthermore, moral equality does not require political equality insofar as the state exercises power over those living *within* its borders, which it cannot do to others; the justifiability of states' institutions is due to those subject to its authority. Thus, far from being morally irrelevant, citizens of a country are those who maintain its political and social institutions (subjects to and authors of them). Thus, moral equality and more broadly liberal principles of justice are not inconsistent with immigration constraints of states (Risse 2005). Christopher H. Wellman's argument, one of the most articulated in favor of closed borders, upholds that legitimate states may choose not to associate with immigrants, as they see fit" (Wellman 2008). This argument rests on three main premises: (1) legitimate states have a right to political self-determination; (2) freedom of association is an essential component of political self-determination; and (3) freedom of association allows one not to associate with others.

Premise 1 upholds that, for example, Sweden cannot punish Norwegian drivers who speed on a Norwegian highway, because intruding in Norway's domestic affairs constitutes a violation of the legitimacy of its state. The legitimacy argument holds against the USA if (hypothetically) it unilaterally decided to annex Canada, and American citizens supported this in a referendum. Legitimacy relies on the doctrine of popular sovereignty, according to which people have a right to rule themselves. While we find the first illustration plausible, we also believe that such a premise is too demanding (e.g. we do not believe that Sweden's legitimacy to self-determination is undermined if constrained by EU laws in domestic affairs, such as labeling its import-export goods veraciously, or international human rights laws, or other regional and international treaties, applying domestically). Most importantly, Laegaard points out that the annexation example is crucially different from immigration: immigration is an *individual* phenomenon that concerns individuals who take residence within a territory, whereas annexation means a state taking over another's territory, subjecting people, and changing its jurisdiction. Annexation is a blatant breach of freedom of association as the annexed people are forcibly incorporated under a new authority, whereas immigration involves individual permission granted (Laegaard 2013).

Premises 2 and 3 provide a more robust, yet limited argument for states having a right not to associate with prospective migrants. The freedom of association right is fundamental in liberal societies as enabling citizens' moral autonomy to collectively decide their own political future, and thus their political autonomy. Philip Cole (cited in Laegaard 2013)—who challenges those defending the right to control membership by subscribing to liberal values— attributes the freedom of association argument a limited role on the ground that states are not associations such as clubs or marriages. When exercising the right to leave a marriage or a club, one does not need to enter a new one to leave the former, while leaving a state necessarily entails entering another. Thus, states are "meta-associations" where autonomous individuals enter all other possible forms of association. Therefore, Wellman's argument for freedom of association seems too demanding, in that it unjustifiably defends the political self-rule against the background of perspective migrants' basic needs. They flee persecution or severe human rights violation, and lack minimally decent life. Self-determination can be overridden in favor of granting asylum, as most theorists assume—unlike Wellman—that states have a moral and legal duty to admit refugees that doesn't undermine self-determination, or so most of us believe when it comes to weighing reasons for the right to freely associate and other rights (Blake 2012). Furthermore, a state cannot justify acting in its interest if its action is impermissibly too harsh toward others, such as poor migrants (Holtug 2011). If one can only save a child drowning, morality dictates saving as quickly as possible *a* child (and possibly all of them), rather than deliberating which one is *the* child to be saved. If we see the adult standing on the shore thinking which child is an insider, or of a 'closer' race in order to save him, we would find it repugnant.

Moreover, according to Laegaard (2013), the associative view is defective in implying that the territorial right of states and the right to freedom of association regard the same entity. States, although they protect individuals' rights, do not enjoy the moral status of individuals. Thus, the state does not enjoy the right to exclude migrants from its territory by virtue of the right of freedom to association. Therefore, migrants' exclusion should be grounded in states' territorial rights, rather than freedom of association rights. However, those that take this direction face circularity insofar as even if states had such territorial rights, ultimately the people are in control of a state's action and the state represents people's interests. Thus, the argument for states excluding immigrants does not follow from Wellman's associative account.

David Miller's thesis grounds the right to control immigration to the territory of the state in the contingent inference that the ability of the state to perform its functions, such as upholding law and protecting human rights, presumes "absolute" control over a territorial jurisdiction, including control to exclude needy foreigners (Miller 2000, 2007). Miller's view is compatible with the assumption: (1) that citizens have special duties toward their fellow citizens and therefore special entitlements to rights within a given territory, and that these same concerns are lesser toward foreigners; and (2) that protecting migrants from violations of human rights when this occurs, but generally setting one's own borders and protecting primarily the national interests, may be considered unjust, but not right-violating.

Contra Miller's argument, however, it can be argued that all other functions that are powers of sovereignty are generally compatible with not exercising control over immigration, resulting in being undermined only if *massive* immigration burdens the state. This is a contingent matter that cannot justify a general right to control immigration for cases where there is no prospect of such consequences as well (Fine 2010: 355), requiring therefore an additional argument that justifies the general right to control migration.[7]

Miller's argument is not solely contingency-based. His normative argument becomes more explicit when unfolding how his view understands the problem of "state's burden."

I suggest that "burdening the state" can be read as three separate premises, each of which has profoundly different implications, some of which are empirical and some are normative. Thus, burdening the state can be taken in the sense of: (1) weakening its economic welfare; (2) undermining its institutional (*qua* liberal democratic) efficiency; and (3) its cultural stability (national identity). There are grounds to assume that immigration can potentially have an impact (positive or negative) on either of the mentioned elements. Miller accepts that the states' economic welfare, institutional efficiency and national identity can be impacted by migration negatively, and positively. Positive effects might include states benefiting economically from migration or from some level of cultural diversity. However, states have the right to ensure that these effects are "positive" in a manner as to fit the national interest.[8]

Thus, Miller has in mind these three interrelated features affecting what he calls *national interest*, which is supposedly to be protected by restricting immigration. However, current empirical studies cannot conclusively establish whether migration impacts negatively or positively *tout court* 1, 2, and 3. If we look at countries such as Canada, the US, and Australia, their wealth and institutions prove a rather positive impact of migration. Miller, however, seems concerned mostly with point 3, because 1 and 2 depend on 3.

Miller's empirical argument, namely justifying immigration restriction when *massive* (or *mass*) *migration* could be understood as numerically burdening: (a) quantitatively, such as half the population of India moving to the UK, if the number of individual migrants is so high as to exceed the number of nationals; or (b) qualitatively, *any* number of individuals, however small or big, can be *perceived* as threatening the national interest.

Claim (a), quantitatively understood, is implausible. The illustration of a "massive" exodus of this form resembles more to a phenomenon of invasion or annexation of a state by another, rather to the phenomenon of contemporary immigration. This is not to say that there are not cases of mass emigration. The contemporary "Syrian refugee crises" (Turculet 2015) is one such case, where two-thirds of the country's population are partially internally displaced and others fled to other countries in the region and in Europe. However, refugees have different claims, morally and legally, than migrants, thus these cases deserve separate theorizing.

Miller gives normative weight to claim (b), according to which immigration is *perceived* as potentially destabilizing to the national culture. The national culture is, in his view, the precondition for flourishing liberal democratic institutions, thus it should be instrumentally preserved to this end. From the lens of this normative standpoint, the *number* of migrants can only *potentially* be the burdening problem, because *any* number of immigrants not sharing the national identity can add to the problem of destabilizing a nation, not by the number itself, but by their lacking of national belonging and not belonging *enough*, or by the willingness of the hosting community to accept diversity (i.e. a conservative community responds differently to diversity than a liberal one). In other words, Miller's primary concern is that the national identity remains "unified" and only derivatively concerned with the number of immigrants. In terms of immigration policies, the counterintuitive implications could be that immigrants that closer resemble nationals are welcome while others "culturally too diverse" face a discriminatorily selective policy. In extremis, it can also encourage policies advocating "absolute" restriction of immigration, even of those whose life is endangered, if the national culture is so reluctant to diversity as to perceive any foreigner as threatening cultural stability.

Miller is emphatically concerned with designing liberal immigration policies to ensure that cultural diversity, brought in by mass immigration, does not undermine trust among citizens. He erroneously speaks of large numbers of immigrants as being the problem of potentially suppressing trust among citizens, where trust is threatened not by the number, but by their *diversity* or *otherness* alone. The following metaphor should build the case. The elephant in the room alters our perceptions by shaping the form and content of *our* democratic conversation (where the room stands for a democratic arena). And this is the case both if we give him the right to a democratic say and if we do not. My argument contra Miller is that we do not need a room half-full of elephants for our conversation to be reframed. As this idiomatic expression shows, only one elephant is sufficient to alter our perceptions. As the metaphor suggests, it might be uncomfortable acknowledging the elephant, the same way it might prove difficult for conservative groups to accept cultural diversity, but comfort or lack of it is not a thick enough metric for something remaining unaddressed or ignored. Miller does not provide normative arguments for not addressing the "elephant in the room problem" at the level of contemporary states.

Now let us consider the second version of the elephant: this elephant will not represent an unanimated truth, but a human person, who has a will and interests of his own. As it often happens by definition in democratic discourse, his views might be in opposition or disagreement with the views of other members. If we assume that those who don't share our national culture in grand masses suppress trust among us, as Miller does, we will assume so even if only one of them is in the room (if the "truth" or novelty is too "overwhelming"). It is not about the number of migrants, but the "change" they are perceived to bring. This idea of conservation has historically condemned heretics who were insiders and outsiders.

Furthermore, if we leave "becoming an insider" up to the decision of insiders and what they can take as "too different," normatively the migrant is not safeguarded even after becoming a citizen against being *perceived* as potentially threatening to the national identity. This is because national identity (or cultural identity) is not gained with legal naturalization. If the truth or the migrant were seen with suspicion until today, culture has not changed all of a sudden after legal naturalization, thus distrust reigns until *perception* of the migrant is one day somewhat more similar to fellow born nationals.

Whatever being a "national" signifies, to whom is left the decision of what this signifies? If we allow for this type of domination[9] of some citizens over some other naturalized citizens, this would lead to opposite conclusions than those reached by Miller. Migration policies should then be designed in such a way that invites as many migrants as needed in a given country to attenuate domination of some citizens over others, by supposedly increasing the number of individuals in the groups that are dominated, up until they are numerically similar to other groups who resided in the place for longer or the longest.

Miller might respond at this point that his proposal foresees a *bilateral* integration, wherein immigrants are expected to integrate culturally by accepting norms of the existing culture in place, but they are also welcome to contribute to reshaping the national culture in an open debate. The end point, though, should be that democratic institutions function properly when immigrants are integrated *within* the national culture, and only then the level of interpersonal trust will be pervasive so as to enable all to trust each other and the laws promoted by their shared institutions. It is unclear, however, why cultural integration in Miller's view, if understood *really* as a bilateral process of co-integration between individuals and collective groups, would ideally entail fewer immigrants to be integrated within an overwhelming majority. What changes if cultural integration takes place ideally between similar in size cultural groups within a state? Miller would most likely claim that the groups would then not integrate, resulting in undermining the national identity that is for him the precondition to democratic institutions. We can then reconstruct Miller's argument by uniting both the national identity and the cultural domination of some citizens over others as an interrelated precondition to flourishing democratic institutions. But this point is counterintuitive, as the democratic order generally is keen to safeguard minorities from the tyranny (cultural and otherwise) of majorities.

To conclude this point, the strategy of grounding trustworthiness in shared national culture is neither prima facie fair to each of the migrants or groups of migrants (undergoing the process of naturalization), nor fostering trustworthy interpersonal relations among citizens (cultural unity can condemn heretic insiders too), which were precisely what Miller considers to be a precondition for democratic institutions.

Lubomira Radoilska (2014) takes this point further by problematizing Miller's normative argument, which I will call "national identity precondition," claiming that:

> The heart of the problem: if political trustworthiness is grounded in sharing a cultural identity rather than membership in a political community, the defensible divide between citizens of the receiving nation and immigrant groups is likely to shift into a pernicious one, between dominant and marginalized groups of citizens.
>
> (Radoilska 2014: 115)

She makes the case of the arrests of the people of Japanese origin in the United States during the Second World War. Those arrested who faced mass detention were identified collectively as "people of Japanese origin" irrespective of being new arrivals in the country or US-born citizens. Being US citizens did not save them, while their ethnicity condemned them. Contra Miller's argument, the inference that might be counterintuitive to many is that cultural identity precedes political membership not only sociologically, which may as well be the case, but normatively. Radoilska argues against Miller that interpersonal trust should not be understood as a double standard—understanding the trust among citizens born nationals an "affective" model, and among citizens who are nationals and those who are not as a "cognitive" model. The problem with this understanding is that perceived outsiders of the national culture enjoy a lesser or entirely passive role in the democratic process.

If we accept her argument, we will then tend to reverse Miller's argument, namely democratic institutions (ensuring equal political power, equal rights, accountability, etc.) are the precondition of a national culture that is necessary for a well-ordered multicultural society. Fully partaking in democratic iterations is a precondition for negotiating cultural integration, rather than all the way around. The national identity as a precondition is not only unfair to the "diverse" (in this sense, the migrant), but also detrimental to democratic order and all that is represented by it. These conclusions indicate that we need to discuss one more important normative dimension—the democratic one.

Porous Borders

In terms of democratic theory, the major problem with Carens' argument for open borders identified by Benhabib is that democracies must be accountable to a specific people, hence a democracy actually requires some kind of political closure (Benhabib 2004: 219). She attempts to reconcile the rights of migrants conflicting with the need for democratic sovereignty, and more broadly to reconcile the demands of universalism and particularism.[10] While accepting that the issue of democratic sovereignty has become a contentious theoretical and political issue, Benhabib challenges the view that there is a conflict between democratic sovereignty and international legal norms regarding human rights. She claims that such a view misunderstands not only what sovereignty is, but also how international and transnational norms function in democracies. Such norms, she claims, enhance rather than undermine democratic sovereignty. While accepting that states do have the right to limit who enters their borders, Benhabib argues that these borders should not be open or closed, but "porous." This is a much more moderate position than that put forward by Carens. Benhabib acknowledges that the migration phenomena have become part of the demos, the decision-making, without borders being open. By "porous borders," Benhabib means that the principles and practices of a community incorporate aliens, refugees and asylum seekers, newcomers, and immigrants into existing polities.

This view—although it accommodates in principle both main concerns, on the one hand, that democracies need some sort of closure and that migration requires accommodation within the demos—is inconclusive in clarifying the right of the contemporary migrant in contrast with the right of the state to restrict the rights of migrants. Benhabib's conclusion is problematic in acknowledging, on the one hand, that borders are de facto porous,[11] but when it comes to explaining normatively the theory of porous borders, on the other hand, collapses into closed borders theory, in line with which states unilaterally set up border policies.

Porous borders theory grants a fundamental human right in line with the Kantian hospitality principle: to sojourn in other territories not only temporarily—as Kant foresees—but also more permanently. This is because residing for a long time in one place should trigger a right to full membership, unlike the Kantian principle of hospitality that grants a cosmopolitan right[12] to migrants to sojourn in other territories rather than be a permanent visitor. The sovereign may refuse the migrant only if this can be done without leading to his or her destruction.[13] Thus, asylum seekers and refugees' claim to admission to a new territory is grounded in the right to hospitality, and anchored in the cosmopolitan order. Moreover, it is legally incorporated in the international human rights regime,[14] and subsequently accepted by states. Benhabib's fundamental human right regards the admission of the asylee and refugee and says little about immigrants whose admission remains "a privilege" in the sense that it is up to the sovereign to grant such "contract of beneficence" (Benhabib 2004: 38). The right to membership of *all* strangers (refugees and immigrants) is inconsistent insofar as she does not explain immigrants' first entrance as she does with the category of refugees. I cannot speak of the rules that apply to me as a Ph.D. student in a given university if I do not first clarify how I got *into* the Ph.D. program of that given university, for rules of the program, such as a leave of absence, or stipend, etc., apply to me.

The Kantian right of hospitality adopted in the porous border theory, however, broadly suggests that denying foreigners the claim to enjoy the land and its resources, when this does not endanger the life and welfare of original inhabitants, would be unjust. If we debunk Miller's position, as Benhabib seems to do, we have no grounds to believe that immigration by definition potentially endangers the style of life and cultural values considered essential for decision-making. Benhabib eschews this view by contrasting the "demos" to the "ethnos."

The question is whether there is a human right to hospitality that applies not only to refugees and asylum seekers, but immigrants as well, on the grounds that the categories morally overlap. Miller, the main closed border theory interlocutor, finds it unproblematic that a country acts in its own national interest (Miller 2007: 163–201, 2012a) when setting border policies that enhance particularistic rights of the state's citizens even though they harm or do not offer equal regard and protection to migrants' rights. In this sense, border policies cannot be considered a violation of a universal human right, precisely because human rights alone do not encompass under their umbrella a set of more *substantive* rights.[15] The idea is that not *everything* citizens enjoy as a right of citizenship by virtue of their status will translate into a human right. Miller correctly points out that not even a fully philosophically grounded human right[16] can ensure a migrant a say with regard to his or her admission in a new territory.

The principle of hospitality is legally unambiguous, as it distinguishes between refugees to whom admission is granted and immigrants, whose admission instead is conditional on democratic decision-making. However, morally, the hospitality principle is ambiguous for distinguishing between migrants and refugees; whereas the latter *deserve* hospitality for escaping war and persecution, the former do not for *simply* escaping poverty. Morally, the categories of migrants and refugees potentially overlap in the sense that their life (e.g. liberties, and so on) can be equally threatened. The hospitality principle does not account for the distinction it takes: it does not apply when one's overall life is endangered by poverty, which can deny many liberties and disrupt one's life and bodily injure migrants, whereas it applies when one's life is disrupted by political persecution, in the case of refugees. The human right to life is not distinguished clear-cut from other basic human rights to subsistence, such as capacity to live a decent life, have adequate well-being for oneself and one's family, including clothing, housing, medical assistance, etc. The Kantian hospitality principle seems too restrictive in that immigrants' entry can be denied based on not leading to one's destruction. A larger scope of the principle would demand the concept of "destruction" to protect individuals beyond cases in which their life is threatened. It would also take into account protection of other human rights that are grounded in the interest of human beings.

Assuming Benhabib is right in asserting that in principle the tension between universalism and particularism[17] is overcome by renegotiation,[18] the question remains whether and which claims immigrants have in new territories. Can democratic iterations support the project of establishing would-be migrants' admission to new countries in their negotiation with sovereign states? Benhabib accepts that sovereignty is a relational concept rather than a self-referential one, explaining this as follows:

> While the paradox that those who are not members of the demos will remain affected by its decisions of inclusion and exclusion can never be completely eliminated, its

effects can be mitigated through reflexive acts of democratic iteration by the people, who critically examine and alter its own practices of exclusion. We can render the distinction between "citizens" and "aliens," "us" and "them," fluid and negotiable through democratic iterations. Only then do we move toward a post-metaphysical and post-national conception of cosmopolitan sovereignty, which increasingly brings all human beings by virtue of their humanity alone under the net of universal rights—while chipping away at the exclusionary privileges of membership.

(Benhabib 2004: 21)

As a result of this, policies regarding access to citizenship ought not to be viewed as unilateral acts of self-determination, but rather as decisions with multilateral consequences that influence other entities in the world community.

The act of renegotiation between the two dimensions, universalism (such as universal moral principles, international laws) and particularism (such as unilateral act of self-determination), occurs by democratic iterations, a concept that shows how commitments to context-transcending constitutional and international norms can be mediated with the will of democratic majorities. In Benhabib's words, democratic iterations are complex processes of public argument, deliberations, and learning through which universalist rights claims are contested and contextualized throughout legal and political institutions, as well as in the public sphere of liberal democracies. Democratic iterations are jurisgenerative as they change established understanding in a polity and establish precedents. Policies regarding access to citizenship ought not to be viewed as unilateral acts of self-determination. However, the implications of concepts such as "democratic iterations" and "negotiation" need clarification.

The fact that formal (laws) and informal (social activism, struggles of social movements, groups and associations in civic society) iterations do in fact bring about change that accommodates new social demands of citizens and noncitizens[19] seems prima facie plausible. The problem of this line of argument, however, is that we cannot know whether the produced change is any more just than the antecedent social situation. Chances via democratic procedures or broadly taking place democratically are not always "good," namely the mere fact that a law is voted by the majority is no guarantee to be neither just generally nor specifically more inclusive of migrants.

Specific principles must be provided to assess when some law or social struggle brings about more rights, more inclusion, and not at too great expense of other rights, etc.—in Benhabib's words, when this is jurisgenerative rather than jurispathos. Even if social changes taking places in this struggle or renegotiation in the democratic arena bring about inclusion of migrants, it remains unclear in Benhabib's view whether migrants have a say on immigration policies and the nature of their claims. Notice that one can be part of any negotiation if he or she is allowed to equally partake in the process, rather than being affected by decisions one has not influenced.

Benhabib (2002: 105–146) assumes that deliberative democracy is the best model of democracy, for it "proceeds from a unitary political framework and can do justice neither to pluralist power-sharing arrangements, nor to cultural secessionists and nationalists demands" (Benhabib 2002: 144–145). Her account of privileging deliberative democracy rests on premises that does not run into the same problems presented by David Miller's liberal-nationalist view when it comes to the self-determination and multicultural dilemmas that states receiving or having already received migrants face, precisely because it envisages some degree of "moral compromise" between all members to lead political actions. Benhabib's deliberative democratic approach presupposes two principles, universal moral respect and egalitarian reciprocity, which are "realized through a range of legal and political arrangements as well a non institutionalized practices and associations in civil society" (Benhabib 2002: 107). These principles are foundational in the sense that they ensure an egalitarian moral claim to all cultural stands, as they precede the national culture and are not vulnerable to the "Cassandra's problem" of undue mistrust (referring to the figure in Greek mythology whose correct prophesies were ignored by the Trojans to their peril). This is to say that there are no individuals whose claims of belonging can be trusted and non-trusted based on their national culture (or lack of it) by some other class of individuals who supposedly have stronger claims and bounds among themselves—such as arbitrary features of their nationality.

Concluding Reflections

Transnational migration poses difficult questions as to how states should regulate the movement of people across borders, via migration policies. However, before addressing how migration policies should regulate migration, more urgent questions loom on the background of our theoretical framework. For example, the right of states to unilaterally regulate migration and migrants' rights are questions that have not been conclusively responded yet. I have highlighted some of the main normative arguments upholding what I consider the major views in the literature: the open, closed, and porous borders theses. It seems that while all theories present valid arguments as to why states must be the authority entitled to the *legitimacy* to deliberate in matters of migration—and that migrants have *justice*-based claims to settle elsewhere—the discussion of migration must take into consideration two more important normative categories; *democracy* and *cosmopolitanism*. Democracy seems to provide the best political arrangement by which means individuals can enter a deliberative process, and in which all views, values, interests, and so on count equally. However, the fact that democracy by definition presumes a bounded polity, and that those whom are members are entitled to choose newcomers, has its limitations. Decisions are not "good" *tout court* in virtue of being democratically made (i.e. by majority rule). Other qualifications must be met, and those are best encompassed by a cosmopolitan moral order of universal moral respect, promising to chip away privileged forms of domination that are instead permitted by our traditional thought. More needs to be said about what a cosmopolitan order prescribes morally and politically.

Acknowledgments

This chapter was written while I was a Marie Curie Fellow at the Migration Research Center Mirekoc and the Department of International Relations at Koc University, Istanbul, Turkey. I am grateful to the Director of the Center, Ahmed Icduygu, and the colleagues from the Center for their support.

Notes

1. I define "transnational migration" as to "pertain to the rights of individuals, not insofar as they are considered members of a concrete bounded community, but insofar as they are human beings *simpliciter*, when they come into contact with, seek entry into, or want to become members of territorial bounded communities" (Benhabib 2004: 10).

2. Consider the example provided by David Miller (2012b: 8): "Your human right to food could at most impose on me an obligation to provide adequate food in the form that is most convenient to me (costs me the least labor to produce, for example), not an obligation to provide food in the form that you happen to prefer."

3. Carens' (1987) view of closed borders is rather strong. Other philosophers (e.g. Walzer 1983: 41) accept that states have a moral obligation to admit the family members of current citizens, refugees, and displaced ethnic nationals.

4. I distinguish between two closed border theories: (1) strong-Westphalian; and (2) moderate-liberal understanding of sovereignty, with (2) considered most valid. (1) regards the cross-border issue as a "private matter," while (2) views states to be increasingly interdependent as they observe common principles, such as international human rights regimes; moreover, (2) postulates that sovereignty is no longer the ultimate and arbitrary authority. Rather, (2) considers that the respect to self-determination is fulfilled when domestic principles are anchored in institutions shared with other states.

5. It is estimated that whereas in 1910 roughly 33 million individuals undertook cross-border movements to settle in countries other than that of their own, by 2000 that number had reached 175 million. From 1910 to 2000, the population of the world grew from 1.6 billion to 5.3 billion, or threefold. Migrations, by contrast, increased almost sixfold over the course of the same 90 years (Benhabib 2004: 5, citing a report from the United Nations Department of Economics and Social Affairs 2002).

6. Basic rights and human rights are conditions that enable the exercise of personal autonomy; as a moral being, you have a fundamental right to justification. Your freedom can be restricted only through reciprocally and generally justifiable norms, which equally apply to all (Benhabib 2004: 133). In the sphere of morality, "generality" means "universality." "Particularity" instead refers to those rights of individuals by virtue of their membership to a community (Benhabib 2004).

7. Fine's argument, found in Laegaard (2013).

8. I distinguish conceptually with the use of benefiting "of" and "from" kinds of benefits immigration brings to a country. Briefly, by "of," I indicate positive effects that are somewhat unexpected, such as young migrants lowering the age of an increasingly aging country, or cultural flourishing cultures and subcultures, which are typical of young multicultural urban areas, such as the much-written-about "hipster" subculture. With the use of "from," I refer to migration policies that are designed instrumentally for a specific expected benefit (i.e. when a state issues a number of visas based on its need of particular specialists, such as doctors or nurses for a given period). This differentiation is fruitful in light of domination theories.

9. The domination is not produced by formal structures: everyone has a right to vote as citizens, as well as other non-political rights, such as right to work. Domination is informal to the extent to which a given culture can be intrinsically gender-biased, and accepts placing women in subordinated roles in society. Domination therefore consists of some being arbitrarily affected in that they do not receive equal treatment and regard.

10. These terms "universalism" and "particularism" have several interpretations in Benhabib's test, and therefore a range of implications. The reader should overlook them for the time being, until I am able to dedicate more space to clarifications.

11. In Chapters 4 and 5 (Benhabib 2004), empirical examples are explained (i.e. extensive discussion on EU borders).

12. The Kantian temporary sojourn right stands on two premises: the capacity of all human beings to associate and the common possession of the surface of the world.

13. The Kantian concept of temporary sojourn is incorporated in the Geneva Convention on the Status of Refugees (1951) as the principle of "non-refoulment," obliging signatory states not to forcibly return refugees and asylum seekers to their countries of origin, if doing so would endanger their life and freedom (Benhabib 2004: 35).

14. By international human rights regime, Benhabib refers to a set of interrelated and overlapping global and regional regimes that encompass human rights treaties as well as customary international law or international "soft law" (namely, international agreements that are not treaties and are not covered by the Vienna Convention on the Law of Treaties): UN treaties bodies under the International Covenant on Economic, Social and Cultural Rights, the Convention of all Forms of Racial Discrimination, the Convention Against Torture and Other Cruel, and the Convention on the Right of the Child; the European Court of Justice, the European Conventions of Human

Rights and Fundamental Freedoms, the European Court of Human Rights, and others. These international norms constrain national sovereignty in a number of ways. For example, state sovereignty is subject to international norms that prohibit genocide, ethnocide, mass expulsion, enslavement, rape, and forced labor. The International Declaration of Human Rights (1948) recognizes the right of movement across boundaries: a right to emigrate, to leave a country, but not to enter a country (Benhabib 2004: 7–11).

15. David Miller's (2012b) conclusion is that such policies might be unjust, but not right-violating.
16. Supra Note 15.
17. Universal human rights have a context-transcending appeal, whereas popular and democratic sovereignty must constitute a circumscribed *demos*, which acts to govern itself. Self-governance implies self-constitution. There is thus an irresolvable contradiction between the expansive and inclusionary principles of moral and political universalism, as anchored in universal human rights, and the particularistic and exclusionary conceptions of democratic closure (Benhabib 2004).
18. Benhabib (2004) explains the concept of democratic iterations as forms of interpretation of the local, the regional, the global, and the national that change constantly. In Chapter 5, she elaborates on a few examples, such as that of the German Constitutional Court that denied the right to vote in local elections to long-term foreign residents in the city of Hamburg. This decision was superseded in 1993 by the Treaty of Maastricht: a democratic iteration that resulted in abolishing of German restrictive citizenship laws. This decision was superseded in 1993 by the Treaty of Maastricht, a democratic iteration that resulted in the abolishment of German restrictive citizenship laws (Benhabib 2004: 21–23).
19. There is no such clear-cut distinction between citizens and noncitizens. David Owen (2014) finds that in the European Union, the general status-class "citizen" comprises many different specific statuses; each of these statuses entails a specific ensemble of rights and duties.

References

Bellamy, R. (2008) "Evaluation Union Citizenship: Belonging Rights and Participation within the EU," *Citizenship Studies*, 12(6): 597–611.

Benhabib, S. (2002) *The Claims of Culture: Equality and Diversity in the Global Era*, Princeton, NJ: Princeton University Press.

Benhabib, S. (2004) *The Rights of Others: Aliens, Residents, and Citizens*, Cambridge: Cambridge University Press.

Blake, M. (2012) "Immigration, Association and Antidiscrimination," *Ethics*, 122(4): 748–762.

Carens, J. (1987) "Aliens and Citizens: The Case for Open Borders," *Review of Politics*, 49(2): 251–273.

Fine, S. (2010) "Freedom of Association Is Not the Answer," *Ethics*, 120: 338–356.

Holtug, N. (2011) "The Cosmopolitan Strikes Back: A Critical Discussion of Miller on Nationality and Global Equality," *Ethics & Global Politics*, 4(3): 147–163.

Laegaard, S. (2013) "Territorial Rights, Political Association and Immigration," *Journal of Moral Philosophy*, 10(5): 645–670.

Miller, D. (2000) *Citizenship and National Identity*, Cambridge: Polity Press.

Miller, D. (2007) *National Responsibility and Global Justice*, Oxford: Oxford University Press.

Miller, D. (2012a) "Grounding Human Rights," *Critical Review of International Social and Political Philosophy*, 15: 407–427.

Miller, D. (2012b) "Border Regimes and Human Rights," *The Law & Ethics of Human Rights*, 7(1): 1–23.

Nozick, R. (1974) *Anarchy, State, Utopia*, New York: Basic Books.

Owen, D. (2014) "Republicanism and the Constitution of Migrant Statuses," *Critical Review of International Social and Political Philosophy*, 17(1): 90–110.

Pevnick, R. (2011) *Immigration and the Constraints of Justice: Between Open Borders and Absolute Sovereignty*, Cambridge: Cambridge University Press.

Radoilska, L. (2014) "Immigration, Interpersonal Trust and National Culture," *Critical Review of International Social and Political Philosophy*, 17(1): 111–128.

Rawls, J. (1999) *A Theory of Justice*, Cambridge, MA: Harvard University Press.

Risse, M. (2005) "How Does the Global Order Harm the Poor?" *Philosophy and Public Affairs*, 33(4): 349–376.

Turculet, G. (2015) "Interest Over Justice in Policy Recommendations: Reflections on the Syrian Refugee Crisis," in E. Chemin, Ö.A. Cetrez, U. Korkut, and D. Chatty (Eds.), *Methodologies of Forced Migration: Past and Present Amongst Refugees in the Mediterranean*, Istanbul: Swedish Institute.

Walzer, M. (1983) *Spheres of Justice*, New York: Basic Books.

Wellman, C. (2008) "Immigration and Freedom of Association," *Ethics*, 119(1): 109–141.

Chapter 7

Managing Ethnic Diversity: The Pakistani Experience*

Muhammad Mushtaq

Ethnic mobilization and conflicts are not new phenomena, but their contemporary global manifestation in frequency and intensity is such that careful reflection and detailed examination is required more than ever to respond to these rising challenges. Since a large majority of nation states are heterogeneous—and this heterogeneity is likely to increase as a result of global migration patterns—ethnic conflict and the resultant political tension are likely to become even more pervasive in the coming years. Hence, the global manifestation of ethnicity has attracted significant attention from social scientists. The management of diversity in multiethnic, multilingual, and multifaith societies is of great interest in the current global situation, from both a theoretical perspective and a practical point of view.

The problem of political instability caused by ethnic conflicts seems to be more acute in developing countries than in the developed world. Empirical studies of developing states suggest some connections between political institutions and the proliferation of ethnic mobilization. For management of diversity in these multiethnic states, policy recommendations suggest a variety of federal and power-sharing arrangements.

Pakistan is an interesting case to examine regarding the limitations of federal settings to accommodate certain identities. In 1971, it became the first postcolonial state to experience a successful secessionist movement, which resulted in the creation of Bangladesh. Even after the separation of Bengal, it has witnessed Bloch insurgencies (1973–1977, 2002–present); Pashtun separatism (1970s); Sindhi regionalism (1980s); and Mohajir's mobilization along ethnic lines (1990s).

A number of alternatives to federation have been proposed in order to more adequately and appropriately manage diversity in Pakistan. Some proposals include consociationalism (McGarry and O'Leary 2005; Adeney 2009), power-sharing (Amin 1988; Cohen 1987), and the reorganization of provincial boundaries (Adeney 2007). Alqama (1997) and Samad (2007) have argued in favor of incorporating excluded and marginalized groups into Pakistan's political structure. Kennedy (1993) has suggested "bold policies to reorganize Pakistan's federal structure" to manage ethnic difference. He has argued in favor of "redesign[ing] territorial boundaries of the constituent units to make them accord more closely with the ethnic landscape of the state" and recommended "more devolution of authority for the proposed homogenous [sic] constituent units."

However, the study presented in this chapter suggests that the discrepancy in theory and practice is the key factor that confines the Pakistani federation's capacity to manage diversity. This argument is in line with Kohli's (2004) approach, which asserts that as a formal federal system increasingly operates as a unitary system, the less capacity that system retains in order to accommodate territorial cleavages. Federations may vary at the level of centralization and in the forms of governance. On the basis of distinctive features, these can be categorized as centralized or decentralized, and as consociational or majoritarian federations. Some federations may adopt a multilevel system of authority and governance, and others may move toward centralized governance.

The Pakistani case suggests that constitutionally, it is a federal state in all respects; however, practically, it operates like a unitary system. In spite of its varied constitutional arrangements, there is a great deal of dissatisfaction between centers of authority and provinces, as well as among provinces. Accordingly, this chapter investigates the relationship between centralization of political power and ethnic mobilization in Pakistan. The evidence suggests that the exclusive design of power structure and relatively centralized governance has marginalized and alienated certain communities in Pakistan. This sense of marginality and lack of power-sharing has mobilized these communities along ethnic lines to seek power. The argument, therefore, is presented that relatively decentralized and inclusive governance is more likely to enable the Pakistani federation to accommodate ethnic identities now and in the future.

Ethnic Composition of Pakistan

Pakistan is a multiethnic state. Each of its provinces is associated with a certain ethnolinguistic group: Punjab with Punjabis; Sindh with Sindhis; Balochistan with Balochs; and Khyber Pakhtunkhwa[1] with Pashtuns. However, there are ethnic and linguistic divisions within every federal unit. Sindh is the most ethnically diverse province of Pakistan. Mohajirs form the majority in urban Sindh. Sindhis—sons of the soil—dominate in rural Sindh. A considerable number of Pashtuns, Punjabis, and Baloch also live in Sindh. Balochistan is the home province of Balochs and Pashtuns. There is also a considerable number of Siraikis and Sindhis in Balochistan. Punjab and Khyber Pakhtunkhwa are also no longer homogeneous provinces. A considerable number of Siraikis now reside in the southern part of the Punjab and Khyber Pakhtunkhwa hosts, including Hindko-speaking and Siraiki populations. Table 7.1 illustrates the heterogeneity of Pakistan according to estimates from the late 1990s.

Ethnic Mobilization in Pakistan

Pakistan has been experiencing ethnonationalist movements since its inception in 1947. The Bengali nationalism, the Pashtun separatism, the Sindhi regionalism, and the Baloch subnationalism have challenged the federal character of the state at various junctures of Pakistani history. Since the 1980s, the Mohajirs (Urdu-speaking community who migrated from India in 1947 and primarily settled in urban centres of Sindh) have been mobilizing

Table 7.1 Pakistan by Mother Language (1998)

Linguistic Group	Pakistan	Punjab	Sindh	Khyber Pakhtunkhwa	Balochistan
Urdu	7.8	4.5	21.1	0.8	1.6
Punjabi	45.4	75.2	7.0	1.0	2.9
Pashto	13.0	1.2	4.2	73.9	23.0
Sindhi	14.6	0.1	59.7	0	6.8
Balochi	3.5	0.7	2.1	0	58.5
Siraiki	10.9	17.4	1.0	3.9	2.6
Others	4.8	0.9	4.9	20.4	5.1
Total	**100**	**100**	**100**	**100**	**100**
Population (Millions)	127.5	73.6	30.4	17.7	5.7

Source: Coakley (2003: 147)

along ethnic lines to protect their so-called interests. A low-profile non-violent assertion has also been seen in southern Punjab. Therefore, with the exception of Punjabis—the most dominant group—all subnational groups felt a certain sense of marginality, and have advocated against the centralization of political power in Pakistan.

Punjab is the most populous and a relatively developed and prosperous region of the country. Its predominance in "armed forces and to a lesser extent in the civil bureaucracy" has been perceived by smaller units as "*Punjabization*" of Pakistan (Talbot 2000: 215). With the military ruling for such an extensive period of time in Pakistan (1958–1969, 1969–1971, 1977–1988, and 1999–2007), it has been argued that this era of reign is "synonymous with Punjabi domination" in Pakistan (Samad 2007). Therefore, "at the core of ethno-regional sentiments" in Pakistan is the perception that the "Punjabi community dominates the politics and society of the state" (Kennedy 1993). It is also argued that Punjab dominates, and as a result has "never seen the need to press for greater autonomy" (Jones 2002).

Bengali Separation

Bengal was not only the heaviest populated province of Pakistan, it also possessed a greater population than the total population of all federating units and princely states of the western wing. Bengalis unequivocally supported the idea of Pakistan skipping over their ethnic identity, but soon agitated for Bengali interests.

The debates in the constituent assembly over the constitutional formulas resulted in distrust between the members from Bengal and western Pakistan. Bengalis were concerned with certain issues such as *lingua franca* and representation in national legislature during the constitution-making process. Contrary to their Punjab counterpart, they demanded autonomy promised in the Lahore Resolution of 1940. The state-building process, however, coupled with

Table 7.2 Instances of Substantial Protest (1947–2006)

Time	Group	Location	Description
1947–1948	Baloch	Kalat and surroundings	First Baloch insurgency of Abdul Karim Khan against the annexation of Balochistan into Pakistan.
1947–1948	Pashtun	Khyber Pakhtunkhwa	Reaction to dismissal of Dr. Khan's government.
1958–1963	Baloch	Baloch countryside	Resistance against one-unit scheme, distant identity.
1950s	Pashtun	Khyber Pakhtunkhwa	Resistance against one-unit scheme. Nevertheless, Dr. Khan accepted the central government's offer and became Chief Minister of West Pakistan.
1973–1977	Baloch	Baloch tribal areas of Marri-Mengal	Baloch insurgency against central government on the dismissal of Mengal's government. This conflict involved more than 80,000 Pakistani troops and some 55,000 Baloch guerrillas (Harrison 1981). The insurgency ended after the overthrow of Bhutto by Zia-ul-Haq.
1973–1974	Pashtun	Khyber Pakhtunkhwa	Resignation of the coalition government of NAP and JUI as a protest against the central government's interference in provincial matters of Balochistan and NWFP.
1980s	Sindhis	Rural Sindh	Movement for the Restoration of Democracy.
1980s	Mohajir	Urban Sindh	Killings in Karachi.
2002–	Baloch	Baloch countryside	Baloch resistance movement: demands for more equitable distribution.

the uncertainty following the partition, led the process of centralization in the nascent state. Thus, the "inability or unwillingness of the central government to devolve authority" led to the separatist and autonomous demands and eventually the separation of East Pakistan, which subsequently formed the contemporary state of Bangladesh (Kennedy 1993). Samad (2007: 94) summarizes the grievances, arguing:

> [t]he exclusion of Bengalis from the center, the tightening grip of Karachi, the country's political and commercial capital, over East Pakistan, the insensitive handling of the language issue and a growing sense of economic exploitation pushed the eastern wing along the road of separatism.

Alqama (1997) has also observed that it was the exclusive design of the power structure that resulted in the marginalization of the Bengali elite. Consequently, this sense of marginality led to the emergence of Bangladesh as a sovereign state in 1971.

Pashtun Separatism

The Pashtuns of Khyber Pakhtunkhwa had a strong sense of distinctiveness. The *Khudai Khidmatgar* (Servants of God) movement of Pashtun nationalists had a popular rural base in predominantly Pashtun districts of the Khyber Pakhtunkhwa. It won both the provincial elections of 1937 and 1946, and formed provincial governments. Pashtun nationalists were not convinced by the two-nation theory of the All India Muslim League and resisted against their inclusion in Pakistan. They demanded an autonomous Pakhtun (Pashtun) state in 1947. Their demand was not entertained, and they boycotted the referendum.[2] Nevertheless, the Muslim League successfully mobilized the public in favor of Pakistan and achieved 99 percent of the polled votes (Talbot 1988).

Pakhtunistan (Pashtunistan) means "different things to different people, ranging from the demand for the formation of a new state incorporating *Pathan* areas on both sides of the Pakistan-Afghanistan border to mere change of nomenclature for the NWFP [Khyber Pakhtunkhwa]" (Kennedy 1993). For example, almost immediately after the creation of Pakistan, the Pashtuns stressed that by "Pashtunistan," they meant regional autonomy of NWFP (Khyber Pakhtunkhwa) (Amin 1988).

Afterwards, the temporal (April 1972–February 1973) sharing of power under the tripartite accord accepted the principle of self-rule by the minority provinces. The assurance of autonomy from the center led the Pashtuns to relinquish their separatist tendencies.[3] For example, Abdul Ghaffar Khan—who previously demanded a separate homeland for Pashtuns—declared, "Our demand for Pashtunistan has been fulfilled" (Amin 1988).

The politics of accommodation—the resultant of tripartite accord—soon broke down. The central government intervened within the minority provinces. Islamabad dismissed the NAP (National Awami Party) government in Balochistan, the coalition government of Khyber Pakhtunkhwa resigned as a protest against the dismissal of the Balochistan government, the central government banned the NAP (alleging that it had been working against the integrity of the country), the Baloch waged a war against the dissolution of provincial government, and Pashtuns pursued a ban on NAP by challenging the decision in the Supreme Court. Accordingly, Pashtun nationalist feelings resurfaced once again. On the question of whether he was "a Muslim, a Pakistani or a Pashtun first," Wali Khan claimed that he was "a six-thousand-year-old Pashtun, a thousand-year-old-Muslim and 27-year-old-Pakistani."[4]

Meanwhile, the gradual migration of Pashtuns into Karachi and urban centers of Punjab resulted in their dominance of the privately owned transport sector and a larger share in employment. They acquired a share in the Pakistani power structure, and their "primary source of incorporation remained the army" (Noman 1988). The majority of Pashtun soldiers and officials receiving jobs belonged to the areas that had traditionally been "strongholds of the Pashtunistan movement" (Jaffrelot 2002). This incorporation and accommodation of the Pashtuns in the power structure resulted in the decline of the Pashtunistan movement. This decline led to the argument that the "Pashtun movement had died down" (Amin 1988). Conversely, evidence suggests that the Pashtun Nationalist Party (ANP) has remained successful enough as to achieve considerable electoral support in Pashtun areas.

In the post-9/11 world, the war against terror has changed the chemistry of the region to a considerable degree. *Talbanization* has resulted in violence and terrorist activities throughout the region. Despite this, the ANP (a relatively secular Pashtun nationalist party) has emerged as the single largest party in the wounded constituency. The verity that Pashtuns, on both sides of the border, had been questioning the legality of the Durand Line makes the case all the more intriguing.

Sindhi Regionalism

The province of Sindh restored its provincial status in 1936 when it was separated from the Bombay presidency. Though Sindh was a Muslim-majority province, the Muslim League remained ineffective in the politics of Sindh until the late 1930s. G.M. Sayeed and Sheikh Abdul Majeed, then the members of the Sindh Assembly, joined the party in 1938 and managed to pass the resolution for a separate homeland for Muslims of the subcontinent during that same year. The Muslim League succeeded in governing Sindh in 1942 and the Sindh Assembly passed a resolution on March 3, 1943, favoring the Lahore Resolution. Shortly thereafter, the Sindh Assembly decided to join Pakistan by 33 votes to 20 (Chandio 2007).

Although Sindh province was not an "ethnically pure region" prior to partition, there was no substantial antagonism by the Sindhis against the Baloch and Punjabi settlers. These peoples adopted the Sindhi language and were "assimilated into the Sindh culture" (Cohen 2005). On the contrary, the Sindhis were worried in 1947 about the influx of "millions of well-educated, mobile, and resourceful *Muhajireens* (refugees)." The Sindh government resisted the policy of central government regarding the settlement of Mohajirs in Sindh. Consequently, the governor dismissed the Chief Minister of Sindh on the recommendation of the central government. Moreover, the immense influx of Mohajirs continued in Sindh, changing the "demographic, political, and economic contours of Pakistani Sindh" in Mohajir's favor (Malik 1997).

Sindhi grievances are not limited to the influx of Muhajireens; they are also based upon the imposition of the one-unit scheme,[5] as well as the allotment of newly irrigated land to non-Sindhis, alleged violation of the pre-independence agreement of water supply between Punjab and Sindh by Punjab, and the underrepresentation of Sindhis in civil and military bureaucracy (Cohen 2005).

The Sindhis remained more marginalized during the one-unit scheme (1955–1969). The Sindhi language was suppressed and many Sindhi medium schools were closed (Rahman 1996). While Sindhi writers were discouraged from practicing their craft and sharing information, Sindhi newspapers disallowed advertising rights. Overall, Sindhi publications were suppressed and widely censored. This policy "created resentment among the people of Sindh." Bhutto, shrewdly, used the "slogans chanted by Sindhi nationalists" in the election campaign of 1970 and won a major victory in Sindh (Chandio 2007).

Bhutto won the election in West Pakistan and acquired power after the separation of East Pakistan in 1971. Bhutto's access to power facilitated the national integration of Sindhis in this decade (Jaffrelot 2002). Bhutto's PPP (Pakistan People's Party) managed to install its government in the provinces of Sindh and Punj; he made the time to listen to many Sindhi grievances, and his policies favored Sindhis considerably. For example, the introduction of the quota system to distribute employment opportunities and placement in educational institutions in urban/rural (40/60 percent) areas of Sindh proved advantageous for the rural Sindhis. Nevertheless, the Sindhis benefited from this scheme at the expense of the Mohajirs.

The removal of the Bhutto government in 1977, and finally his execution through a judicial trial by a Punjabi-dominated Supreme Court bench in 1979, produced nationalist feelings in rural Sindh once again. These nationalistic feelings gained momentum during the MRD's (Movement for Restoration of Democracy) national campaign against the military dictatorship of Zia-ul-Haq (then President and Chief Marshal Law Administrator) in 1983. The unrest spread to a much grander scale, resulting in ferocity in the Sindh interior. Soon, "radical students and groups of peasants and workers" joined the movement, which "took the army four months to quell" (Noman 1988). This struggle in Sindh has been seen for the participation in government and more equitable share in the economic progress of the province. The removal of the first government favorable to Sindhis, and its replacement by the Punjabi–Pashtun-dominated army, fueled ethnic antagonism in the province. The articulation of regional aspirations was formulated through the demand for confederation, outlined by the ex-governor of Sindh, Mumtaz Bhutto (Noman 1988: 184).

In the post-Zia democratic era, the PPP resumed its political character again, and the "Daughter of Pakistan" (Benazir Bhutto) managed to defuse nationalist feelings in the wounded Sindhi community. While the PPP dominated rural Sindh, Sindh's nationalist parties were unable to challenge PPP support. These parties "never attracted the support of more than 5% or 6% of the electorate nor have they ever won any directly elected National Assembly seats" (Jones 2002). Nevertheless, the PPP continue to promulgate the cause of Sindhi nationalism at the provincial level (Waseem 2006) and "many PPP candidates in Sindh are just as nationalistic as their counterparts in the parties devoted to Sindhi issues" (Jones 2002). Despite their weak organization, Sindhi nationalists have not abandoned their struggle, and they continued to express simmering resentment with respect to Punjab's role in their affairs (Jones 2002). The Sindhis resent the murder of Bhutto during the election campaign of 2008 at Rawalpindi, a Punjabi town near Islamabad. However, Asif Ali Zardari (Bhutto's husband) and Nawaz Sharif (former Prime Minister and most popular leader of Punjab) have managed the issue successfully.

Mohajir Identity Politics

The Punjabis and Mohajirs dominated politics in the early years of Pakistan. While Punjabis remained overrepresented in the army and administration, Mohajirs dominated the civil bureaucratic scene and political decision-making centers (Jaffrelot 2002). This relatively privileged position of the Mohajirs led them to identify themselves with the Pakistani state and Islamic ideology overall, and to become hostile toward regional ethnic movements (Alavi and Harris 1989). Conversely, in the post-Liaquat era (1951), "Mohajirs gradually lost ground to Punjabis." Additionally, the military *coup d'état* of Ayub Khan in 1958 "initiated a new Pathan–Punjabi axis," and hence, "those (Mohajirs) who regarded themselves as makers of the Pakistan had begun to recede to the background" (Jaffrelot 2002).

The Mohajirs disconcerted against the discriminatory policies in Sindh during the Bhutto era. Contrary to the other provincial assemblies, the Sindh Assembly passed a Language Bill in 1972. Under the law, the learning of the Sindhi language was mandatory for provincial officials. The Mohajirs saw this discriminatory move as a denial of their right to employment. As a result, Karachi witnessed massive demonstrations. Introduction of the quota system to distribute government jobs and placement in educational institutions in urban/rural (40/60 percent) areas was also limited to Sindh. In this regard, it is quite evident that the Sindhis benefited from this scheme at the expense of the Mohajirs.

During the period of 1973–1986, the Mohajirs' representation declined from 33.5 percent to 18.3 percent, and from 30.1 percent to 18.2 percent in overall official positions (Kennedy 1993). Still, the "ethnic composition of the military–bureaucratic oligarchy" gradually shifted even further in favor of Punjabis and Pashtuns at the expenses of Mohajirs. This development "exacerbated age-old dissatisfaction," and consequently the "sense of relative deprivation" set the stage for Mohajir identity politics (Samad 2002).

The rise of the MQM (Mohajir Qaumi Movement or Mohajir National Movement) in 1984 on the national scene was quite sudden and dramatic (Alavi and Harris 1989). It is "an urban, youthful, and organizationally well-knit party." Its leadership and most of its activists represent the lower middle classes who have experienced unemployment (Malik 1997). Since the late 1980s, the MQM remained dominant in urban Sindh. It has achieved remarkable electoral support in Karachi and Hyderabad (the major urban centers of Sindh).

The MQM (formerly known as the Mohajir Qaumi Movement or Mohajir National Movement, and renamed the Muttahida Qaumi Movement or Joint National Movement) entered into and left alliances with Bhutto and Nawaz Sharif at both the federal and provincial levels in Sindh between 1988 and 1999, which was the period between the Zia-ul-Haq and Pervez Musharraf military dictatorships. During this time, Karachi and Hyderabad witnessed bitter ethnic conflict that led to bloody military action. According to one study, political violence in Karachi between 1985 and 1998 resulted in approximately 9,000 deaths (Zaffar Abbas, cited in Samad 2002).

Although the MQM was given a new designation, its leadership "adopted a more inclusive outlook away from *Mohajirism*," yet the voting pattern in Sindh suggests that "it relied essentially on the Mohajir vote" (Waseem 2006).

Baloch Nationalism

The colonial period in Balochistan includes British Balochistan (Pashtun-majority areas and the Bugti-Marri tribal areas), the Kalat state, and the states of Kharan, Makran, and Lasbella. The ruler of the Kalat state, Mir Ahmad Yar Khan, declared independence on August 15, 1947—one day after Pakistan was formally established. Both houses of the Kalat Assembly endorsed this decision and rejected accession with Pakistan. Ultimately, Khan had to sign accession papers in order to formally join Pakistan. The Baloch nationalists resisted the annexation of the Kalat state, and Prince Abdul Karim initiated an armed movement in the Jhalawan region (Breseeg 2004).

Subsequently, under the one-unit scheme, the government of Pakistan amalgamated Punjab, Sindh, NWFP, and Balochistan into a single province. The second Baloch insurgency began against this centralizing policy of the government. This time, however, Mir Noroz Khan Zahri led the resistance campaign. Though he exemplified determination in his fight, he finally agreed to surrender before an offer of safe conduct by the army. However, he was arrested with his colleagues and later died while in custody (Harrison 1981).

Balochistan had waited a long time to receive provincial status. Upon the dissolution of the one-unit scheme in 1970, Balochistan was finally granted the status it sought for so long. The Baloch and Pashtun nationalists contested in the first general elections of Pakistani history in 1970 under the banner of the NAP. The Baloch nationalists performed well and managed to install their government in Balochistan. However, Attaullah Mengal's government was dismissed in February 1973 on the grounds of lawlessness and for failing to comply with central government directives. This sparked sharper confrontation with the center and led to an insurgency that climaxed from 1973 to 1977 (Jetly 2004). According to Harrison (1981: 36), "[t]here were around 55,000 Baloch fighters, including 11,500 organized combatants, fighting against the over 80,000-strong military force that was called out to quell the resistance."

Zia-ul-Haq adopted a relatively softer approach by relaxing the detained Baloch leaders. He made positive gestures toward nationalists by announcing a general amnesty for the guerrillas. Despite the sense of marginality and suppression, the nationalist feelings in Balochistan subsided as a result of representative democracy during the 1990s. However, since the military coup of 1999, a low-level insurgency has challenged central control over the province once again. Due to further military rule—this time under Musharraf—deprived of representative participatory institutions and with their natural resources exploited by Islamabad, Bloch alienation stands at a record high. Although regional parties and leaders currently struggle to gain political, economic, and social rights within a democratic, federal, and parliamentary framework, militants have once again picked up the gun.[6]

Military action and conciliatory efforts remained simultaneously intact in Balochistan during the latest round of insurgency. Acting as the decisive power in Musharraf's hand, the parliamentary committee remained powerless to implement its recommendations. Bugti's[7] personal resistance fueled the flames of the conflict.

Siraiki Movement

Within Punjab, three well-known groups/regions may be recognized on a linguistic and geographical basis—the Punjabi-speaking central Punjab; the Pothowhari-speaking northern Punjab; and the Siraiki-speaking southern Punjab. The three regions differ in their level of socioeconomic development, representation in the civil military bureaucracy, and access to power.

It is the civil-military officers, administrators, and businessmen from the central and the northern Punjab that together make "the Punjabi ruling group" (Shackle 1977). The Siraikis of the southern Punjab—a relatively poorer and marginalized region—popularly term the central and northern Punjab "jointly" as the "Upper Punjab." The term, perhaps, denotes the deprivation and marginality of southern Punjab vis-à-vis upper Punjab. Samad (2007: 116) has rightly observed that "the Siraiki-speaking areas have made a conscious and explicit attempt to distance themselves from the dominant groups in Punjab."

Siraiki identity is still a very recent phenomenon, and the people who are considered to be Siraiki-speaking have a different history. The people of Bahawalpur belonged to a princely state that became a part of Punjab in 1970. *Riyasti* remained the language of majority in this region. Multan remained a part of Sindh earlier and *Multani* was the language of the area. The people of Dera Ghazi Khan and the surroundings had a distinct language—*Derewal*—and have historically "tended toward Baloch identity" (Ahmed 1998).

Siraiki identity evolved, more or less, parallel with its twin centers of Bahawalpur and Multan. A variety of literary and cultural organizations surfaced during the 1960s and the early 1970s, and the movement largely remained cultural in character. Though the movement remained apart from cohesive political mobilization, some individual voices rose in favor of a separate Siraiki *Suba* (Siraiki province) upon the extinction of the one-unit scheme (Shackle 1977).

Siraiki political parties had no appeal for the majority of Siraiki-speaking people. Despite their efforts to strengthen support for the Siraiki movement by stressing the marginalization of the Siraiki-speaking community, they lacked electoral support and performed poorly in various general and local elections. The local aristocracy holds prominent positions within mainstream parties, and is well incorporated in the Punjabi ruling class. This incorporation has led Feroz Ahmed to suggest that Siraikis will become increasingly amenable to resolving their problems in multiethnic contexts (Ahmed 1998: 276).

This survey of ethnonationalist movements suggests that it was the policy of centralization that created a sense of Punjabi domination and marginality in smaller units across the federation. The Punjabi-dominated federal authorities intervened and dismissed various provincial governments, ignoring their right to self-governance. The 1973 Constitution of Pakistan qualifies the minimum level of legislative decentralization, and evidence suggests that Pakistan is gradually moving toward fiscal decentralization. However, Pakistan currently lacks political decentralization.

Federal Settings in Pakistan

The British government allocated a considerable degree of autonomy to the provincial governments throughout the subcontinent during their rule. Adeney (2007: 32) explains that "all the constitutional plans proposed between 1916 and 1946 were drafted under the assumption that there would be provincial governments with a certain amount of autonomy."

A more or less formal federal system was introduced in the Government of India Act of 1935. Legislative, administrative, and financial powers were divided between the center and the provinces. However, the center retained an authoritative position vis-à-vis the provinces. The governor general was a custodian of imperial interests and held extraordinary powers to regulate British India. Provincial governors, the agents of the governor general in the provinces, also possessed the power to dominate across the provinces.[8]

Muslims of India demanded a separate homeland. Eventually, India was divided, and the Muslims of India were granted a separate homeland by way of Pakistan in 1947. The new state inherited the colonial institutions and political practices of its former colonial parent nation, and adopted the Government of India Act of 1935 with certain amendments as an interim constitution. This was repealed by the first Constitution of the Islamic Republic of Pakistan on March 23, 1956. This constitution was short-lived, and abrogated as a result of martial law in 1958. Ayub introduced his constitution in 1962, and stepped down in 1969. He abrogated the constitution of 1962 and handed over the government to Yahya, then the Commander in Chief of the army. After the separation of East Pakistan in 1971, the National Assembly of Pakistan enacted the 1973 Constitution of Pakistan.

It has been argued that "constitutional distribution of the legislative and executive powers and of financial resources between two orders of the government" is the key feature of every federation throughout the modern world (Watts 1999: 155). Thus, this section will, primarily, focus on the distribution of legislative powers, the administrative relations between federation and provinces, and the distribution of financial resources between federation and provinces of Pakistan.

Legislative Distribution and Decentralization

The Government of India Act of 1935 was amended in order to strengthen control over federating units in 1947. These amendments made the central government "one of the most powerful governments in the world" (Sayeed 1954). The constituent assembly of Pakistan passed the "objective resolution" in which basic principles for the constitution were laid down. The resolution recommended that a federal system of government be established and applied within the state of Pakistan. Nevertheless, the Basic Principles Committee suggested a strong center be established instead.

In the 1956 Constitution, the distribution of legislative powers between the federation and the federating units were enumerated in three lists. The federal list included 30 items, the provincial list 94 items, and the concurrent list 19 items. Furthermore, residuary powers were granted to the provincial legislature (Khan 2005). The division of legislative powers suggests that this constitution was relatively decentralized. This constitution was abolished by the administration that ruled during the period of martial law in 1958. The Ayub regime (1958–1969) introduced the second Constitution of Pakistan in 1962. The 1962 Constitution provided a single list of federal subjects. The list consisted of 49 items, including defense, external affairs, interprovincial trade and commerce, national economic planning, currency, and foreign exchange (Khan 2005).

The Legal Framework Order of the Yahya regime (1969–1970) suggested a relatively decentralized federalism. It stated that *all* powers, including legislative, administrative, and financial, would be distributed between the federal government and provinces, and that the provinces would have maximum autonomy, with maximum legislative, administrative, and financial powers. It also stated, however, that the federal government would also have adequate powers, including legislative, administrative, and financial powers, to discharge its responsibilities in relation to external and internal affairs and to preserve the independence and territorial integrity of the country.

Before the 18th constitutional amendment in the 1973 Constitution, the distributions of legislative powers were enumerated in two lists. The federal list was divided into two sections. The first section had 59 items and the second section had eight items. The concurrent list comprised 47 items (Khan 2005). The constitutional provisions suggest that Pakistan fulfilled the minimum requirements of legislative decentralization. Equally, and contrary to conventional wisdom, the comparative study of the legislative decentralization in selected federations reveals that Pakistan, even before the 18th constitutional amendment, was not a deviant case in terms of legislative decentralization.

The selected federations were classified on the basis of their constitutional provisions relating to legislative distribution. The cluster analysis was based on 30 variables in 11 federations. The analysis classified these federations into three broad clusters. Pakistan stands in the first cluster with Canada, the United States (US), Australia, Germany, India, Malaysia, and Belgium. Hence, the comparative results suggest that Pakistan fulfills the minimum criteria of legislative decentralization. Nevertheless, the post-18th constitutional amendment federation of Pakistan is more decentralized since the concurrent legislative list has been abolished and the federating units have been provided with much autonomy.

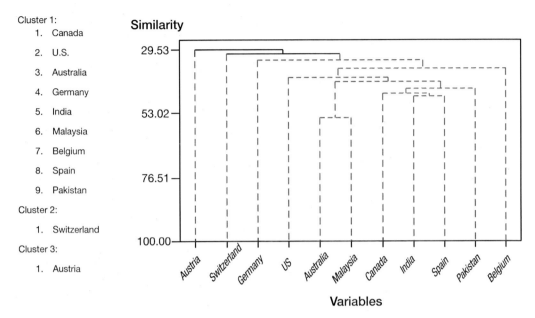

Figure 7.1 Hierarchical Cluster Analysis

Fiscal Distribution and Decentralization in Pakistan (1971–2006)

The ratio of provincial/subnational revenues and expenditures to the national revenues and expenditures respectively are the best indicators for various levels of fiscal decentralization. Generally, "the expenditures focus on the amount of government activity that governments undertake, and revenues focus on the quantity of resources that pass through them" (Schneider 2003).

The following comparative analysis of fiscal decentralization in some states suggests that Pakistan lies almost in the middle of the 18 states compared. Although it is fiscally less decentralized than Canada, the US, Germany, and India, it ranks higher than Malaysia, South Africa, Spain, and Belgium. Thus, the outcome suggests that Pakistan fulfills the minimum requirement to be considered as a fiscally decentralized state.

Moreover, the study of fiscal decentralization for the period 1971–2006 shows a gradual trend toward fiscal decentralization. The author has attempted to quantify fiscal decentralization. Two variables have been used: (1) ratio of provincial revenues to central revenues; and (2) provincial expenditures to central expenditures. Figures 7.2 and 7.3 show the gradual trends toward fiscal decentralization in Pakistan with reference to the first and second variables respectively.

The Pakistani federation had adopted a revised criteria for the distribution of funds among provinces in the 7th NFC Award. Previously, the funds were distributed among the provinces on population basis. The revised formula is more acceptable for the smaller provinces.

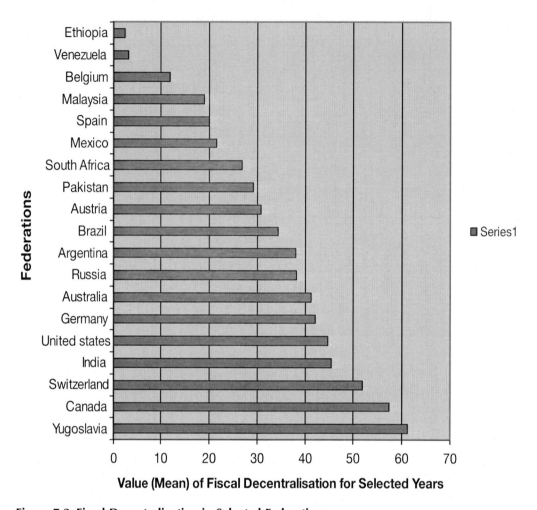

Figure 7.2 Fiscal Decentralization in Selected Federations

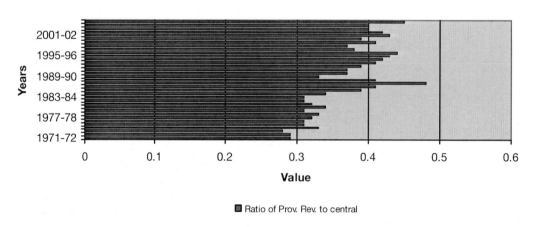

Figure 7.3 Fiscal Decentralization (1)

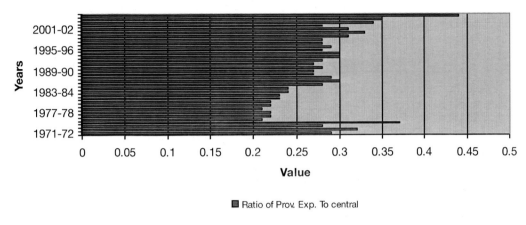

Figure 7.4 Fiscal Decentralization (2)

Political Distribution and Decentralization

Some scholars have measured political decentralization by "tracking regional and local elections over time" (Rodden 2004). This indicator, however, does not seem to fit with the Pakistani case due to its unique political culture.[9] Therefore, in this study, political distribution or decentralization will discuss matters regarding the working relationship between the federal government and the provincial government.

In Pakistan, "the central government very frequently dismissed and reformed the ministries in the provinces." Congress ministry in NWFP (Khyber Pakhtunkhwa) had "the support of 33 members out of 50." It was replaced by a Muslim League ministry in spite of the fact that assurance was given for cooperation in this regard (Hussain 1989). The Sindh assembly opposed the decision of the central government to take Karachi out of the control of Sindh and passed a resolution unanimously. The Chief Minister of Sindh had to pay for this resolution and he was dismissed shortly thereafter.

During the Ayub regime (1982–1969), there was no federation in Pakistan; all powers were vested in the president. Governors were appointed among the provinces by the president without any approval or consultation by any other organ of government. They worked as agents of the president. In practice, the federation operated as a unitary system (Hussain 1989). This centralization alienated Bengalis and they eventually broke away from the federation in 1971. The Constitution of 1973 was introduced on August 14, 1973, in the new Pakistan.

Bhutto (1973–1977) dismissed Balochistan's provincial government and the provincial government of NWFP resigned in protest. Still, Bhutto managed to capture all political power in the remaining provinces, including Punjab and Sindh. An overwhelming majority was achieved in these provinces and no responsibility was assigned to local leadership at the provincial level. Many favorable ministries were replaced in Punjab. Thus, under Bhutto's rule, the Sindh and the Punjab provinces were also denied their autonomy just as they were in NWFP (Khyber Pakhtunkhwa) and Balochistan (Hussain 1989).

Zia removed the Bhutto government in 1977. During the new regime (1977–1988), various amendments changed the nature of the constitution. They resulted in a substantial departure from the parliamentary and federal principles laid down in the 1973 Constitution.

Table 7.3 Central Government Intervention in Federating Units

Year	Description
1947	Congress ministry in NWFP (Khyber Pakhtunkhwa) had "the support of 33 members out of 50." However, a Muslim League ministry replaced this.
1947	Sindh Assembly opposed the decision of central government to take Karachi out of the control of Sindh and passed a resolution unanimously. The Chief Minister of Sindh had to pay for this resolution and he was dismissed soon after.
1948	Inclusion of Kalat state into Pakistan.
1955	One-unit scheme (amalgamation of provinces and states into the province of West Pakistan).
1962–1969	Ayub's presidential period (federal system operated like British vice regal system of 1930s).
1970–1971	Military action in East Pakistan and its separation.
1972–1973	End of tripartite accord and dissolution of Balochistan government. Khyber Pakhtunkhwa government resigned as protest.
1977–1988	Constitutional amendments by a military regime undermined the parliamentary and federal nature of the constitution.
1988–1993	Dissolution of provincial assemblies (1988, 1990, 1993).
1994	Governor rule in Khyber Pakhtunkhwa and installation of favorable government.
1995	Governor rule in Punjab and installation of new government.
1999	Removal of Nawaz Sharif government along provincial government.
2002	17th Amendment has undermined the federal character of the state.

The presidential unitary form of government operated instead of the parliamentary federal form of government during this era (Hussain 1989).

In the post-Zia era (1988–1999), central interventions in provincial matters remained intact. Various provinces experienced governor rule and the replacement of ministries by central authorities. Table 7.3 offers further detail in this regard. Musharraf assumed power in a bloodless *coup d'état* in October 1999. Centralizing policies of the regime resulted in unrest and Balochistan experienced another insurgency.

Conclusion

This chapter suggests that Pakistan fulfills the minimum requirements in order for it to be considered a federation. The 1973 Constitution of Pakistan distributes legislative, administrative, and financial powers between federation and federating units. The degree of legislative and fiscal decentralization in the Pakistani case, compared with contemporary federations, reveals that it is not a deviant case. Although Pakistan might appear relatively centralized, it is political centralization, rather than legislative or fiscal, that matters most.

This chapter further argues that ethnic mobilization and political instability in Pakistan is the result of discrepancy in the theory and practice of federal arrangements. Though the Pakistani federation fulfills the minimum criteria of federalism, its operative procedures are more akin to a unitary system. Various central governments have intervened in provincial affairs, and these interventions were justified by Article 149 of the Constitution, which "authorizes the federal government to intervene in a province to protect it from internal disturbance and to ensure that its government is carried on in accordance with the Constitution."

Furthermore, the survey of politics of identity in Pakistan suggests that the centralization of political power is the key factor connected with political mobilization within the state of Pakistan. Much of the mobilization and many of the interventions against provincial and regional matters were limited to the groups that thought they were deprived of their right to self-rule. These protests were prominent in particular regions against the centralization of political power. Therefore, it is safe to argue that Pakistan needs a relatively more decentralized federal design that demonstrates the essence of federalism. Such a design would be the embodiment of self-rule and shared rule.

Notes

* This chapter is a revised version of Mushtaq (2009).

1. Originally, the name of this province was North-West Frontier Province (NWFP) but it was renamed as Khyber Pakhtunkhwa through a constitutional amendment in 2010.
2. The Pashtuns perused Lord Mountbatten—Governor General of India—to include a third option in the referendum: a right to opt for Pashtunistan, a state for their own, next to the options to join either Pakistan or India.
3. In the general elections of 1970, the Pakistan Peoples Party of Zulfiqar Ali Bhutto got victory in the Punjab and Sindh. Jamiat-ul-ulmai Islam (JUI) and NAP—the representative of Pashtun and Baloch nationalists—were the leading parties in NWFP and Balochistan. The three leading parties entered into the tripartite accord and decided to respect the mandate of each party in its respective jurisdiction.
4. For detail, see Supreme Court of Pakistan (1975), p. 27.
5. Under this scheme, all administrative units of the western wing of Pakistan were amalgamated into one unit, namely West Pakistan.
6. For detail, see the Asia Report No. 119 by the International Crisis Group (2006), p. 1.
7. Bugti was a Baloch leader who was previously Governor and then Chief Minister of Balochistan.
8. The British introduced various constitutional formulas in India. These constitutional formulas include the *Indian Councils Act of 1861*, *India Councils Act of 1892*, the *Government of India Act of 1909*, *India Act of 1919*, and the *Government of India Act of 1935*.
9. To gauge political decentralization in Pakistan, intervention of central government in provincial matters is a better indicator than provincial or local elections in such regions.

References

Adeney, K. (2007) *Federalism and Ethnic Conflict Regulation in India and Pakistan*, New York: Palgrave.
Adeney, K. (2009) "The Limitations of Non-Consociational Federalism: The Example of Pakistan," *Ethnopolitics*, 8(1): 87–106.
Ahmed, F. (1998) *Ethnicity and Politics in Pakistan*, Karachi: Oxford University Press.
Alavi, H. and Harris, J. (1989) *Sociology of Developing Societies: South Asia*, London: Macmillan Education.
Alqama, K. (1997) *Bengali Elite Perception of Pakistan, the Road to Disillusionment: Uneven Development or Ethnicity*, Karachi: Royal Book Company.

Amin, T. (1988) *Ethno-National Movements in Pakistan: Domestic and International Factors*, Islamabad: Institute of Policy Studies.
Breseeg, T.M. (2004) *Baloch Nationalism: Its Origin and Development*, Karachi: Royal Book Company.
Chandio, A.A. (2007) "Politics of Sindh under Zia Government: An Analysis of Nationalists vs. Federalists Orientations," unpublished Ph.D. dissertation, Bahauddin Zakariya University Multan, Pakistan.
Coakley, J. (2003) *The Territorial Management of Ethnic Conflict*, London: Frank Cass.
Cohen, S.P. (1987) "State Building in Pakistan," in A. Banuazizi and M. Weiner (Eds.), *The State, Religion, and Ethnic Politics: Pakistan, Iran, and Afghanistan*, Lahore: Vanguard, pp. 299–332.
Cohen, S.P. (2005) *The Idea of Pakistan*, New Delhi: Oxford University Press.
Harrison, S.S. (1981) *In Afghanistan's Shadow: Baloch Nationalism and Soviet Temptation*, New York: Carnegie Endowment for International Peace.
Hussain, F.A. (1989) "The Problem of Federalism and Regional Autonomy in Pakistan," unpublished M. Phil dissertation, London School of Economics, University of London.
International Crisis Group (2006) *Pakistan: The Worsening Conflict in Balochistan*. Islamabad/Brussels: International Crisis Group, available at: http://www.crisisgroup.org/~/media/Files/asia/south-asia/pakistan/119_pakistan_the_worsening_conflict_in_balochistan.pdf (accessed August 12, 2009).
Jaffrelot, C. (2002) *Pakistan: Nationalism without a Nation*, London: Zed Books.
Jetly, R. (2004) "Baloch Ethnicity and Nationalism (1971–1981): An Assessment," *Asian Ethnicity*, 5(1): 7–26.
Jones, B.O. (2002) *Pakistan: Eye of the Storm*, London: Yale University Press.
Kennedy, C.H. (1993) "Managing Ethnic Conflict: The Case of Pakistan," *Regional and Federal Studies*, 3(1): 123–143.
Khan, H. (2005) *Constitutional and Political History of Pakistan*, Karachi: Oxford University Press.
Kohli, A. (2004) "India: Federalism and Accommodation of Ethnic Nationalism," in U.M. Amoretti and N. Bermeo (Eds.), *Federalism and Territorial Cleavages*, Baltimore, MD: Johns Hopkins University Press, pp. 281–299.
McGarry, J. and O'Leary, B. (2005) "Federation as a Method of Ethnic Conflict Regulation," in S. Noel (Ed.), *From Power-Sharing to Democracy: Post Conflict Institutions in Ethnically Divided Societies*, Montreal: McGill Queens University Press, pp. 263–296.
Malik, I.H. (1997) *State and Civil Society in Pakistan: Politics of Authority, Ideology and Ethnicity*, London: Macmillan Press.
Mushtaq, M. (2009) "Managing Ethnic Diversity and Federalism in Pakistan," *European Journal of Scientific Research*, 33(2): 279–294.
Noman, O. (1988) *The Political Economy of Pakistan 1947–1985*, London: KPI.
Rahman, T. (1996) *Language and Politics in Pakistan*, Karachi: Oxford University Press.
Rodden, J. (2004) "Comparative Federalism and Decentralization: On Meaning and Measurement," *Comparative Politics*, 36(4): 481–500.
Samad, Y. (2002) "In and Out of Power but Not Down and Out: Mohajir Identity Politics," in C. Jaffrelot (Ed.), *Pakistan: Nationalism without a Nation*, London: Zed Books, pp. 63–84.
Samad, Y. (2007) "Pakistan: From Minority Rights to Majoritarian," in G. Pandey and Y. Samad (Eds.), *Fault Lines of Nationhood*, New Delhi: Roli Books, pp. 67–138.
Sayeed, K.B. (1954) "Federalism and Pakistan," *Far Eastern Surveys*, 23(9): 139–143.
Schneider, A. (2003) "Decentralization: Conceptualization and Measurement," *Studies in Comparative International Development*, 38(3): 32–56.
Shackle, C. (1977) "Siraiki: A Language Movement in Pakistan," *Modern Asian Studies*, 11(3): 379–403.
Supreme Court of Pakistan (1975) *Supreme Court judgment on dissolution of NAP*. Rawalpindi: Directorate of Research, Reference and Publications Government of Pakistan.
Talbot, I. (1988) *Provincial Politics and the Pakistan Movement: The Growth of the Muslim League in North-West and North-East India 1937–47*, Karachi: Oxford University Press.
Talbot, I. (2000) *Pakistan: A Modern History*, London: Hurst & Company.
Waseem, M. (2006) *Democratization in Pakistan: A Study of the 2002 Elections*, Karachi: Oxford University Press.
Watts, R.L. (1999) *Comparing Federal Systems* (2nd ed.), Montreal: McGill University Press.

Chapter 8

An Abuse of Culture: North Korean Settlers, Multiculturalism, and Liberal Democracy*

Minkyu Sung

In a 2004 interview with a South Korean scholar, a North Korean settler in South Korea remarked, "I've realized I'd have to *die* in order to survive in this society" (cited in Yoon 2009: 148, emphasis added). His use of the word "die" is not so much about literal physical death as it is about a removal of his North Korean identity marker in his daily encounters with his South Korean neighbors. Sociologist In-Jin Yoon's (2012) recent survey reveals that only four out of 10 North Korean settlers in South Korea believe their North Korean background, culture, and knowledge are worth keeping and passing down to their descendants. The survey also reports that 87.1 percent of those settlers have no hesitation confirming that they have been trying their best to become "genuine South Koreans" since entering the country (Yoon 2012: 47). One of the implications of these survey results is that settlers' successful social adaptation to their adopted country, South Korea, has something to do with a pious denial of their North Korean origins in identity. Embracing "South Korean values" seems essential to their survival in South Korean society. *But is this act of embracing more than mere acceptance? Is it about subjection?* In her ethnographic survey on North Korean refugees' account of the famine in mid and late 1990s North Korea, Fahy (2011: 21) reports that their memories of the homeland are not entirely negative. She suggests, "As they compete for a living in a society that mostly rejects them and their past, they may more readily call up positive memories of their former lives as sources of comfort and national pride." This chapter on the discursive formation of North Korean settlers via multiculturalism and liberal democracy feeds on the interpretation of their negotiation in social life, ambivalence in cultural identity, and resilience from painful memory.

North Koreans in South Korea are expected to remain a vivid entity through which South Koreans can understand and experience what North Korean-ness is or what genuine Korean values are. Policymakers, church ministers, nongovernmental organization (NGO) activists, and TV talk show hosts bring North Korean settlers to seminars, confessions, and testimonies to uncover and confirm the ruthless, horrible, and miserable face of the North Korean regime (Green and Epstein 2013). Many scholars and activists have recently challenged and criticized the realist approach to North Korean-ness, which presumes that there are intrinsic and objective properties of North Koreans to be observed, experienced, and measured (Ryang 2012). One dominant critique of this approach comes from, and draws on, critical reflections on the idea of a cultural "Other" (Sung 2009). It reasons that North Koreans and their culture are never intrinsically homogeneous, nor are they merely identified with South Korean national culture. As this postmodern diagnosis has gained traction in the recognition of North Koreans in South Korean society, policymakers, as well as scholars and activists, have begun to expand the critical interpretation along the lines of multiculturalism.

North Koreans at the Crossroads of Multiculturalism in South Korean Society

This multicultural exploration of North Korean settlers was largely inspired, it seems to me, when in 2006 the South Korean government proclaimed that the South Korean state was no longer a single ethnic nation, but a "multicultural nation." Late 1990s South Korean society witnessed large-scale labor and marriage migration from Third World countries. As with other nations such as Canada, Australia, the UK, and the US, the South Korean government's multicultural policy on foreign (im)migrants has undergone intense public and scholarly debate. South Korean multiculturalism literature has generally focused more on individual (im)migration cases than on a theoretical elaboration of multiculturalism in the South Korean context (Lee 2013).

One consequence that can be drawn from the debates at this point is that scholars and activists have applied to North Korean settlers an idea of multiculturalism that has not been made theoretically nuanced. It should be acknowledged that they have reached a consensus that multiculturalism in South Korea should avoid (im)migrants' mere integration into their host society. But their theoretical speculation is still unclear about why we should be committed to the idea of multiculturalism for North Korean settlers (and about how it helps those settlers not simply to survive, but also to develop a meaningful sense of belonging to their second homeland). The reason is that as Korean nationalism's filial, bloodline narratives regarding the nation's membership, which have "Othered" foreign ethnic populations residing in South Korea, have also done so to North Korean settlers, scholars and activists hope that multiculturalism remedies the predicament of North Koreans in the same manner that it works for other foreign groups (Jung 2007; Park 2007).

However, the discussion of the impact of multiculturalism on North Korean settlers has issues that need to be addressed. First, multiculturalism for North Koreans is still understood as a means of integration. Although the idea of integration through multiculturalism has constantly been challenged empirically and conceptually, the conceptual commitment to integration for multicultural recognition still remains strong. For example, Yoon (2013) claims that a multicultural school curriculum should be offered to school-age North Korean settlers who (would) fail in social adaption because integration into their host society is considered the final measure through which to understand the extent to which they successfully adapt themselves to society. Tolerance that can be learned through multicultural education, insists Yoon, can help to decrease the school dropout rates of North Korean teenagers in South Korea.[1] But research shows that household income and family ties would have a strong sociological implication for these students' educational success.[2] Only some would imagine the best or most viable outcome of successful adaptation to be integration. The idea of *maladaptation* in multiculturalism has been critiqued in that it unscrupulously posits the adaptation/integration combination as the precondition of a multicultural society (Lee 2006; Yoon 2009, 2012; Lee 2010).

Second, multiculturalism for North Koreans brings with it its own liabilities on that conceptual commitment. While it spans a diverse range of definitions, multiculturalism is fundamentally a claim to a community membership, sharing with each member an ethnic, cultural, and historical origin and background. When North Korean settlers are recognized as a multicultural group in South Korea, it is quite unclear what communitarian criteria they can create or use to inform South Koreans. *Would North Koreans be willing to accept their ethnic status as being different from that of South Koreans?* It appears South Koreans hope (and utilize) multiculturalism as a better means of mutual understanding. If they do so, they should be prepared to accept North Korean-ness or North Korean values not as something they want to exploit or remove, but as something they appreciate and maintain. But as discussed above, North Koreans in South Korea fear when they are publicly treated as culturally and ethnically different from South Koreans. In addition, when the postnationalist multicultural reflection, which is a criticism of the homogeneity of the nation, is addressed to North Korean settlers, it can confound them in such a way that they are expected to refute the workings of Korean nationalism for themselves. Although it is possible for them to understand and accept nationalism's exclusive dimension to non-nation/ethnic members, it is hardly possible—if not impossible—for them to admit that they can be discriminated against in a way similar to how other ethnic (im)migrants are treated by South Koreans. This is because they believe their strong blood tie should make them a member of the nation, which is what they have been taught in North Korea as well.

Recently, some South Korean scholars have begun to respond to this multiculturalism–nationalism aporia. My argument is that this aporia cannot be resolved unless those settlers' subject formation in liberal democracies is challenged. To explain further, in what follows, I critically evaluate the multicultural duty imposed on North Koreans in South Korea of being liberal and being (post)national. Examples from policy texts are used to help illustrate the contentious nature of this aporia.

Engaging Multiculturalism

Scholars who have conducted research on North Korean settlers in South Korea have recently brought to the fore multiculturalism in order to address the *maladaptation* view of those settlers. Specifically, they claim that the socio-functionalist idea of adaptation has a strong tendency to describe (im)migrants only as individuals who have a *lack* of something required for their host society's accommodation. Preoccupation with (im)migrants' adaptation thus irreversibly makes them the maladapted and ignores differences in their identity and culture from members of their host society. These scholars believe multiculturalism can remedy the flaws in recognition by considering equality in identity and culture between host members (i.e. South Koreans) and migrants (i.e. North Koreans).

For example, Yoon (2009: 59) dubs the application of multiculturalism to North Koreans as "host society members' affirmative will to equality and difference for North Koreans." Sociologist Lee (2011: 68, 72) insists, "Multiculturalism can help those settlers to negotiate difference and diversity," thereby gaining "equal access" to (South) Korean culture. These scholars' deliberate use of terms such as equality, equal access, and difference refers to the multicultural institutions, laws, and policies through which settlers can secure and expand their participation in the South Korean public sphere. This multicultural politics of recognition does not allow North Koreans to use their own North Korean cultural membership against their members' individual autonomy in society to transcend their culture's restrictions and limitations. Yoon (2009: 55) claims, "North Koreans should not be recognized as 'a particular existence'" in Korean culture and society. Lee (2011: 73) warns of "the individual's isolation in his or her culture and community" when multiculturalism is enacted.

This multicultural allegiance to liberalism is an attempt to resolve the multiculturalism–nationalism aporia on North Korean settlers. This strand of liberal multiculturalism takes up the postnationalist approach to North Korean settlers—to which both Yoon and Lee subscribe—as a critical response to the discrimination those settlers have faced as a result of Korean nationalism. These settlers fear to speak in North Korean accents in public because the cultural difference costs them stigmatization as alien, North Korean. No matter how South Koreans take this to be (in)tolerable, North Koreans' accents are arguably already rendered *in*tolerable to themselves. In that sense, postnationalist reflections can help South Koreans critically evaluate their own unjust, discriminatory behaviors and attitudes toward North Koreans. However, as discussed above, for North Korean settlers, the narrative of pedigree is always a strong resource to confirm and legitimize their South Korean citizenship status and social provisions.[3] Suspecting they would appreciate postnationalist reflections on themselves, postnationalist liberal multiculturalists (i.e. multiculturalism drawing on liberal postnationalism) may inevitably admit that those settlers hardly refuse the legitimacy of Korean nationalism that works for them.

Neither postnationalist liberal multiculturalists nor North Korean settlers want to make a claim to communitarian recognition of their culture and difference. For both, North Koreans in South Korea cannot be compared to Québécois in Canada in that the former (have to) accept assimilation and the latter never do. Indeed, the postnationalist liberal approach does not entirely deny the necessity of a national identity that both South and North Koreans are expected to share. In this sense, postnationalist liberal multiculturalism regarding North Korean settlers is not anti-nationalist, but rather nationalist apologetic. Its main concern, as shown in the introduction, is with how stable *liberal* institutions are established and maintained well enough to sustain and foster a *national* identity. Liberalism's entrenched conception of individual autonomy is utilized not simply to compete with nationalism, but to prompt it (Mason 1999). In this multicultural scheme, North Koreans in the South feel obligated to carry within themselves a multicultural double duty of being liberal and national. However, as shown below, it is uncertain how liberal autonomy can substantially rescue them from baneful self-denial in adaptation. Postnationalist liberal multiculturalism complicates rather than resolves the multiculturalism–nationalism aporia.

Making Room for North Koreans

The promise of the autonomous self idealized for market-driven liberal democracies selectively works for North Korean settlers, insofar as they incessantly encourage/train/demonstrate themselves to make that promise—which I want to call *encouragement rhetoric*. When they are put to work within the liberal democratic scheme, their North Korean sociocultural values and lifestyles are not simply embraced, as they expect them to be. Due to abnormal behaviors and language uses that disqualify them as non-self-autonomous citizens incompatible with the South Korean standard virtues in society, North Korean markers become the cause of a crisis of recognition. North Koreans are constantly encouraged to make the promise, but they can never fulfill and complete that promise unless they root out their innate traits of being North Korean. The encouragement rhetoric is a "crisis policing" on recognition, tackling North Korean sociocultural values and lifestyles as "both the cause and mode of legitimacy" (Black et al. 2012: 141) with which those settlers can be disqualified from, as well as accepted in, South Korean society.

As with many South Korean citizens, North Korean settlers are expected to constantly embrace a self-reliable and self-responsible character best suited to market-driven democracies. The Korea Hana Foundation (KHF), which was established by the Lee Myung-Bak government in November 2010, has produced those settlers' adaptation policy initiatives and operated various programs to support them. This institution regularly runs seminars and workshops, publishing and updating research papers, reports, and magazines on North Korean settlers' adaptation to society. A KHF report titled *Consumption Patterns of North Korean Women Defectors and Measures to Promote Rational Consumption Behavior* says:

> It has been found true that the blatantly conspicuous and excessive consumption patterns of North Korean settlers in South Korea have been a result of the abrupt collapse of scarcity in their original lifestyles since they began to experience a liberal market society. Their consumption desires that were repressed in the totalitarian country have just exploded and prompted them to make themselves an abnormal consumer through impulse buying and conspicuous consumption.
>
> (Kim and Kim 2011: 21)

This diagnosis implies that the ideal citizen of liberal market democracy should develop autonomous skills for rational consumption lifestyles. The brutal repression North Koreans must have experienced in their homeland has had a fatal impact on their adaptation process in South Korea. Adaptation fails, in this diagnosis, not because consumption in the market is bad, but because bad consumption is made in the market. The market is presumed to be the main domain of adaptation that never fails to transform these abnormal defectors into self-reliable and self-responsible citizens. Thus, the key in the liberal scheme is not to change the domain in which defectors live, but to change them to be qualified for the domain. Abnormal is not the market, but the individual who cannot properly lend him or herself to it.

In this policy report, an excessive consumption behavior of North Koreans is also manifested in female North Koreans' enthusiasm for interior design and their attitude toward social status achievements associated with material wealth in a capitalist society. Those female North Koreans are interested in interior design as self-fulfillment, a ritual they had in

North Korea (Kim and Kim 2011: 158–161). This ritual practice is questioned because South Koreans suspect that those settlers do not stint on interior design that would not suit their low-income household budget (Kim and Kim 2011: 13). And even if North Koreans decided to defect to "a capitalist society that they strongly desired," their approval rate of respect for the wealthy is unacceptably low—only 37.7 percent (Kim and Kim 2011: 251, 264). It has been perceived in this report that North Koreans are lavish with intolerable citizenship disqualifications for liberal market democracies. Failure to fulfill the liberal market criteria conjures up a crisis of recognition.

North Korean language use is another main target for contentious potential conflicts that should be eliminated in the encouragement rhetoric. The 2013 revised edition of *Manuals for North Koreans' Successful Social Adaptation* (KHF 2013) takes up host language integration, instructing North Korean settlers in a wide range of topics such as cell phone use and rational consumption habits. The term "host language" sounds strange here because both North and South Koreans use Korean. Apparently, in the South, there are different, unique dialects having their own local linguistic terms, intonations, pronunciations, and accents in the administrative provinces and geographical regions. Although South Koreans generally are taught the "standard Korean," which is defined as modern Seoul language, in schools and media campaigns, South Koreans from other provinces and regions are never publicly forced into the standard Korean. But North Koreans in South Korea are obligated to hide, and even eliminate, their North Korean accents in order to aid South Koreans' understanding of them. The instructions about this are designed not so much for mutual understanding as for an integration paradigm. The manuals say:

> The North Korean pronunciations of the Korean consonants ㅅ [s] and ㅆ [ts] sound like 쉬 [ʃui] to South Koreans. This sort of difference marks you as North Korean defectors.
>
> (KHF 2013: 90)

North Koreans should be informed that in general, South Koreans make a slight high tone at the end of each sentence when they speak. North Koreans mostly feel extremely awkward about the standard Korean because they never speak that way in North Korea, and thus often tend to refuse the standard manner. But they should be advised that conforming to the standard Korean can help them more carefully listen to their (South Korean) conversation partners and make the conversation much smoother (KHF 2013: 84).

In these assimilationist instructions, North Koreans can hardly find any *equal access* to South Korean society. *Being national* to them means merely conforming to *South Korean* values. As Cronin (2012: 186) rightly remarks, "Each language is, by definition, an invitation to discover the rich, complex, and nuanced world inhabited by its speakers." There is no such realm for South Koreans when they talk with North Koreans and listen to what they speak in North Korean. In the liberal–nationalist scheme, North Korean values are never embraced, but are merely *culturalized* in that North Koreans become hierarchically measured against the South Korean standard virtues (cf. de Leeuw and van Wichelen 2012). They are always morally encouraged to make North Korean ways recognizable to South Koreans. However, the encouragement that they (have to) subscribe to and provide brings them back to the haughty orders of assimilation and integration that it promises to avoid and refute.

In an interview with the author (conducted September 5, 2014), Sindong Kim, a senior teacher who has been working at Yeomyung School—an alternative school for North Korean refugee teenagers that has currently been certified by the Seoul Metropolitan School District Board since its start in 2004—says:

> the school strongly recommends that teachers in class, or in interaction with their students outside the classroom, include North Korean terms when teachers feel it harder for their students to understand South Korean terms they are describing. North Koreans are usually confused when they hear from South Koreans who tend to include a lot of English words in speaking Korean. Teachers here [at Yeomyung School] believe that this would help to facilitate their students' adaptation, *their successful survival in multicultural South Korea.*

This cultural adaptation strategy for educational purposes is clearly stated in the school's Korean language curriculum whose main scope is to help those North Korean students expose themselves to "diverse border-crossing experience of speaking both North and South Korean, through which they can become a future unified Korea's leaders" (Yeomyung School 2014: 44–45). The school's "unified Korean language" curriculum, however, mandates "corrections of wrong Korean language uses from North Korea" for every school grade at the school (Yeomyung School 2014: 50). Yosep Park, a North Korean refugee activist, insists, in an interview with the author (conducted on September 5, 2014):

> What would be the cost incurred for this assimilationist brand of multiculturalism is clear to me: *Loss of self.* Why we can't just be seen as Koreans—hailing from the North—living in South Korea, like other international people living in South Korea?

There is reason to belive from the above testimonies that becoming South Korean, identified in a privileged level in cultural adaptation, means removing North Korean settlers' identity marks.

Conclusion

In this chapter, I have shown that the concept of multiculturalism, when applied to North Korean settlers in South Korea, falls short of a viable solution to the identity negotiation process these settlers continually undergo while living in South Korea. In the liberal national formulation of multiculturalism, North Korean values and lifestyles cannot be cherished as a way to help those settlers express or take pride in their culture. As Green and Epstein (2013) have illuminated, it is when they express pain, sorrow, anger, and frustration regarding their experiences in North Korea and during their refugee life that they can be hailed as brave, autonomous, reliable, and responsible citizens. Their agency of resilience is merely approached as an illness through psychiatric intervention (Sung 2010). When they demonstrate their ineptitude to retain sentimental codes suited to South Koreans, they prove themselves to be mentally disordered, having alexithymia (Ha 2012).

This is an abuse of culture that, as I have sought to demonstrate, depoliticizes these settlers. North Koreans in South Korea are often mobilized to witness the persistent cruelty of human rights abuses committed by the North Korean regime, which has been considered a significant contribution to the strengthening of liberal democracies. But they are rarely invited to give critical commentary about the liberal democratic regime in which their subject formation as competent citizens is always questionable. As an important part of the community, they should be considered on their own mettle under any circumstance. To catch a glimpse of the insight into North Koreans as *avant la lettre* for unification of the nation, *South Koreans, "Others"* to them should be better prepared to respond to the political implications that are made and carried through multiculturalism ventriloquizing the ideal liberal citizenship that they can never attain without a constant denial of the self.

Acknowledgments

This research was supported by the National Research Foundation of Korea Grant funded by the Korean Government (NRF-2013S1A5A8022807).

Notes

* This chapter is a revised version of Sung (2015).

1. North Korean settler teenagers' middle and high school dropout rates are five times higher than their South Korean counterparts (Yoon 2013: 168).
2. In 2007, only 4.6 percent of North Korean settlers in South Korea reached an annual average household (standard four family members) income of US$24,000; approximately seven out of 10 North Korean settlers were eligible for government low-income subsidies (Yoon 2009: 132, 140).
3. The South Korean Citizenship Law grants South Korean citizenship status to North Koreans upon their entry to the country. Abiding by the North Korean Settler Support Special Act, the Low Income Household Support Law qualifies and guarantees North Korean settlers 1.5 times higher monthly low-income benefits than South Korean low-income households.

References

Black, L., Sinha, S., and Bryan, C. (2012) "New Hierarchies of Belonging," *European Journal of Cultural Studies*, 15(2): 139–154.

Cronin, M. (2012) "Who Fears to Speak in the New Europe? Plurilingualism and Alterity," *European Journal of Cultural Studies*, 15(2): 182–194.

de Leeuw, M. and van Wichelen, S. (2012) "Civilizing Migrants: Integration, Culture, and Citizenship," *European Journal of Cultural Studies*, 15(2): 195–210.

Fahy, S. (2011) "'Like Two Pieces of the Sky': Seeing North Korea Through Accounts of the Famine," *Anthropology Today*, 27(5): 18–21.

Green, C.K. and Epstein, S.J. (2013) "Now on My Way to Meet Who? South Korean Television, North Korean Refugees, and the Dilemmas of Representation," *The Asia-Pacific Journal: Japan Focus*, 11(41), available at: http://japanfocus.org/site/view/4007 (accessed December 14, 2015).

Ha, J. (2012) "A Psychiatric Diagnosis of North Korean Settlers' Emotions in Communication," *Unification Humanities Journal*, 53: 303–329.

Jung, J-H. (2007) "North Korean Settlers: Minority Nationals in a Post-National Division and Multicultural Era," in K-S. Oh (Ed.), *Multiculturalism in South Korea: Realities and Issues*, Paju, South Korea: Hanwool, pp. 135–166.

KHF (2013) *Manuals for North Koreans' Successful Social Adaptation*, Seoul, South Korea: KHF.

Kim, B-W. and Kim, Y-H. (2011) *Consumption Patterns of North Korean Women Defectors and Measures to Promote Rational Consumption Behavior*, Seoul, South Korea: KHF.

Lee, H-Y. (2010) "New Citizens' Participation and the Politics of Recognition: A Study on Oral Accounts of North Korean Settlers' Identity Formation," *Korean Sociology*, 44(1): 207–241.

Lee, J-W. (2006) "A Qualitative Study on the Socialization of North Korean Settler Teenagers in South Korea," *Society and Education*, 45(1): 195–219.

Lee, S-J. (2011) "When Multiculturalism Speaks to National Reunification," *North Korea Economy Review*, October 15, pp. 62–78.

Lee, Y-J. (2013) "On a Theoretical Reconstruction of the Multicultural," *Culture/Science*, 74: 165–187.

Mason, A. (1999) "Political Community, Liberal-Nationalism, and the Ethics of Assimilation," *Ethics*, 109(2): 261–286.

Park, H-S. (2007) "Multiculturalism and New Identity: On a Postcolonial Perspective," in K-S. Oh (Ed.), *Multiculturalism in South Korea: Realities and Issues*, Paju, South Korea: Hanwool, pp. 111–134.

Ryang, S. (2012) "North Koreans in South Korea: In Search of Their Humanity," *The Asia-Pacific Journal: Japan Focus*, 10(25), available at: http://japanfocus.org/-Sonia-Ryang/3771/article.html (accessed December 14, 2015).

Sung, M. (2009) "The 'Truth Politics' of Anti-North Koreanism: The Post-Ideological Cultural Representation of North Korea and the Cultural Criticisms of Korean Nationalism," *Inter-Asia Cultural Studies*, 10(3): 439–459.

Sung, M. (2010) "Psychiatric Power of Neo-Liberal Citizenship: The North Korean Human Rights Crisis, North Korean Settlers, and Incompetent Citizens," *Citizenship Studies*, 14(2): 127–144.

Sung, M. (2015) "An Abuse of Culture: North Korean Settlers, Multiculturalism, and Liberal Democracy," *Asian Social Science*, 11(4): 48–54.

Yeomyung School (2014) *Yeongmyung School's 2014 Curriculum Guidelines*, Seoul, South Korea: Yeomyung School.

Yoon, H. (2013) "Facilitating Multicultural Education for North Korean Settler Youth," *Diaspora Studies*, 7(2): 161–186.

Yoon, I-J. (2009) *North Korean Migrants: Life, Rituals, and Policy*, Paju: South Korea: Jipmoondang.

Yoon, I-J. (2012) "North Korean Migrants' Acculturation and Social Adaptation," *Research on Korean Studies*, 41: 37–61.

Chapter 9

Dictators, Trade, and Development: The Mediterranean MENA Development Model and Euro-Mediterranean Economic Relations

Eugenio Dacrema

This chapter aims to provide a preliminary description of the development model that spread in most Mediterranean MENA countries[1] during the 1990s and 2000s and the influence that Euro-Mediterranean relations had on its development. Particular attention will be paid to the shortcomings of this development model fostered by the intensification of the Euro-Mediterranean economic relations and their contribution to the 2011 wave of uprisings. The first part will summarize the crucial political and economic changes that occurred in the region at the beginning of the 1990s. The end of the Cold War and launch of the Barcelona Process marked the beginning of a new era and the shaping of a new developmental model for most of the Mediterranean MENA countries. Utilizing the framework of the domino effect theory of regional trade developed by Baldwin (1997), this chapter will provide an explanation for the rapidity by which numerous bilateral agreements have been signed by the EU and by nearly all of its southern partners in the past two decades. Furthermore, a brief description of the particular historical context in which the Barcelona Process was initiated will highlight additional factors that both led to its rapid development and resulted in its key shortcomings.

The second part will deepen the analysis of the particular political and economic features of most Mediterranean MENA regimes. In particular, it will take into account the motives that led several autocratic regimes to embrace bilateral agreements that entailed a significant opening of their economic systems, a process that according to some theories would eventually lead to a democratic transformation of their systems (Ahlquist and Wibbels 2012). In order to provide a satisfying explanation for this phenomenon, this chapter will utilize the innovative theorization developed by Wen-Chin Wu of Taiwan University. This theorization provides a convincing framework to analyze the relationship between authoritarianism and trade openness, treating the latter as a tool in the hands of autocrats to fix the socioeconomic inequalities within their societies. Moreover, the political developments that have occurred since 2011 in the Mediterranean MENA (Middle East and North African) countries will be taken into account. The final part of this chapter aims to provide an explanation for the occurrence of these political developments using an economic perspective. It will be argued that although many regimes pursued trade openness and entered into intense trade relations with the EU in order to stabilize their power, some specific features of the trade rules imposed by the EU on its partners may have generated unintended conditions that fostered instability among those authoritarian regimes.

Therefore, while the first part will provide a summary of the region's economic and political developments in the last two decades, the second part will explore further the preference formation within authoritarian regimes and the factors that can lead them to open their economies (despite fears of facilitating instability and democratic transitions). In particular, it will explore the reasons why such instability and (partial or complete) democratic transitions actually occurred in some countries—highlighting the specific characteristics of the prevalent development model adopted by most Mediterranean MENA states in the 1990s and 2000s. Finally, it will take into account some specific characteristics of the trade treaties negotiated within the regional framework of the Euro-Mediterranean Partnership and the European Neighborhood Policy and the influence they had in shaping such a development model and in sparking the social grievances that led to the wave of political instability in 2011. The chapter will focus especially on the case of Tunisia, Egypt, and Syria—three countries characterized by different cultural, economic, and historical backgrounds. However, despite their differences, these three countries embarked into important economic reforms and development plans after the end of the Cold War according to very similar development models. Finally, all these countries experienced violent turmoil in 2011.

Background

Before Barcelona: The MENA Region at the Beginning of the 1990s

At the beginning of the 1990s, the Mediterranean part of the MENA region went through significant political and ideological transformations sparked by the end of the Cold War and the bipolar world order. The MENA had been deeply divided between the two international political fields; countries such as Syria, Libya, Algeria, and Egypt (until the 1970s) had been at various degrees close to the Eastern bloc, while Jordan, Morocco, Tunisia, Lebanon, and the Gulf monarchies had sided with the US and Western Europe. In addition to these international rifts, the region had also been divided by internal fractures. Until the 1970s, the pan-Arab ideologies (Nasserism and Baathism) that gained predominance in several countries (Egypt, Iraq, and Syria) had been opposed to the conservative block led by Saudi Arabia and the region's monarchies. After the crisis of pan-Arabism sparked by the defeat of Nasserist Egypt in the 1967 Six Days War, at the end of the 1970s a new regional fracture emerged between Khomeini's revolutionary Iran and the Sunni powers once again led by Saudi Arabia.

The end of the Cold War brought a change in paradigm and a crisis of the ideological order. Furthermore, it imposed a radical revision of the economic order that until that moment had been dominant in the region. Since the beginning of the 1980s, most of the region's oil-producing countries—especially the minor producers such as Syria and Egypt—had already been going through significant budgetary troubles due to the fall of international energy prices. The end of the Cold War also entailed the end of the financial and military assistance that many regimes had enjoyed from the two blocks in exchange for their support.

Therefore, for most of the non-oil producers and minor oil producers of the region, a radical economic restructuring became necessary in order to sustain their national budgets. Furthermore, the ideological quagmire in which several regimes—especially those that had been funded under the pan-Arab flag—found themselves in need of constructing a new national narrative in order to support and justify their power. It is in this context that the beginning of new season in economic and political relations between the European Community (EC) and the countries of the South Mediterranean shore was inaugurated by the Conference of Barcelona and the launch of the Barcelona Process in 1994.

After Barcelona: The Euro-Mediterranean Partnership and the European Neighborhood Policy

In the last two decades, the process initiated in Barcelona sparked rapid developments in the economic relations between the EU and the southern shore of the Mediterranean Sea; this significantly altered the trade structure of the Mediterranean MENA countries. Several regional initiatives—first the Euro-Mediterranean Partnership and later the more comprehensive European Neighborhood Policy—were launched, aimed at deepening economic integration along with political coordination in key matters such as immigration and security policies. The Barcelona Process' main target was the gradual creation of a free trade area between the EU and South (and South-East) Mediterranean countries and among the South Mediterranean countries themselves. The first characteristic emerging from the relationships built in this period between the EU and the southern shore is its bilateral nature. In fact, the lack of any other regional organization able to speak and act on behalf of the countries of the southern shore made it necessary to negotiated bilateral treaties with the South Mediterranean countries. This stems also from the deep political heterogeneity characterizing the MENA partners. Existing supranational entities such as the Arab League (or later on the Union of the Maghreb) were able to create only tenuous political and economic links between their members—making it impossible for the EU to treat them as credible counterparts (Tino 2012).

Since the beginning of the Barcelona Process, the strategy of the newly founded Euro-Mediterranean Partnership encompassed the negotiation of bilateral treaties (Association Agreements) between the EU and each South Mediterranean country. All agreements had the same structure and long-term objectives aiming at the establishment of a full-fledged free trade area by 2010. Each agreement included a political, an economic, and a cultural dimension. The political and cultural dimensions sought to strengthen cooperation on issues such as regional security, the control of the migration flows, and the promotion and development of local civil societies in the framework of—at least theoretically—shared values such as democracy and respect for human rights. The economic dimension of the agreements has been by far the most important, and it has encompassed the gradual elimination of tariff barriers in the industrial sector (and, more slowly, also a limited integration in other crucial sectors such as agricultural productions, services, and capital flows) (Tino 2012).

The Euro-Mediterranean Partnership (EMP)—the organization founded as first result of the Barcelona Process—has had the declared objective of deepening and developing the pan-Mediterranean economic relations on both the north–south (EU–South Mediterranean countries) and the south–south (among the South Mediterranean countries) vectors. In order to achieve the second target, the EU encouraged the creation of regional organizations such as the Union of the Maghreb (UoM) and the strengthening of the existing ones such as the Arab League. Since 2004, the Association Agreements and the Euro-Mediterranean Partnership have been overlapped and relaunched by the European Neighborhood Policy (ENP). This new framework has not substantially modified the approach and the priorities of the previous agreements. The new "plans" (bilateral agreements with no legal binding force) signed under the ENP—now called "Action Plans"—have maintained the same pillars of the Association Agreements and have privileged the economic dimension.

The results obtained so far by the Barcelona Process and the ENP in the Mediterranean neighborhood are controversial. The two European initiatives have been the first regional frameworks that successfully brought Israel and all Arab countries of the South Mediterranean shore to the same table. Moreover, in the last two decades, every South Mediterranean country has signed at least one bilateral agreement with the EU in the framework of the Barcelona Process (with the exception of Syria; negotiations for a first bilateral treaty were interrupted by the beginning of the civil war in 2011). The cooperation in security and migration matters has achieved considerable results in limiting and regulating the migration flows and enhancing the exchange of information between intelligence and counterterrorist agencies. At the same time, the economic north–south exchanges have witnessed a remarkable and steady increase in the last two decades, making the EU the first economic partner of all South Mediterranean countries (see Figures 9.7, 9.8, and 9.9 in the Appendix).

Despite these considerable successes, the European policies of economic integration in the Mediterranean region show today at least three shortcomings. First, the bilateral approach chosen at the beginning of the Barcelona Process led to the emergence of significant differences in the depth of economic integration reached by each country in its relations with the EU. Countries such as Tunisia and Morocco have signed several subsequent treaties and have rapidly deepened their bilateral relations with the European common market; others, such as Algeria, Lebanon, and Libya, have witnessed a significantly slower pace of integration in the framework of EMP and ENP. Second, the objective of developing the south–south economic integration along with the north–south integration has essentially failed. While nowadays the EU is by far the most important trade partner for every southern Mediterranean country, the MENA region is among the least economically integrated areas of the world (Tino 2012). Finally, the numerous conditions included in the bilateral treaties that aimed to enhance the democratic level of the southern Mediterranean countries' political systems have so far emerged as inefficient, often sparking harsh criticism against the presumed hypocrisy of the EU institutions in dealing with autocratic regimes (Bouris 2011).

In the 1990s and especially the 2000s, the new "rhetoric of development" supported by the remarkable economic figures in most Mediterranean MENA countries seemed to strengthen these countries' authoritarian regimes instead of leading them toward a gradual democratic transition. Only in 2011, after the wave of protests that temporarily shook the stability of nearly all the South Mediterranean regimes, did this picture seem to fade and the idea that economic development and openness could eventually spark democratic transition were relaunched. Today, this idea appears at least simplistic as only Tunisia seems to have achieved a stable democratic system; Libya and Syria have spiraled into civil war and Egypt seems to have returned to a Mubarak-like military regime under the current order ruled by President al-Sisi. In order to understand what led to the rapid success of the EU Mediterranean trade and financial initiatives, the rapid economic openness enacted by the southern shore's authoritarian regimes, and to the wave of political destabilization in 2011, it is necessary to take into account numerous factors. Among them, the features of the development model that spread in the region in the last two decades and the specific characteristics of the Euro-Mediterranean trade and financial links are worthy of examination.

The Domino Effect Theory: The European Union and Mediterranean MENA Countries

The domino effect theory surged in the second half of the 1990s in order to provide an explanation to a growing trend in the international trade system: the increasing number of regional organizations and trade areas in almost all parts of the globe (Baldwin 1993). The formation of a preferential trade area or the development of an existing one diverts trade and investment to new recipients and begets the creation of political economic forces in non-member nations (Baldwin 1997). If, for example, a specific country is granted privileged low- or no-tariff access to another country's market by a bilateral agreement or the accession to a regional trade organization, other countries traditionally exporting toward the same market may be hurt by the new conditions granted to a competitor. This may lead them to ask for the same conditions through their integration in the same regional organization. If such an organization includes a fairly big and rich market—such as the European or the American market—this dynamic can come to involve a great number of countries.

The end of the Cold War led the European Union to look eastwards and to begin the enlargement process towards most of the Eastern European countries previously part of the Soviet-led Eastern bloc (Baldwin 1997). Therefore, in the same years in which the southern Mediterranean autocratic regimes were looking for new rhetorical and concrete basis for their stability, the EU enlargement process toward East Europe was going to grant significant market privileges to countries that they saw as direct competitors. For this reason, almost all those regimes saw the Barcelona Conference in 1994 as an important chance to avoid such risks—especially countries such as Tunisia and Morocco that had traditionally maintained significant economic relations with the northern shore. They were followed by the rest of the Mediterranean MENA countries that had similar resources. By the beginning of the new century, the European Union became the first trade partner of all South Mediterranean counterparts. Therefore, the domino effect triggered by the subsequent Association Agreements and Action Plans can be explained by the will of a group of countries characterized by the same resources and factors not find to themselves in a position of comparative disadvantage vis-a-vis the EU market.

The domino effect described by Baldwin seems to hold in this case, and explains the success and rapidity that characterized the first two decades of the Barcelona Process. However, the domestic dynamic described by Baldwin to explain the push toward the Domino Effect can be considered straightforward only regarding democracies. In the case of authoritarian regimes, the issue requires a different explanation, especially in the case of the Mediterranean MENA countries and the specific political climate and economic conditions at the beginning of the 1990s. The following section provides a description of the motives behind trade openness policies in autocratic regimes and the specific development model that was applied in the Mediterranean MENA countries after the end of the Cold War.

Preferences and Open Trade in Autocratic States

In the classic domino effect theory at the domestic level, the protagonists are the exporting firms that are stimulated to engage in greater pro-integration political activism if their country is excluded from a trade agreement involving a market in which they have conspicuous interests. Such a stimulus increases with the number of countries accessing the trading block from which their country is excluded. Therefore, if the block includes important markets and is truly open, then this process is only impeded by significant resistance to becoming a member (Baldwin 1997). However, such a dynamic is significantly more straightforward within democratic systems than within authoritarian ones.

If, on the one hand, an authoritarian regime can be willing to avoid damages to its economic interests triggered by the formation of a trade agreement from which it is excluded, on the other hand different dynamics may lead to the formation of such interests—not necessarily primarily involving its exporting firms. As demonstrated by some recent studies (Dutt and Mitra 2002; Wen-Chin Wu 2014), one of these possible dynamics can involve the need on the part of one regime to balance the economic inequalities within its society in order to avoid increasing discontent.

Different Approaches to Inequality

Stability and the ability to preserve its own rule are the first objectives of every authoritarian regime. Therefore, discontent—its extent and the sectors of the society in which it spreads—is a crucial indicator to measure the stability and health of those regimes. However, the lack of direct methods to monitor the level of discontent toward governmental policies leads dictatorships to resort to proxy indicators. According to a vast literature, inequality is an efficient substitute and empirical results demonstrate that this indicator often triggers measures and policies in authoritarian regimes (Schofield and Levinson 2008; Gallagher and Hanson 2009). Meltzer and Richard (1981) developed a widespread model examining the role of inequality as a factor of instability in authoritarian regimes. According to this model, the "red line" of a regime's stability is the income of the mean earner; if the income of the mean earner is higher than of the median earner, the latter will support a redistribution that damages the richer social classes in the society. In a dictatorship, where such a dynamic is slow or even impossible since the rich classes are usually composed by the loyal and powerful supporters of a regime, it can transform into a revolt and a possible democratic transition. According to the two authors, its high chance to success is determined by the fact that it also includes the middle classes, which are considered determinants for the successful outcome of a democratic transition as well.

However, several other studies contest the universal validity of the Meltzer–Richard model. Boix (2003), for example, supports the existence of a linear negative relationship between inequality and the prospect of democratization. According to his model, democratization becomes likely only either in an equal society or if the richest citizens are free to move their assets abroad. In the second case, they would be keener to accept the redistribution stemming from democratization. Moreover, Acemoglu and Robinson (2006) proposes an inverted relationship in which rich citizens have stronger incentives to resist democratization if inequality is high, while poorer citizens have fewer incentives to start a revolution if inequality is low—since they would gain little from redistribution.

Authoritarian Regimes and Inequality in the MENA Region

Despite the different approaches, the largest part of the existing literature tends to stress the role of inequality as a crucial factor for the stability of an authoritarian regime (Wen-Chin Wu 2014). Over the past decades, the empirical observations of the MENA region's authoritarian regimes have highlighted similar patterns of power management that have been commonly labeled as "neo-patrimonialism." As described by Toby Dodge (2012), the recurrent scheme of neo-patrimonialist regimes is based on the "concentric circles" dynamic that links the ruling elite to a series of exponentially wider patron–client circles. Therefore, neo-patrimonialism as a governing method is structurally unstable. It is characterized by an unequal access to government resources and by the creation and recreation of dispossessed constituencies. In this way, inequality becomes an intrinsic element of the management of the state. In order to avoid inequality to fuel rebellions, it has been traditionally handled in two main ways: repression or temporary top-down distribution of resources. The resources necessary for the second method come from different sources depending on the historic period and on the endowment of natural resources of every single country. States endowed with significant amounts of hydrocarbons—the Gulf monarchies, Algeria, Libya, but also minor producers such as Egypt, Jordan, or Syria—have been able to enact top-down distributive policies in moments of their history characterized by high oil prices. Minor producers and states lacking hydrocarbon resources have often had to resort to other means. For example, international donations were particularly conspicuous during the Cold War, when major powers "compensated" their local allies for their foreign postures by channeling them resources in order to guarantee the stability of their regimes. This framework changed conspicuously with the end of the Cold War.

The beginning of the 1990s represents a turning point for many MENA region regimes. The amount of donations to the region in the previous decades began to fall dramatically, and local dictators had to resort to new means in order to guarantee their regimes' stability. It is in this period that the policies of market opening began to spread across the entire region, even in countries that until a few years before had ran a Soviet-style centralized regime characterized by a planned economy—such as in Syria or Algeria. According to Wen-Chin Wu (2014), such a fast change can be explained by the role that trade openness has in stabilizing authoritarian regimes. The author utilizes the Heckscher–Ohlin model, which predicts that countries benefit from exporting goods produced with domestically abundant factors. In the case of non (or minor) hydrocarbon-producing MENA countries characterized by authoritarian regimes, the abundant factor is labor. Therefore, by opening their economies, dictators favor distribution toward the poorer social classes—without harming the richer ones that are usually their main loyal base (Wen-Chin Wu 2014).

Wen-Chin Wu's (2014) argument is similar to the one formulated by Dutt and Mitra (2002), who predict that an increase in inequality will lead to lower trade barriers in countries characterized by labor abundance. According to the authors, dictators pursue economic openness in order to address growing inequality—since they cannot resort to democratic elections as a feasible means to reconcile the political dynamics that led to such an inequality status (Dutt and Mitra 2002; Wen-Chin Wu 2014). Wen-Chin Wu's empirical findings demonstrate that a rise in inequality results in more trade openness in dictatorships and not in democracies. Such findings are particularly relevant if compared to the mainstream literature regarding trade openness and democratic transition. According to Ahlquist and Wibbels (2012), the exposure to global trade leads to a boost in the probability of a democratic transition, since economic growth is one of the main engines triggering democratization. Moreover, following Alquist and Wibbels' argument, countries with similar endowments—such as the Mediterranean MENA countries—will face a similar push toward democratization if exposed to an economic shock. The so-called "Arab Spring" in the aftermath of the world financial crisis (which entailed also a sudden decrease in global financial and trade flows) seems to prove their argument. Nevertheless, in their empirical research, the two authors do not find any significant correlation between labor abundance or international trade and democratization once they control for regional forces of democratization, while Wen-Chin Wu's results appear robust. Therefore, it is necessary to resort to a more convincing narrative if we want to pinpoint the specific factors explaining what occurred in the Mediterranean MENA countries in the last two decades and in particular the factors that led to the "Arab Spring."

Especially in the beginning of the 1990s—just after the end of the Cold War—all the Mediterranean MENA countries enacted long-term plans of progressive trade and financial liberalization. In most cases, such plans were accompanied by a "development" rhetoric that fits Wen-Chin Wu's theory on the relation between trade openness and dictatorships. This also fit with the new global political climate that had brought to an end the period of strong ideologies characterizing the internal dialectics of the Arab world. After the end of the postcolonial rhetoric and pan-Arab ideology, most of the Arab republican regimes embarked into a new political rhetoric in which the words "development" and "progress" had a central importance. Foreign donations and ideology were no longer sufficient to offset the discontent stemming from the growing inequality in their societies. In order to avoid the destabilizing forces that inequality could trigger, they devised new radical economic plans that entailed deep trade and financial openness—especially toward their Western (especially European) partners. Therefore, the behavior of these regimes correlates almost completely with Wen-Chin Wu's theory. In the ensuing years, several Mediterranean MENA countries actually showed significant improvement in their inequality rates (see Figure 9.1 in the Appendix). Nevertheless, their unemployment rates remained high and their economic fundamentals showed significant shortcomings. In 2011, the "Arab Spring" led to the toppling of several dictators in the region, and in the case of Tunisia and Egypt to a partial or a radical democratic transition—for a time.

What Went Wrong? The Structural Shortcomings of Authoritarian Regimes in the MENA Region and the 2011 Wave of Protests

Neo-Patrimonialism and Paths of Economic Development in the MENA Region: An "Imitation Game"

As we have seen, neo-patrimonialism is an authoritarian regime type that characterized the MENA region in the last decades. Its main features have been defined by the work of several scholars in the 1990s and 2000s, but the field witnessed a new development in the beginning of the 2010s (Hinnebush 2006; Schwarz 2008; Bank and Richter 2010; Dodge 2012). The first organic conceptualization of neo-patrimonialism was provided by Pawelka and his study on the Egyptian regime. According to the author, neo-patrimonialism is characterized by a scheme that has the ruler at its center. Around it, several societal elites are structured and ordered according to their personal distance from the ruler. A similar hierarchy applies to the different societal sectors. According to their distance from the core, they are ordered within the society in a hierarchy of priority. Such a scheme is therefore formed by a series of concentric circles having the ruler at its center and a series of dyads—personal contacts—linking every circle with the previous one. The personal nature of these links is based on loyalty and only secondarily on expertise and competence. The ruler appoints personalities that he considers most loyal to key posts. These posts provide these subjects with a certain amount of power and rents they can distribute among their own clients, who will do the same thing in a progressively smaller scale until the last circle. Pawelka and other scholars (Bank and Richter 2010) identify three main features characterizing the dynamics within this scheme. First and foremost, there is personalism; these links are based on the client's individual loyalty to the patron. The second is emanation; the decisions taken by elite members gain importance and effectiveness only if they are backed by the patron of this elite. In this way, the elite is nothing more than a means for the patron to fulfill his or her own will. The third characteristic is power balance; neo-patrimonialist regimes are characterized by a systematic rotation of key figures and by the intersection of institutional authorities. This constrains the formation of alternative coalitions within the ruling system (Bank and Richter 2010).

Finally, a fourth characteristic, "elite pluralism and competition," is of particular importance for this chapter. Neo-patrimonialist systems are characterized by fragmented elites competing with each other for the favor of the ruler. Grounds for such competition include the provision of political ideas that are accepted by the ruler (Bank and Richter 2010). Through this mechanism, in the 1990s, new suggestions and ideas for economic development spread within the regimes of the region. In the ensuing 15 years, a common pattern emerged—although in different moments in the different countries—leading to trade openness and financial liberalization. This was due to the emergence of new similar intellectual elites within the economic circuits of the region's regimes. In some countries such as Tunisia or Syria, they emerged alongside the rise to power of a new generation of leaders such as Ben Ali and Bashar al-Assad. With the help of these new leaders, the new intellectual elites replaced the old ones. This was achieved mainly by exploiting the incapacity of the old elites to cope with the transformed international political climate that did not allow the regimes to keep on with the old patterns of power administration. New ways to face inequality and the pressure of the West for democratization were necessary. These new elites used the recipes of the Washington Consensus—which in the 1990s enjoyed its popularity peak among the world's economic circles—and added some very specific "ingredients" imported by the experience of other authoritarian countries, creating a new "hybrid" model that was applied at different degrees in all the Mediterranean MENA countries. The most important characteristic of the process that led to the emergence of this new model is the imitation dynamic that we can observe among the different countries of the region. These new elites had intense contacts with each other and often implemented measures borrowed from the experience of their counterparts in other countries. Such a process led to the formation of a model that has common features from Morocco to Syria.

The first of these features is trade openness. In all Mediterranean MENA countries, trade openness was achieved mainly through the Barcelona Process and the Association Agreements (and later the Action Plans) with the EU. Some countries also developed secondary trade links, such as the trade agreement of Morocco with the US or the FTA developed by Turkey, Lebanon, Syria, and Jordan by the end of 2010 (which was immediately suspended due to the beginning of the Syrian civil conflict). The second is a partial opening to foreign capitals. All countries carried out a partial liberalization of the financial sector, often with mixed results. The banking sector remained largely in the hands of the state, while new rules were introduced in order to ease FDI inflows and portfolio investments. Nevertheless, the investment climate remained largely uncompetitive due to the impossibility of enacting deep reforms in the national bureaucracies. Third, the partial privatization of some strategic sectors such as telecommunications, construction, and tourism created a system in which most of these companies remained fundamentally public and a source of ongoing corruption. Due to their fundamental importance for the economies, the property of such sectors was transferred to private subjects close to the regimes. In some cases, they were directly part of the dictator's family—such as the Syrian telecommunications tycoon Rami Makhlouf, cousin of Bashar al-Assad—while others were close to the regime's first neo-patrimonialist circle such as the "Gamal Klan"—the group of Egyptian tycoons orbiting around Hosni Mubarak's son Gamal Mubarak—or the "Trablesi Klan"—the circle of businessmen linked to the family of Ben Ali's wife Laila Trablesi.

Finally, the economic administration of all these regimes was characterized also by the state's influence in directing the allocation of foreign FDIs. Imitating the Chinese model of free trade zones (FTZs), many MENA countries adopted similar measures in order to concentrate and direct the inflows of foreign productive investments. Several countries such as Tunisia or Egypt built from scratch entire technological cities provided with the necessary infrastructures to host the installation of new industries and offices. These zones were all geographically localized, usually close to the most important economic centers. In general, the state's supervision on the inflows of investments (both private and public) led to the prioritization of some urban areas—where the circles of the regimes had usually their main headquarters—and to the neglect of the countryside and the areas least endowed for the trade with the most important economic partners (mostly the EU).

Increasing disparities among regions within the same country widened dramatically and became a common feature of the development model spread among the Mediterranean MENA countries. In Tunisia, for example, the 1990s saw a continuous deepening of the economic imbalances between the coastal area—the so-called "Sahel"—and the internal regions. Such disparities were partially the heritage of the colonial era, during which the French colonizers settled mainly in the Mediterranean areas leaving basically untouched the rest of the country. However, the development plan applied by the regime of Ben Ali during the 1990s and 2000s deliberately expanded such imbalances: almost all the new FTZs—in Tunisia known as "technopoles"—were concentrated in the Sahel along with almost all the investments for new infrastructures. The same dynamic was witnessed in Egypt. In the 1990s, Cairo and Alexandria became the sole centers of the country's plan of development, leaving other large areas of the country—such as the south and the Sinai Peninsula—largely neglected. FTZs were developed in these two main cities that became the sole industrial centers of the country. In Syria, the development investments were entirely directed toward the two main urban areas, Aleppo and Damascus, while the rest of the country remained largely in the grip of underinvestment and desertification. Although it is impossible to know the exact details of this imitation game, it is possible to track imitation as one of the features that characterized the shaping of this development model that by the mid 2000s came to a similar form in these countries despite their specific differences.

Looking at the effects on the economic growth of these countries and on their general economic performances, it is easy to understand why such a model was considered for a long time a successful choice. The economies of these countries grew steadily in the last two decades, and for a long while they were able to cope with the dramatic demographic growth and the consequent constant increase in the labor market's demand (see Figures 9.2, 9.3 and 9.4 in the Appendix). Investments—both portfolio and FDIs—grew steadily along with pro capita income. These data made most observers consider these countries' regimes solid and stable thanks to their economic performance.

However, in 2011, this widespread opinion turned out to be wrong. Starting from Tunisia, almost all Mediterranean MENA countries witnessed a wave of protests that ousted the dictators in Tunisia, Egypt, and Libya, and sparked protracted civil conflicts in Libya and Syria. It should be noted that most rebellions originated in cities located in the neglected countryside of these countries or from neighborhoods inhabited by immigrants coming from those areas: in Tunisia, the protests started in Sidi Bouzaid, a countryside village, and then spread into the Tunis neighborhoods of Dwar Hicher and Grand Tadhamoun, inhabited largely by people immigrated from the southern and internal regions.

In Egypt, the demonstrations spread in the peripheral quartiers of Cairo and Alexandria where immigrants from the southern regions were mostly located despite the narratives in the international media that highlight Tahrir Square as the center of turmoil. In particular, the people living in these quartiers started a long chain of strikes in the industries where they were—usually informally—employed paralyzing the country's industrial sector. In Syria, the city of Daraa', located in a region largely neglected by the Assad regime's development plans, was the scene of the early protests. In particular, in the previous decade, Daraa' had witnessed a significant immigration from the southeastern countryside where lands lost gradually productivity due to the process of desertification against which the regime never provided any contrasting infrastructural plan.

As we have seen, the neglect of the agricultural countryside was the result of the development model applied by all the Mediterranean MENA countries in the previous two decades with few differences from a country to another.

Almost all countries—especially the ones that started the application of this model earlier—had entered into the European Framework of the Euro-Mediterranean Partnership or the Neighborhood Policy. Even Syria, which had entered only into the negotiation phase in the same time span, had developed its trade and financial relations with Europe to a great extent, with the EU becoming Syria's first trade partner in the 2000s. Therefore, although there are certainly several domestic conditions that led the Mediterranean MENA countries' development model to privilege the big urban areas at the expense of the agricultural countryside, some specific characteristics of the kind of trade agreements imposed by the EU on its partners may have had a determinant influence in the shaping of this model.

Euro-Mediterranean Trade Relations and the "Manipulation" of Comparative Advantage

Before the Barcelona Process and Euro-Mediterranean Partnership, tariffs constituted a significant part of the public sector's revenues in several MENA Mediterranean countries. In small countries such as Tunisia, for example, they constituted one-fifth of the public budget, and the loss for the state revenues was estimated in 1995 at 3.5 percent of GDP (Jbili and Enders 1996). In order to maintain the large expenditures in distributive policies (such as food and fuel subsidies), such losses should have been compensated by an increase in domestic taxes. However, as we have seen in the paragraph regarding the structure of the neo-patrimonialist regimes, authoritarian regimes have always been reluctant to apply a complete and functional taxation system on the country's private sector. On the other had, the end of distributive policies risked damaging the very target of the trade openness policy (i.e. wealth redistribution toward the poorer social classes). The result of these contradictory trends led to growing budget deficits in Tunisia and other Mediterranean MENA countries and scarce public investment capacity due to the growing share of the public debt that they kept on devolving to nonproductive subsidiary policies. Therefore, in all these countries, public investment in infrastructures and the development of tradeable sectors had been subjected to narrow limits and long delays.

In particular, it led the regimes to concentrate expenditures on areas that required less investment to yield short-term results, such as the already-developed areas of the Sahel in Tunisia or the biggest urban centers in Egypt and Syria. Therefore, large long-term investments such as the anti-desertification infrastructure plans in Syria were left largely neglected due to the heavy budget constraints and the need to obtain immediate results from the new economic policies. To the imbalances triggered (and widened) by the quick elimination of the trade tariffs, it is necessary to add the effects caused by another important characteristic of the EU trade agreements: the exclusion of agricultural products. Prior to the Barcelona Process, most of the trade between the EU countries and the southern shore was composed of agricultural products. In particular, Morocco, Tunisia, and Syria have been traditionally endowed with a great share of fertile lands. At the same time, Egypt has always been one of the major producers of high-quality cottons and other textile materials despite having a limited amount of cultivable lands.

Nevertheless, in the first decade of the Barcelona Process, the EU imposed the almost complete exclusion of agricultural products from the trade agreements signed with the southern

Mediterranean countries. Especially in countries already heavily dependent on the EU market such as Tunisia, this entailed an indirect "distortion" of the country's comparative advantage toward its main trade partners. In fact, after the beginning of the Barcelona Process, sectors that were previously highly competitive and employed a significant amount of labor became suddenly uncompetitive in comparison with other sectors—such as industrial intermediate products—that were previously negligible. Investment in the agriculture sector's development became relatively unprofitable and the salaries started to lose relative purchase power in comparison with the salaries in other sectors.

This dynamic exacerbated migration trends from the countryside toward the urban centers, where vast new neighborhoods were created to host the impoverished migrants. The already poor quarters of Cairo, Alexandria, Damascus, Tunis, and Aleppo witnessed a dramatic acceleration of immigration flows. When, in the 2000s, the new agreements with the EU entailed a tariff reduction also for agricultural exports toward the EU market, the primary sector in the southern shore was already heavily damaged from the previous decade. Furthermore, the EU Common Agricultural Policy (CAP) new standards entailed high-quality requirements for the products imported into the European market. Origin controls, quality controls, and packaging rules became the new non-tariff barriers heavily hindering the inflows of agricultural products from the Mediterranean MENA countries. While for European producers the technological developments required to comply with the CAP requirements were significantly subsidized by the EU, southern Mediterranean producers were incapable of obtaining the necessary investments; moreover, often the size of their internal markets made impossible the development of the economies of scale necessary to reach those technological levels. The two features of the EU agreements described above had a determinant influence in shaping the conditions that led to the 2011 turmoil. They heavily hindered the redistribution effects triggered by the trade openness promoted by the regimes of the Mediterranean southern shore, and fostered the structural social and geographic disparities already present within those countries' societies.

Conclusion

The first aim of this chapter has been to analyze the successful and rapid enlargement of the Barcelona Process framework in the light of Baldwin's domino effect theory. We have seen that the domino effect theory is suitable to explain the dynamic that led to the fast widening of the trade relations between the EU and its Mediterranean MENA counterparts. However, a close analysis of these countries' authoritarian regimes and their neo-patrimonialist structure helped to outline some specific features that led those regimes to open their economies and engage in the Barcelona Process. Moreover, with regard to the specific analysis of the policies of trade openness that spread throughout the South Mediterranean shore, this chapter provided an economic perspective to analyze the formation of a specific regional model of economic development. In particular, some features of this model—such as the structural imbalances that have widened within the South Mediterranean societies along the last two decades— have been taken into account in order to pinpoint the reasons that led to the instability wave in region at the beginning of 2011. This chapter has endeavored to outline the most important factors that sparked such instability and found at least part of their origins in two main elements of the Euro-Mediterranean trade framework: the rapid and bilateral elimination of import tariffs and the exclusion of agricultural products from the trade integration process. Both elements deeply influenced the development strategies of the Mediterranean MENA countries and the formation of their development model. Their coupled effects contributed to the structural socioeconomic shortcomings that were fundamental to inciting the wave of rebellions affecting the entire MENA region in 2011.

Notes

1. In this chapter, this definition includes the countries of the MENA region having a Mediterranean coast with the exception of Algeria, Libya, and Israel. The particular economic features of these three countries make them exceptional in comparison with the rest of this region's economies.

References

Acemoglu, D. and Robinson, J. A. (2006) *The Economic Origins of Dictatorship and Democracy*, Cambridge: Cambridge University Press.

Ahlquist, J.S. and Wibbels, E. (2012) "Riding the Wave: World Trade and Factor-Based Models of Democratization," *American Journal of Political Science*, 56(2): 447–464.

Baldwin, R.E. (1993) *A Domino Theory of Regionalism*, Geneva: University of Geneva.

Baldwin, R.E. (1997) "The Causes of Regionalism," *The World Economy*, 20(77): 865–888.

Bank, A. and Richter, T. (2010) *Neopatrimonialism in the Middle East and North Africa: Overview, Critique and Alternative Conceptualization*, Hamburg: GIGA (German Institute of Global and Area Studies) Conference.

Boix, C. (2003) *Democracy and Redistribution*, Cambridge: Cambridge University Press.

Bouris, D. (2011) "The Limits of Normative Power Europe: Assessing the Third Pillar of the Euro-Mediterranean Partnership," *Political Perspectives*, 5(2): 80–106.

Dodge, T. (2012) *From the Arab Awakening to the Arab Spring: The Post-Colonial State in the Middle East*, London: London School of Economics.

Dutt, P. and Mitra, D. (2002) "Endogenous Trade Policy through Majority Voting: An Empirical Investigation," *Journal of International Economics & Politics*, 20(3): 289–334.

Gallagher, M. and Hanson, J.K. (2009) "Coalitions, Carrots, and Sticks: Economic Inequality and Authoritarian States," *Political Science & Politics*, 42(4): 667–672.

Hinnebusch, R. (2006) "Authoritarian Persistence, Democratization Theory and the Middle East: An Overview and Critique," *Democratization*, 13(3): 373–395.

Jbili, A. and Enders, K. (1996) "The Association Agreement between Tunisia and the European Union," *Finance and Development*, 33(3): 18–20.

Meltzer, A.H. and Richard, S.F. (1981) "A Rational Theory of the Size of Government," *Journal of Political Economy*, 89(5): 914–927.

Schofield, N. and Levinson, M. (2008) "Modeling Authoritarian Regimes," *Politics Philosophy & Economics*, 7(3): 243–283.

Schwarz, R. (2008) "The Political Economy of State Formation in the Arab Middle East: Rentier States, Economic Reform, and Democratization," *Review of International Political Economy*, 15(4): 599–621.

Tino, E. (2012) "Le Relazioni Euro-Mediterranee e la Pan-Mediterranean Free Trade Area alla luce della Primavera Araba," *Osservatorio Europeo, La Comunita' Internazionale*, Fascicolo, 3–4(2012): 541–566.

Wen-Chin Wu (2014) "When Do Dictators Decide to Liberalize Trade Regimes? Inequality and Trade Openness in Authoritarian Regimes," *International Studies Quarterly*, 59(4): 790–801.

Appendix

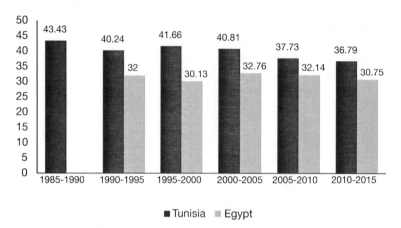

Figure 9.1 Gini Index Trends for Tunisia and Egypt—1985–2015

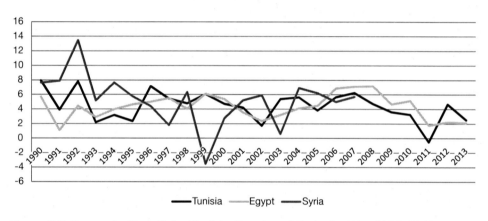

Figure 9.2 Economic Growth for Tunisia, Egypt, and Syria (in %)—1990–2013

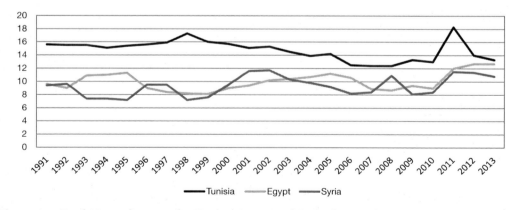

Figure 9.3 Total Unemployment for Tunisa, Egypt, and Syria (in %)—1991–2013

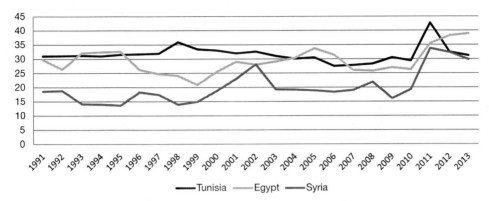

Figure 9.4 Total Youth Unemployment for Tunisia, Egypt, and Syria (in %)—1991–2013

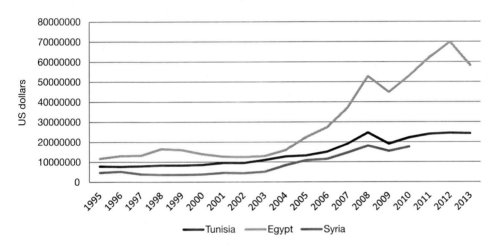

Figure 9.5 Total Imports from the World for Tunisia, Egypt, and Syria—1995–2013

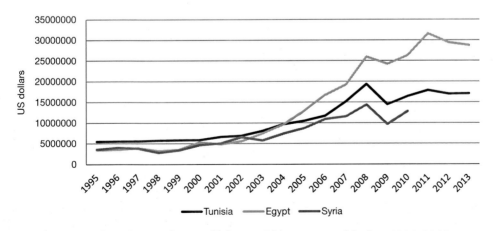

Figure 9.6 Total Exports to the World for Tunisia, Egypt, and Syria—1995–2013

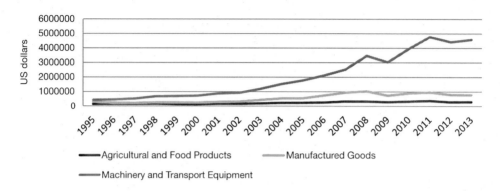

Figure 9.7 Tunisian Exports to the European Market by Sector

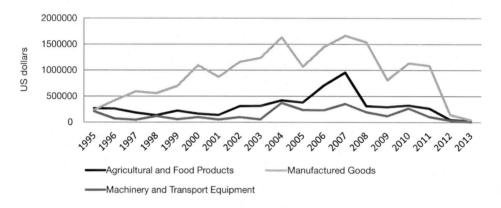

Figure 9.8 Syrian Exports to the European Market by Sector

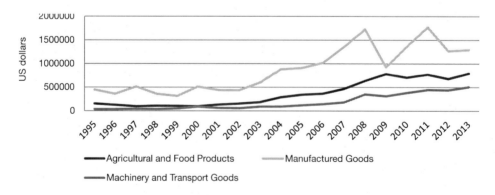

Figure 9.9 Egyptian Exports to the European Market by Sector

Chapter 10

Regional Security and Democratic Transitions: An Alternate Perspective

Barbara Buraczynska

This chapter examines how states' military security environment influences their internal political structures, and the possibility that domestic power centralization within them might depend on the frequency and intensity of their conflict involvement. In the extant literature, the relationship between war participation and regime type has typically been analyzed through the prism of the second image, a level of analysis in international relations that aims to explain interstate hostilities by the domestic makeup of states. The most prominent and appraised of these approaches is democratic peace theory. According to its premises, democracies tend not to engage in war with one another due to their strong normative commitment to peace and mutual respect for other liberal governments, as well as a public accountability for war not observed among other types of regimes. Despite extensive criticism from system-level explanations of war such as neorealism, democratic peace theory remains one of the most influential approaches to the causes of conflict in the field of international relations, and continues to inform security strategies of many liberal states. The idea that democracies are inherently peaceful, despite finding little support in quantitative research to date, has been explicitly stated to be a major inspiration for the US policies of military interventions with the aim of democratizing the target nation. Despite much contestation from both the theory's proponents (Russett 2005) and critics (Rosato 2003), and the low success rate of implanting democracy externally (Downes and Monten 2012), politics of democratization remain high on the list of US security priorities.

The following work will explore an alternative approach to the study of regime type and conflict involvement. It will present evidence that the relationship between government style and war participation might have been approached from the wrong angle, and argue that the causal arrow between democracy and peace ought to be reversed. It is likely that protracted periods of interstate peace within a region, coupled with a host of other favorable conditions, foster democratic transition. If the external conditions of war and peace affect power distribution within a state, the process of decentralization and, ultimately, of regime change cannot take place without stabilizing its regional security situation. Both military and financial efforts to democratize a target state are likely to result in failure.

The chapter will proceed as follows: first, an outline of democratic peace theory (hereafter DPT) will be presented, along with a brief account of how it has shaped the US policy of democracy promotion abroad. DPT will then be critically appraised to demonstrate that the current explanation of the inter-democratic peace is overly reductionist and lacks empirical support. An alternative approach, the reversed second image theory (hereafter ReSIT) will be introduced, providing evidence from recent literature that international conflict hinders democratic transition on both societal and political levels. Finally, the chapter will discuss the implications of ReSIT for the practice of forceful democratization. It will be suggested that external regime imposition through military intervention is unlikely to succeed and the practice should be abandoned in favor of peacekeeping efforts and building stable alliances between the target states and their neighbors. Less intrusive forms of supporting democratization should be approached with caution and never without prior efforts to alleviate the tensions between the target state and the adjoining countries.

Democratic Peace Research

Traditionally, the study of international conflict has been confined to three levels of analysis conceptualized by Kenneth Waltz (1959). These prisms explicate how human nature, domestic structures of states, and the international system explain the existence of wars. The *first image* explicates the effects of inherently corrupt human condition on the outbreaks of interstate disputes. The *second image* aims at explaining wars between nations by studying their political and societal organization. The *third image*, espoused by Waltz himself, sees conflict as a result of competition in a state of perpetual anarchy. The absence of central authority demands that states compete for resources in order to secure their survival. All three approaches are monodirectional in nature and aim solely at explaining the occurrence of war. The second image, domestic structures of states, has ironically become one of the most influential accounts for interstate hostilities, despite being explicitly rejected by Waltz (1959).

In the wake of the fall of the Berlin Wall and the inability of mainstream theory to explain the sudden collapse of the Soviet Union, the first and third levels of analysis (occupying crucial roles for classical and structural strands of realism, respectively) have become increasingly criticized for their inability to explain rapid changes to the international system. The ideological struggle against communist states during the Cold War years has persuaded many that the cause of overly aggressive foreign policies has wrongly been attributed to structural forces, and can instead be ascribed to particular regime characteristics. Concerns about the aggressive nature of authoritarian governments expressed in the wake of the Second World War by many public figures[1] have become almost axiomatic. It was thought that only the spread of representative forms of governance could bring about a more peaceful international environment, a condition that was to be accomplished by policies of forceful and economic democracy promotion around the world.

Early quantitative research has provided strong empirical evidence that democracies can be distinguished by a special, amicable relationship with each other—a phenomenon known as dyadic peace (Babst 1972; Doyle 1983a, 1983b; Rummel 1983). In attempts to explain why representative regimes do not engage in war with one another, scholars have reached for the writings of Immanuel Kant, who theorized the possibility of perpetual peace between republican states (Kant 1975). Kant's explanation for the scarcity of conflict between democracies stems from the notion of accountability inherent in all just, representative regimes. Republics, to what are understood as modern democracies today (Brown 2009), are less likely to go to war without, because conflict results in immense costs in blood and treasure to the people within. The anticipated burden of these losses makes the public innately war-averse. The low costs of monitoring the actions of political actors, coupled with the freedom to publicly voice potential discontent, increase the chances that elected officials will be punished for their aggressive foreign policies. Political leaders, being accountable for their actions to the public, are less likely to engage in hostile actions against other states due to fear of being punished by losing their office. The accountability feature of democracy guarantees a great degree of caution in the manner elites choose to develop their foreign strategies (Doyle 1983a).

Despite its immense normative appeal, the above proposition (termed as the *structural constraints* argument) remains highly problematic. The logic of accountability suggests that democracies ought to be more peaceful toward all forms of governments (monadic peace), not merely in relation to each other (dyadic peace). Given the fact that virtually all conflict demands the sacrifice in human life and vital resources, public opposition to armed struggles should hold regardless of the political nature of the adversary. Nevertheless, representative states have been repeatedly shown to engage in as many wars as authoritarian regimes (Chan 1997; Bueno de Mesquita et al. 1999, 2003; Quackenbush and Rudy 2009).[2] If the logic of *structural constraints* was correct, the fear of domestic consequences of war ought to inhibit conflict not only toward democracies, but also more despotic regimes. The overwhelming number of empirical studies discounting the existence of monadic peace has led the DPT research community to devise an alternative explanation for the scarcity of war between liberal states. In order to "rescue" the premise of democratic pacifism and account for the existence of dyadic peace, a *normative constraints* argument has been constructed (Doyle 1986; Russett 1993; Dixon 1994). Liberal democracies recognize each other as just and legitimate, and therefore accommodate each other when crises emerge. Mutual trust and respect between representative governments is contrasted with their mistrust and enmity toward despotic regimes. Free states tend to be suspicious of autocracies because they expect that the oppressive manner in which they treat their subjects will be externalized to their interaction on an international level. The *normative constraints* proposition attempts to explain why democracies —while peaceful and accommodating toward each other—are as hostile as other regimes during mixed regime conflicts.

Influence on Democracy Promotion

Despite criticism from both supporters and opponents of democratic peace research, the institutional and normative arguments outlined above have helped to shape and maintain the idea that encouraging democratic transitions in politically unstable regions might in time result in reduced chances of interstate conflict (Russett 2005). While DPT research has had a profound impact on the policies of democracy promotion adopted by the subsequent administrations of US presidents, it would be incorrect to attribute the practice of forceful regime change to the theory alone. Advancement of democratic norms and values has been an inherent part of US foreign policy since the state's inception, with a strong base in

Calvinism and the Enlightenment (Poppe 2010: 5; Saito 2010). American exceptionalism, the belief in the special and unique role the US was to play in world history (Restad 2012: 54), has led to the conviction that the New World ought to disseminate its democratic values abroad.

Perhaps the most crucial role of DPT—apart from providing academic grounds for the normative aspects of democracy promotion—was its inspiration for the belief that promoting democratic values abroad is synonymous with the promotion of US national security interests. The assumption was that once democratic, targets of military intervention would eventually become vital US allies. The identification of representative governments with peace and stability led the Bush Administration to believe that a representative Iraq would be free of terrorist threats and illegal weaponry (Desch 2007–2008: 22; Poppe 2010: 13–16). The Bush presidency was explicit in its statements that the pursuit of democracy in the Middle East was more important than achieving order and stability, and that America was willing to accept the turmoil caused by the forceful regime change, which was seen as a natural outcome of democratic transitions (Desch 2007–2008: 22–25). His views run parallel to the previous administration's policy agenda. President Clinton strongly believed that democracy and security are tantamount: "As we help democracy expand, we make ourselves and our allies safer. Democracies rarely go to war with each other or traffic in terrorism" (Clinton 1996: 270). Similar stances on democracy promotion were also assumed by Presidents Harry Truman and Ronald Reagan (Rice 2005).

Despite arguments to the contrary, the policy of democracy promotion has been continued by the Obama Administration since assuming its office in 2009. While Obama's Cairo and UN General Assembly speeches stressed the importance of self-determination of national regimes and expressed the view that democracy ought not to be imposed from the outside (Obama 2009a, 2009b), this rhetorical shift finds little reflection in US foreign policy practice. Obama's approach, while not military in nature, is akin to the stance taken by the Clinton Administration: democracy is to be spread through financial aid and economic incentives (Poppe 2010). According to Freedom House, the requests for foreign aid with the intention of supporting just and democratic governance have increased to a record level of $3.3 billion in 2011 (Poppe 2010). Neither of the previous presidents has ever requested such large sums of money with the intention of supporting democratic transitions abroad. Although the amount has fallen to $2.87 billion between financial years 2012 and 2014 (Trister 2013), it remains at a surprisingly high levels considering the economic constraints imposed on the US as a result of the 2008 financial crisis. It is also likely that future US administrations might resume forced democratization efforts with the intention of securing a strong economic and military bond with the Middle East and other regions vital to its geopolitical interests.

In summary, the two basic premises of DPT are that the institutional makeup of representative systems prevents the elites from engaging in conflict, and that liberal values promoting peace between democratic dyads have had a profound impact on the foreign policy of the United States. In an attempt to secure its strategic interests and increase stability in the Middle East, American officials have pursued the policy of forceful democratization in the region.

Despite being adopted by and widely acclaimed among Western states, democracy promotion as conflict resolution remains highly problematic. Its assumptions rest on a shaky foundation of inconsistent theory and scant empirical support. The next section of this chapter will briefly outline the *structural* and *normative constraints* arguments of DPT and discuss the main logical and empirical controversies associated with the approaches. The chapter will argue that theoretical and practical inconsistencies within democratic peace theory render the practice of forced democratization an inappropriate tool for conflict resolution. It will then proceed to propose an alternative way to approach the relationship between conflict and democracy and the reversed second image theory, discussing its implications for regional security promotion.

Democratic Peace Theory: A Reappraisal

Given that democratic peace theory remains one of the most influential areas of research in international relations today, it is perhaps unsurprising that it has had such a great influence on the foreign policies of Western states. Nevertheless, despite the fact that dyadic peace between representative regimes has been considered almost axiomatic, there is a growing consensus among certain researchers that DPT does not provide a sound explanation for the phenomenon of dyadic peace. The following section will review these claims, arguing that neither structural nor normative constraints arguments can fully account for the scarcity of conflict between democracies. It will be concluded that, first, accountability is not a uniquely democratic feature, and second, that democratic citizens (despite what is often claimed by theorists) have little incentive to oppose international conflict. Finally, it will be shown that democratic norms and values are not universally respected by liberal regimes. It is more likely that trust is only awarded to political allies and does not depend on a state's regime type. The chapter will then proceed to present a different account of why liberal regimes tend to be more pacific in their interactions with other free governments. It will be proposed that reversing the causal arrow between democracy and peace sheds new light on the relationship between regime type and conflict involvement. Long-term stability and the absence of external military threats to the state allow it to decentralize power within, fostering democratic transitions.

Structural Constraints

As demonstrated in the earlier sections of this chapter, the most elementary explanation of democratic peace is the *structural constraints* argument: the notion that separating legislative and executive bodies within a state hinders the aggressive tendencies of political elites by holding them accountable to the public.

First, although the public is thought to oppose international conflict due to its high costs, interstate hostilities have been shown to increase the chances of a widespread spike in patriotism and support of the war effort, leading to the so-called "rally around the flag" effect, with a hawkish public often forcing their governments to adopt more hard-line policies against their enemies. Examples include the reactions of the British public to the 1853–1854 Crimean War and the American public during the 1812 war with Spain (Mueller 1973; Levy 1988; Morgan and Cambell 1991). More recent examples of the "rally around the flag" phenomenon include the events that followed the 9/11 attack on the Twin Towers, with the American public largely in favor of the war that ensued: eight in 10 people supported the 2001 ground war in Afghanistan (Moore 2001). Rosato (2003: 594–595) provides an explanation for why the general population might be so easily swayed in favor of interstate conflict. With the exception of the First and Second World Wars, democratic fatalities have exceeded 0.1 percent of the populace in only 6 percent of all militarized disputes. Most people are not directly affected by war, or know anyone who is, and therefore have little incentive to strongly oppose war—especially if it is endorsed by the state elites. The first pillar of *structural constraints* argument, that citizens will always see it in their best interest to oppose war, remains unconvincing in face of the evidence provided above.

Second, the *structural constraints* argument is based on the idea that democratic officials closely follow public opinion in hopes of retain their seats in the upcoming elections. However, it is often the citizens who form their ideas about war by following the cues from politicians. According to the "elite cue" theory, the public is more likely to form their opinion about foreign affairs based on elite preferences rather than performing a rational cost–benefit analysis of war (Berinsky 2007, 2009). In his study of six major American wars, Berinsky (2009) demonstrated that the public tends to rely on party politics when shaping their attitudes toward war. In the case of the Iraq War, the Democratic Party supporters—initially divided on the issue—only began strongly opposing the war when it started being portrayed as a "Republican" or "Bush war" (Berinsky 2007: 986).

These observations contradict the bottom-up assumption of most democratic peace research, suggesting that instead of following public opinion, political elites might in fact be shaping it. While the elite cue theory cannot fully explain all aspects of the war support dynamic, it runs counter to the DPT assumption that casualties and economic costs of war are the main factors driving public opinion on conflict involvement. Nevertheless, one might assert that to a certain extent, the democratic officials are still somewhat accountable for their actions and therefore more careful in their foreign policy dealings than the average autocrat. As a result, it might appear surprising that a great deal of modern research into authoritarian regimes reveals that the assumption of "free reign" and lack of accountability is largely unfounded.

The evidence shows that not only are authoritarian leaders held accountable, but they are also likely to face more severe punishments for adopting unfavorable policy choices (Escribá-Folch 2013). This misconception results from a belief that all autocratic systems resemble personalist regimes. In fact, most IR researchers who study the effects of regime type on conflict involvement incorrectly infer that all authoritarian governments function in a similar fashion purely by virtue of not being representative. The faulty generalization is made on the basis of a limited sample of highly publicized accounts of personalist regimes such as the ones of Adolf Hitler, Kim Jong-Il, or Idi Amin, where the heads of state had a blank check on initiating political violence (Weeks 2012: 326). However, leaders of military, single-party, or dynastic regimes often rely upon support from political elites who are largely independent from those in direct position of power (Bueno de Mesquita et al. 2003; Weeks 2008, 2012; Ezrow and Frantz 2011).

This "selectorate" frequently controls large portions of state apparatus such as security organs, providing them with means of staging a potential coup or even reducing leaders' capability to punish them for dissent (Weeks 2008: 41; Ezrow and Frantz 2011). Elites in a number of Middle Eastern dynastic regimes distribute their members along a wide range of crucial posts, making them remarkably resilient to internal power shifts—including the change of a monarch; examples include Bahrain, Kuwait, and Qatar (Herb 1999: 8–10). Similarly, the "selectorate" in military and single-party regimes tend to remain in their positions even if the leader is ousted from power. In their case, the lack of personal connection to the head of state guarantees relative security: most USSR party officials retained their offices after ousting Khrushchev precisely due to a lack of personal ties; similarly, the members of the military junta in Argentina have succeeded in ousting three chiefs of state between 1976 and 1983 because military hierarchies played a more important role than personal connections (Weeks 2008: 42).

More importantly, democratic peace research fails to acknowledge that despotic rulers face more severe punishment for unfavorable policy outcomes such as losing a war, making them potentially more cautious in their foreign strategy dealings. As shown by Escribá-Folch (2013), almost half of all authoritarian rulers have faced death, imprisonment, or exile as a result of losing an interstate military conflict between 1946 and 2004. Compared to the prospect of simply losing office—as it is often the case in democratic states—the severity of punishment is much higher in authoritarian regimes. Despotic leaders should be considered to have more incentives than their democratic counterparts to avoid potential conflict (Rosato 2003; Escribá-Folch 2013).

The above analysis makes it clear that fostering democratic change is unlikely to contribute to regional stability by reducing aggressive policies. It is evident from the experiences faced by many transitioning countries such as Afghanistan and Iraq, as well as established democratic regimes such as Israel that they are unlikely to engage in less conflict as a result of their internal structure. Making the officials accountable to the public—although desirable for the sake of democracy itself—is unlikely to make states more peaceful because there is no guarantee that the peace would be desired. Nationalism, ethnic tensions, grievances, and economic deprivation are likely to make people turn to parties that promise violence as a solution to their problems. If the public is opposed or indifferent to conflict, propaganda, and scaremongering are likely to change their minds, especially in regions when war is a commonplace strategy for resolving disputes. It is perhaps unsurprising that there is little empirical support for the existence of monadic peace.

Although it is clear that democracies are unlikely to be more peaceful in general as the *structural constraints* argument would predict, some still believe that representative states (while aggressive toward authoritarian regimes) are unlikely to ever engage in war with one another on account of their shared liberal values. According to this argument, encouraging democratization might not make states more peaceful in general, but two newly democratic states would almost definitely be able to keep the peace with one another. The next section will appraise this *normative constraints* argument, and challenge the idea that liberal values are guarantors of peace.

Normative Constraints

In an attempt to rescue the premise of democracy as an inherently peaceful regime, many scholars have attempted to explain the lack of empirical evidence for monadic peace caused by *structural constraints* by pointing to the apparent absence of trust and respect between mixed regime dyads. Democracies do not recognize authoritarian states as just and deserving of respect so disputes between mixed dyads are more likely to escalate to a full-scale war. Conversely, representative government officials trust other liberal states to prefer peaceful conflict resolution and to accommodate their demands, resulting in lasting amity between democracies: dyadic peace. Nevertheless, the argument for normative constraints dissuading liberal states from engaging in war is hardly convincing. Using the example of covert military operations, the analysis below will demonstrate that democracies do not always award each other the consideration necessary for the formation of a lasting peace, and that geopolitical concerns are often more important to liberal states than values such as trust and respect. If democracies value strategic goals more highly than liberal ideals, then the lack of war between democratic states must be the outcome of something different from their political organization.

First, the history of covert US interventions against other democratic regimes makes it evident that liberal states do not necessarily trust and value fellow regimes when their geopolitical interests are at stake. The forcible removal of legitimate and democratically elected governments in Iran (1953), Guatemala (1954), Indonesia (1950s), Chile (1973), Nicaragua (1980s), and many more calls the sincerity of liberal values into question (Forsythe 1992; Lilley and Downes 2010). Anti-communist sentiment and the desire to surpass the political influence of the Soviet Union during the Cold War seem to have been held in higher regard than the promotion of just and legitimate regimes abroad. More strikingly, perhaps, the liberal US not only disrupted the democratic processes in those states, but also forcefully installed regimes that turned out to be far more oppressive in the long run (Rosato 2003: 591; Forsythe 1992: 387). During the 1957 invasion of Indonesia, "at least some of US concern stemmed from Sukarno's implementation of proportional democracy," which could potentially grant communist parties greater share in the policymaking process (Forsythe 1992: 388). Democratic values were clearly considered secondary to the geopolitical concerns of the Cold War era. The "privilege" of nonintervention and respect is awarded to political allies, rather than democracies more broadly. The history of such operations poses a great threat to consistency of the normative constraint argument. According to DPT scholars, democracies, as legitimate and just regimes, ought to be free from foreign interference and invasion (Doyle 1983a: 230). For the "norms and values" explanation of dyadic peace to hold up to scrutiny, democracies ought not to use any form of coercion—overt or covert—to replace or disrupt a justly elected government (Reiter and Stam 2002: 160). Given that democratic states have used covert action against legally elected leaders, the "norms and values argument" should be used with caution when explaining dyadic peace.

The above analysis has shown that the flaws in the causal logic of both structural and normative arguments of DPT render it an unsatisfactory explanation for the absence of conflicts between representative states. First, the *structural constraints* argument makes hasty and often incorrect assumptions about the differences in political leaders' accountability within democratic and authoritarian regimes. Second, the spike of nationalism often accompanying foreign conflict counters the proposition that the public is inherently war-averse. The level of general support for various military conflicts in the past implies that belligerent leaders are unlikely to be punished for aggressive foreign policies. Third, the logic of the *normative constraints* argument is often contradicted by double standards of international conduct found in inter-democratic relations. The privilege of non-intervention, instead of being granted to fellow democracies, is often given to political allies based on purely strategic considerations. It is evident that democratic norms and values cannot account for mixed regime war if democracies and autocracies can successfully cooperate with each other despite adhering to opposing norms of domestic conduct.

Nevertheless, the overwhelming empirical evidence for the existence of dyadic peace cannot be ignored. If neither structural nor normative premises of DPT can account for the dearth of conflict between democracies, an alternative approach has to be considered. The next section will explore reversed second image theory and present the argument that it is peace that fosters democratic transitions, not the reverse. Frequent conflict occurrence, especially of territorial nature (Gibler 2007) tends to centralize power within affected states and might eventually result in full institutionalization of authoritarian modes of governance. Only by managing interstate disputes in unstable regions is it possible to encourage democratic transitions that ought to happen organically, rather than be forced through by external parties.

Reversed Second Image Theory

Despite the prominence of democratic peace theory in explaining the links between regime type and conflict engagement, it has long been suggested that the arrow of causality between democracy and peace ought to be reversed. Many scholars have hinted at the possibility that lack of international conflict could facilitate democratic transitions, making the "empirical law" of democratic peace spurious (Thompson 1996; Chan 1997: 84; Gibler 2007: 509). External threats are likely to encourage leaders to develop large standing armies, aimed at defending states' territorial integrity. The following section will proceed by briefly reviewing the literature on the links between geopolitical location and the centralization of domestic authority structures, with particular attention given to resource scarcity and border security. It will then turn its focus to more recent research suggesting a strong relationship between violent territorial disputes and the existence of authoritarian governments (Gibler 2007; Gibler and Tir 2010). The section will expand on how the presence of large military, the costs of war, and territorial disputes might affect the state at both societal and elite levels by facilitating oppressive modes of governance and reducing political polarization. Finally, the chapter will move on to exploring the implications of ReSIT on the practice and theory of democracy promotion.

The idea that external factors could influence the domestic organization of states is not a novel one, although it has not received much attention from the research community. Until very recently, the Waltzian imposition of the three levels of analysis in the study of international relations (Waltz 1959) has greatly limited the capacity of reverse causality theories to account for internal structures of states. Most research, confined to either Marxist, realist, or liberal approaches, has become monodirectional in nature. Such monodirectionality is a hurdle to sound theoretical development and might possibly explain why research puzzles such as democratic peace have not yet been properly accounted for. This is because traditional approaches obscure the possibility of endogeneity between key variables, presenting the world in an overly reductionist fashion. The research community has placed focus on how the individual, the state, or the international system might explain war occurrence, but have failed to account for the possibility that either of these levels could have a reverse relationship with military conflicts. Fortunately, the advent of severe criticism directed at the premises of democratic peace (Layne 1994; Spiro 1994; Schwartz and Skinner 2002) has led many to pursue the possibility of a reversed causality between conflict and autocratic structures.

One of the earliest theories on the links between environmental factors and regime structures is Wittfogel's (1957) work on "hydraulic civilizations." Wittfogel theorized that scarcity of certain resources might have contributed to the development of autocracies in early communities and demonstrated that authoritarian structures might have arisen from the need to manage irrigation waters in zones of high aridity. The high demand for extremely scarce resources might have led to centralized forms of redistribution and ultimately contributed to the development of more despotic polities. The lack of control over vital supplies eased the imposition of oppressive structures on the general population by the ruling classes (Wittfogel 1957: 154).

Midlarsky (1995) has taken Wittfogel's (1957) theory further by investigating how not only rainfall, but also the number of sea borders, affects the likelihood of democratic development in Sumer, Mesoamerica, Crete, and China. The most crucial part of the investigation was the consideration that a high proportion of sea borders minimizes the threat of war from rival settlements. In earlier analyses, certain peninsular and island states such as Sri Lanka, Jamaica, Greece, Ireland, or Malaysia had exhibited levels of democracy that were too large to be predicted by domestic variables such as economic development, trade, land scarcity levels, or the lack of domestic violence. Coincidentally, the high proportion of sea borders was also correlated with the low international conflict participation and relatively low size of the army (Midlarsky 1995: 237). The conclusion offered was that low levels of military threat in states insulated by large bodies of water somehow contribute to their democratic development. This point is supported by Thompson (1996), who later suggested that zones of peace, likely to be enforced by extensive sea borders, often preceded democratic progress in early European states. These cooperative niches were insulated from aggressive regional geopolitics and therefore less likely to be threatened by war (Thompson 1996: 142). Furthermore, Midlarsky (1995: 238) has found that a high number of sea borders is highly correlated with a relatively small military as compared to states with many territorial frontiers. These findings conform with earlier theories (i.e. Gourevitch 1978) on how the expanding number and presence of the military personnel within a state could lead to more authoritarian modes of governance.

An extensive army presence as a result of poor geopolitical location provides several ways to concentrate domestic power and facilitate autocratic structures. First, during protracted periods of external threats, the army is likely to start occupying a special role within the state and help the leader to maintain his power position in times of public discontent, as mentioned in the case of Prussia above (Hintze 1994: 193). The more powerful the army, the easier it is to suppress the dissidents at a very low cost to the ruling elites. Second, in line with the resource scarcity argument outlined earlier in this section, the army is likely to require a sizeable portion of supplies and monetary resources in order to properly defend the territory at risk of foreign attack. Protracted conflicts impede economic growth and, in more extreme circumstances, lead to a shortage of vital supplies and high levels of taxation (Gibler and Tir 2010). Resource deficits are likely to result in more authoritarian and centralized forms of redistribution (Midlarsky 1995; Gibler 2007). In a war-torn economy, the costs of adopting a representative system and redistributing the few goods available to the poor become much higher than the costs of "using the army to pursue a strategy of exclusion and suppress competing social groups" (Gibler 2007: 514).

Aside from high resource expenditure and the pacifying effects of standing armies, conflicts tend to reduce polarization among the elites and the public. First, on a societal level, the threat of violent clashes with neighboring states results in a rallying effect among the public. War is a form of a public good that cannot be enforced if citizens are allowed to maximize their own utility. Certain prerogatives (i.e. freedom of speech, financial security, or even the right to survival) are expected to be given up to secure the collective interest of winning a battle (James et al. 1999: 7). If people are willing to sacrifice their lives to secure a victory, they are also very likely to temporarily "suspend" many of their rights and privileges. The need for safety and security is likely to override the less fundamental need for freedom and self-actualization (Maslow 1954). Undeniably, in wartime, there is a significant increase in tolerance for state actions typically considered reprehensible. Over prolonged periods of time, these mechanisms are likely to become institutionalized and develop into a permanent feature of the regime under threat.

Second, on the elite level, external threats are likely to result in unification of the otherwise polarized elites (Gibler 2010: 520–524). The opposition is likely to lose its bargaining power as a result of conflict, making it easier for the leader to expand and consolidate his or her influence. When faced with salient external threats such as territorial conflict, political rivals of the incumbent ruler are faced with two options: they can either continue opposing the government's policies, risking defeat in war (and, potentially, foreign occupation), or they can temporarily back their opponents in order to avoid power fragmentation and secure a swift victory. Given that the debilitated bargaining position of opponents results in weaker checks on the executive power, opportunistic political leaders are likely to take advantage of their newly acquired autonomy and increase their influence by consolidating power (Bueno de Mesquita et al. 2003; Gibler 2010: 526).

Correspondingly, the absence of military conflict and a stable security environment reduces the need for a unified national and political front. In the long term, under an absence of salient threats, the opposition might proceed to question the *raison d'être* of centralized political power and as a result attempt to increase their bargaining position. If the opposition is successful and other necessary conditions are satisfied, these changes might lead to a process of democratization. Although the absence of exogenous threats cannot be seen as a guarantee of democratic transition, it might be a factor that significantly increases the likelihood for its occurrence (Thompson 1996: 144).

Territorial Conflicts

Although a large proportion of the literature on the links between external threats and domestic power centralization concerns early civilization and state formation periods (Gourevitch 1978; Hintze 1994; Midlarsky 1995; Thompson 1996), it is likely that protracted military conflicts continue to shape internal state structures. Recent studies of modern regimes suggest a strong relationship between zones of peace and the development of democratic societies. The key to explaining the dearth of war between democracies is to understand which military conflicts are likely to be of most significance to the states involved. Research on issue salience suggests that disputes arising from territorial feuds are perceived as the most threatening. Land is critical for nations' identity, security, and prosperity (Gibler 2007: 510). Border issues are also most likely to result in the highest number of casualties (Senese and Vasquez 2003) and are least likely to be settled without resorting to violence (Vasquez 1995; Gibler 2010: 521). Lack of territorial disputes between states is most likely to result in decentralization of power and ultimately lead to democratic transitions. Much of the extant literature demonstrates that democracy is a symptom, rather than a cause, of the lack of land feuds between neighboring countries. Liberal regimes were shown to have stabilized their borders *prior* to becoming democratic, which would explain why there are virtually no wars between them (Gibler 2007, 2014; Gibler and Tir 2010, 2014). The phenomenon of dyadic peace can be easily explained by the fact that "rarely are disputes between democracies over issues of much consequence; and rarely, if ever, do these disputes target their homeland territories" (Gibler 2014: 129).

In summary, external threats, especially those arising as a result of territorial disputes, tend to have a centralizing effect on domestic power distribution. Large standing armies provide the elites with means of suppressing dissent and help them hold on to scarce resources, placing them in a position of power. The prospect of military defeat reduces political polarization at both societal and elite levels, leading to increased support for government actions that would normally be considered unacceptable. Protracted territorial disputes and interstate wars lead to the consolidation of authoritarian structures and formation of stable autocratic regimes. Conversely, ReSIT suggests that peaceful resolution of territorial disputes occurs prior to democratization. Authoritarian regimes are likely to lose their *raison d'être* in stable security environments and eventually begin democratizing as a result of lasting peace. Since a vast majority of interstate wars occur between neighboring states, it is perhaps unsurprising that democracies virtually never fight each other. They are likely to have settled their border issues long before democratization occurred.

Implications and Conclusion

The findings of ReSIT have significant implications for both the theoretical and practical aspects of democratization. First, they elucidate some of the mechanisms responsible for democratic and authoritarian regime transitions, many aspects of which are still somewhat confounding to the research community. Accounts of democratization should, by now, be "parsimonious and compelling" yet are instead plentiful, inconsistent, and largely descriptive in nature (Geddes 1999: 117, 2003). This is not to say that the continuous presence of external threats is the sole or most significant factor in accounting for centralized forms of government. Yet the discovery of the links between territorial conflicts and authoritarianism should certainly be considered as crucial, along with economic development, societal homogeneity, or past experiences with representative forms of government (Downes and Monten 2012). The reversed second image theory can certainly help to uncover some essential links between regional security and the prospect of future democratization.

Second, reversed second image theory helps identify some of the reasons why democratization efforts—whether by military, economic, or diplomatic means—have been shown to be ineffective. In the past, many scholars have argued that in the case of post-2003 Iraq, failures to liberalize the state were failures of implementation and not the principle of democratization itself. According to these arguments, the inability to fully commit to democracy culminated in the breakdown of civil order and mass violations of human rights. The problem was rooted in the fact that the US has acted as an occupant force rather than a liberator (Zunes 2007). Others point out that "Iraq became a hole of instability" not as a result of forced regime change, but the fact that not enough troops were deployed in order to "secure peace" (Diamond 2005: 279, 285). Nevertheless, as suggested by the reversed second image theory outlined above, it is likely that authoritarianism in the Middle East might have its roots in unresolved territorial feuds between neighbors in the region. Iraq has a history of military disputes over locations considered vital to its strategic interests: the Shatt-al-Arab region between Iraq and Iran and the Bubiyan and Warbah islands between Iraq and Kuwait— neither of which have been settled by a peaceful territorial transfer, adding to existing tensions between neighbors. Moreover, Iraq, like many states within the area, has national boundaries that hardly correspond to the population within: a remnant of the post-World War I order. The native Shia population is split between Iraq and Kuwait, while the Kurdish people have been arbitrarily divided between Iraq, Iran, and Turkey.

Finally, the theory offers some insight into the dangers of relying on democratic transitions to enforce regional peace. Attempts to make Middle Eastern states more placid are highly unlikely to succeed. The promise of democratic peace has persuaded various political figures that a change in regime would solve territorial disputes, and democratization has been treated as a panacea for regional conflict. Israeli Prime Minister Benjamin Netanyahu was convinced that encouraging democratic changes in Palestine was more important than peace talks as part of the Oslo accords: a belief that had an immense impact on both the US and Israeli approaches to the Israeli–Palestinian conflict (Ish-Shalom 2006: 582–584). Prioritizing regime transition over peacekeeping and diplomatic efforts to solve interstate feuds is likely to continue escalating the tension in the region. If the United States and Israel genuinely care about the promotion of liberal values across the Middle East, they should focus their attention on resolving the conflicts between the Jewish state and Palestine, Syria, and Lebanon. If democracy is truly to be achieved in the region, it cannot be treated as a means of advancing US strategic interests. Human rights, political representation, and personal freedoms need to be viewed as ends in themselves. They can only be achieved by encouraging peaceful means of dispute solving between neighboring states, rather than engaging in military interventions. Military threats cannot lead to democratization because, by their very nature, they tend to centralize domestic power distribution. Institutions and laws can be enforced and imposed, but they are doomed to remain inefficient if the target state is not provided with basic military security.

Notes

1. The argument that democracies are more peaceful than autocracies has been voiced by US President Woodrow Wilson, US Senator Robert Taft, US President Dwight Eisenhower, and many other democratic politicians in the United States and Europe (Waltz 1959: 7–9).
2. See also: Dixon (1994), Maoz and Abdolali (1989), Maoz and Russett (1993), Russett and Monsen (1975), Small and Singer (1976), Chan (1997), Weede (1984), and Wright (1965). For the argument suggesting that democracies *are* more peaceful than autocracies, see Rummel (1983, 1995), Benoit (1996), and Rousseau et al. (1996).

References

Babst, D.V. (1972) "A Force for Peace," *Industrial Research*, April 14: 55–58.

Benoit, K. (1996) "Democracies Really Are More Pacific (in General): Re-examining Regime Type and War Involvement," *Journal of Conflict Resolution*, 40(4): 636–657.

Berinsky, A.J. (2007) "Assuming the Costs of War: Events, Elites and American Public Support for Military Conflict," *Journal of Politics*, 69(4): 975–997.

Berinsky, A.J. (2009) *In Time of War: Understanding American Public Opinion from World War II to Iraq*, Chicago, IL: University of Chicago Press.

Brown, G.W. (2009) *Grounding Cosmopolitanism: From Kant to the Idea of a Cosmopolitan Constitution*, Edinburgh: Edinburgh University Press.

Bueno de Mesquita, B., Morrow, J.D., Siverson, R.M., and Smith, A. (1999) "An Institutional Explanation of the Democratic Peace," *American Political Science Review*, 93(4): 791–807.

Bueno de Mesquita, B., Morrow, J.D., Siverson, R.M., and Smith, A. (2003) *The Logic of Political Survival*, Cambridge, MA: MIT Press.

Chan, S. (1997) "In Search of Democratic Peace: Problems and Promise," *Mershon International Studies Review*, 41(1): 59–91.

Clinton, B. (1996) *Preface to the Presidency: Selected Speeches of Bill Clinton, 1974–1992*, compiled and edited by S.A. Smith, Fayetteville, AR: University of Arkansas Press.

Desch, M.C. (2007–2008) "America's Liberal Illiberalism: The Ideological Origins of Overreaction in US Foreign Policy," *International Security*, 32(3): 7–43.

Diamond, L. (2005) *Squandered Victory: The American Occupation and the Bungled Effort to Bring Democracy to Iraq*, New York: Owl Books.

Dixon, W. (1994) "Democracy and the Peaceful Settlement of International Conflict," *American Political Science Review*, 88(1): 14–32.

Downes, A.B. and Monten, J. (2012) "Forced to Be Free? Why Foreign-Imposed Regime Change Rarely Leads to Democratization," *International Security*, 37(4): 90–131.

Doyle, M.W. (1983a) "Kant, Liberal Legacies and Foreign Affairs: Part 1," *Philosophy and Public Affairs*, 12(3): 205–235.

Doyle, M.W. (1983b) "Kant, Liberal Legacies and Foreign Affairs: Part 2," *Philosophy and Public Affairs*, 12(4): 323–353.

Doyle, M.W. (1986) "Liberalism and World Politics," *American Political Science Review*, 80(4): 1151–1169.

Escribá-Folch, A. (2013) "Accountable for What? Regime Types, Performance, and the Fate of Outgoing Dictators, 1946–2004," *Democratization*, 20(1): 160–185.

Ezrow, N.M. and Franz, E. (2011) *Dictators and Dictatorships: Understanding Authoritarian Regimes and Their Leaders*, New York: Continuum International Publishing Group.

Forsythe, D.P. (1992) "Democracy, War, and Covert Action," *Journal of Peace Research*, 29(4): 385–395.

Geddes, B. (1999) "What Do We Know About Democratization After Twenty Years?" *Annual Review of Political Science*, 2(1): 115–144.

Geddes, B. (2003) *Paradigms and Sand Castles: Theory Building and Research Design in Comparative Politics*, Ann Arbor, MI: University of Michigan Press.

Gibler, D.M. (2007) "Bordering on Peace: Democracy, Territorial Issues, and Conflict," *International Studies Quarterly*, 51(3): 509–532.

Gibler, D.M. (2010) "Outside-In: The Effects of External Threat on State Centralization," *Journal of Conflict Resolution*, 54(4): 519–542.

Gibler, D.M. (2014) "Contiguous States, Stable Borders, and the Peace Between Democracies," *International Studies Quarterly*, 58(1): 126–129.

Gibler, D.M. and Tir, J. (2010) "Settled Borders and Regime Type: Democratic Transitions as Consequences of Peaceful Territorial Transfers," *American Journal of Political Science*, 54(4): 951–968.

Gibler, D.M. and Tir, J. (2014) "Territorial Peace and Democratic Clustering," *The Journal of Politics*, 76(1): 27–40.

Gourevitch, P. (1978) "The Second Image Reversed: The International Sources of Domestic Politics," *International Organization*, 32(4): 881–912.

Herb, M. (1999) *All in the Family: Absolutism, Revolution, and Democracy in the Middle Eastern Monarchies*, Albany, NY: State University of New York Press.

Hintze, O. (1994) "Military Organization and the Organization of the State," in J.A. Hall (Ed.), *The State: Critical Concepts, Volume 1*, London: Routledge, pp. 181–202.

Ish-Shalom, P. (2006) "Theory as a Hermeneutical Mechanism: The Democratic-Peace Thesis and the Politics of Democratization," *European Journal of International Relations*, 12(4): 565–598.

James, P., Solberg, E., and Wolfson, M. (1999) "An Identified Systemic Model of the Democracy-Peace Nexus," *Defence and Peace Economics*, 10(1): 1–37.

Kant, I. (1975) *Perpetual Peace: A Philosophical Essay*, London: Allen & Unwin.

Layne, C. (1994) "Kant or Cant: The Myth of the Democratic Peace," *International Security*, 19(2): 5–49.

Levy, J.S. (1988) "Domestic Politics and War," *Journal of Interdisciplinary History*, 18(4): 653–673.

Lilley, M.L. and Downes, A.B. (2010) "Overt Peace, Covert War? Covert Intervention and the Democratic Peace," *Security Studies*, 19(2): 266–306.

Maslow, A.H. (1954) *Motivation and Personality*, New York: Harper & Row.

Maoz, Z. and Abdolali, N. (1989) "Regime Types and International Conflict, 1816–1976," *Journal of Conflict Resolution*, 33(1): 3–35.

Maoz, Z. and Russett, B. (1993) "Normative and Structural Causes of Democratic Peace, 1946–1986," *American Political Science Review*, 87(3): 624–638.

Midlarsky, M.I. (1995) "Environmental Influences on Democracy: Aridity, Warfare, and a Reversal of the Causal Arrow," *Journal of Conflict Resolution*, 39(2): 224–262.

Moore, D.W. (2001) "Eight of 10 Americans Support Ground War in Afghanistan," *Gallup*, available at: www.gallup.com/poll/5029/eight-americans-support-ground-war-afghanistan.aspx (accessed July 20, 2014).

Morgan, T.C. and Campbell, S.H. (1991) "Domestic Structure, Decisional Constraints, and War: So Why Kant Democracies Fight?" *Journal of Conflict Resolution*, 35(2): 187–211.

Mueller, J.E. (1973) *War, Presidents, and Public Opinion*, New York: Wiley.

Obama, B. (2009a) "Remarks by the President on a New Beginning," Cairo University, Egypt, June 4.

Obama, B. (2009b) "Remarks by the President to the United Nations General Assembly," New York, September 23.

Poppe, A.E. (2010) *Whither To, Obama? US Democracy Promotion After the Cold War*, Frankfurt: Peace Research Institute, Report No. 96.

Quackenbush, S.L. and Rudy, M. (2009) "Evaluating the Monadic Democratic Peace," *Conflict Management and Peace Science*, 26(3): 268–285.

Reiter, D. and Stam, A.C. (2002) *Democracies at War*, Princeton, NJ: Princeton University Press.

Restad, H.E. (2012) "Old Paradigms in History Die Hard in Political Science: US Foreign Policy and American Exceptionalism," *American Political Thought*, 1(1): 53–76.

Rice, C. (2005) "The Promise of Democratic Peace: Why Promoting Freedom Is the Only Realistic Path to Security," *Washington Post*, December 11, available at: http://instructional1.calstatela.edu/tclim/F11_Courses/Rice-the_Promise_of_Democratic_Peace%20copy.pdf (accessed July 20, 2014).

Rosato, S. (2003) "The Flawed Logic of Democratic Peace Theory," *American Political Science Review*, 97(4): 585–602.

Rousseau, D.L., Gelpi, C., Reiter, D., and Huth, P.K. (1996) "Assessing the Dyadic Nature of the Democratic Peace, 1918–88," *American Political Science Review*, 90(3): 512–533.

Rummel, R.J. (1983) "Libertarianism and International Violence," *Journal of Conflict Resolution*, 27(1): 27–71.

Rummel, R.J. (1995) "Democracies ARE Less Warlike Than Other Regimes," *European Journal of International Relations*, 1(4): 457–479.

Russett, B.M. (1993) *Grasping the Democratic Peace: Principles for a Post-Cold War World*, Princeton, NJ: Princeton University Press.

Russett, B.M. (2005) "Bushwhacking the Democratic Peace," *International Studies Perspectives*, 6(4): 395–408.

Russett, B.M. and Monsen, R.J. (1975) "Bureaucracy and Polyarchy as Predictors of Performance: A Cross-National Examination," *Comparative Political Studies*, 8(1): 5–31.

Saito, N.T. (2010) *Meeting the Enemy: American Exceptionalism and International Law*, New York: New York University Press.

Schwartz, T. and Skinner, K.K. (2002) "The Myth of the Democratic Peace," *Orbis*, 46(1): 159–172.

Senese, P.D. and Vasquez, J.A. (2003) *The Steps to War: An Empirical Study*, Princeton, NJ: Princeton University Press.

Small, M. and Singer, J.D. (1976) "The War-Proneness of Democratic Regimes, 1816–1965," *Jerusalem Journal of International Relations*, 1(4): 50–69.

Spiro, D. (1994) "The Insignificance of the Liberal Peace," *International Security*, 19(2): 50–86.

Thompson, W.R. (1996) "Democracy and Peace: Putting the Cart before the Horse?" *International Organization*, 50(1): 141–174.

Trister, S. (2013) "Investing in Freedom: Democracy Support in the US Budget," *Freedom House*, available at: http://www.freedomhouse.org/sites/default/files/Policy%20Brief%207-22-13%20 Investing%20in%20Freedom%20-Democracy%20Support%20in%20the%20U.S.%20Budget.pdf (accessed July 20, 2014).

Vasquez, J.A. (1995) "Why Do Neighbors Fight? Proximity, Interaction, or Territoriality," *Journal of Peace Research*, 32(3): 277–293.

Waltz, K.N. (1959) *Man, the State and War*, New York: Columbia University Press.

Weede, E. (1984) "Democracy and War Involvement," *Journal of Conflict Resolution*, 28(4): 649–664.

Weeks, J.L. (2008) "Autocratic Audience Costs: Regime Type and Signalling Resolve," *International Organization*, 62(1): 35–64.

Weeks, J.L. (2012) "Strongmen and Straw Men: Authoritarian Regimes and the Initiation of International Conflict," *American Political Science Review*, 106(2): 326–347.

Wittfogel, K.A. (1957) *Oriental Despotism: A Comparative Study of Total Power*, New Haven, CT: Yale University Press.

Wright, Q. (1965) *A Study of War* (2nd ed.), Chicago, IL: University of Chicago Press.

Zunes, S. (2007) "Iraq: The Failures of Democratization," *Foreign Policy in Focus*, available at: http://fpif.org/iraq_the_failures_of_democratization/ (accessed July 20, 2014).

Chapter 11

Democracy and State Constitutionalism: The Quest for "Good Governance" in Bangladesh

Sayed Javed Ahmad and Scott Nicholas Romaniuk

Introduction

Since becoming an independent state, Bangladesh has had limited success with democracy. The state has repeatedly faced challenges with the democratic process and its democratic political system, and even found itself in political, social, and economic chaos. Thus, an indication has emerged that something very wrong is being done, and that if this practice continues, then Bangladesh will continue to fail in its struggle to achieve a peaceful and democratic future. In spite of the fact that government is expected to be inherently "good," the opposite has, more often than not, characterized the Bangladeshi political scene. The term "good governance" is currently permeating all levels of Bangladeshi society. This buzzword is typically contrasted with the term "bad governance," according to various criteria. So what is "good governance"? The terms "governance" and "good governance" are increasingly being used in development literature. Governance can be seen as constituting the decision-making process and the implementation of decisions. Thus, public institutions conduct public affairs, manage public resources, and guarantee the realization of human rights in accordance with its fundamental and underlying principles and values. Good governance accomplishes this in a manner essentially free of abuse and corruption, and with due regard for rule of law, political integrity, openness, fairness, and a plethora of other democratic values deemed necessary for the positive and constructive functioning of any progressive society.

In accordance with the United Nations Economic and Social Commission for Asia and the Pacific (UNESCAP), good governance has eight major characteristics: (1) participation;

(2) consensus orientation; (3) accountability; (4) transparency; (5) responsiveness; (6) effectiveness and efficiency; (7) equitability and inclusion; and (8) following the rule of law. These elements, when implemented and practiced as intended by UNESCAP, assure that corruption is minimized, the views of minorities are taken into account, and the voices of the most vulnerable in society are heard in decision-making processes. Most importantly, however, these factors are responsive to the present and future needs of society.

This chapter considers the need for "good governance" and presents a picture of how to begin addressing the state of political disorder that regrettably characterizes contemporary Bangladesh. It may be accurately stated that the present political parties operating in the country represent the root cause of the problem of "bad governance." Accordingly, this chapter attempts to demonstrate the direct link between poor governance and political party-based government.

The Constitution as a Foundation

Since a constitution is an important guiding force in any stable and democratic state, it is therefore important to analyze this document to determine what guidance might exist for Bangladesh to achieve a state of "good governance" and to fully ascertain which tools and mechanisms are available in this quest. Even though the constitution of Bangladesh is a readily available document, it is very much neglected by political party members; as a result, various violations can periodically be observed in local news headlines across the country.

The constitution is a very readable document and the concepts presented therein are quite clear and straightforward. The preamble of the constitution of Bangladesh begins with the proclamation of independence to establish the sovereign People's Republic of Bangladesh, pledging that the high ideals of absolute trust and faith in the Almighty Allah, nationalism, democracy, and socialism meaning economic and social justice shall be fundamental principles of the constitution and the future of the country as a stable democratic state. The fundamental aim of the state is to realize, through the democratic process, a society that is inclusive and free from exploitation—a society in which the rule of law, fundamental human rights, and freedom, equality, and justice (political, economic, and social)—will be secured for all citizens. It is also the duty of all Bangladesh citizens to maintain the constitution's supremacy as the embodiment of the will of the people of Bangladesh so that every man, woman, and child may prosper in freedom and may make a full contribution toward international peace and cooperation in keeping with the progressive aspirations of humankind.

For the sake of clarity, it is necessary to review some of the passages from the Constitution in order to obtain a more nuanced understanding of the importance of this document and what it really embodies:

> **Duties of Citizens and of Public Servants.**
> (1) It is the duty of every citizen to observe the Constitution and the laws, to maintain discipline, to perform public duties and to protect public property.
> (2) Every person in the service of the Republic has a duty to strive at all times to serve the people . . .
>
> **Supremacy of the Constitution**
> (1) All powers in the Republic belong to the people, and their exercise on behalf of the people shall be effected only under, and by the authority of, this Constitution.

(2) This Constitution is, as the solemn expression of the will of the people, the supreme law of the Republic, and if any other law is inconsistent with this Constitution and other law shall, to the extent of the inconsistency, be void.

From the above passages, it is clear that the Constitution is regarded as the source of laws, and that the civil servants are instructed to strive to meet not only the needs, but also the demands, of the people. The Constitution acknowledges that "the people," which includes politicians, are the source of all powers in a republic through solemn expression of the will of the people. Any contradictions with the Constitution should, therefore, be seen as a negative force in progressive democratic societies.

Strangely, many government officials are not fully aware of precisely what the Constitution contains as they are the product of an educational system that does not place emphasis on learning the particulars of the Constitution. This reality raises an important question: How can government officials be expected to appropriately run and operate the government without knowing and understanding the provisions within the Constitution?

Democracy and Human Rights

Underlying the will of the citizens of Bangladesh, Part 2 of the Constitution states:

> The Republic shall be a democracy in which fundamental human rights and freedoms and respect for the dignity and worth of the human person shall be guaranteed, and in which effective participation by the people through their elected representatives in administration at all levels shall be ensured (International Relations and Security Network [ISN]).

According to Sami (2008), the Constitution of Bangladesh provides for a parliamentary system of government with a unicameral legislature on a modified Westminster model (British model). The members of the legislature (the Jatiyo Sangsad or the National Parliament) are elected by universal adult suffrage. A member who the president feels commands the confidence of the majority in the parliament is invited to be the prime minister (PM). The cabinet is headed by the prime minister who selects the ministers to be appointed by the president. The president is the head of the state and "executive actions" of the state are taken in "the name of the president." But "all executive powers" are vested in the prime minister. The constitution provides for a powerful and strong prime minister and the presidency is largely a ceremonial office. In the exercise of "all his functions" except for the appointment of the prime minister and the Chief Justice of the Supreme Court, the president is obliged to act in accordance with the "advice of the prime minister."

While the Constitution provides for a powerful and strong prime minister, the presidency remains largely a ceremonial office. In the exercise of "all his functions" except for the appointment of the prime minister and the Chief Justice of the Supreme Court, the president is obliged to act in accordance with the "advice of the Prime Minister." The president cannot dismiss the PM; he does not have the power to dissolve parliament, except on the advice the PM. The president is also the Supreme Commander of the Armed Forces for Bangladesh, and has the prerogative of mercy and can grant pardon, remit, and suspend or commute any sentence. In these areas too, he acts on the advice of the PM. In spite of the fact that the president can seemingly act only on the advice of the PM, it is clear that the president is absolved of a great deal of accountability and has the luxury of acting in a manner that is conducive to mere semi-transparency in political terms. Thus, in this context, the political system in Bangladesh, despite the democratic rhetoric encapsulated in the Constitution, is exceptionally "managed" and has undergone a drastic political wardrobe change.

A president's service is limited to two five-year terms, but in the case of the PM, there is no limit to service, whereas the PM is more powerful than the president. Therefore, the PM needs to act in accordance with the proper values that any democracy in Western society would demand; this includes dignity and honor to ultimately ensure a practice based on the idea of "good governance." Unfortunately, however, no qualifying criteria are established in the constitution for this very post.

Structure of the Bangladesh Government

As every modern state or nation is built on some sort of government foundation or framework, it is the character of such an established framework that will essentially dictate the nature in which that body governs.

The government of Bangladesh was founded along the Western model of democracy. Bangladesh is a democratic government with a federal/parliamentary system under the overall authority of the PM. However, the practice of this parliamentary democracy is further questionable in this country, as the so-called "checks and balances" are virtually nonexistent in a political party-based government. The Legislature, Judiciary, and the Executive are the three major power structures in the Bangladesh governmental system, seemingly independent from one another and supposedly functioning without any political influence from external factors. However, in reality, there exists a great deal of interference by the political party-based governments in these governmental organs influencing the decisions and policies by political interest groups. This state now symbolizes only a single piece amid many in the mosaic of illiberal democracy across the Asian map. Dyer (2007) characterized the state of democratic decline in the region in these terms:

> Two steps forward, one step back. Thailand's democracy has now given way to military rule, and democracy in the Philippines isn't looking too healthy either. But nothing compares with the fall from grace of Bangladesh, which is usually ranked among the five most corrupt countries in the world by Transparency International.

The political groups that are presently taking advantage of the manner in which the system is set up and exploiting national resources influence the power organs of the government. The so-called "Separation of Power" has fizzled out before it was even given a chance to fuel the democratic growth of Bangladesh, as appointments operating at top levels are made by the party in power, thus positioning the candidates of their choosing. Different power organs of the government are discussed in the following pages in order to piece together a clearer understanding of how they were meant to work and how they actually function. As such, a comparison of theory and practice will be employed in the following sections of this chapter.

The theoretical diagram (Table 11.1) provides an understanding of the process of governance in Bangladesh; however, the reality is that the political party in power influences every sector at that particular time. No matter what party holds power or enters into a situation of power in the country, the scenario is the same. Since the political party in power appoints ministers, the government tends to empower its best and most reliable employees regardless of their background and qualifications. All the high-level appointments such as the

Table 11.1 Present and Proposed Constitutional Provisions

Serial No.	Present Situation	Proposed Plan
1	There is a powerless president.	The president will exercise real power as the head of the government of Bangladesh.
2	There is a PM.	The new system will see the removal of the PM and the end of prime ministerial power completely.
3	There are various "ministers" for different ministries.	There will be a "chairperson" for different councils heading a ministry.
4	There is a presidential election, and the president appoints the prime minister.	There will a presidential election and there will also be independent council elections for chairmanship and formation of board of directors.
5	The president is the chancellor of all the universities throughout Bangladesh.	A president or chancellor would be appointed to each university throughout Bangladesh.
6	The PM appoints the ministers.	The chairperson would be pre-qualified by his council members.
7	The chairpersons are selected electorally.	The chairperson will be an appointed position selected through competitive merit to ensure appropriate appointments.
8	Civil servants enjoy a sense of semi-permanency.	No such notion will exist in this context.
9	There is unrest in the general public lifestyle due to strikes (herbals).	There will be no need for any of them as there will be no political parties to call for.
10	Foreign elements influence political parties.	Leadership will not be untrammeled, as international accountability can help to ensure that leadership and governmentality is consistent with the democratic principles as they were established in the Constitution.
11	There is open and hidden competition among the political parties to gain and stay in power.	There will be no such "power" to fight, as all citizens would participate in the political and democratic process at will.
12	The peoples of Bangladesh have become politically, socially, and culturally disconnected and are characterized by general disunity.	The establishment of a coherent and leadership-centric system of government is a critical mechanism for facilitating a greater sense of unity among the peoples of Bangladesh, including its diaspora.
13	Every five years, before the new election, the CTG intervenes and addresses the issues left over by the previous administration.	There will be no need for the caretaker government to intervene.

Table 11.1 *continued*

Serial No.	Present Situation	Proposed Plan
14	When the political scene deteriorates, the military intervenes with frequent declarations of martial law.	The martial law concept would be closely tied with the right of *habeas corpus*. The adoption of the Canadian-style Emergencies Act would ensure that a declaration of an emergency would have to be reviewed by ministers, and that any temporary laws enacted under the Act would be subject to the provisions as established in the Constitution.
15	Corruption remains relatively uncontrolled and unaddressed within the political system.	All appointments shall be on the basis of fair competition and on merit. Besides, there will be no permanency of jobs.
16	Due to the five-year term of the party-based government, many long-term projects and plans go unfulfilled after a new administration assumes power, which results in financial loss.	Decisions taken at council by members of council can ensure the continuation of projects approved under the previous administration.

Chief Justice of the Supreme Court are made in accordance with the tradition of political influence. As a result of this process, it can be safely argued that the overall neutrality of the Bangladesh government is grossly compromised from the moment the government is established after each election by the winning party without exception. The government in power largely influences the lower-level elections such as Parishad and Upazila. It favors its own party members so that they may be elected. The purpose behind this is to have a group of people in the government who are like-minded and who would not oppose any decisions the government makes regarding policy design and implementation. In this regard, all decisions taken and passed by the government in power might appear inherently democratic and as if the citizens of Bangladesh support this; however, this is done by way of their close-knit network.

The overwhelming control on power disallows those bureaucrats situated in the center of the political structure to function independently and in a neutral manner as the constitution of Bangladesh intends for them to function. Moreover, to minimize resistance at the bureaucratic level, civil service recruitments are also politicized, favoring party-supporting candidates to work for the government, and thus destroying the core concept of checks and balances that are supposed to exist throughout various government organs. These apparent manipulations of power provide the party-based government supreme authority in every early sector; it therefore remains completely unchallenged. Even the political parties established as the official opposition of the ruling body ultimately succumb to this process of monopolization of power. Each party, acting in accordance with the genuine interests of the state and those living within it, can appropriately be considered victims of an illegitimate system. The result is a system that fails to operate democratically and clearly fails to bring an appreciable breath of political voice to the table. At the present time, the scenario is such that even in a redefined state system, the matter goes unresolved where the local government, private sector, and civil society are considered active partners in power checks and balances.

While local governments are mostly elected under the favored umbrella of the political party in power, actors that function as an intricate part of the private sector are also greatly influenced by the political parties. In fact, many development projects implemented by the government are used as "bait" to keep others in the business sector under a perpetual state of pseudo-control. It is very common in Bangladesh to see people functioning as part of the business world belonging to a political party, and assuming a major share of the tender-based development project allocations. In return, they are loyal to the political parties in power by offering generous donations or subsidies during times of elections, as well as preceding or subsequent struggles for dominance within the government. Finally, civil society is the only group that remains in a position to oppose the government, although their influence remains rather insignificant as to the whole picture that they barely impact the decision-making process.

The Executive

Part 4 of the Constitution deals with "the Executive," where the powers and duties of the president, PM, and ministers are outlined. One point worth analyzing is that within the Constitution, the masculine gender is used for the president and the PM, which is considered a "sexist expression" in the contemporary period. If the Constitution of Bangladesh is to truly be modeled along Western lines and reflect the true standards, principles, and values as do states in the Western democratic world, the language component of this and other texts will certainly require further adjustment in order to reflect the essential reality and diversity of this society. The masculine expressions are illustrated in the following, quoted from the Constitution with emphasis added:

The President
(1) There shall be a President of Bangladesh who shall be elected by members of Parliament in accordance with law.
(2) The President shall as Head of State, take precedence over all other persons in the State, and shall exercise the powers and perform the duties conferred and imposed on *him* by this Constitution and by any other law . . .
(4) A person shall not be qualified for election as President if *he* (1) is less than thirty-five years of age; or . . .

Tenure of office of Prime Minister
(1) The office of the Prime Minister shall be vacant if *he* (1) resigns from office at any time by placing *his* resignation in the hands of the President; or (2) if *he* ceases to be a Member of Parliament . . .

In other words, a female candidate is not permitted to hold the position of president or PM in Bangladesh. The implications of the vocabulary used in the constitution spur public and scholarly interest in the political and legal legitimacy of Khaleda Zia and Sheikh Hasina holding power. In order to legitimize their presence in government, the Constitution should be amended in order to properly neutralize the innately "sexist expressions" embedded within it.

When Bangladesh's Constitution was enacted in 1972, international experts of the legal profession saw it as one of the most progressive democratic constitutions in the modern world, particularly in the developing world. The document was noticed in the Third World as one of the most inspiring constitutions that would set in motion a wave of progressive political ambitions, especially for populations seeking and fighting for self-determination. Although the constitution was written in a relatively modern period of history by Western standards, it was written at a time when the developing world in Southeast Asia was undergoing strident and turbulent change. At that point, nobody anticipated that Bangladesh would ever have a female president or PM. Therefore, it is no mistake on the part of the authors of the Constitution that the words "he" and "she" were written into the document. Acting upon what was prevalent and seen as widely acceptable in 1972, Bangladesh's Constitution is clearly failing to inspire the progressive change that it might seem to superficially claim.

The Constitution of Bangladesh can also be seen as a factor that is radically altering the power-sharing struggle between men and women in Bangladesh society in a negative way, and is creating new problems for those struggling with women's empowerment. Women were traditionally seen as the homemakers in Bangladesh society rather than independent entities competing with males over positions of power, especially in government sectors. Eliminating the gender-based terms would not, however, eliminate the universal truth and natural biological differences between a man and a woman, but it would represent a fundamental step helping to re-establish the Constitution of Bangladesh as the liberalizing force that it was seen as approximately four decades previously.

While the president is the supreme leader of the Executive, according to the Constitution, the PM enjoys most of the power and is allowed to act in reference to the president if required. The president, on the other hand, does not normally engage in any sort of decision-making without consulting with the PM. Having so much power for a select position that normally comes from a political background represents a point of contention regarding the roles as outlined in the Constitution. The process leaves ample room for political parties to position peoples of their liking without challenge. It is a serious blow to accomplishing a government with expected checks and balances adequately set in place.

The Judiciary

Part 6 of the Constitution explains how the Judiciary should be set up. The Constitution envisages the separation of the Judiciary from other organs, which is a critical arrangement to enable a nation's political system to function properly. Clause no. 22 of the Constitution sums this up as:

> **Separation of Judiciary from the Executive**
> The State shall ensure the separation of the judiciary from the executive organs of the State (Common LII).

Previous governments have demonstrated how the political party-based arrangements ignored this constitutional mandate and openly violated it without any direct opposition or recourse for such action. Only during the caretaker government (CTG) had the Judiciary again been separated from the influences of the other organs.

The notion of a separate and independent Judiciary is one of the cornerstones of the Constitution of Bangladesh. The separation of the Judiciary from the Executive finally became operative November 1, 2007, when the CTG formulated relevant rules and amended the Code of Criminal Procedure Ordinance in 2007. This was a response to the Court's 12 directives in the historic Masdar Hossain case. The separation of the Judiciary represented the fulfilment of a constitutional obligation that was long overdue, and is largely seen as the outcome of the Judiciary's proactive stance as successive political governments failed to realize this much-needed constitutional mandate. This shows how vulnerable Bangladesh was as a nation, whereby citizens remained largely unaware of governmental activities and how the governing powers have traditionally sought to manipulate the citizens that they have been elected to govern.

Bangladesh's political elite has invested a great deal of effort in maintaining their power. Manipulation of the general population has gone hand in hand with this form of corruption given that it is a tactic that helps to ensure that power remains in the hands of those governing. The Chief Justice, for example, is an appointed position by the elected government, which is one of the steps to control the Judiciary indirectly. In this regard, there is no guarantee that the appointed person would not be politically biased and operate in a politically neutral manner. Through this manipulation of the power structure, the political government manages to cast a blind eye to the Constitution, knowing very well that the common citizens are ignorant about the Constitution and their nominated Chief Justice is there to shield them. This message is reflected in the following passage:

> The existence of a judicial system as the ultimate interpreter of the Constitution and the Law is an indispensable feature of a democracy governed by Rule of Law and not by Rule of Power. The Judiciary, therefore, operates through Rule of Law for protecting legal and Fundamental Rights . . . It is neither the Cabinet nor the party in power but the uniform policy expressed in the form of well-deliberated laws and regulations made in a transparent manner that should decide the issue in resolving those conflicting interests so that the entire community can pursue a common goal, despite their competing interests and values. The only safeguard for democracy is therefore the Rule of Law. It is the judiciary, which is the final arbiter in enforcing the Rule of Law. When the government of the day tends to break or bend the law breaking its oath, it causes imbalance in the system of governance. If the executive and the political elite want to wield its absolute power, it can push it as far as it can go by neutralizing the judiciary through allurement or intimidation or by packing the court with nominees of one's own choice. Once they are allowed to do so, this becomes not only the end of democracy, but also will likely result in the break down of all institutions—leading the country towards chaos and anarchy.

The Legislature

By definition, the Legislature is a deliberative body of persons, usually elected, empowered to bring about change or to repeal the laws of a country or state. The Legislature is the branch of government that retains the power to make laws, as distinguished from the Executive and Judicial branches of government. This is the hub of the political majority in which most positions are held by the political party selections that are disguised in elections.

The parliament is one of the important components of the Legislative body in government; of the parliament, the Constitution states the following:

> **Establishment of the Parliament**
> (1) There shall be a Parliament for Bangladesh (to be known as the House of the Nation) in which subject to the provisions of this Constitution, shall be vested the legislative powers of the Republic: Provided that nothing in this clause shall prevent Parliament from delegating to any person or authority, by Act of Parliament, power to make orders, rules, regulations, bye-laws or other instruments having legislative effect.
> (2) Parliament shall consist of three hundred members to be elected in accordance with law from single territorial constituencies by direct election and, for so long as clause (3) is effective, the members provided for in that clause; the member shall be designated as Members of Parliament.
> (3) Until the dissolution of Parliament occurring next after the expiration of the period of ten years beginning from the date of the first meeting of the Parliament next after the Parliament in existence at the time of the commencement of the Constitution (14th Amendment) Act, 2004, there shall be reserved forty five seats exclusively for women members and they will be elected by the aforesaid members in accordance with law on the basis of procedure of proportional representation in the Parliament through single transferable vote: Provided, that nothing in this clause shall be deemed to prevent a woman from being elected to any of the seats provided for in clause (2) of this article.
> (4) The seat of Parliament shall be in the capital.

Since parliament is the power hub state government in Bangladesh, a fierce power struggle between the political parties can be witnessed within this particular phase of the election process. The political government in power attempts to remain in power "by hook or by crook." This manner of situation was witnessed during the end of the previous political tenure whereby the power struggle between the parties became so intense that the armed forces of Bangladesh were forced to intervene in order to install the CTG. Eventually, a relatively fair election was held under the CTG in 2008; however, the result was somewhat disappointing for a great deal of Bangladeshi citizens given that it was the Awami League (AL) that came to power with a majority in the parliament, and assumed nearly 250 seats of 300. As a direct consequence of this political outcome, AL will always represent the majority party in the state's political system, and thus are free to exercise power with relatively little opposition.

Many are now witnessing the power play of the AL government whereby attacks are being carried out against opponent party members. Violent acts of intimidation have become a common tactic in this game, as well as the looting of domiciles as acts of revenge for past incidents. The community has also witnessed attempts by AL supporters to artificially impact local government elections. Resultantly, a greater breadth of power plays should be expected in nearly every sector of government and business as time passes. This is inevitable under a political party-based government system. It is very common to see the winning party undertake a great effort to nullify many decisions taken by the earlier government upon its ascendance to power. This rivalry attitude in the political party-based government exemplifies little more than negative strides for the entire state of Bangladesh instead of maintaining, and even strengthening, a progressive political posture.

Compared to Western democratic systems on which the Bangladesh system of democracy was designed, the outcome is wholly undesirable and signals a strong swing from Western democratic practice. This is a result of the fact that the practice of lawmaking represents an area of legislature that is supposed to be fulfilled through parliament. The negative influence of this political scenario ultimately has dire consequences for Bangladesh, and would negatively impact any nation seeking to advance itself as a democratic state. Constant evaluation of the laws that were passed during the political party-based governments are an extremely critical operation in order to reveal just how many of them are on par with the Constitution. This mechanism is equally important for the enablement of political watchdogs to assess and potentially reveal the number of parties that are in violation of these laws. In terms of accountability and ongoing political monitoring, the notion of implementing such a tactic raises the question of who or what ultimately is responsible for balancing and keeping the fair and democratic political practice of the government in check.

The Ministry and Bureaucracy

A constitutional body is in place to ensure the functionality of the Constitution, as well as to protect it from violation by any party attempting to gain power or corrupt the political process currently in place in Bangladesh. However, in spite of the rules by which all parties are supposed to and expected to play, previous governments in the state of Bangladesh have seen their power neutralized through politicization by installing their politically influenced employees who turn a blind eye to constitutional violations by the government. During the CTG, the government struggled to empower the Election Commission as the independent entity it should be, under which the election was finally held.

A similar situation was witnessed at the Bangladesh Public Service Commission (BPSC), where civil service recruitment was put on hold as a result of unfair recruitment processes regarding political influence. A classroom discussion meeting with the Chairman of the BPSC revealed how blatant the government could be at times in forcing them to give into their demands under unfair pressure. The bureaucratic structure presents the hierarchy and chain of command. This chain of command is fairly ineffective if bureaucrats who succumb to external influence are positioned there. Subsequently, good and fair officers would be forced to submit to the political will and influence and face severe consequences if they chose to resist this sort of pressure.

Possible Solutions and Recommendations

The objective of this chapter is not to simply present a discussion about the problems currently playing out in the political and democratic process of the Bangladeshi government; rather, it seeks to put forth viable options and present potential solutions to the unfair and heavily undemocratic practice that takes place in this state on a daily basis. The ultimate goal, therefore, is to establish fresh dialogue in this domain and compel scholars and practitioners alike to join a growing cadre of those willing to maintain the democratic path that Bangladesh chose to pursue when the country was still in its infancy.

Focusing on and considering the present scenario of Bangladesh, it is clear that the country is in a position where those wishing to be a part of a positive democratic movement for the country are no longer sure what course of action is most appropriate. It would seem as though Bangladesh has played around with all known political systems and has arguably failed through those systems to achieve its desired end. Bangladesh also does not enjoy the necessary resources and immediate support system necessary for the formulation and implementation of an absolutely new and untried system. However, in spite of this relative disconsolate representation of Bangladesh, there are vital steps that should be taken to correct the current political disorder and depravity.

Democracy and the Political Parties

The recent record of policymakers in Bangladesh demonstrates that they are no longer in a position to offer and maintain good government/governance. As a result, Bangladesh now seeks to establish a system of good governance without any practical means set in place or in motion to achieve this end. In many cases, professionals within the government system in Bangladesh talk about good governance but their actions embody almost a complete reversal of the ideals as established in the Constitution; as a result of the imagery established through this negative practice, a notion has now developed in the minds of many Bangladeshi citizens that "goodness" does not pay. Perhaps the strongest reason for this change in the mindset of many Bangladeshi is the absence of "reward and recognition" for goodness and fairness in the current system in addition to the absence of proper accountability for criminal activities.

Evidence of this mindset and the subsequent corruption is apparent in the country's Judiciary, in which "officers of the High Court Division take bribes from 500 to 15,000 taka just to push cases up the queue on the daily cause list" (Haque 2011). Many of the political elite in the country have become so greedy that we do not mind selling Bangladeshi values and morals to anyone; although vote-buying, for example, is not the sort of practice that can be easily measured in any state, payments have been accepted for voting in certain ways in Bangladesh. "This is particularly true," according to Hossain (2008: 1), "because they [politicians] so often depend on poor people behaving like automatons in the polling booth, programmed to deliver the right vote." This simple act embodies the idea that people are willing to sacrifice their principles for material gain in the hope that the sale of votes will enable them to live better.

The idea of good governance is not a simple end that can be acquired with relative ease; it takes a great deal of time, effort, and dedication by state actors, as well as external actors, to achieve the objectives that are necessary for the functioning of a liberal and democratic state. This is a realistic dream that could only be fulfilled if certain conditions are met. Greed has played a dominant role in Bangladeshi politicians becoming subservient to foreign elements. The Niko incident provides a valuable case in point, depicting the negative consequences of government misconduct that had a serious impact on the legitimacy of management within the economic sector. The presentation of gifts by Niko presented to BAPEX caused general outrage among the public in Bangladesh, while in April 2008 roughly 20 officials (including two former prime ministers) were charged "in connection with corrupt Niko deals with the government" (Trace International 2011).

The past several decades of governance in the state of Bangladesh have greatly brought into question the primary objectives and motivations of those who seek to govern and continue governing in upcoming years. According to Chowdhury (2008), a silent majority asserts that the Bangladeshi politicians' culture of corruption mainly imprisons the vast majority the citizens of Bangladesh in a world of poverty. In spite of messages of morality, equality, democratic values, and ongoing rhetoric in consideration of greater rights for ethnic and religious minorities throughout Bangladesh, a sharp stroke of injustice and poor governance can be seen on a daily basis. Akash (2009) explains that lack of proper governance in the country has made even the most essential professional practices difficult and dangerous to perform. "Each day," according to Akash, "to be a journalist in Bangladesh is becoming dangerous and risky. There is no press freedom there. The torture and killing of journalists is common; yet even in this horrible situation, journalists continue to work there." Even though it claims that the media is free, in reality the practice represents a completely different situation, and represents a severe impediment to the progression and promulgation of human rights overall.

Moreover, political parties are not accustomed to the idea of sharing power and working together. A quote from a letter of a fellow citizen by the name Ekram Belal was published in the *Daily Star* on February 13, 2008, that reflects a sense of consternation:

> My worry is one of Newton's laws of physics, which is also applicable to our corrupt politicians and the democratically elected governments. Forces of change will be gone with the departure of this current CTG and the evil forces of inertia will be back and will try to take the country and run it their old way . . .

Strategies for Reform

Dr. Kamal Hossain (2008) penned a significant contribution to the subject matter under the title "Making Democracy Work: What We Need to Do," in which he depicted the ugly picture of the political party-based democratic system in Bangladesh. He contends that the Bangladeshi have bitter experiences of how the fruits of victory of their struggle for freedom and the establishment of their own state and own constitution have been lost due to the selfish pursuit of power by those governing that same state. For people to become empowered, remain empowered, and to enjoy the fruits of victory, institutions need to be built while checks and balances need to be established, maintained, and strengthened in order to prevent the usurpation of power by government that could subsequently lead to disempowerment of people and their continuing independence.

Although one of the ultimate goals of social advocates in and throughout Bangladesh is the establishment of free and fair elections, in order to grant Bangladeshi citizens the capacity to choose honest and competent representatives who would genuinely represent them, elections alone cannot ensure a working democracy unless democratic institutions are strengthened and are allowed to function effectively. A democratic culture enabling active participation by people, tolerance, and mutual respect must be nurtured.

Over time, political parties became centralized and their nomination process for candidates degenerated into a form of auction or selling of nominations to the highest bidder. Potential candidates were questioned not about their qualifications or how they were equipped to serve the people to whom they were elected to lead, but on how much money they could spend in the elections. Even though there have been numerous attempts by the government to combat vote-buying, its attempts have not proven very successful. A business owner in Chittagong stated that "[w]e want to see an end to violence and terrorism . . . In the past, we've had to give payoffs to local political activists just to run a business or do other things in society" (Magneir and Alam 2008). In a country where the government has had to resort to the deployment of half a million soldiers to mitigate the possibility of civil unrest turning devastatingly violent, the sort of corruption experienced by common Bangladeshi—which can be accurately classified as endemic—is the source of democratic disempowerment in the country and a means of considerably stunting a democracy that is still relatively in its infancy. Even mafia-like structures spread through the country and the word "godfather" found its place in common parlance even in the countryside as small arms continued to proliferate, with the connivance and protection of powerful coteries. This type of corruption takes place at both the top and the bottom levels of government, and has taken a myriad of forms in the political system. The relationship between the state and the types of corruption that destabilize its liberal democratic foundations have been addressed by Muzaffer Ahmad, a supporter of Transparency International—Bangladesh (TI-B), who explains:

> Recent studies have distinguished between grand corruption where bribe recipients are few at the top level of the government and petty corruption where multiple and numerous bribe recipients are at the low levels of government. Similarly there can be multiple bribers and few bribers. Susan Rose-Ackerman, using this dichotomy has identified four polar cases i.e. Kleptocracy, bilateral monopoly, competitive bribery and Mafia domination. The case of Kleptocracy has been described well by Moncur Olson . . . where 'Monopolist' bribe taker maximizes gain by restricting output of the economy while he strives for productive efficiency. This is presumably what has happened in the Telephone Sector and Energy Sector of Bangladesh where supply did not respond to demand in order to maximize rents in licensing at the top level of the government. While people have looked at rent seeking at the bottom tier, the decision makers have worked with the levers at hand. When the resource base is poor, legal framework is unclear and civil servants loyalty is not guaranteed, then the decisions become selective and incremental till marginal increment in private gain is negligible.

In instances involving government intervention, police were prevented from taking action against such protected armed cadres in campuses and other arenas, as they were compelled to enforce law in a partisan manner, harassing and persecuting the poor and vulnerable, as well as the political opponents of those in power, while extending impunity to their protégés. Land-grabbers who enjoyed political patronage deployed police forces to forcibly occupy lands, as well as to evict poor slum dwellers that comprise some 40 percent of Dhaka's population. Those who practiced corrupt politics in order to patronize and protect extremist elements within government also misused agencies responsible for law enforcement. Acts of terrorism were routinely covered up, investigations delayed, and effective law enforcement obstructed. There can be no rule of law where there is selective enforcement of law and the injection of the virus of "*dolliokoron*" (grouping) into national institutions responsible for law enforcement and national security.

There is a proverb in Bangla that loosely translates into "If you have two Bengalis, you will have three political parties." This is evidenced in the existence of over 100 political parties. "Most of these are small, fringe parties formed mostly by a small coterie of like-minded intellectuals or politicians who usually have broken away from larger groupings" (www. virtualbangladesh.com/the-vitals/politics/, February 2016). The idea of "grouping" is fatal for us. Grouping divides and leads to conflicts. As a single nation of Bangladesh, we should do away with all the groupings and unite under a single philosophy, which is best for all of us.

Thus, the time has come to abolish all political parties and ban all party-based political activities in Bangladesh. We should accept and move forward with a new concept of democracy that is plain and simple. All we should care about is "one nation, one goal." Banning of political parties would resolve 80 percent of our political problems; the remaining 20 percent can be handled by amending the Constitution to accommodate the new system.

In the absence of political parties, there will be no political candidates. Therefore, there will be no need for any political elections for candidates. Chowdhury (2008) wrote in an article entitled "Blueprint for Democracy," which appeared in the *Daily Star* on February 15, 2008, which stated that the success of democracy depends on various factors. Education is perhaps number one on the list; then comes human rights. This would include freedom of expression, right to information, tolerance for each other's philosophies, and rule of law. All these factors have to come together to bring success to democracy. The need for the achievement of fundamental changes in the democratic realm, as well as the placement of democracy on the right track so that it does not get derailed again, cannot be gainsaid. Since little to no democratic integrity exists within the political parties themselves or their activities, the need to understand how they can advocate "democracy" when they do not practice it needs to be fulfilled. Chowdhury (2008) opines on this point of issue in the following statement:

> First, let us talk about reform in political parties. We do not want political parties to be headed by hereditary leaders. Let not political parties be used as family property . . . The parties must remain committed to resolving all matters through democratic means. Finally, they must also spell out as to who can or cannot contest an election. Any criminal record should automatically disqualify a person, and the person must also meet some minimum criteria in respect of age, education.

At this point, by disagreeing with Chowdhury, the abolishment of all political party activities in Bangladesh is advocated. It is clear that the political parties are undemocratic; instead of hoping that they would become democratic and passing laws to make them or force them to behave, let us simply say "no" to that failed concept.

A New Model

Considering the nature and situation of Bangladeshi people, the best workable solution would be a "Council Based Democratic System." This means that instead of elected officials in the government, all we need is a group or council of "experts" independently formed to head the respected ministry. "The Economic Council" should run and monitor the affairs of concerned governmental ministry. "The Agricultural Council" would look after the affairs of the Ministry of Agriculture.

The graduates of the universities would automatically become members of the respective councils and they would have their own elected or mutually selected or nominated board members for a term—say, five years. Non-graduates or graduates of other disciplines who are interested in becoming a member could be allowed membership to ensure participation and contribution in the area. The routine council sessions will be held at the house of parliament in regular intervals and will be broadcasted through our media of all kinds, so that the members at large or distant members could also participate in decision-making processes for the nation.

The idea is similar to the "Citizen Council" suggested below, but better. To counter a single party or a powerful leader from monopolizing power, a modified form of Athens Council may be in order. Besides voting for the candidates of different parties, a Citizen Council composed of prominent citizens may be formed. This will include civil society members—academics, lawyers, journalists, business people, union members, and other citizens who want to contribute to public life. Under this system, there would be no need for wasteful nationwide elections, and all decisions would be taken in broad daylight through open sessions; meeting agendas and minutes will be passed on to the concerned ministry for execution or implementation. This system would not allow any anyone to intervene in any democratic processes, or get a chance to hold positions for which they are not qualified. Experts in a democratic way would govern all matters. All decisions will be taken on the basis for what is good for the nation. No personal interests would get preference at any point, as a parliamentary system will be in place.

In such a system, the process would be constant and the vision of the nation will be long term and effective. There would be no chance for any interference in long-term projects and national strategies, as there would be no change in government, ever. The whole nation would be focused into one single direction and follow a track smoothly without any distraction. This process will replace the parliamentary elections.

The President

We need a national leader or a president. The leader who would represent the nation could be an elected one, elected by the citizens in open competition. The main criterion will be to elect the best candidate(s) based on their academic record, personality, and other competitive aspects the may possess. This position could be for a five-year term, but would not hold much power in reality because, in a council-based democratic system, the country is actually run by the citizens behind the scenes. A decision of the president would not be required. In fact, the country would function even if we did not have a president; still, we should have one, to be our ambassador to the world community.

Presidential Election

Every five years, there will a presidential election nationwide in an open competition among the interested and independent candidates whose candidature would be approved by the security council of the country after all background checks, managed and organized by the Election Commission. This would prevent the crooks and criminals from becoming candidates. There would be a day-long election when eligible voter citizens would cast their votes. The majority vote would bring the successful presidential candidate to take oath ceremoniously. There will be no other national elections besides this presidential election. All other elections will be held internally within the council members of the respective councils.

National Security Council

Under this setup, the existence of a National Security Council (NSC) is recommended. An increasing threat of global terrorism, as well as from homegrown terrorists, is now on the horizon that did not exist before. Recently, we have witnessed one such incident at the Pilkhana Bangladesh Rifles (BDR) Headquarters on February 25–26, 2009, where almost 100 military officers were murdered in a mutiny. On May 29, 2009, *Prothom Alo* reported that during the period of 2001–2007, about 1,300 BDR soldiers were recruited under the political backing. Therefore, can we conclude that the mutiny at BDR was politically triggered to seek revenge on the officers who harassed the politicians during the CTG? If that is really the case, then we are all involved in a tremendous hate crime and the whole country is in terrible danger.

Many countries are now adopting the concept of an NSC. Bangladesh too needs to adopt one. It is argued that if some institutional structure such as the National Security Council consisting of civilian and military leaders is constituted, military leaders could have some say in the running of the state power and military officers would be less prone to take over political power directly. It should be mentioned here that General Ershad established a National Security Council consisting of a few senior ministers of his government and three chiefs of armed forces. However, Ershad had no commitment to the cause of national security, and Ershad's NSC atrophied and soon died. For the defense of the country, the establishment of a civilian-led NSC may better manage the international and national forces that dominate its actions.

Parliament

The Parliament House will be used for regular National Council assemblies and there will be no more fixed or permanent parliamentary committees as we have today. A special committee will be formed at the time of National Council Sessions on an ad hoc basis by the respective ministries holding the sessions. In other words, all the entry doors for crooks, criminals, and ineligible candidates will be closed for good. Only competent candidates with proven track records will take office. The president could preside over the meetings or sessions.

Local Government

There would be no election at the local level. A government office would be there to handle all activities at the local level where all citizens/voters living within that area would be members. Any member moving from one location to another must do so by notifying the local government office so that his or her membership could be transferred to the new location or jurisdiction of his or her new residency. This way, the mobility of a citizen could be tracked, which would eventually help the government in implementing social safety net programs effectively. Now that we have already created a national database of our citizens in order to prepare and issue the voter registration card (which is also our national identification card), through this mechanism the information on the database could be constantly updated.

On February 15, 2008, speakers at a meeting said that transparency, accountability, and citizens' participation in different development works and in formulation of budgets have become essential for good local governance, as well as poverty reduction. They also stressed that self-reliance is needed to strengthen local government and this becomes possible when citizens are sure of good returns. The views were exchanged at the meeting for sharing achievement of Sharique, a local governance program with Inter Cooperation of Care Bangladesh at Nanking Darbar Hall. Several union parishad chairmen and members, in a special discussion arranged for sharing their experience, stated that the Sharique program is helping union parishads manage public affairs more effectively.

Citizens' participation at the local government level is crucial in national decision-making processes. Attempts have been made at the root level to motivate and encourage citizens to participate without much success. However, in the newly proposed model, for a valid quorum, one-third of the total members would be required to validate a meeting or session. Now here we are talking about direct democracy.

In addition to challenges to traditional patterns of governance arising from globalization and from the power of networks, there is yet another set of challenges that would produce very different styles of governing. This collection of related challenges endeavors to deinstitutionalize governance and to more directly involve citizens in making binding policy decisions. The assumption undergirding these ideas is that the public can—and more especially should—have more direct influence over decisions than they can exercise in respective democracy, to focus on citizens themselves as the principal source of governance. The people who know and understand the issues deeply should be allowed to have their say in policy devising in the council meetings at the parliament. This is one of the ways to go for digital Bangladesh.

System Comparison

One may wonder why a system based on the "Council of Experts" is advocated. In order to gain an understanding of this, it is necessary to first take into consideration the sort of role that the Council fills. On January 11, 2008, *Star Weekend Magazine* published an article entitled "Developing Bangladesh through Research," in which it is acknowledged that for a developing country, research is probably the single most important tool in maintaining pace with the rest of the world as it develops and adjusts to emerging demands. Although research is not typically seen as the most engaging or exciting of professional fields, all development work would simply fall apart without it. One organization that has been consistently engaging in this tedious and often under-recognized area for the last 50 years is the Bangladesh Institute of Development Studies (BIDS).

BIDS is mandated to function as an agency for initiating and conducting study, research, and dissemination of knowledge in the fields of economic development, population studies, and human resources, in addition to many other social issues related to policy, planning, and national development. BIDS serves as a conduit for dissemination of research findings through its library information system, publications, website, and seminar programs, conducting training and workshops and generally engaging proactively with the broader national and international communities. BIDS researchers also directly contribute to the formulation of development policies through participation in government committees and task forces. In short, BIDS serves as a resource center for the community at large, and thus represents an essential ingredient for the proper functioning of a robust and engaging civil society and social activism.

BIDS appears to be the just one amid a sea of organizations carrying out research activities on "real-life" issues facing each and every person living within Bangladesh. Ideally, institutions of higher education such as the public and private universities of Bangladesh were also supposed to conduct research activities and publish their subsequent findings and data in local and international journals so that this work may be used in national development. In reality, however, rarely is any extensive research from academics at various Bangladeshi universities applied to national development. This is reflected in the sentiment as expressed by Rahman (2007) that unless enough indigenous knowledge capital, which is also globally competitive, is generated, it may be very difficult for Bangladesh to face the growing onslaught of global policy intervention. Research is one area that has been thoroughly neglected in Bangladesh. The universities in Bangladesh are producing too many artificially intelligent young people disintereed in questioning the world around them; as a result, the impact of research in various fields that comprise the domain of social sciences has become soft.

Theoretical ideas are rarely developed and utilized in explaining the contemporary realities facing Bangladesh and its citizens. In fact, very few qualified scholars and researchers participate in international symposiums, workshops, seminars, and conferences in Bangladesh. Part of the reason for this situation could be that not many opportunities or financial assistance are offered in this area. Additionally, under a politically based government system, most of the international participation invitations are passed to the party members who might not fully connect with the scholarship presented. Indeed, this may be reinforced with the notion that Bangladesh has failed in implementing a coherent or even a proper policy in the context of education, which is progressively seen as "something that is received rather than achieved and it has increasingly become dependent on certificates" (*Viewspaper* 2015). In other words, under a political party-based government system, true and qualified people are left out of these opportunities, which is a matter of loss for the nation overall.

Many of the academic scholarships are granted to civil servants, whereas they were mainly intended for the university teachers. The doctorate route is normally an academic track to prepare an academic or an educator for research work that normally spans for anywhere from two years to six years, and for anyone attempting to contribute new and fresh ideas and research in a manner that has not been seen before in that particular field. Therefore, these scholarships should go to the college and university teachers who are appointed and hired to do research work and develop effective teaching methodologies. If the country fails to support potential researchers, then pressing the issue of pursuing an advanced education might be a hard sell to the peoples among the general population. The result might be a detraction of burgeoning minds in the professional fields, particularly in government. The developed countries spend a large sum of their financial budget on research activities as a means of maintaining their competitive edge in the world.

The people who are in the best position to understand and address the problems of governance in Bangladesh are resident Bangladeshi themselves. Therefore, it is important to engage local researchers and consultants toward resolving such problems. Rahman expresses the same view when he states that changing economic and social conditions have gradually shifted the focus to many areas relating to globalization, macroeconomic issues, agriculture and rural development, water resources management, poverty and inequality, food security, microcredit, health, nutrition, education, energy, environment, gender, empowerment, migration, urbanization, and other development issues. BIDS can make an important contribution to the national policy agenda, as it has a Parliamentary Charter—lending it wide and effective autonomy in the choice of research issues. The research output of BIDS provides valuable input to the policymakers and development practitioners for designing appropriate development interventions.

The contribution of BIDS to the country's development process, however, remains contingent upon the choice of relevant agenda and proper use of its research output by the end users. The gap between research and policymaking has historically remained quite significant in Bangladesh. The aim is to spread the research activities under the control of all councils and ministries into various fields instead of centralizing it under BIDS alone. Different councils will publish their own journals (the *National Journal of the Economic Council*) consisting of the best research outcomes that could be considered in the council sessions for policymaking, which can then be published online for the public to read and review. BIDS—along with the public libraries and universities—could play an important role in facilitating the researchers by arranging and supplying reference materials through their existing library facilities on a membership basis. This arrangement would eliminate any possibility of influence in research and idea generation. In absence of political influence, there will be no secret or unwanted interference.

The Awami League (AL) party has won the Members of Parliament (MP) elections overwhelmingly, assuming nearly 250 seats out of 300—the product of which has been an overtly noticeable imbalance within parliament as the opposition parties suffered a loss of power. The session quorum will not be affected and any decision taken by the majority vote by AL will pass even if the whole of opposition walks from parliament, as we have recently noticed in the case of Constitution amendments despite opposition from the opposing groups.

In order for Bangladesh to accommodate the suggested changes, the Constitution would have to be modified. A thorough exposure and propaganda of this concept would have to be undertaken to earn people's support as this concept will face fierce resistance from the political parties. Some bold steps may have to be taken to get this implemented as H.M. Ershad did. Sami (2008) reminds us by saying that in 1991, when the presidential system was discarded, it was incongruously decided that some of the prime minister's executive powers, privileges of the presidential system and some trappings of the presidency would be retained. Some of these measures were innovative creations of President Ershad to perpetuate his dictatorial stranglehold on the civil and military establishment at the expense of the powers of other ministries.

Most of these are not compatible with the temperament of the traditional parliamentary system and are unfriendly to the concept of joint cabinet responsibility and authority. There have been calls for a "Review of the Constitution" by many. One such editorial was published by Rashid (2008), who said that Chapter IIA of the constitution—which envisages a non-party caretaker government between the elected outgoing and the incoming governments—was incorporated in the Constitution in 1996 because the political parties could not trust the ruling party to hold parliamentary elections.

The functions of the caretaker government are enumerated in Article 58D, where, in case of necessity, the government can make policy decisions. Furthermore, since this caretaker government was installed under unusual circumstances during political turmoil, chaos, and lawlessness, it has to fight against what the government has recently described as the three "Ms"—money, muscle, and the misuse of power. The Constitution had undergone 14 amendments to this day, and these amendments have changed the Constitution of 1972 so much that it has lost the substance, spirit, and character of the Constitution of the founding fathers. The first severe blow to the Constitution came in 1975, when the system of government was turned into presidential from parliamentary. This constitutional change from parliamentary to presidential (and making a one party-state) destroyed the fundamentals of the 1972 Constitution.

Successive military regimes under martial law had also amended constitutional provisions as they wished through Presidential Orders or Proclamations. The Constitution is based on certain expected assumptions and conduct from office holders. Those expectations had been totally ignored in practice in the past. The ruling party leaders did not interpret or use the provisions of the Constitution in good faith. The 37 years of governance have demonstrated the pitfalls and deficits of the provisions of the Constitution. Some of the amended provisions are totally against the democratic norms of the Constitution and need to be deleted. What is imperative is that provisions of the Constitution must be made explicitly clear, with checks and balances on the separation of powers among the organs of the state executive, legislative, and judiciary. Simply put, the government runs the administration, parliament enacts laws, and judiciary interprets the laws. Each organ has its own limits of power enumerated under the constitution, and that is the essence of constitutional democracy in a republic.

Conclusion

A growing momentum of support appears to be in the making within Bangladesh society for modifying the present Constitution of Bangladesh in order to reflect the interests of the general population. Such revisions, in light of the country's past experience, should take into account the political, social, and cultural environment of a perpetually evolving state. A constitution is not a "one-size-fits-all" phenomenon that can simply be transplanted in the country from another. In this context, the establishment of a Constitution Review Commission calls for urgent attention for national interest in the state of Bangladesh. As is evidenced by the analysis and reasons presented in this chapter, it is clear that Bangladesh simply does not meet the basic criteria for a political party-based democratic system.

The argument was presented that the concept of political party-based democracy should be abandoned. In order to protect the integrity of "good governance" in Bangladesh, a nonpolitical party approach seems to be an appropriate response to the current state of affairs in this country. If the echelon is cleaned and remains stable, then the remaining branches would subsequently enjoy a better outcome in the immediate and distant future. Elimination of party-based politics would further yield multidimensional benefits for the country, as well as for its roughly 164 million inhabitants. Bangladesh might very well make the same mistake that it did when it broke from the political path that was outlined in the original Constitution in 1971 if it fails to respond to the contemporary demands of its peoples. The primary objective is to develop and provide the nation with a more positive and effective political framework that could be considered for implementation, particularly given the egregious state of affairs that Bangladesh currently finds itself in.

References

Ahmad, M. (n.d.) "Governance, Structural Adjustment and the State of Corruption in Bangladesh," www.ti-bangladesh.org/oldweb/index.php?page_id=332. Accessed February 2016.

Akash, J.A. (2009) "Lack of a Free Media in Bangladesh," www.jaakash.wordpress.com/page/14/?app-download=ios. Accessed February 2016.

Belal, E. (2008) "Corrupt Politicians," *The Daily Star*, February 13.

Chowdhury, F.R. (2008) "Blueprint for Democracy," *The Daily Star*, February 15.

Common L. II. "Constitution of the People's Republic of Bangladesh. Bangladesh Constitution Contents, Part II."

Dyer, G. (2007) "Bangladesh: When Democracy Goes Bad," www.gwynnedyer.com/2007/bangladesh-when-democracy-goes-bad/. Accessed February 2016.

Haque, S.M. (2011) "Anti-Corruption Mechanisms in Bangladesh," Asian Human Rights Commission (AHRC), Kowloon, Hong Kong.

Hossain, K. (2008) "Making Democracy Work: What We Need to Do," *The Daily Star 17th Anniversary Special Edition*, February 16.

Magneir, M. and Alam, N. (2008) "Foes of Bangladesh Victor Call Vote 'Farcical'," *Los Angeles Times*, December 31.

Rahman, N. (2007) "A Price Too High to Pay," *Star Weekend Magazine*, May 9.

Rashid, H. (2008) "Review of the Constitution," *The Daily Star*, June 18.

Sami, C.M.S. (2008) "Dispersal of Power for Checks and Balance," *The Daily Star 17th Anniversary Special Edition*, February 16.

Star Weekend Magazine (2008) "Developing Bangladesh through Research," *Star Weekend Magazine*, 7(12), January 11.

Trace International (2011) "Niko Resources," www.traceinternational.org/compendium/. Accessed February 2016.

Viewspaper (2015) "Bangladesh: The Race for Education," www.theviewspaper.net/bangladesh-the-race-for-education/. Accessed February 2016.

CIVIL SOCIETY

II

Chapter 12

Taking Steps toward an Understanding of "Civil Society with Chinese Characteristics": An Exploration through the Eyes of Chinese Faith-Based Organizations

Caroline Fielder

While the concept of civil society is not new, what is understood by it remains widely contested. Although debates persist over terminology and the universality of civil society as a concept (Guan 2005), it nevertheless continues to act as a term garnering considerable interest (Schwartz 2003: 3). In the Chinese context, although there are still some voices warning against attempts to create a Western-style civil society in China, it appears that despite periodic crackdowns on discussions around the term, either in the media or in education, "most people—even those in government—seem ready to embrace civil society 'with Chinese characteristics'" (Simon 2012).

Although some scholars have suggested that the People's Republic of China (PRC) is devoid of civil society (i.e. Alagappa 2004), others suggest that there is mounting evidence of a budding civil society taking root within the Chinese context (i.e. Yu 2008; Deng 2011). While such differing opinions may simply reflect divergent opinions, they also reflect changes in approaches to what is understood by civil society in the Chinese context and to how it is studied. Whether there is civil society in China, whether it resonates with models from elsewhere, or if it is predominantly characterized by difference (and if predominantly different, it still can be considered as a valid form of civil society) are all questions that this chapter seeks to answer.

Thus, an analysis of some of the ways in which civil society has been both theorized and operationalized within the context of the PRC in the years since the start of the Opening and Reform period in the late 1970s is here undertaken. It is necessary to begin this endeavor by unpacking some of the assumptions made when using the concept in China, and looking at various terms commonly used within the Chinese language to express the term "civil society." The chapter then explores some of the ways in which civil society has been theorized in recent times by both Chinese and foreign scholars, drawing on the historical context that has helped to shape these viewpoints. Finally, the chapter takes a look at some of the ways in which the concept is being operationalized from a grassroots perspective, through an exploration of the ways in which the newly emerging sector of faith-based and religiously inspired charitable organizations[1] are now engaging in charitable and social service work. This latter section is based on information gathered during extensive fieldwork undertaken within China and draws on materials and observations gathered from over 43 organizations across the five officially recognized religious traditions[2] in both rural and urban China. In order to condense the dense array of information provided by such a wide spectrum of organizations, my analysis of the sector draws on the work of Michael Edwards and applies a framework of his that has gained popularity in China since its translation into Chinese. This framework analyzes civil society from the perspective of associational life, the good society, and the public sphere. As such, this section echoes his central quest to discover whether civil society should be described as "a noun (a part of society), an adjective (a kind of society), an arena for societal deliberation or a mixture of all three?" (Edwards 2004: 4), and applies it to the Chinese context.

Terminology

The term civil society is often seen to have "multiple meanings and counter-meanings," which, while "open to interpretation" (Yu 2008: 137), are nevertheless "connected by a deep structure of discourse" (Heins 2004: 499). In the Chinese lexicon, there are numerous ways in which civil society can be expressed, and understanding some of the differences between these different terms helps us gain a more nuanced understanding of the ways in which civil society is conceived of by Chinese people.

Modern commentators have proposed that the correct translation for the term civil society is *gongmin shehui* (Wang 2011: 10). Literally translated with *gongmin* meaning citizen and *shehui* meaning society, this term emphasizes the role of the citizen. Although the term *gongmin* finds its roots in Han Fei's doctrine of self-interest, the *Wudu* (*The Five Vermin*),[3] the translation and use of the specific term *gongmin shehui* meaning civil society is a relatively new one, dating back to the reform era. As such, the term is seen as being a particular form of social life emerging from urbanization and industrialization. Yu Keping[4] has written extensively on the term and suggests that it is widely thought to include an emphasis on "the political dimension, namely citizens' political participation and checks on state power" (Yu 2008: 137). Taken together, these show that the term is reminiscent of Hegel's interpretation of civil society, which recognizes the benefits that the provision of a space for civil society has on society, but also recognizes the need for that space to be closely managed by the state in order to check any potential social disintegration (see Hegel 1991).

While *gongmin shehui* is the preferred translation in the PRC and is particularly "en vogue with younger academics" (Yu 2008: 137), other terms have been commonly used when translating civil society in the wider Chinese context. The term *shimin shehui* was the preferred term used in Marxist classics. Literally translated as "society of urban dwellers," it provides a precise translation of the German term Bürgerliche Gesellschaft, but He Baogang notes that in the Chinese context it also carries with it additional undertones. The first is that it is seen to apply to urban residents only. Second, it not only refers to those living in cities, but "may refer narrowly to business people, as *shi* means market" (He 2010: 232). As such, the term has been linked to the oppression of the bourgeoisie (Yu 2008: 137), and therefore can carry with it negative connotations.

Two other prominent terms that have been used to translate civil society include the terms *minjian shehui* and *wenming shehui*. *Minjian shehui* (literally "people and their space society") can also be translated as "popular society" (Ma 2006: 18) or "society not associated with the government." The latter comes from the term *min* (people) and is contrasted with that of *guan* (officials or government). Although this implies a "deep-rooted dichotomous structure of 'society against officials' or 'popular society opposes or even confronts the officials'" (Ma 2006: 21). Richard Madsen has argued that in general, when the term *minjian shehui* is used, it does not necessarily follow that popular groups will act independently of the state and can indeed be assumed to be guided and supervised by the state (Madsen 2008: 6). Other scholars have suggested that the term has gone through numerous changes, as the state–society relationship has evolved over time, with expansion of social space both within and outside of the state system (Liang 2004: 188).

It is also important to note that within the PRC, the term *minjian shehui* is often seen as a Taiwanese formulation. The term was indeed chosen in the late 1980s by advocates for political reform within Taiwan, arguably for the very reason that it suggests a popular, grassroots uprising against an unjust form of leadership (Deng 1997). As such, its use is imbued with an inherent sense of confrontation. Although this term *minjian shehui* is more inclusive than the term *shimin shehui* in that it includes the peasantry, this recent history and the implications that such a vision of civil society involves a "democratic strategy" (Chen Kuide, cited in He 2010: 232) explains why the term is often restricted in its use to either a historical context or in reference to the Taiwanese context.

The term *wenming shehui* literally means "civilized or enlightened society" (Des Forges 1997: 70) and emphasizes the meaning of "civility against violence" (He 2010: 233). It is the least-used of the terms but at times when sensitivities around the use of other terms such as *gongmin shehui* have surfaced in the media,[5] it has not been uncommon for this term to be used; appearing, for example, on NGO websites as a translation for civil society. This term is less commonly used in scholarly circles, however. One reason for this may be because the term *wenming* (civilization) has been closely associated with the state discourse on societal transformation in post-Mao China through Deng Xiaoping's "Two Civilizations" program (*liange wenming*). This program sought to "civilize" society through a range of public education campaigns, but it has also been criticized because "actions were also taken to hide the most visible manifestations of the reform's failure to benefit all members of Chinese society" (Broudehoux 2004, cited in Boutonnet 2011: 101). The program also establishes a clear distinction between "material civilization" (*wuzhi wenming*) and "spiritual civilization" (*jingshen wenming*) (Boutonnet 2011: 79) and becomes problematic for those for whom civil society incorporates both a material and a spiritual dimension.

Therefore, the preferred term for civil society, *gongmin shehui*, indicates an inherent assumption that civil society is a byproduct of industrialization and carries with it an assumption that citizens (both urban and rural) will play a prominent role in the ongoing development of society through their active participation in public issues. Citizens have access to the public sphere, but while they have a responsibility to check the power of the state within that sphere, it is also assumed that the state will also manage and direct that sphere in order to preserve social stability. The relationship between the state and citizens is seen as being mutually beneficial and is not seen as antagonistic.

Theoretical Underpinnings of Civil Society with "Chinese Characteristics"

Although a brief overview of the lexical differences in terminology can provide us with a sketched outline of what is understood by civil society in Chinese society, an overview of the theoretical underpinnings of the term can add depth to that picture. As such, the following section provides a brief overview to some of the most significant discussions shaping this discourse.

In sharp contrast to political theorists in Eastern Europe who developed an understanding of civil society that "had its origins in the internal contradictions between state, society, and the Church; the presence of the Soviet army on their soil and the looming Soviet threat; the consistent downward trend of wages and poor living standards lasting for over two decades" (Adlakha n.d.: 4), the concept of civil society was first advocated in China at a time of extraordinary public optimism. Within China itself, impressive strides had been made in the struggle against poverty. After years of being cut off from the outside world, China was also in the process of opening itself up to the world and its markets and early responses from the international community were welcoming and encouraging. Although there was debate among scholars and within leadership circles about the potential effects that unfettered capitalism could have on China's future, the process of reform also encouraged a more positive attitude toward debate and discussion within the public sphere.

He Baogang has identified four different approaches that Chinese scholars have taken to theoretically underpin the Chinese understanding of civil society in post-reform pre-1989 China. He termed these four approaches: the reconstructed Marxist approach; the citizenship approach; the neo-authoritarian approach; and the civil discourse approach (He 2010: 197–240).

As the name suggests, the reconstructed Marxist approach sought to embed civil society within a revised understanding of Marxist ideology—suggesting that when civil society is seen as a central concept within Marxism, it provides the state with an opportunity to entrust power to the people (Rong 1987). As such, the emancipatory qualities of civil society, rather than its antagonistic, anti-government potential, were the focus of this approach.[6]

The second category identified by He, the citizenship approach, focused on the changing perceptions within society to the idea of citizenship. This approach recognized the Chinese preference for self-identifying with the "masses" over the individual and suggested that this led to a "pervasive culture of dependency on the state" (Liu and Wang 1988). Drawing on the work of Rousseau and others, scholars taking this approach hypothesized that the modernization of Chinese society would eventually encourage a drive toward a form of individualized citizenship—which would manifest itself in a growing awareness among citizens of their own rights, but would place these in the context of the wider community and as such would lessen any sense of dependency on the leadership (Liu and Wang 1988).

This approach emphasized the development of "competent citizens" (Almond and Verba 1980) who were aware of their own sense of duty in relation to society at large. They knew their own rights and the responsibilities of government, and would seek to engage in healthy dialogue for the greater good of society. A focus on the duties and responsibilities of citizens sought to engender increased levels of civic cooperation and trust; however, these ultimately endorsed, rather than opposed, the authority of the state.

The third approach identified by He Baogang was the neo-authoritarian approach, an approach that saw civil society as being an intrinsic part of the changing economic realities of China. According to this approach, scholars argued that the development of private enterprise would inevitably lead to the emergence of a middle class and that any forthcoming economic freedoms would provide a fast track to modernization and the emergence of civil society. This approach emphasized the role of private property rights in securing democratic rights. It should be particularly noted, however, that any notion of wider applicability to broader elements of society—including the peasantry—would be at the discretion of the state (Kelly 1991).

The final approach identified by He was the civil discourse approach. It is quite common to hear of civil society being formed discursively—that is, "it is through a group's discursive practices that the society 'discovers' itself and formulates its values, character and ultimately its ethos" (Kluver and Powers 1999: xi). In the Chinese context, a civil discourse approach specifically sought to reflect the ways in which new, Western, scientific approaches had influenced Chinese society. One such example was the way in which public discourse on social and political norms were now to be encouraged in an emerging environment free of government control. It is important to note, however, that this approach did not promote a Habermasian view of the public sphere in the sense of being a space that was open to all to participate on an equal basis. Instead, discussions were to be limited to the "counter-élite structures" of the urban-based intellectuals and students (Chamberlain 1993: 200).

These approaches, like the nuanced distinctions apparent in the various terms used to translate civil society, make it possible to identify a diverse range of approaches and a plurality of views during the 1980s.

The social upheaval in Eastern Europe and the events in Tiananmen Square in 1989 brought an abrupt end to the open atmosphere that had been so prevalent during the earlier part of the decade. The events of 1989 also caused discussions to change direction. As Brook and Frolic have pointed out, although the relationship between state and society in China had long been a topic of Western intellectual interest, the events in Tiananmen Square on June 4, 1989, "renewed anxieties among Chinese and non-Chinese scholars alike about how to understand the state–society relationship" (Brook and Frolic 1997: 3). These events also served to recalibrate the intellectual compass of enquiry with respect to civil society, creating distinct communities of interest—each of which brought with them distinct and fixed ideas on how civil society should be conceived.

Within academic circles in China itself, in the direct aftermath of Tiananmen, discussion on civil society came to an abrupt end and Xi Zhaoyong's report of May 1990 was effectively the last major study on civil society to be published in China for two full years (Ma 1994: 186). During the next few years, research into China's civil society continued but was undertaken only by Chinese scholars in exile and by foreign researchers looking at China from the outside. Perhaps unsurprisingly, this brought with it a distinct perspective and limited the variety of voices that had previously been heard on the topic.

In the case of those Chinese intellectuals forced overseas into exile after the summer of 1989, many were greatly influenced by their own personal experiences. This shaped the ideological underpinnings of their contribution but also shaped the manner in which they publicly engaged with the question of civil society. For many, this meant that they focused less on theoretical questions and instead became more focused on exploring practical ways in which civil society could be brought into being. In the minds of many of those exiled, the events of June 4 reinvigorated a personal calling to encourage others to join forces in order to defend any nascent forms of civil society (Hua 1990, cited in Ma 1994).

For many, civil society became a political end goal in its own right. Exiled away from their homeland, the issue of cultural difference became their daily reality, and for many of these scholars the sense of civil society needing to be in a form that was culturally appropriate to the Chinese context became all the more urgent. As such, a number of scholars reflected on China's own history and looked into its heritage in order to find resources that could be used in the building of a culturally suitable form of civil society (McCormick et al. 1992).

For many Western scholars, 1989 was also a critical juncture for studies of civil society in China. Like their Chinese counterparts, research into the historical origins of civil society also dominated the first wave of research undertaken by foreign scholars after 1989—but for very different reasons. Stimulated by Habermas' understanding of the "public sphere" (Habermas 1987), these early studies explored the politicization of the elite and lower classes in the late Qing period through an attempt to identify "political terms" used in the late Qing period (Rowe 1990; Rankin 1993).

The historical nature of these early studies also reflected a generational predisposition of Sinologists toward historical studies (Madsen 1998). Nevertheless, they reinforced their Chinese counterparts' desire to discover the origins of modern civil society within a Chinese rather than a foreign context. Although these studies were later critiqued by both Western and Chinese scholars—who argued that the concepts were too value-laden and historically determined to be helpful in understanding modern Chinese realities (see, for example, Huang 1993; Wakeman 1993)—they did provide a sense of historical perspective and unity in approach (if only at surface level). They also injected vigor into the search for civil society "with Chinese characteristics," while also providing scholars with a valuable vantage point from which to reflect on and analyze the important events of 1989.

While many of these studies traced evidence of civil society back to pre-Liberation China (Gold 1990)—suggesting that any evidence of civil society was merely a re-emergence of something previously evident in society—there was another group of scholars who broke away from the historical focus, and concentrated their analysis on the contemporary situation.

Some of this research suggested that the events of 1989 reflected sweeping social changes that had the effect of wiping away tradition. As a result, autonomous groups had begun to emerge and their presence was seen to provide evidence of a new form of civil society (McCormick et al. 1992). Although such forms of civil society were undeniably still weak, these scholars argued that over time, they could be strengthened through the development and implementation of new market systems (Ostergaard 1989). Arguably shaped by the discourse taking place outside of China on civil society (which stressed an anti-government stance and the state–society dichotomy), some Western scholars found evidence for strong forms of civil society in the nature of the pro-democracy demonstrations of 1989. These included examples such as vibrant public expression of opposing political views and the role of intellectuals as mediators between state and the demonstrators (Strand 1990). They also included the active participation in demonstrations of members from all sectors of society, who were noted as showing "extraordinary self-discipline" (Sullivan 1990).

As these studies became increasingly framed (either consciously or subconsciously) around an antagonistic model of civil society, the confrontational nature inherent in the conceptualization of civil society within these studies began "to block a vision for a constructive future" (Yang 2003: 197). This tendency for researchers to situate discussions of Chinese civil society within what was arguably a Western model was seen as exceedingly problematic by Chinese scholars (Deng and Jing 1992). Deng Zhenglai has been particularly vociferous on this point and has argued that the fundamentally antagonistic state–civil society lens is in desperate need of revision. Within the Chinese context in particular, he has reasoned that the partisan arguments put forward by Western scholars are not suited to the Chinese situation and need to be replaced by a framework that allows for a more "mutually enhancing" relationship to surface (Tan 2003: 207).

Heath Chamberlain has also made similar arguments about the understanding of civil society in overseas scholars' writings on China, and has proposed a revised model of civil society that takes note of earlier discourses taking place in China and that recognizes the peculiarities of the Chinese context. His proposed model was based on a structure of state–society relations that distinguishes civil society from society at large. Although such a view has echoes of a "third sector" common to many other models, this Chinese-appropriate model differs from its Western counterparts by acknowledging the role of the state and dynamics in state–society relations in China and by positioning civil society as being "as much a creature of the state as it is of society" (Chamberlain 1993: 204).

Such an approach recognizes the dangers inherent in the various approaches that seek to apply imported models of civil society directly onto the Chinese context, but it is not without its own flaws. The first problem with Chamberlain's model is that it does not specifically classify what lies within each of the three realms. For example, in China, does civil society lie (as it does in many Western interpretations) between state and family? If so, this may be problematic given the Confucian tendency to view all relations in familial and kinship terms (Tan 2003: 194). The second issue with this model is that it suggests fixed boundaries. Yang Fenggang has argued that this is inappropriate, as it belies the reality of the civic sphere in contemporary China. Instead, he proposes the adoption of a dynamic model of three social sectors: the state, the for-profit sector (capital), and the not-for-profit sector (voluntary associations) (Yang 2003: 198).

Like Chamberlain, Yang's version shares features with other tripartite models of civil society but again his differs in that rather than depicting the three areas as being distinct spheres (which at best attempt to balance excesses in the other spheres, and at worst work in opposition), he proposes a model that recognizes the interactive, fluid relationship that exists between the three, making them interconnected and interdependent. Yang's model supports the view held by other Asian societies that the state can be constructively involved in the creation and development of civil society but that it can also play a role in constraining the excesses of civil society, ensuring that it remains a "good society." This resonates with the implicit terms of reference contained within the preferred term *gongmin shehui*. Yang's model also makes a clear distinction between the not-for-profit sector and the for-profit sector, acknowledging that both have a potential role in civil society being outside the state, but recognizing too their markedly different functions in society (Yang 2003: 199).

Far from seeing the state's influence on civil society as a negative—potentially diminishing the ability of civil society to be independent or to affect political change—both Chamberlain and Yang's models re-emphasize qualities inherent in the Chinese understanding of *gongmin shehui*. One such point is that the very nature of the close, almost symbiotic, relationship between state and civil society not only provides legitimacy for civil society within wider society at large, but also provides tangible "touch points" between state organs and civil society, which can then serve as "a process for holding to account those charged with collective responsibility" (Hay 2007: 62). Although this draws out the inherent and often overlooked importance of this to the Chinese psyche and echoes Hegel's depiction of civil society, such a view is in stark contrast with many more modern Western interpretations that suggest that only fully autonomous (and at times antagonistic) forms of civil society can truly affect lasting political change.

Thomas Metzger has highlighted other differences between Western and Chinese understandings of civil society. He writes:

> In this western tradition "civil society" refers to an un-utopian political order in which morally and intellectually fallible citizens organize themselves to monitor an incorrigible state, seeking either to minimize state intervention in their lives or to use some state intervention to check allegedly oppressive elites outside the state. In Chinese writing, however, this un-utopian, "bottom-up" definition of "civil society" has been filtered out and replaced by a tradition-rooted, utopian, "top-down" view according to which moral-intellectual virtuosi—whether a political party free of selfishness or "true intellectuals"—take charge of a corrigible state or at least are allowed by the latter to guide society.
> (Metzger 1998: 1)

This highlights the assumption made in China that civil society is constructed in a top-down manner, with the sense that civic space is an "invited space" controlled or regulated by the state. While some scholars have dismissed ideas that this constitutes any form of civil society, suggesting instead that it is a form of "political corporatism" (Unger and Chan 2008), where activities become "embedded" within the existing institutional infrastructure (Ho and Edmonds 2011), this understanding does resonate with Chinese and wider Asian patterns of thought. He Lichao has argued that a common theme in East Asian models of civil society is that they have predominantly been encouraged to grow in a top-down manner, often developing at the behest of the state, usually as a result of the state's inability to meet the challenges of decentralization. He goes on to argue that market liberalization in the 1990s brought about a large number of social and economic challenges that various Asian states did not have the capacity to then respond to. As a result, they were forced to relinquish civic space, yielding control and a share of their power, in return for cooperation and even partnership with civic organizations in order to address escalating social issues (He 2007: 4).

This pattern has been increasingly evident in China in recent years with local government opening up key areas of social service provision to civic organizations for tender. This reflects preferences for state and society to work together but also adds a slightly new dimension. This contract-based system necessitates a separation between social organizations and government, with the former initiating changes and the latter supervising and evaluating the changes (Jia and Su 2009). Critics have suggested that this top-down model lacks real autonomy and can therefore result in a lack of critical space due to the balance of power remaining firmly in the hands of the party-state (Pei 2008). While this concern may be worth noting, it is also worth remembering that the roles of "close ally" and that of a "critical friend" are not always seen as contradictory, and that such formal ties can—and do—provide channels through which issues and concerns can be voiced, and by which social change can be brought about over time.

Although there has been a clear move from attitudes that sought to uncritically impose Western models wholesale (in the 1980s) through to ones that yearn to develop a more indigenous model, finding a definitive theoretical model of civil society appropriate to the Chinese context remains a difficult challenge. Michael Edwards (2004: vii) has argued that "recognition that civil society is contested territory—in both theory and reality—is the first step in rescuing a potentially powerful set of ideas from the conceptual confusion that threatens to submerge them." Moreover, Richard Madsen has pointed out that many models of civil society used to describe China have hitherto ignored the moral element, making no distinction between moral communities and special interest groups within civil society. He argues that this is a mistake— especially in light of the moral crisis affecting Chinese society—and suggests that both scholars and policymakers should pay increasing attention to the development of moral associations (Madsen 1993).

Despite the centrality of a distinctively moral space of human interrelations to the concept of civil society in much of Asian thinking on civil society (He 2007), such an approach has been deemed sensitive by the Chinese authorities and so research in this area has hitherto been difficult. According to Professor Yang Fenggang, however:

> Within the third sector of Chinese society, religious institutions deserve special attention. They are closest to the so-called "moral associations" in Tocqueville's terms. Religions are social institutions with long traditions in China. Under the rule of the Chinese Communists, for several decades, all religions were treated as pre-modern superstitions and suffered cruel suppression. However, we have seen the great revivals of all religions in China since the beginning of economic reforms.
>
> (Yang 2003: 204)

The sections that follow explore three different dimensions of civil society, each of which is a fruitful site of analysis in its own right but may provide an incomplete picture when looked at in isolation (Edwards 2004: vii). Looking at the associational life, the good society, and the public square in turn will help to build up a picture of how civil society is currently being operationalized in China.

Civil Society as "Associational Life"

Social organizations have had a long history in China, dating back to the Sui, Tang, and Song dynasties, with trade guilds,[7] lineage associations, and cultural and religious groups providing rudimentary forms of "social organizations" (Rankin 1993; Des Forges 1997; Zhang 2003). Records from Marco Polo's travels to China in the late thirteenth century showed his delight at finding a vibrant associational life in the Chinese city of Hangzhou (Goody 2001) and in more recent times there has been much written about the rise in organized voluntary activity alongside the creation of increasing numbers of private nonprofit organizations (Wang 2005; Xu and Ngai 2011). However, surprisingly little has been written about the significant growth that has taken place within the faith-based sector or the emergence of religiously inspired social service organizations over the past decade.

In a speech made at a conference on "building a 'harmonious society' in China" in 2005, Yang Fenggang identified four types of faith-based organizations (FBOs) present in China: faith-based social service organizations; social service enterprises; grassroots FBOs; and informal associations of religious believers (Yang 2005).

The first category of faith-based social service organizations are registered as separate and independent social service organizations. A growing number of these organizations are now registered as private foundations, which confers a number of rights, including the ability to fundraise. While some of these have long histories in China that date back to pre-Liberation, even new organizations within this group have become notable players and have grown into some of the most powerful and well-managed civic organizations in China today. They are predominantly staffed by professional aid or management experts who are generally sympathetic to the religious basis on which the group is founded but who may or may not have any personal religious convictions themselves. These organizations often have the capacity to run a variety of large-scale programs and activities ranging from poverty relief to capacity-building and disaster relief. Some of the larger organizations have access to policymaking bodies; for example, through the appointment of senior staff to bodies such as the Chinese People's Political Consultative Conference (CPPCC). Programs are often delivered and funded through a mixture of both religious and secular partners.

The second category is that of social service enterprises. These organizations are predominantly established (and often funded and staffed) by religiously motivated individuals. Due to the cumbersome nature of regulations, in a similar way to many secular civic organizations a number of these enterprises cannot be registered as nonprofit organizations, and as such register as a for-profit company even though they have no intention of making money out of their work. These organizations vary hugely in scope, and operate in a variety of fields.

The third type of FBO is perhaps the most extensive and most disparate of the groups, that of the grassroots FBOs that are often attached in some way to churches, mosques, and temples. Many of these are funded at a local level, by local members of the religious community; however, some receive supplemental external funding from both Chinese and (often religious) overseas funding sources. These organizations are abundant but they are rarely accounted for as separate legal entities by the Ministry of Civil Affairs due to their registration status, which often groups them under a religious community, making them appear less autonomous than their practice may actually reflect. As such, they do not appear in the statistics despite their far-reaching impact in the community. These grassroots FBOs not only provide mutual assistance to their members, but often also provide social services to the wider community at large. However, such social service programs run by churches, mosques, and temples are rarely reported by the media due to restrictive policies toward religion, and many remain unknown to researchers. Moreover, once they have been successfully piloted, many of the social service programs of religious organizations are later co-opted by the local state agencies, who have the capacity to roll them out on a larger scale. This means that successful programs can appear to the public as governmental instead of nongovernmental programs.

The last group is the most fluid, and is that of informal associations of religious believers that make moral and ethical issues their primary concern. These groups bring people together around a shared theme or area of common interest—such as a group of business leaders who support one another in making ethical decisions in the workplace, an HIV/Aids self-help group, or a group of foster parents. More than just self-help groups, these groups seek ways by which to operationalize their shared religious beliefs, often seeking ways of "mainstreaming" them into people's daily lives and everyday practices. Such groups cannot register directly with the government because of their informal and voluntary basis.

Although Yang's typology is a helpful starting point highlighting the diversity of the sector, it also reveals a number of contradictions. First, the need to register as a business or the need for organizations to be grouped under other religious institutions highlights the ongoing antipathy that some sectors of the state still show toward the charitable sector in general and the FBO sector in particular. Although charity has enjoyed a rich and extensive history in China,[8] after Liberation (as rapid ideological changes swept through Chinese society) charity not only became a redundant concept but also became viewed as an element of a corrupt capitalist system and an instrument of the ruling class' subjugation of the poor. While currently legally sanctioned, religious organizations have had a tumultuous past in China's recent history. However, changes in recent policy indicate an attempt to rehabilitate both.

The publication of the "Opinions on Encouraging and Regulating Religious Entities to Engage in Charitable Activities" in February 2012 implicitly recognizes the sensitivities surrounding religious organizations working in the charitable sector. Heralded as a breakthrough document, this paper was co-signed by a number of different government agencies[9] and explicitly calls on religious organizations to become involved in social service work. By implication, the range of signatories indicates the difficulties some groups have had to gain official recognition and can be seen as a public statement of encouragement.

Other recent changes to policy, such as the announcement in May 2014 by the Chinese Ministry of Civil Affairs to extend the so-called "Guangdong experiment" to NGOs in other areas of China by simplifying the registration process and by providing direct registrations for civic organizations may also impact on the FBO sector. The dual registration system that was previously applied rigorously to all NGOs was particularly cumbersome for FBOs (given their dual status as both religious and social organizations) and was previously assumed to provide conclusive evidence of the state's control over the sector (Kang 1999). Arguably the changes now remove the need for FBOs to find alternative means of operating (such as registering as a for-profit business, as many have previously done). As such, it remains unknown if a change in the typology will occur as a result of all groups now registering openly as an association, social enterprise, or foundation. However, the exclusions of Xinjiang and Tibet from these exemptions may indicate that such changes will not be imminent. If that is the case, this may have interesting implications on issues such as transparency within the sector and governance.

With scandals ravaging the nonprofit sector in China in recent years, the issue of good governance is an increasingly critical one to both the authorities and the general public.

Yu Keping has suggested that "good governance equals the return of state power to society" and that it is "indicative of a high level of cooperation between the state and society and government and citizens" (Yu 2008: 140).

Some of the larger FBOs currently registered as foundations have been able to contribute their considerable experience to discussions on self-regulation guidelines for the nonprofit sector. Although not legally binding, the "Self-Discipline Declaration of China Private Foundations," issued in February 2012, has served as a good benchmark *in lieu* of more legally binding legislation from the Ministry of Civil Affairs. In light of recent charity scandals and the findings of the People's Daily China Charity Transparency Report of 2011—which found only 8 percent of those interviewed were satisfied with the level of transparency provided by the charitable sector (Simon 2012)—such contributions are aiding to rebuild trust in the wider charitable sector.

The importance of establishing such trust cannot be underestimated for, as Ho (2012) has argued:

> Some regions in China have seen their rule of law suspended by the rule of the rich, the well-connected and the powerful. A mature civil society would serve as a counterbalance to those who would ill-serve the public. Besides its ability to prevent the emergence of despotism, a developing civil society can also help to alleviate the moral and social vacuum caused by commercial development and the creation of markets.

Civil Society as "Good Society"

In light of Ho's comments, it is easy to see why the nature of civil society is becoming so important to the discourse on civil society and to practitioners in the field. Civil society as "good society" concerns itself with a vision of how civil society should look and feel. This can easily be explored by asking those working for FBOs what kind of a world they are working toward. This simple question elicits a range of different answers, including descriptions of a changed society, or even an idealized world. At other times, responses focus on the kind of society they seek to eliminate and in this regard importance is often placed on mechanisms that provide governance and oversight, but which also ensure fairness and equity in society.

Many of the FBOs I visited saw themselves as acting as "microclimates" where values and attitudes held dear to people within the organization could be nurtured and encouraged in others. These values varied across organizations and groups. Some groups sought to inspire generosity by providing opportunities to give to good causes; others sought to break down stigma by working with the marginalized in society. Yet others sought to inspire compassion or a sense of social justice. While there were differences, it was more common to find similar values being espoused across organizations, irrespective of religious background or scope of projects.

FBOs see an important part of their role as being repositories of values and see it as their role to share those values with others. They recognize that their exposure to particular constituency (of volunteers, for example) varies, and as such they seek opportunities to optimize the impact of their message and reinforce their values as often as they can. FBOs come into contact with some groups of volunteers on a fairly regular basis, for example early retirees who regularly devote many hours a week to FBO work; novice monks attending training; or young people attending a summer camp, where intense periods of time could build up a strong relationship of trust. In these cases, considerable time was spent nurturing relationships, sharing and developing core values through exposure to project work. Maintaining contact with volunteers, even those who have only been able to spend short periods of time with the FBO, is regarded as a priority, so that this opportunity is not lost.

In some communities, FBOs are seen to have a pivotal role. This is particularly the case in certain ethnic regions where religious organizations and FBOs are seen as integral to the social makeup of the community, providing important contact points at critical stages in life. In such areas, it is much easier to mainstream values into society through village festivals centered on religious celebrations or training courses run through the local mosque, temple, or church, which are often seen as a rite of passage and which large parts of the community would attend.

In some projects, FBOs seek to reach out to those living on the margins of society, such as migrant communities, orphans, or those living with HIV/AIDS. In these cases, contact with a particular group is maintained over an extended period of time, but where such contact is maintained over a distance care is taken to build a sense of community between project recipients. This happened, for example, in some microfinance projects where recipients are encouraged to apply for funds in groups, or in the case of fostering projects where children are placed in towns or villages again in groups so that the new foster carers are close to others in a similar position, encouraging and enabling each family to be able to overcome any problems through mutual support. These kinds of projects not only seek to nurture values within that particular group, but also seek to provide them with a sense of solidarity where deeper discussions, which touch on issues of public concern, can be addressed.

FBOs often see the very nature of their work as value-laden. As such, it is not just the content of the project that is important, but the way in which the work is undertaken. Growing numbers of FBOs serve as mediating institutions, seeking to address issues with the relevant authorities directly, or liaising on behalf of third parties. In cases where migrants have left home, because of broken relationships, FBO staff may also serve as mediating institutions between estranged family members, seeking to bring about long-term reconciliation.

Many FBOs across the religious divide see the "good society" as being one that is built on love and compassion for others. While love is easy to talk about, it is much less easy to operationalize. This is especially the case where charity has traditionally been kinship-based and where society is seen as having low levels of trust among strangers (Fukuyama 1996). For many FBOs, love and compassion can be nurtured through people-to-people contact, and so volunteering opportunities are increasingly being offered as a means of creating links, and bonds between different strata of society.

Civil Society as the "Public Sphere"

The last dimension, which I cover in this subsection, is that of civil society as the public sphere. Habermas (1989) viewed the public sphere as a space in which citizens freely engage in discussion on matters that relate to the common good, for the purpose of engaging in debate and creating public opinion. In other words, the public square is seen as an important transmission mechanism, between the formation of a "good society" and the "associational realm."

While it has been argued that "from the Ming dynasty onward there was a continuous, slowly developing, public sphere in China, involving both state and social power" (Rankin 1993: 158), it has also been argued that in modern society, there has been a distinct lack of public sphere in Chinese society, and that what little space does exist does not always welcome public debate.

FBOs are often frustrated about the way in which much of the public media is reluctant to publish their stories, or cover events in which they were involved. Although their access to the media is much less restricted, even those registered as foundations often find themselves excluded from the public's view. Such restricted access to media outlets has prompted some FBOs to find other ways in which to give voice to their issues, such as direct action. Although a few FBOs have their own publications, ranging from newspapers to newsletters and websites, many of these have limited circulation due to their religious nature.[10] Undertaking research on topics of public interest is another mechanism used by FBOs to engage in public debate. Collaborative projects with universities are increasingly being entered into so that the experience and contacts of the FBOs can be used to inform the research undertaken by academics, and so that any findings from collaborative research can be published in a format that maximizes public exposure.

In addition, issues such as the role of charity in society and the changing discourse on disability have also been brought into the public eye through FBO project work. One example of where this has happened was through the Saturday morning baking classes offered by the social enterprise bakery run by young adults with learning disabilities. By offering opportunities for citizens to engage with the young disabled bakers in a practical manner, issues of disability, and stigma attached to disability, can be addressed in a direct and personal manner.

Increasingly, FBOs are using websites as a means of engaging with the public both at home and abroad (using English-language sites to appeal to foreign audiences in some cases). Proponents of this approach emphasize that use of the Internet not only provides the FBO with access to a much wider public, but that it also enables FBOs to bypass any media prejudice by enabling them to write their own content and publish and update stories on a regular basis. Although stories are often removed from websites, placing them online even for a short time can gain them exposure. However, the use of the Internet means that not all citizens will have equal access to information, and therefore potentially adding to the ways in which already marginalized sectors of society are becoming increasingly excluded from access to information and full participation in society.

As China finds itself increasingly integrated into global mechanisms, questions around the vitality of its civil society are often used as a mechanism to test how open Chinese society is becoming. Moreover, with religion becoming an increasingly important feature within international development circles, FBOs have sometimes unwittingly been propelled onto the international stage. This offers FBOs the opportunity to be part of a global civil society through linkages such as volunteer programs or short-term development programs. On an organizational level, there have been increasing openings for China to be represented in international settings by FBO representatives. These links help to portray a different side of China to that which is often portrayed in the media, and offers opportunities for China to showcase alternative development models to those currently in circulation. Active participation in international meetings also helps to counter arguments that voice concerns over ongoing religious repression in the Chinese context.

Conclusion

An exploration of the work undertaken by FBOs and the "civic competencies" that they are building in society seems to indicate that "civil society with Chinese characteristics" (perhaps unsurprisingly) means different things to different groups. Using an analytical tool that sees civil society as a three-dimensional process incorporating an end goal (the good society), a means of getting there (the associational realm), and a space where these can be discussed (the public sphere) enables us to not only see the malleability of the concept, but to also see its great potential to the Chinese people at a time of immense social change.

Although civil society is contested as an idea, evidence suggests that it continues to be widely discussed at all levels of Chinese society. Despite periodic clampdowns, growing numbers of publications indicate that the topic of civil society does in fact matter a great deal to Chinese citizens. Perhaps even more importantly, on a daily basis thousands of workers and volunteers are using their time and energy to engage in projects and programs that are making a real impact in the lives of strangers. Our theoretical models may currently be inadequate to describe what is occurring, but we would be foolish to conclude that that means it does not exist. Closer links between practitioners, policymakers, and academics, and an openness to observe and analyze what is happening on the ground, will help us gain more clarity in the future.

Given the difficulties raised in theorizing the concept, and based on the evidence garnered through this cursory glance at the emerging FBO sector in China, the question of whether civil society remains a useful concept in the Chinese context demands to be asked. My answer is that it does. Over the coming years, as the sector and the legislative framework that manages it develop, it may become easier to discern its shape, but in the meantime I conclude with the words of Michael Edwards:

> Warts and all, the idea of civil society remains compelling, I think, but not because it provides the tidiest of explanations or the most coherent of political theories—it doesn't and probably never will. It remains compelling because it speaks to the best in us—the collective, creative and values-driven core of the active citizen—calling on the best in us to respond in kind to create societies that are just, true and free.
>
> (Edwards n.d.)

Notes

1. The terms faith-based organization (FBO) and religiously inspired organization will be used interchangeably throughout the text, despite the recognition that there are problems associated particularly with the use of the term FBO in the context of some religious traditions. In this chapter, the terms are used to cover a range of organizations that have been purposefully set up to do charity, to provide social services or public goods. These organizations are distinct from "venues of religious activity" such as temples, churches, and mosques, which are registered through the Religious Affairs Bureau—although in some cases their registration may be linked.
2. The five officially recognized religious traditions in China are Buddhism, Catholicism, Daoism, Islam, and Protestantism.
3. This was a discussion on the concepts of *gong* and *si*, where *si* was described as "acting in one's own interest" and *gong* is simply that which opposes *si* (see Goldin 2001).
4. Yu Keping is a political analyst. He has worked as Director of the Center for Chinese Government Innovations at Beijing University and has also served as Director of Central Compilation and Translation Bureau for a number of years. He has written a number of influential books, including

Democracy and the Rule of Law in China (2010), *Democracy Is a Good Thing* (2008), and *Globalization and Changes of Governance in China* (2008).

5. As the Arab Spring took hold of the Middle East, the Chinese government's response to the rapid rise in civic organizations and public protests within its own boundaries was to ban the use of the term *gongmin shehui* in the media (January 2011). More recently, a policy directive issued in May 2013 banned the topic *gongmin shehui* (and six other topics) from instruction in university classrooms.
6. Central to this was a discussion spearheaded by Shen Yue, who argued that the mistranslation of key ideological terms had corrupted the Chinese interpretation of Marx's original teachings (Shen 1986), leading to serious misunderstandings in the ways in which civil rights were understood within Chinese society. Shen argued that a more authentic translation would remove any association with the bourgeoisie and would enable the concept of civil rights to be extended to a much wider sector of society. Although such a view was a radical departure from previous views, the republication of the article in state-run media (Ma 1994: 183) indicates that these views found approval within the political hierarchy.
7. There has been much controversy about the terminology *huiguan* and its translation as "guild," resulting in a controversy about the basic nature of these organizations. For more, see Goodman (1995).
8. See, for example, *The Art of Doing Good: Charity in Late Ming China* (Handlin Smith 2009).
9. The cosignatories were the State Administration of Religious Affairs, the United Front Work Department of CPC Central Committee, National Development and Reform Commission, Ministry of Finance, Ministry of Civil Affairs, and the Taxation Bureau.
10. The 2001 Regulation on the Administration of Printing Enterprises details both general provisions imposing restraints on printing and also specifies tighter restrictions on the printing of materials for "religious use" (*zongjiao yongpin*) and internal reference publications with religious content (*zongjiao neirong de neibu ziliaoxing chubanwu*).

References

Adlakha, H.K. (n.d.) *Chinese Civil Society and the Anatomy of the Wenzhou Model*, available at: www.asianscholarshiorg/asf/ejourn/articles/Hemant%20Adlakha2.pdf. Accessed March 25, 2012.

Alagappa, M. (2004) *Civil Society and Political Change in Asia: Expanding and Contracting Democratic Space* (1st ed.), Palo Alto, CA: Stanford University Press.

Almond, G.A. and Verba, S. (Eds.) (1980) *The Civic Culture Revisted: An Analytic Study*, Boston, MA: Little, Brown.

Boutonnet, T. (2011) "From Local Control to Globalized Citizenship: The Civilizing Concept of *Wenming* in Official Chinese Rhetoric," in C. Neri (Ed.), *Global Fences: Literatures, Limits, Borders*, Lyon: Université Jean Moulin, pp. 79–103.

Brook, T. and Frolic, B.M. (1997) *Civil Society in China*, Armonk, NY: M.E. Sharpe.

Broudehoux, A.M. (2004) *The Making and Selling of Post-Mao Beijing*, New York: Routledge.

Chamberlain, H. (1993) "On the Search for Civil Society in China," *Modern China*, 19(2): 199–215.

Deng, Z.L. (1997) *State and Society: Study of Chinese Civil Society*, Chengdu: Sichuan People's Press.

Deng, Z.L. (Ed.) (2011) *State and Civil Society: The Chinese Perspective*, Volume 2 of Series on Developing China—Translated Research from China, Singapore: World Scientific.

Deng, Z.L. and Jing, Y. (1992) "Building Chinese Civil Society," *Chinese Social Sciences Quarterly (Hong Kong)*, 1: 1–22.

Des Forges, R.V. (1997) "States, Societies and Civil Societies in Chinese History," in T. Brock and B.M. Frolic (Eds.), *Civil Society in China*, Armonk, NY: M.E. Sharpe, pp. 68–98.

Edwards, M. (n.d.) "Civil Society: Pedagogies for Change," *Infed Ideas. Thinkers. Practice*, available at: www.infed.org/association/civil_society.htm. Accessed June 2, 2012.

Edwards, M. (2004) *Civil Society*, Cambridge: Polity Press.

Fukuyama, F. (1996) *Trust: The Social Virtues and the Creation of Prosperity*, London: Penguin.

Gold, T. (1990) "The Resurgence of Civil Society in China," *Journal of Democracy*, 1: 18–31.

Goldin, P. (2001) "Han Fei's Doctrine of Self-Interest," *Asian Philosophy*, 11(3): 151–159.

Goodman, B. (1995) *Native Place, City and Nation: Regional Networks and Identities in Shanghai, 1853–1937*, Berkeley, CA: University of California Press.

Goody, J. (2001) "Civil Society in an Extra-European Perspective," in S. Khilnani and S. Kaviraj (Eds.), *Civil Society: History and Possibilities*, Cambridge: Cambridge University Press, pp. 131–146.

Guan, L.H. (2005) *Civil Society in Southeast Asia* (1st ed.), Copenhagen: NIAS Press.

Habermas, J. (1987) *Theory of Communicative Action: Lifeworld and System: A Critique of Functionalist Reason: 002*, Boston, MA: Beacon Press.

Habermas, J. (1989) *The Structural Transformation of the Public Sphere*, Cambridge: Polity Press.

Handlin Smith, J. (2009). *The Art of Doing Good: Charity in Late Ming China*, Berkeley, CA: University of California Press.

Hay, C. (2007) *Why We Hate Politics*, Cambridge: Polity Press.

He, B. (2010) "The Ideas of Civil Society in Mainland China and Taiwan, 1986–92," in Z.L. Deng (Ed.), *State and Civil Society: The Chinese Perspective*, Singapore: World Scientific Publishing, pp. 197–240.

He, L. (2007) *In Search for an East Asian Model: Comparative Civil Society Study in China, Japan and South Korea*, New Orleans, LA, available at: www.allacademic.com/meta/p143194_index.html. Accessed June 3, 2013.

Hegel, G.W.H. (1991) "Elements of the Philosophy of Right," in A. Wood and H.B. Nisbet (Eds.), *Hegel: Elements of the Philosophy of Right (Cambridge Texts in the History of Political Thought)* (new ed.), Cambridge: Cambridge University Press.

Heins, V. (2004) "Civil Society's Barbarisms," *European Journal of Social Theory*, 7(4): 499–517.

Ho, C. (2012) "Relaxed NGO Registration to Boost Growth of Civil Society," *China Daily*, avaialble at: www.chinadailyapac.com/article/relaxed-ngo-registration-boost-growth-civil-society. Accessed June 20, 2012.

Ho, P. and Edmonds, R. (Eds.) (2011) *China's Embedded Activism: Opportunities and Constraints of a Social Movement*, London: Routledge.

Hua, Y. (1990) *Zai ping xin quanwei zhuyi (On New Authoritarianism Again)*, Beijing: Zhongguo zhiqun (China Spring).

Huang, C.C. (1993) "Public Sphere/Civil Society in China? The Third Realm between State and Society," *Modern China*, 19(2): 216–240.

Jia, X.J. and Su, M. (2009) "Final Report on Government Procurement of Public Services People's Republic of China," *Asia Development Bank Technical Assistance TA 4790-PRC: Facility for Reform Support and Capacity Building*, available at: http://unpan1.un.org/intradoc/groups/public/documents/un-dpadm/unpan042435.pdf. Accessed March 17, 2013.

Kang, X. (1999) *Quanli de Zhuanyi: Zhuanxing Shiqi Zhongguo Quanli Geju de Bianqian (The Transfer of Power: The Change of Power Structure in China during the Transitional Period)*, Hangzhou: Zhejiang People's Publishing House.

Kelly, D. (1991) "Chinese Marxism Since Tiananmen: Between Evaporation and Dismemberment," in D.S.G. Goodman and G. Segal (Eds.), *China in the Nineties: Crisis Management and Beyond*, Oxford: Clarendon Press, pp. 19–34.

Kluver, R. and Powers, J.H. (Eds.) (1999) *Civic Discourse, Civil Society, and Chinese Communities*, New York: Ablex Publishing.

Liang, Z. (2004) "Rethinking Civil Society in China: An Interpretative Approach," in D. Bell and H. Chiahark (Eds.), *The Politics of Affective Relations: East Asia and Beyond*, Oxford: Lexington Books, pp. 169–200.

Liu, Z. and Wang, S. (1988) "Cong qunzhong shehui zouxiang gongmin shehui" (From Mass Society to Civil Society), *Zhengzhixue yanjiu (Political Research)*, 5: 1–5.

Ma, S.Y. (1994) "The Chinese Discourse on Civil Society," *The China Quarterly*, 137: 180–193.

Ma, Q.S. (2006) *Non-Governmental Organizations in Contemporary China: Paving the Way to Civil Society?* London: Routledge.

McCormick, B.L., Shaozhi, S., and Xiaoming, X. (1992) "The 1989 Democracy Movement: A Review of the Prospects for Civil Society in China," *Pacific Affairs*, 65(2): 182–202.

Madsen, R. (1993) "The Public Sphere, Civil Society and Moral Community: A Research Agenda for Contemporary China Studies," *Modern China*, 19(2): 183–198.

Madsen, R. (1998) "Five generations of American Sinologist research on China state society relationship," in Y.-M. Lin and J. Tu (Eds.), *Social Change in China's Reform Era. (Jingji tizhi shehui wangluo yu zhive liudong)*, Hong Kong: Oxford University Press, pp. 77–89.

Madsen, R. (2008) "Confucian Perspectives of Civil Society," in D. Bell (Ed.), *Confucian Political Ethics*, Princeton, NJ: Princeton University Press, pp. 3–19.

Metzger, T.A. (1998) *The Western Concept of the Civil Society in the Context of Chinese History (Hoover Essays)*, Stanford, CA: Hoover Institute Press.

Ostergaard, C. (1989) "Citizens, Groups and a Nascent Civil Society in China: Towards an Understanding of the 1989 Student Demonstrations," *China Information*, 4: 28–41.

Pei, M. (2008) "China's Repression of Civil Society Will Haunt It," *Financial Times*, August 4, available at: http://www.ft.com/cms/s/0/46316820-6232-11dd-9ff9-000077b07658.html#axzz3vkRDJNgq. Accessed June 5, 2012.

Rankin, M.B. (1993) "Some Observations on a Chinese Public Sphere," *Modern China*, 19(2): 158–182.

Rong, J. (1987) "The Weakening Tendency of the State's Political and Economic Functions: From the Point of View of Relationships between State and Society," *Zhengzhixue yanjiu (Studies in Political Science)*, 2: 19–25.

Rowe, W. (1990) "The Public Sphere in Modern China," *Modern China*, 16(3): 309–329.

Schwartz, F. (2003) "Introduction: Recognizing Civil Society in Japan," in F. Schwartz and S.J. Pharr (Eds.), *The State of Civil Society in Japan*, Cambridge: Cambridge University Press, pp. 1–23.

Shen, Y. (1986) "Zichanjieji quanli ying yi wei shimin quanli" (Bourgeoisie Rights Should Be Translated as Towns People's Rights), *Tianjin Shehui Kexue (Tianjin Social Sciences)*, 4: 9–14.

Simon, C.W. (2012) "A Look Back at Developments Affecting Civil Society in China in 2011 (and a Sneak Peek at 2012/2013)," *Philanthropy News Alliance Magazine*, available at: http://philanthropy news.alliancemagazine.org/a-look-back-at-developments-affecting-civil-society-in-china-in-2011-and-a-sneak-peek-at-20122013/. Accessed January 13, 2013.

Strand, D. (1990) "Protest in Beijing: Civil Society and Public Sphere in China," *Problems of Communism*, 39(3): 1–19.

Sullivan, L. (1990) "The Emergence of Civil Society in China, Spring 1989," in T. Saich (Ed.), *The Chinese People's Movement: Perspectives on Spring 1989*, Armonk, NY: M.E. Sharpe, pp. 126–144.

Tan, S. (2003) "Can There Be a Confucian Civil Society?" in Kim Chong Chong, Sor-hoon Tan and C.L. Ten (Eds.), *The Moral Circle and the Self: Chinese and Western Approaches*, Chicago, IL: Open Court.

Unger, J. and Chan, A. (2008) "Associations in a Bind: The Emergence of Political Corporatism," in J. Unger (Ed.), *Associations and the Chinese State*, Armonk, NY: M.E. Sharpe, pp. 48–68.

Wakeman, F. (1993) "The Civil Society and Public Sphere Debate: Western Reflections on Chinese Political Culture," *Modern China*, 19(2): 108–138.

Wang, H. (2005) "CPPCC Members: NGOs, an Irreplaceable Force in China's Harmony-Prone Drive," *Xinhua News Agency*, avaialble at LexisNexis.

Wang, M. (2011) *Emerging Civil Society in China, 1978–2008*, Leiden: Brill.

Xu, Y. and Ngai, N. (2011) "Moral Resources and Political Capital: Theorizing the Relationship Between Voluntary Service Organizations and the Development of Civil Society in China," *Nonprofit and Voluntary Sector Quarterly*, 40(2): 247–269.

Yang, F. (2003) "The Decline and Reconstruction of Morality in Chinese Society," in G. Mclean and J.K. White (Eds.), *Imagination in Religion and Social Life*, Washington, DC: The Council for Research in Values and Philosophy, pp. 197–215.

Yang, F. (2005) "Chinese Faith-Based Organisations: Case Studies, Analysis, and Trends," speech given at Pew Forum on Religious Life Conference *Building a "Harmonious Society" in China: Non-Governmental and Faith-Based Organizations as Agents of Social Change and Stability*, September 26.

Yu, K. (2008) *Globalization and Changes in China's Governance*, Leiden: Brill.

Yu, K. (2011) *Democracy is a Good Thing: Essays on Politics, Society, and Culture in Contemporary China.* The Thornton Center Chinese Thinkers Series. Washington, DC: Brookings Institution Press.

Zhang, Y. (2003) *China's Emerging Civil Society*, Center for Northeast Asian Policy Studies, the Brookings Institution, Washington, DC, available at: www.oycf.org/Perspectives2/22_093003/2b.pdf. Accessed March 12, 2012.

Chapter 13

Redrawing Boundaries: Neoliberal Governmentality and the Politics of Active Citizenship*

Abhilash Babu

The long-standing discourse on the issue of active citizenship plays a central role in the current debates on development. Of the various methods employed to encourage and promote active citizenship in communities around the world, the concept of "people's participation"—a concept that has experienced astounding growth since the 1970s—has been reinvented as a highly democratic and effective tool in development. The term became a buzzword in the development agenda of national and international agencies in the recent past, with consensus among the international and local development experts that only those governance mechanisms that could achieve the agreement of all citizens through a deliberative democratic process would be successful. It ensures that citizens' concerns are included into the planning, implementation, and monitoring process.

The concept of people's participation can also be viewed as a new (invisible) technology of governance or a new paradigm for an ordered rule for collective action (Provan and Milward 1995; Peters and Pierre 1998; Stoker 1998). In general, it will be seen as a vital component to the overall concept and practice of civil society in the contemporary period; one that strengthens the overall legitimacy and robustness of democratic states. The concept requires, however, redefinition of the roles of the citizen and the state. While the process is not a linear one, it is a pluralistic strategy including the state, civil society, and local community to include the "people's voice" in the field of national and international development. Within the context of water governance, people's participation plays a central role in planning, implementation, and managing of various projects. It begins as a modest physical participation in the construction of political, social, and economic systems, and develops into general community participation and community management in these and many other domains.

Within this process, responsibility for service provision gradually moves from the national government to local peoples. Part of this discursive formation is entrenched within the debates on the failure of "big government" and a centralized approach to basic service delivery—including water as a vital commodity. Accordingly, a decentralized approach through people's participation emerges as an alternative. What is inherent in celebrating this model is the valorization of "active citizenship." The study presented within this chapter centers on the case of the World Bank-aided "Jalanidhi" project of Kerala, which was implemented with the active participation of local peoples.

The discussion within this chapter focuses predominantly on various strategies applied by supporting agencies to create consensus among its various sections. During the course of this study, discussions that have taken place at the field level with the staff of supporting agencies, politicians, elected representatives, bureaucrats, and local peoples on the nature of resistance of the local people and how it had been contained or included in the project are reflected upon. Drawing from the concept of "governmentality" by Michel Foucault, the argument is made that remote government technologies of the state—by promoting localism and active citizenship—shape the regime of action in water supply through a variety of discourses, which redefine rights as duties and how "resistance and negotiation" are ultimately marginalized within society.

Kerala's Water Scenario

Kerala is situated in the southernmost part of the Indian subcontinent and the "Kerala Development Model" has won accolades throughout the world as a successful model in the field of development, in spite of the rather weak economic performance of this state. Kerala has a wide network of rivers, rivulets, and springs that are spread across the state with two major rainy seasons caused by the Southwest and the Northeast Monsoon. The state receives approximately 3,000 millimeters of rain annually, of which 60 percent is obtained during the Southwest Monsoon, 25 percent during the Northeast Monsoon, and 15 percent during the summer months (Government of Kerala 2008). The people of Kerala have practiced a wide range of traditional water management technologies that have been efficient and eco-friendly over recent years, and these provide real inspiration for further development within the state and in other regions as well. The state has recently made use of a crude form of modern drip irrigation. Regarding the increasing scarcity, some of the traditional water management practices of Kerala still have relevance in the modern period. The major fresh water source, traditionally in use for domestic and irrigation purposes on the Malabar Coast, was the open well. Streams, springs, and ponds were also incorporated into the innovative system of water management along with the wells in select regions. At present, in excess of 70 percent of the population within Kerala depends on open wells for meeting their domestic water consumption requirements and demands. Given that Kerala may be one of the geographical locales with the highest density of open wells, there exists the possibility of positively expanding on Kerala's system of water management that is currently in place. Location-specific soil and water conservation measures, appropriate for different physiographic zones of Kerala, were developed over recent decades, while an integrated approach concerning land–water–biomass, appropriate for the humid tropical region, slowly evolved. Wherever freshwater sources—either surface or ground—were not available, the collection of rainwater stood as one viable and often relied-upon source of water.

2010 marked a distinct change in Kerala's climate, with the numerous reported cases of sunstroke within different regions of the state. This change is not accidental; it has been a result of unmindful development interventions, the changing of lifestyles, and disregard of traditional technologies. Changes that have taken place within agricultural patterns and practices, an increase in the building of structures, the burgeoning number of vehicles on Kerala's road networks, pollution of rivers and other water sources, and high density of population (to name a few negatively impacting elements) have caused tremendous damage to the environment—particularly in the availability of safe drinking water.

The drinking water system in Kerala can be broadly classified into three categories. The first category centers on the private sector with open wells, bore wells, and ponds that have been constructed and maintained by individual households and institutions. Water supplied through private tankers and bottled water also falls within this category. The second category is comprised of piped delivery of drinking water supply, wells, and ponds, all of which are maintained by *panchayats* or the Kerala Water Authority (KWA), either independently or through foreign monetary and technological assistance. The third category is of recent origin, and involves the provision of drinking water supply through beneficiary participation.

The State and the Drinking Water Sector in Kerala

The concept of public water supply began in Kerala with Willingdon Water Works of Trivandrum of the erstwhile princely state of Travancore (Pilllai 1946). Even though *panchayats* have their own mechanisms, the KWA is one of the major public sector drinking water supply institutions in the region; traditionally, water has been predominantly the responsibility of the state. There are frequent media reports on peoples protesting in front of the *panchayat* office or blocking roads used for the transportation of drinking water during the summer season, especially in rural areas. Hence, it is evident that many remain highly reliant on the state to provide their drinking water, and perceive water as a fundamental right of the people and the duty of the state to ensure its availability. In public finance literature, the budgetary allocations required for the provision of drinking water and sanitation in rural India is earmarked mainly for the poor. Naturally, the allocations—governed by non-market principles—are not offered on the basis of investment criteria such as social rates of return/cost–benefit ratio.

In Kerala, the state-led drinking water supply is divided into two categories: (1) urban; and (2) rural. While the urban water supply is more organized and well maintained, rural areas are still far behind in meeting current drinking water demands. Regions characterized by extreme terrain, as well as distant locales, still experience acute water scarcity, which represents a serious concern for those perceiving water as a fundamental human right and one necessary for maintaining basic human security. The spatial distribution of households, lack of funds, and geographical specifics make state intervention in the rural sector increasingly difficult to ensure that these needs are met and fulfilled as best as possible.

Despite having an average annual rainfall of roughly 3,000 millimeters in addition to the highest density of open wells in the world, Kerala suffers from high inequity in terms of drinking water access. The state has the lowest water-to-person ratio in the country, which is even lower than that of the high water-scarce state of Rajasthan. According to the government of Kerala's economic review in 2006, 84.21 percent of the urban and 65 percent of the rural populations have been covered by piped water supply (Government of Kerala 2006). There is a large rural–urban divide in the case of piped water supply, which has been mainly provided by the state (National Family Health Survey 1998–1999). Historically, groundwater has been considered private property in India; thus, he or she who owns the land essentially owns the water below that land as well. Even the progressive governments of Kerala do not properly address the issue of unequal land rights, which is also a major reason for inequitable access to water and this unevenness within the context of ownership over water.

The Paradigm Shift

Recent developments within the state-led drinking water sector have resulted in a paradigm shift synchronized with the neoliberal path adopted by the Indian state, particularly since the 1990s. Instead of being seen as a duty to be fulfilled by the state, the provision of water is perceived of as a commodity. According to the guidelines of the Asian Development Bank (ADB), all street taps should be converted to a household connection with meters or installed meters for street taps. The Action Plan of the World Bank for Kerala also suggests working toward the reduction of non-revenue water to only 20 percent within six years, and a full recovery of the cost within this period. A parallel development exists in the form of the degeneration of the KWA as a result of the aforesaid issues that plague the authority in all areas of its operations. While meeting the costs with the revenue from the non-plan grant from government and water charges is becoming an increasingly difficult task, these costs continue to rise due to an increase in salaries, pensions, and material and electricity costs. The repayment of Housing and Urban Development Corporation Ltd. (HUDCO) and Life Insurance Corporation of India (LIC) loans and interest also increases liability in the same context. Even as three distinct increases have been recorded in electricity charges over recent years, the cost of water is increasing further due to the Kerala State Electricity Board's (KSEB) classification of the KWA.

The discourse surrounding drinking water supply within the state underwent a moral turn in the early 1990s. This fundamental turn may be likened to the global discourse on resource management with community participation. Development of new concepts, including "scarce resource," "environmentalism," "sustainability," "social capital," "basic water requirement (BWR)," and "equity" are all pivotal terms in the major shift that had taken place. This can be attributed to the new liberal regime and macro-political debates centering on state inter-vention in basic welfare services. The rationale of huge investment in water supply and the long-term water planning through extensive water infrastructure development has been under scrutiny recently. This change is largely due to social, political, and economic transformations, which have increasingly limited the acceptance of traditional approaches in this field. Economic efficiency has been the mantra of the planners while this paradigm shift has brought the resurgence of concepts such as "civil society" and "social capital" well within the orbit of development.

Part of this paradigm shift involved the new perception of rights and duties of the state and citizens. The responsibility of social justice has been transferred to the market and civil society with the passage of time; it is in this changing cultural and political context that the participatory strategies for sustainable water management evolved as an alternative. Furthermore, the participatory strategies for sustainable water management gained legal recognition in the government of India's Water Policy of 2002; it envisages the active participation of the user communities in drinking water supply. The introduction of the Panchayatiraj Act in 1993 stood as a profound morale boost to this shift. The *panchayati raj institutions* (PRIs) have become the focus of planning and implementation ever since.

Decentralization initiatives present a formal institutional structure and platform for establishing consensus among local peoples regarding the question of development, now and in the future. The major shift in the participation debate can be found in once being used to attain the rights from the state, while that same technology is currently being adopted by government authorities. Under Article 243G of the Constitution, the state legislatures may, by law, endow the *panchayats* with the powers and the authority necessary to enable them to function as institutions of self-government. The government order issued by Kerala (Government of Kerala 1998) states that peoples' participation is necessary for the implementation of various development schemes. Peoples' participation is also a legal necessity, as has been clarified by the High Court of Kerala (1997) in its judgment, whereby it ruled that the *panchayats* are not selecting authorities, but rather they are merely approving authorities in the case of beneficiary selection.

Of no less importance is the fact that the paradigm shift in water supply has also been attributed to the environmental and economic outcomes of large water supply projects. The extensive contamination of the available water resources, due to large-scale urbanization, unscientific interventions, and uncontrolled population growth, has been a political issue from the early 1990s in Kerala. Water-borne seasonal diseases have received wider attention with the growth of the popular media, as well as in the advent of a growing literate population. The discourse on personal hygiene and the practice of safety have been emphasized in the government's advertisements, as well as by NGOs. In the case of public water supply, the responsibility of the government ends with the supply of safe water. Subsequently, state apparatuses have been severely criticized for their inefficiency, lack of accountability and transparency, and apathy amid the general population's discontent over management.

Decentralization of Water Supply: The New Jalanidhi Alternative

The *Jalanidhi* project of the Kerala Rural Water Supply and Sanitation Agency (KRWSA) was initiated in 1998 in the four northern districts of Kozhikode, Palakkad, Malappuram, and Thrissur, with the assistance of the World Bank. The specific development objectives of the project are as follows:

1. Demonstrate the viability of cost recovery and institutional reforms by developing, testing, and implementing the new decentralized service delivery model on a pilot basis.
2. Build the state's capacity for improved sector management in order to scale up the new decentralized service delivery model statewide.

It is the first government-initiated, community-based rural water supply scheme in Kerala that has been organized by the state through NGOs. The project, which is expected to cover three lakhs of households benefiting a population of over 15 lakhs in the 80 selected lowest levels of local self-government/*grama panchayats*, has a total expected outlay of Rs. 450 Crore.

Of this, 15 percent of the capital costs are borne by the beneficiary community, 10 percent by the *grama panchayats*, and 75 percent is the share of the government. However, as a measure of reducing the financial burden on the state, the beneficiary communities are expected to meet the maintenance costs alone.

The World Bank-aided project has been implemented with the participation of the *panchayat*, NGOs, and the user communities. The project was conceived of as a demand-driven one and has been implemented only in areas where interested *panchayats* and groups of people show their willingness toward voluntary and monetary participation. The newly created autonomous body of the KWA and sanitation agency (KRWSA) was the implementing agency at the top level. The primary function of the *panchayat* is to coordinate the project and convince local peoples of the benefit of the project. The NGOs are required to provide expertise from the social and engineering fields. The social workers mobilize the community while the engineers provide technical assistance. The tenure of the project was two years, with nearly half of that time invested in the generation of awareness, as well as organizing user groups—referred to as beneficiary groups in project parlance. The rationale for using the service of an NGO is the efficiency, accountability, and speedy implementation of the project compared to the bureaucracy.

The project involves a preplanning phase of three months, which consists of *Grama panchayat* selection, selection of NGOs, and the signing of a tripartite agreement between KRWSA, *panchayat*, and NGOs. The 12-month planning phase focuses on the training and capacity-building of various officials involved, elected representatives of *grama panchayats*, officials of NGOs, organization of beneficiary groups (BGs) and their registration, the collection of data through participatory rural appraisal techniques such as transect walks, resource mapping, pre-feasibility studies that include identification of sources, water availability tests using the services of geologists, and yield tests of the existing sources that could be used for the project, among others. The implementation phase consists of eight months, which includes procurement of materials and construction of wells, ponds, and tanks. This phase is also inclusive of a four-month post-implementation phase for monitoring. At this stage, the project is fully transferred to the beneficiary committees. Henceforth, the project is fully under the responsibility of the BGs.

Following the implementation of the project, all the public taps would be removed or made part of the project. The *panchayat* or NGO has no further role in drinking water supply in that *panchayat*. It is one of the frequently referred-to sustainable water management projects operating with the participation of the user community, implemented and celebrated as a successful rural community movement in order to achieve sustainable drinking water. Responsibility for the planning and implementation of this plan lies with local peoples. The Jalanidhi initiative is repeatedly romanticized in the literature on water supply as an alternative to the failing state-run and private schemes.

Governmentality and the Micropolitics of Service Delivery in the Water Sector

Governmentality is a neologism stemming from the writings of Michel Foucault[1] and has been given different connotations, not straying from the central theme, by a proliferating body of scholarship.[2] It is an alternative analysis of political power and government in modern societies and can be comprehended as "the conduct of conduct" and "governmentalization of the state" (Foucault 1979: 20). The discourse on governmentality starts from the vantage point of how political power is exercised not through sovereign powers, but by working through individual freedom, which is made compatible with the requirements of social life (Neale 1997: 4). It is a "general term for any calculated direction of human conduct" (Dean 1999: 3), and is a "political technology" of the state by problematizing the specific domains it needs to govern (Murdoch and Ward 1997).

In contrast with the traditional political theories on power (which focus on the Machiavellian conceptions of rule), governmentality focuses on conceived power as something, which circulates. "It is not localized here or there, never in anybody's hands, never appropriated as commodity or piece of wealth" (Gordon 1980: 98). With the notion of governmentality, power in modern societies is exercised through institutions, procedures, analyses, and reflections, as well as calculations and tactics (Foucault 1979: 20). Governmentality involves the regulation of "bodily and other visible activities," the operation of which ultimately relies upon the "production of knowledge about those subjected," which Foucault called the "disciplinary power" (Hannah 1997: 171). The term "government" was used in a comprehensive sense that goes beyond the political tracts to cover the philosophical, religious, medical, and pedagogical texts (Lemke 2002: 2).

Apart from administration, government responds to such items as "problems of self control, guidance for the family and for children, management of the household, directing the soul, and so forth" (Lemke 2002: 2). This implied a greater control of its population and also the new concern for the biological well-being of the population, including disease control and prevention, adequate food and water supply, sanitation, shelter, and education, to name a few, which Foucault qualifies as "biopolitics." It is more concerned with the structuring and shaping the field of possible actions of subjects and relations between technologies of self and technologies of domination. Governmentality is composed of three components, which Darier (1996) explains as:

> [f]irstly, a centralization around the government (Army, education, governmental ministries and/or departments, justice and so on; secondly, an intensification of the effects of power at the levels of both the entire population and of the individuals (*omnes et singulatim*) and thirdly, the emergence of new forms of knowledge useful for the implementation of the centralization/intensification elements.

Foucault (1979) used the example of panopticon[3] that reflects all these three aspects of the new governmental mechanism. It represents an enduring mechanism of surveillance that opposes traditional perspectives on political power and enables reflection upon: "[the] proliferation of a whole range of apparatuses pertaining to government and a complex body of knowledge and 'know-how' about the government, the means of its exercise and the nature of those over whom it was to be exercised (Nikolas and Miller 1992: 174).

What is most important in applying the governmentality paradigm in the context of the present study is the fact that it draws attention toward the formation of knowledge that constitutes an "active citizen" image of a participant in participatory development projects. This is analyzed in the context of neoliberal regimes of power that promote individualization (under the guise of collective action). The new governmental mechanism shapes the field for proposed actions of the individuals by production, systematization, and rationalization of specific knowledge on the community and on the environment. Developments within the discourse on environmental sustainability deserve much attention in this new governance system.

The newly forged global–local linkages by global resource managers criticize the human ecologist's inability to see beyond territoriality and locality (Goldman 1997: 6). The "self interested small producer"[4] metaphor is inappropriate for explaining the environmental degradation (Goldman 1997: 8). The common inquiry has, at the conceptual level, shifted from local to global (Goldman 1997: 15). The human ecologist, development expert, and the global resource manager's views converge at the point that its use should be institutionalized by "managerialism" driven by either local or global linkages. The result is a renewed emphasize on the "rational human being" and his or her capacity to make change in his or her own life; if put differently, reinventing the potential for calculated individual action. In conformity with this point of view, international and national development initiatives focus on democratic local institutions as the basis for effective local environmental decision-making, in which individuals and communities have or can develop the skills and desire to make and effectively execute development projects.

To complicate the picture, these organizational structures, levels, and networks can be seen as overlapping or penetrated by "scapes" in which people, money, images, ideas, and the perpetual flow of technology (Appadurai 1996). This process is neither uniform nor universal, and the state—scaled at various levels—retains prime importance in setting and controlling the parameters for regime formation. Under pressure from market forces and neoliberal political forces, many states are undergoing transformations, which are evident in the reduced state authority in favor of market liberalization, regionalization, and localization. In India, the state power in the development sector, drawing authority from the 73rd and 74th amendments, has been decentralized and acted through the enhanced choices and freedoms of citizens. The focus has shifted to a people-centered approach and "active citizenship." The hitherto followed centralized delivery of service through governmental institutions and bureaucratic control has been spelled out as inefficient, and the failure of the development intervention since independence has given legitimacy to the decentralized approach. The debates, in tune with the argument of the international development agencies and academia, were diligently maneuvered to include citizens' voice within the general framework of development processes.

Governmentality and the Reinvention of Active Citizenship

Citizenship is an historical and comparative category that has evolved over the past 200 years and has taken many different turns in the different countries of the world. In his classic study entitled *Citizenship and Social Class*, T.H. Marshall (1950) described its evolution as consisting basically of the progressive expansion of certain rights: civil, political, and social. With the French Revolution, it became a socially acknowledged category (Beteille 1999: 2589). It was a part of the popular recognition accrued to participatory development or participatory governance methods, which emphasized the political participation of citizens and included their voice in development (Gaventa and Valderrama 1999; Cornwall 2000; Goetz and Gaventa 2001; Gaventa 2002). Some government authorities have promoted the notion of citizenship as a civic identity in an attempt to draw citizens together under a new form of commonality (Meekosha and Dowse 1997), while others have argued for the need to address the exclusions created by the linkage of citizenship to nation states (Ellison 1997; Newell 2000). Beyond simple participation, the term "citizenship" has been cobbled together by questions of rights, state responsibility and the responsibility of non-state actors, and mechanisms of power relations, as well as multiple dynamics of inclusion and exclusion (Gaventa 2002: 6). As Gaventa states:

> Many of these questions have been theoretically explored within the academic literature on citizenship, which often distinguishes between the liberal, communitarian and civic republican traditions which differed fundamentally based on individual freedom, differences in Identity and individual obligations in participation.

In order to analyze citizenship within the framework of governmentality, citizenship is usually seen as a right that enables peoples to act as agents (Lister 1998: 228). Thus, the concept of agency is the critical focus of any analysis on citizenship in this context. It defines a person as a competent member of any given society irrespective of its size and character, and as a consequence shapes the flow of resources to persons and social groups (Hickey and Mohan 2003: 11). Expressing citizenship or agency should therefore be considered the extension of control over the resources that involve a broader range of sociopolitical practice (Hickey and Mohan 2003: 11). This implies the involvement of active citizen participation rather than passive or withdrawn citizenship from development activities. Active citizenship may also be understood as peoples' propensity "to recognize their moral responsibilities to care and provide for their needy neighbors and to meet their obligations to encourage their talents and skills in the management of public and welfare services" (Kearns 1992: 20).

In the context of effectiveness of a primary representative, democracy is increasingly challenged (Saul 1997), laying a platform for the collaborative local action for the common good (Cox 2000), owing to difficulty of the elected representatives in engaging in the diverse issues in their constituency. Within the governmentality framework, active citizenship is a means of providing remote government where the state increasingly relies on individual capacity and subjectivity, instead of directly engaging through its apparatuses. It seeks to decentralize its power to the lower echelons of society but often undermines the inherent inequalities in social, economic, cultural, and political terms. The following section analyses the various aspects of theoretical possibilities against the backdrop of fresh and emerging water governance in Kerala in which drinking water supply is decentralized with citizens participation and "disciplining" of the space.

Panoptic Governance

In the water sector, control and surveillance operate on two levels. The first is the macro-level (the policy level), and the second is the micro-level (the local level). Institutional centralization is made very powerful through the establishment of a separate ministry of water resources, groundwater departments, and engineers. State control over natural resources is evident in the Water (Prevention and Control of Pollution) Act 1974, the Water (Prevention and Control of Pollution) Cess Act 1977, and the Environment (Protection) Act 1986. The Accelerated Rural Water Supply Program (ARWSP) in 1972–1973, the Minimum Needs

Program (MNP) during the fifth five-year plan (1974–1975), the "International Water Supply And Sanitation Decade (81–90) Program" in 1981, and the Technology Mission for drinking water in 1986—which was renamed Rajiv Gandhi National Drinking Water Supply Mission in 1991—were also intended to the "biopolitical" control of the population with the support of scientific and technological knowledge.

Surveillance through policy stems from the water policies of India (1987, 2002, and 2012) and Kerala and the international agreements. The water policies of India relate to the declared statements as well as the intended approaches of the central and state governments for water-resource planning, development, allocation, and management. They also include statements not only gravitating toward the overall policy framework, but also in terms of specific policy issues such as project selection, water pricing and cost recovery, and user and private participation. However, this all takes place under the "super panopticism" of the agenda of the international agencies. For example, the basic philosophy of the Jalanidhi project is taken from the 1999 Cochin Declaration on Rural Water Supply Policy Reforms, which spoke of:

- adopting "Demand–Responsive Approaches through use of participatory processes";
- changing the role of government from provider to facilitator;
- establishing financial viability and sustainability of rural water supply services; and
- promoting integrated water resource management.

According to the website of Jalanidhi, the project is conceptualized as a demand driven one, with active participation of the local community in planning, implementation, monitoring, and day-to-day functioning of the project. This will be owned, operated, and maintained by the users themselves on a total cost–recovery basis. The plan reveals the strong commitment of the government's policies to international discourses and agencies related to the governance of water. As early as 1977, the United Nations Water Conference held at Mar del Plata, Argentina, confirmed that "[a]ll people have a right to have access to drinking water." The New Delhi Declaration of 1990 endorsed the principle of "some for all rather than more for some," which reflects the fundamental human rights principle of universality. It marks the official birth of the community management paradigm in India. The Dublin Statement on Water and Sustainable Development (1992) states that water is an "economic good."

As explicit in the international policies on development, efficiency and sustainability are the major two aspects that external agencies adopt as a viable solution to the scarcity of drinking water. It is also reflected in both the national water policies in 1987 and 2002, stating that "efforts to develop, conserve, utilise and manage this important resource in a sustainable manner have to be guided by the national perspective." Nonetheless, the issue of efficiency and sustainability has been manifested through the proxy of "community participation" or "user participation."

In line with this, the Kerala water policy (Government of Kerala 2008) states:

> [a]ccess to water is a human right. As water is a common heritage having economic value, the responsibility for its regulated use and conservation is vested with every citizen and community ... it is important to make sure that the right of every citizen to equitable access to water for his or her basic needs is protected and enforced through appropriate policy, legislative and program initiatives.

It asserts that water is a human right but it is the duty of the citizen to determine its availability and use.

The Kerala water authority, established in 1986 and responsible for the public drinking water supply, is now almost redundant due to corruption and bureaucratic apathy. It ensures public participation though the inherent dangers behind it invite concern. For example, the 2007 Kerala water policy states that water has an economic value. The entire debate centers on the economical sustainability of water with the strategies of cutting off subsidies and efficient cost-recovery mechanisms. The discourse points to the efficient use of water using business management principles and its reliance on individual rationalities and market mechanisms in the water governance (Salskov et al. 2000: 3). The role of the expert has been changed from a technocratic approach to a social-centric approach.

The concept of technology has also shifted to new environmentally sustainable technologies that prevent over-exploitation of water. It is evident from the project documents that the regime of action is defined and the rules are fixed for government regarding water.

Strategies of Spatial Disciplining

Disciplining power of modern government systems has long been a focal concern of governmentality. It analyzes emergence of the modern social state, the forms of modern exercise of power, and its different expressions (Fejes and Nicoll 2008: 13). The emergence of neoliberal states and its governing apparatuses closely fits in the governmentality framework of analyses. The shaping and disciplining of the conduct of the population and management of the territory is exercised through an interface of power/knowledge put forward by Foucault (1980).

The project has adopted the basic tenets of the Cochin Declaration (WSP 1999), which promulgates a demand-responsive approach, as well as changing the role of government from one of "provider" to one in which it acts as "facilitator." Subsequently, the projects are implemented in regions where people have come forward and demanded water under this scheme. The demand is created through well-articulated participatory development strategies, including awareness-generation programs conducted by NGOs and other agencies, whether they work together on this issue or independently. The experts are divided into two sections. One section constitutes social workers predominantly armed with critical education in the field of social work and similar disciplines, and who are responsible for the community empowerment or capacity-building programs. The second section is primarily technical and comprised of engineers and other personnel with training in similar fields of practice. The social workers' responsibility is to bring the community into a common platform where they instil their "expert knowledge" in order to ensure the active participation of each citizen.

A noted feature of these awareness programs is imparting "critical consciousness"[5] of the individual responsibility (Freire 1973) and creating contempt toward government-run mechanisms for the supply of drinking water. Drawing inspiration from the Participatory Rural Appraisal[6] (PRA) of Chambers (1983), the empowerment programs included various techniques such as transect walks, videos, and participatory resource mapping. During the exercise, people were encouraged to identify the problems and possibilities related with drinking water in their locality independently. Through this process, the individuals are subjected to formulate knowledge on their locality.

The following step involved networking and liaising in different regions. The participants are made subject to self-criticism through questions such as: Have you noticed the broken pumps and public taps that cause leakage for days in your locality? Have you ever done anything to rectify that? The debates are carefully directed toward lack of responsibility of the people in rectifying it and the inefficiency of the government institutions. The moderator from an NGO notes their irresponsible behavior in lack of monitory and physical participation and community monitoring.

Exhorting to put aside political difference in the overall running of the projects is another noted characteristic of these awareness programs. Promoting health consciousness is a further component of the project. The participants are made aware of what is perceived of as poor health habits and practices they are following. Water samples would be collected from the project villages and checked in laboratories, and revealing the possibility of leakage of faecal matter from septic tanks and open areas to the drinking water sources. Experts targeted behavioral changes of the community in matters of hygiene—such as the importance of washing hands after defecation and dangers of open defecation—through specialized education programs. It also includes inculcating contempt toward such governmental institutions such as the water authority, and in rural areas *panchayat* wells and ponds. This may be interpreted as tactical, whereby the state is encouraging citizen participation by projecting public drinking water supply as inefficient at the same time as it promotes "pastoral care" through various means of influence. It is articulated through the individual's will to rectify/control his or her own actions in availing the drinking water while coaxing him or her to remain loyal to the governing authority.

Redefining Rights and Duties

Once consensus is reached among the participants, politicians, and defying voices, participants are encouraged to organize as small beneficiary groups. This implies that the right to a minimum requirement of water would be realized only if they perform their duty as "active participants" during the course of the project. These groups are the manifestation of social capital hailed by the World Bank in its literature and are interpreted as proxies for the ineffective centralized supply-driven water supply by the state, which currently lacks accountability and efficiency. Here, the individual is responsible for his or her own basic water requirements, and he or she should thus act in tandem with the dynamic of the group to which he or she forms a part.

The user group often consists of 10–20 households and follows its own set of rules and responsibilities as proscribed by the funding agencies operating though grassroots-level NGOs. Each group is registered under the Charitable Societies and Registration Act and has a president, secretary, and treasurer placed in their respective positions as a result of majority decision, and trained in the necessary tasks to conduct the group's operations. They receive their training from a range of NGOs. In all cases, people who had economic, cultural, and political capital were selected for these positions. "Less active" individuals have little to no voice in the decision-making process. Decisions are taken by the selected leadership of the group, the NGO worker/representative, and other officials.

Bringing concepts such as cost recovery, efficiency, and effective utilization greatly supplements business management principles, while water is conceived of here as an economic good that has to be managed with minimal state intervention. It is contingent upon the concept of "rational economic man" in neoclassical economics. Here, each individual is responsible, self-controlled, and would monitor each other's actions. This panopticism is more effective than direct state control, and local spaces are literally under surveillance without using violence, which is the ultimate form of governmentality.

Through the "technologies of self," the state can efficiently exercise the biopolitical management of its populations with minimum cost. The state, which has the authority and responsibilities over its citizenry, has started widening its horizon to include these "scapes" to the efficient delivery of safe minimum water requirements. The image of the local people has been deliberately transformed from passive receptors of benefits to active citizens who have greater control of their livelihood and have been granted more decision-making power on issues related to their communities in order to meet the political ends of the state.

The normalization process of citizen participation has two dimensions. First, it upholds the notion that water is an economic good, for which each individual has to pay for; second, it is the duty of the citizen to actively participate in its delivery and monitoring. Pivotal to the debates on active citizen participation in cost-efficiency and user-community charging is the redefinition of the role of state in development. The state eventually has become a mere facilitator, rather than a legitimate provider of rights and justice.

Active citizenship for sustainable economic development calls for the institutionalization of communities for the effective utilization of human capital and resources. Here, supplying economic goods and assisting the overall progress of society becomes a duty of the community. Naturally, this has immense political implications, as it breaks the Hobbesian social contract. Active citizenship strategies reorganize some of the fundamental rights, such as social and economic security, as well as the right of poverty or of being in poor health, which the community surrendered before the state in a social contract, to duties of the community. However, this breaking of the social contract is not generally visible, because it is reinforced by a well-built discursive formation that includes the notion of economism, debates on ethnic market, and social capital. With the discursive restructuring, some of the central concerns of development—such as social justice, economic inequality, and democracy—are evidently marginalized. Moreover, active citizenship strategies for sustainable development operate amid a political climate of consensus, at least in the economic sphere. This can certainly develop a kind of democracy based on popular participation, but without the inconvenience of contestational politics, as Harriss (2001) observed. For him, participatory strategies for sustainable development increasingly eschew the conflicts of values and ideas necessary for democratic politics and practice to function and operate freely.

Conclusion

The concept of governmentality introduced by Michael Foucault to analyze the modern forms of power can be applied to a variety of social issues. Governmentality coincides with the concept of active citizenship, which can be used as a tool to implement the "remote control" technologies of government and government authority. This chapter used the case of water and sanitation to show inherent dangers of valorizing the concept of active citizenship in decentralized water supply. The analysis based on the World Bank-aided Jalanidhi project shows the implication of these concepts at the grassroots level. These target-based projects constantly encourage the participation of the people.

While the idea centers upon the inclusion of so-called "unheard voices," the underlying agenda seeks to find alternatives to avoid the responsibilities of government. The state was seen to have eventually become a mere facilitator, rather than a legitimate provider of rights and justice. A participatory strategy for sustainable economic development calls for the institutionalization of communities for the effective and positive utilization of human capital and resources. Here, supplying economic goods and assisting the overall progress of society, including its various constituents, becomes a duty of the citizen/community. Naturally, this has immense political implications, as it breaks the Hobbesian social contract. Participatory strategies reorganize some of the fundamental rights and duties of the community. However, this disconnect is not visible by and large, as it is reinforced by a well-built discursive formation. With the discursive restructuring, some of the central concerns of development such as social justice, economic inequality, and democracy are evidently marginalized.

The entire process is a pedagogically inclined one, which includes conscientization at the local level through various levels of awareness programs. It is in tandem with such factors as the global discourse on health, hygiene, and basic water requirements; more specifically, it is a process of implementation of the preconceived ideas developed by the global discourse on water governance. It uses culturally imbibed techniques or customization of the objectives at the local level, set by the transnational funding organizations.

"Participatory Rural Appraisal" techniques are a classic example of promoting the active participation of citizens to meet the political ends of the state. In short, it serves the dual purpose of enhancing people's involvement in the projects and softens the dissenting voices by the strategies of inclusion. The conceptualization and spreading of the concept of active citizenship redefines the "right" of the citizens over water as a "duty" of the citizen, and ultimately marginalizes resistance and negotiation in society.

Notes

*   This chapter is a revised version of Babu (2009).

1.   For more details, see Foucault (1979, 1981).
2.   Mitchell Dean (1999) has offered a conceptual clarification on this topic in his book *Governmentality* (see also Miller and Rose 1990; Hindess 1996; O'Farrell 1997).
3.   An efficient prison model designed by Jeremy Bentham involves an annular ring of black-lit cells surrounding a central observatory tower from which each prisoner is potentially visible to unseen guards (see Foucault 1977).
4.   Garrett Hardin's parable imagines a set of pastoralists who destroy the future viability of their pastoral commons by each of them selfishly deciding to increase their herd size for individual short-term benefit, until the commons becomes overgrazed (see Hardin 1968).
5.   The term "critical consciousness" was coined by Brazilian educator Paulo Freire in the 1960s. Freire defined critical consciousness as a state of in-depth understanding about the world and resulting freedom from oppression, which was at first applied mainly in the field of adult education. Freire explored liberating educational methods that he believed could promote the development of critical consciousness, a process that would lead to their emancipation and advancement. His theories have greatly influenced thinking about participatory development (Freire 1973).
6.   Participatory rural appraisal (PRA) comprises a set of techniques aimed at shared learning between local people and outsiders. During this time, PRA has moved from the margins to the development mainstream, opening up space for a diversity of meanings and applications. During the 1990s, it was adopted in accordance with the general debate on governance as a new form or even substitute of the traditional government and considered as a strategy to open up spaces otherwise closed off to citizen engagement. For more details, see Chambers (1983).

References

Appadurai, A. (1996) *Modernity at Large: Cultural Dimensions of Globalization*, Minneapolis, MN: University of Minnesota Press.

Babu, A. (2009) "Governmentality, Active Citizenship, and Marginalization: The Case of Rural Drinking Water Supply in Kerala, India," *Asian Social Science*, 5(11): 89–98.

Beteille, A. (1999) "Citizenship, State and Civil Society," *Economic and Political Weekly*, 34(36): 2588–2591.

Chambers, R. (1983) *Whose Reality Counts? Putting the Last First*, Harlow: Longman.

Cornwall, A. (2000) *Beneficiary, Consumer, Citizen: Perspectives on Participation for Poverty Reduction*, Stockholm: Swedish International Development Cooperation Agency (SIDA).

Cox, E. (2000) "Creating a More Civil Society: Community Level Indicators of Social Capital," *Just Policy: A Journal of Australian Social Policy*, 19/20: 100–107.

Darier, E. (1996) "Environmental Governmentality: The Case of Canada's Green Plan," *Environmental Politics*, 5(4): 587–588.

Dean, M. (1999) *Governmentality*, London: Sage.

Dublin Statement (1992) *The Dublin Statement on Water and Sustainable Development*, available at: www.gdrc.org/uem/water/dublin-statement.html (accessed April 13, 2007).

Ellison, N. (1997) "Towards a New Social Politics: Citizenship and Reflexivity in Late Modernity," *Sociology*, 31(4): 697–711.

Fejes, A. and Nicoll, K. (2008) *Katherine Foucault and Lifelong Learning*, Canada: Routledge.

Foucault, M. (1977) *Discipline and Punish: The Birth of the Modern Prison*, New York: Vintage Books.

Foucault, M. (1979) "Governmentality," *Ideology and Consciousness*, 6: 5–21.

Foucault, M. (1980) *Power/Knowledge: Selected Interviews and Other Writings 1972–1977*, New York: Pantheon.

Foucault, M. (1981) "Omnes et Singulatim: Towards a Criticism of 'Political Reason'," in S. McMurrin (Ed.), *The Tanner Lectures of Human Values*, 11, Salt Lake City, UT: University of Utah Press, pp. 225–254.

Freire, P. (1973) *Education for Critical Consciousness*, New York: The Seabury Press.

Gaventa, J. (2002) "Introduction: Exploring Citizenship, Participation and Accountability," *IDS Bulletin*, 33(2): 1–18.

Gaventa, J. and Valderrama, C. (1999) "Participation, Citizenship and Local Governance," Background Paper for Workshop: *Strengthening Participation in Local Governance*, Mimeo, Brighton: IDS, pp. 21–24.

Gianpaolo, B. (2003) "Emergent Public Spheres: Talking Politics in Participatory Governance," *American Sociological Review*, 68(1): 1.

Goetz, A.M. and Gaventa, J. (2001) *From Consultation to Influence: Bringing Citizen Voice and Client Focus into Service Delivery*, IDS Working Paper 138, Brighton: Institute of Development Studies.

Goldman, M. (1997) "Customs in Common: The Epistemic World of Commons Scholars," *Theory and Society*, 26(1): 6.

Gordon, C. (Ed.) (1980) *Power/Knowledge: Selected Interviews and Other Writings 1972–1977*, Brighton: Harvester Press.

Government of Kerala (1998) Order G.O. (P) No. 181/98/LAD, dated Thiruvananthapuram, September 2.

Government of Kerala (2006) *Economic Review*, available at: www.kerala.gov.in/index.php?option=com_content&view=article&id=3338&Itemid=2921 (accessed December 23, 2008).

Government of Kerala (2008) *Kerala State Water Policy*, available at: http://kerala.gov.in/docs/policies/wp_08.pdf (accessed October 8, 2008).

Hannah, M.G. (1997) "Space and the Structuring of Disciplinary Power: An Interpretive Review," *Geografiska Annaler*, 79(3): 171–180.

Hardin, G. (1968) "The Tragedy of the Commons," *Science*, 162: 1243–1248.

Harriss, J. (2001) *Depoliticizing Development: The World Bank and Social Capital*, New Delhi: Left Word Books.

Hickey, S. and Mohan, G. (2003) *Relocating Participation within a Radical Politics of Development: Citizenship and Radical Modernism*, draft Working Paper prepared for conference on participation: "From Tyranny to Transformation? Exploring New Approaches to Participation in Development," Manchester University.

High Court of Kerala (1997) O.P. No. 18175/1996-L, April 4.

Hindess, B. (1996) *Discourses of Power: From Hobbes to Foucault*, Oxford: Blackwell.

Kearns, A.J. (1992) "Active Citizenship and Urban Governance," *Transactions of the Institute of British Geographers*, 17(1): 20–34.

Lemke, T. (2002) "Foucault, Governmentality, and Critique," *Rethinking Marxism*, 14(3): 49–64.

Lister, R. (1998) "Citizen in Action: Citizenship and Community Development in Northern Ireland Context," *Community Development Journal*, 33(3): 226–235.

Marshall, T.H. (1950) *Citizenship and Social Class*, Cambridge: Cambridge University Press.

Meekosha, H. and Dowse, L. (1997) "Enabling Citizenship: Gender, Disability and Citizenship, Australia," *Feminist Review*, 57: 49–72.

Miller, P. and Rose, N. (1990) "Governing Economic Life," *Economy and Society*, 19(1): 1–31.

Murdoch, J. and Ward, N. (1997) "Governmentality and Territoriality: The Statistical Manufacture of Britain's 'National Farm'," *Political Geography*, 16: 307–324.

National Family Health Survey (1998–1999) "Source of Drinking Water by State 1998–99," in McKenzie David and Ray Isha (2005) Household Water Delivery Options in Urban and Rural India, Working Paper No. 224, Stanford Centre for International Development, available at: http://web.stanford.edu/group/siepr/cgi-bin/siepr/?q=system/files/shared/pubs/papers/pdf/SCID224.pdf (accessed December 8, 2009).

Neale, A. (1997) "Organizing Environmental Self-Regulation: Liberal Governmentality and the Pursuit of Ecological Modernization in Europe," *Environmental Politics*, 6(4): 1–24.

New Delhi Statement (1990) *1972–2006: From Stockholm to Mexico*, UNESCO, available at: www.unesco.org/water/wwap/milestones/index.shtml (accessed March 3, 2007).

Newell, P. (2000) "Environmental NGOs and Globalization: The Governance of TNCs," in R. Cohen and S. Rai (Eds.), *Global Social Movements*, London: Athlone Press, pp. 117–134.

Nikolas, R. and Miller, P. (1992) "Political Power Beyond the State: Problematics of Government," *The British Journal of Sociology*, 43(2): 173–205.

O'Farrell, C. (Ed.) (1997) *Foucault: The Legacy*, Brisbane: Queensland University of Technology.

Peters, B.G. and Pierre, J. (1998) "Governance without Government? Rethinking Public Administration," *Journal of Public Administration Research and Theory*, 8(2): 223–243.

Pilllai, V. (1946) *The Travancore State Manual Chapter* 6, State Gazetteer Department GoK [reprinted in 1996].

Provan, K. and Milward, H.B. (1995) "A Preliminary Theory of Interorganizational Network Effectiveness," *Administrative Science Quarterly*, 40(1): 1–33.

Salskov, I., Dorte, H., Krause, H., and Bislev, S. (2000) *Governmentality, Globalization and Local Practice: Transformations of a Hegemonic Discourse*, available at: http://ep.lib.cbs.dk/download/ISBN/x648030775.pdf (accessed September 27, 2007).

Saul, R.J. (1997) *The Unconscious Civilization*, Sydney: Penguin.

Stoker, G. (1998) "Governance as Theory: Five Propositions," *International Social Science Journal*, 50(1): 17.

WSP (1999) "Politicians for Reform", Proceedings of the State Water Ministers' Workshop on Rural Water Supply Policy Reforms in India Cochin, Kerala (India), December 7–8, available at: www.wsp.org/sites/wsp.org/files/publications/327200791643_sa_reform.pdf (accessed May 25, 2006).

Chapter 14

Public Corruption and Civic Disclosure: Natural Resources and Indonesia

Mark S. Williams

The fight against corruption is an imperative of contemporary Indonesian *demokrasi* and *reformasi*. "*Korupsi, kollusi, dan nepotisme*" (corruption, collusion, and nepotism)—or, as it is more commonly known in Indonesia, "KKN"—acted as a rallying cry that helped usher in democratic reform in Indonesia. However, the failure of the state to remedy the conditions of KKN represents the greatest threat to the legitimacy of Indonesia's newly founded democratic institutions. The discontent of KKN played a significant role in the revolution that swept Suharto from power and in the defeat of the first three presidents who came after him. This imperative to fight against corruption has been driven by both the public resentment over the injustices KKN produces and a fear in Indonesian civil society that KKN is discouraging international investment, thereby prohibiting Indonesia's economic development.

Susilo Bambang Yudhoyono (SBY) made the fight against KKN a central feature of his politics, leveraging his anti-KKN stance into winning the first directly contested presidential election in Indonesian history. He went on to win a second consecutive electoral victory. After a seven-year span when Indonesia went through four presidents, SBY brought stability to the young democracy, serving the maximum number of terms as president allowed under Indonesian law, from 2004 to 2014. The stability of the SBY years was deeply connected to his early national strategies toward the eradication of corruption, such as his empowerment of the Komisi Pemberantasan Korupsi (the Corruption Eradication Commission—KPK). Anti-KKN politics helped to earn SBY the public trust. This trust, however, proved to be ephemeral as the Indonesian public began to doubt the effectiveness of the anticorruption measures over the final two years of SBY's presidency; even more worryingly, the public lost confidence in the promises of the republic as a democracy.

Corruption is difficult to measure, and so too is it difficult to measure the progress made in the fight against it. Public disclosure in corruption cases is now recognized as a central mechanism to empower anticorruption institutions by informing civil society of the sectors that have proven to be the most corrupt. This chapter overviews the lack of public disclosure on corruption cases in Indonesia, the third most populous democracy in the world but a country that has only been democratic since 1998. It chronicles the auspicious sentiment expressed during the first term of SBY's administration—when the KPK appeared to have the institutional momentum to make a discernable impact on the corrupt practices found in the republic—to a state of frustration and despondency less than a decade later. Analysis of the investigations and the prosecutions of the KPK demonstrate that the most important institution in this young democracy's anticorruption campaign has been reluctant to provide much disclosure to civil society on the extent of corruption in the natural resource sectors.

Corruption, Natural Resources, and Disclosure

Perhaps this contradiction between global governance and the global political economy is no more evident than in the international trade of natural resources. Corruption plagues forestry (Irland 2008), mining (Petermann et al. 2007), energy (Shaxson 2007), and the natural resource sector generally (Robbins 2000). A parsimonious model advanced by Klitgaard (1988) to explain the pervasiveness of corruption in natural resource sectors posits that corruption occurs where rents are high, public officials have discretion in their allocation, and these officials are not accountable to any system of public disclosure.

The stakes are particularly high in cases of corruption in natural resource management because in addition to the profound human misery corruption inflicts on societies (Siverson and Johnson 2014), it has also been shown to lead to rapid ecological degradation (Pellegrini and Gerlagh 2006; Koyuncu and Yilmaz 2009). So systemic is corruption in the natural resource sector, it has even been debated whether corruption is the leading cause of the "natural resource curse" (the relationship between high rents earned through natural resource exports and sluggish overall economic growth) (Sachs and Warner 2001; Mehlum et al. 2006; Kolstad and Søreide 2009).

Corruption of natural resource sectors persists in spite of anticorruption becoming an issue of increasing attention for civil society (Elliot 1997: 1; Wang and Rosenau 2001). There have been notable increases in the amount of media coverage on corruption, as well as in public awareness. Transparency International (TI) became one of the major voices calling for disclosure in the fight against corruption in the mid-1990s, employing a "name and shame" strategy of disclosing and humiliating national governments that expect kickbacks and bribes (Haufler 2010: 620). Other notable institutions that have arisen in this context of using disclosure to fight corruption include the Organisation for Economic Co-operation and Development's (OECD) "Convention on Combating Bribery of Public Officials in International Business Transactions," the United Nations Convention Against Corruption (UNCAC), and, most significantly, the Extractive Industries Transparency Initiative (EITI).

The original idea behind EITI was to have corporations involved in extractive industries (oil, gas, and minerals) disclose the taxes and fees paid to governments, and for governments to disclose revenue earned. However, the focus of EITI quickly moved away from corporate disclosure and has instead become almost exclusively preoccupied with governmental disclosure (Haufler 2010: 65). As of early 2014, EITI has grown to 27 compliant members (roughly half of them located in western Africa) and 17 candidate countries. The criticism is that the "promotion" of disclosing revenue has not led directly to "adoption" as the extractive sector continues to be opaque (Haufler 2010: 58).

Disclosure to the public is dependent on national anticorruption institutions and legislation rather than at work at the international level, and these efforts have been "hollow" (Brown and Cloke 2004; Meagher 2005; Bukovansky 2006; Heineman and Heimann 2006). Kolstad and Wiig (2009: 522) have demonstrated that there exists a statistical correlation between low transparency of public disclosure by national institutions and high levels of corruption. The trend is especially discernible in countries that are dependent on rents from natural resources. This relationship exists because corruption is not as risky without public disclosure. Public officials do not have any little incentive to be clean, and it is easy for these public officials to gain access to rents without oversight mechanisms. Furthermore, the corrupt practices of institutions can influence civil society, weakening trust and undermining social norms of citizenship, community, fairness, and justice, and create a vicious cycle where corruption is expected (Kolstad and Wiig 2009: 522).

So foundational is disclosure as a mechanism in UNCAC, EITI, and the OECD that there is even talk of a "transparency turn" going on in international politics (Gupta 2010: 2). The fight against corruption requires what Gupta (2010: 2) calls "governance by disclosure," and what Florini (2010: 123) refers to as "regulation by revelation."

The Politics of Corruption in Indonesia

The years of Susilo Bambang Yudhoyono's (SBY) presidency in the Republic of Indonesia, from 2004 to 2014, represent the first period of relative stability in the *demokrasi dan reformasi* (democracy and reform) era (1998–present). During this period, Indonesia had experienced some modest progress in its fight against corruption. Transparency International's "Corruption Perceptions Index" is not a precise measure of corruption, quantifying graft, bribes, or missing money. It is instead a measure based on the perception held by international investors of how corrupt the public sector is in countries throughout the world. Corruption in Indonesia is interpreted by surveyed investors as less severe compared to 1999–2000, but there persists a belief that corruption has only modestly decreased from the final years of Suharto's New Order.

Suharto held the reins of power for three decades through a twin spectre of fear and the promise of economic development. Fidelity to the Orde Baru (New Order—name of the Suharto regime to differentiate it from the Sukarno years, derided by Suharto as the Orde Lama, or Old Order) on a doctrine of stabilitas nasional (national stability) resonated within a society traumatized by the revolutionary and genocidal events that occurred between late September 1965 and early 1966. Suharto rejected Sukarno's destabilizing politics of the romantik, dialektik, and dynamism (romanticism, dialectic conflict, and a spiritedness). With an authoritarian grip on power, Suharto demanded the same rejection of revolutionary politics from society, destroying the Partai Kommunis Indonesia (Communist Party of Indonesia—PKI) and demanding an uncompromising adherence to the Pancasila (Five Principles of the Indonesian Constitution) as the asas tunggal (sole foundation) of republican life. In return, Indonesians were promised physical security, political and economic predictability, and above all, economic growth. Stability came not entirely from the Indonesian fear of national disintegration (which had scarred the politics of the archipelago since the early years of the early twentieth century's "national revival"), but also from a hopefulness rooted in *pembangunan ekonomi* (developmental economics).

After the crippling inflation of the mid-1960s was brought under heel, the New Order boasted of its fantastic economic growth rates, auguring an auspicious future for the republic. It also feigned concern for corruption. In 1970, soon after he had become president, Suharto appointed "the Commission of Four" to deal with corruption. The commission had no direct powers over the investigation of corruption cases. Instead, they were to act as an advisory panel to Indonesia's new president, who quickly dissolved the commission within two months (Setiyono and McLeod 2010: 348). Shortly thereafter, student activists at the University of Indonesia—including Emil Salim, one of the five members of the so-called "Berkeley Mafia"—organized protests against the dissolution of the commission. The New Order grudgingly responded to the demonstrations by granting committee powers to the activists, but never offering much support to their investigations and relying on internal dysfunctions to prevent them from becoming an efficacious institution in the republic. Charges of corruption gripped the New Order during the early to mid 1970s, culminating in the *Malari* incident—a wave of demonstrations that met Japanese Prime Minister Kakuie Tanaka during his state visit to Jakarta. Later, during the 1980s, a "Petition of Fifty" was circulated to the public. It was drafted by a number of politicians and retired military officers who condemned the graft of Suharto and his extended family. The drafters of the petition were ultimately intimidated out of public life, or co-opted back into the power structure of the New Order.

It was during the mid 1990s when anticorruption returned to Indonesian public discourse, and this time there was no dismissing it. Amien Rais, the chair of Muhammadiyah (the oldest Islamic organization currently active in the republic, and at approximately 30 million members, the second largest) first used the phrase *korupsi, kollusi, dan nepotisme* (KKN). His critique centred on the corruption of the Suharto family and the ostensibly unscrupulous mining contracts that were being signed with international investors. When the Asian Financial Crisis hit, KKN became a common refrain from the demonstrators, uniting liberal, Islamic, nationalist, socialist, and Christian organizations for the common purpose of overthrowing the government. The fight against corruption was stated in one World Bank report as "at the heart" of *reformasi* (World Bank Group 2003: i).

The catastrophe of the Asian Financial Crisis proved to be the existential threat to Suharto that could not be overcome. Post-*reformasi* Indonesia is similarly faced with an existential threat in the form of large-scale financial volatility, yet the republic escaped the 2008 Global Financial Crisis mostly unscathed. There does persist a *milieu* of existential threats to the democratic institutions of Indonesia during the early twenty-first century, such as Islamist groups who reject the nondenominational sentiment of the Pancasila, hyper-nationalistic forces within the military, and the tense relationship between Java and the Outer Islands. Still, the greatest existential threat to Indonesia's democracy is KKN.

Suharto's successor, B.J. Habibie, the final vice president of the New Order, lasted a year and a half as president, before he too was booted out of office in the shadow of corruption charges. Habibie's government allegedly requested US$60 million from Bali Bank for his party in the upcoming election, money that Indonesia received from the IMF for its post-crisis stabilization fund. Indonesia's second president of the *reformasi* period, Abdurrahman Wahid—known as "Gus Dur"—similarly lasted only a year and a half. Gus Dur lost the confidence of the MPR (People's Consultative Assembly), the DPR (People's Representative Council), and the general public over the revelations that he had accepted US$2 million from the Sultan of Brunei for his election campaign and that US$3.5 million had gone missing from the National Food Logistics Agency. With nearly half of his cabinet under investigation on corruption charges, a defiant Gus Dur was also forced out of office. The third president of the republic of this time, Megawati Sukarnoputri, enjoyed more success than her two predecessors —lasting in office for three and a half years (though there was no direct election for the office of the president).

It was during these turbulent years that the first post-*reformasi* anticorruption institution was hastily assembled. In 2000, the Office of the Attorney General launched the Joint Investigating Team for Corruption Eradication (Tim Gabungan Pemberantasan Tindakan Korupsi—TGPTK). The objective of the TGPTK was to investigate the complex and politically sensitive corruption cases where the courts did not have the confidence of the Attorney General. The TGPTK was only intended to function as a stopgap measure before a comprehensive and independent anticorruption institution was to be officially announced within the next two years. However, lacking the power and initiative to launch investigations into sensitive cases, and forced into an irreconcilable debate over what cases could not be trusted to the courts, the TGPTK was barely able to last one year before it was decommissioned (Butt 2011: 383).

The TGPTK's intended successor, the Komisi Pemberantasan Korupsi (Corruption Eradication Commission—KPK) was established with Law No. 30 in 2002. Measures afforded to the KPK to strengthen the institution included its independence from the government, the ability to take the initiative on what cases are investigated, a mechanism that prohibits cases to be dropped after investigation begins (to limit the impact of bribes on the institution), and a tribunal for prosecutions where defendants found guilty are automatically directed to Indonesia's Anti-Corruption Court (Pengadilan Tindak Pidana Korupsi—Tipikor). Tipikor can then initiate a criminal trial based on the KPK investigation and prosecution.

Eventually, for Megawati, public discontent over the slow economic recovery after the Asian Financial Crisis, the appearance of showing too much solidarity with the Bush Administration in the months after the 9/11 terrorist attacks, and the perceived unwillingness

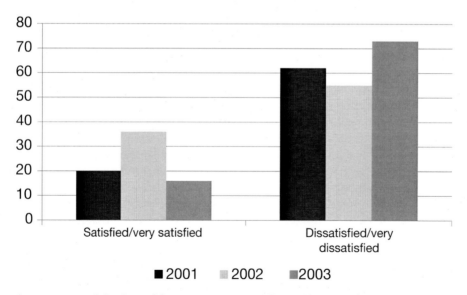

Figure 14.1 Satisfaction with Government Handling of KKN, Percentage

of the Megawati government to take action on KKN provided the context for the electoral victory of Susilo Bambang Yudhoyono (SBY).

The Indonesian Fight Against Corruption

The KPK was established under the auspicious pretext that the Indonesian state was finally going to dismantle the corrupt institutions of the New Order under an independent institution. The KPK became operational one year after Law No. 30 was passed, and it has since been faced with a truly daunting task.

Up until 2012, all public complaints (thousands of them in number) were being assessed by the KPK. Throughout its first decade of operations, they found the majority of complaints received to be "actionable" (Figure 14.2). Not every case was actually investigated—as subsequent figures will show, only a tiny minority of them were—but the overwhelming number of cases that were interpreted by the KPK as having "a high probability of convictions" is staggering.

Additional initiatives of the early years of the SBY Administration—intended to be delivered on an anti-KKN platform—included a Presidential Decree on the Acceleration of Corruption Eradication in Indonesia (5/2004), and the *National Action Plan for Corruption Prevention and Education, 2004–2009* (DAN-PPK). Public sentiment during the early years of the KPK was very hopeful, with majority of respondents under the impression that corruption in Indonesia would decrease over the next three years in late 2003 and in 2004.

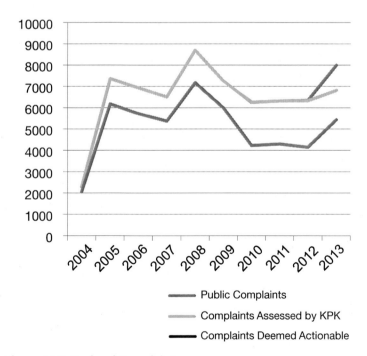

Figure 14.2 Scale of Complaints

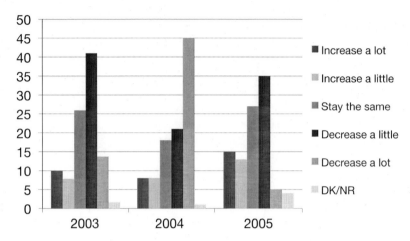

Figure 14.3 Corruption Over the Next Three Years

2004 was a particularly promising year, with 45 percent of Indonesians under the impression that corruption was going to "decrease a lot" and 21 percent with the belief that it would decrease a little. By 2005, however, public hopefulness for developments to dismantle corruption began to deflate—as only 5 percent of respondents chose "decrease a lot" (although more respondents thought that corruption was set to "decrease a little" than any other possibility) (Figure 14.3).

Between 2004 and 2007, under the chairmanship of Taufiqurrahman Ruki, the KPK pursued its fight against corruption incrementally—investigating mid-level officials in national and regional governments. Simon Butt (2011) describes this period of time as characterized by the KPK's unwillingness to go after the "big fish" of Indonesian corruption, either in contemporary cases or those that pertained to the Asian Financial Crisis a decade prior (Butt 2011: 384).

Despite this tempering of enthusiasm by 2005 for the KPK (largely due to the public coming to understand the slowness of the pace of the KPK), anticorruption measures continued to represent the one area related to the economy that showed positive polling for SBY in August 2005.

In another IFES survey from 2010, 72 percent of Indonesians in the poll responded that they were aware of the KPK (IFES 2010: 11). For those who identified as aware of the KPK, a generally positive impression for the anticorruption institution was revealed.

The KPK polled slightly higher than the courts and the municipal government; far higher than the DPR and only slightly below mayors, governors, and SBY himself.

The signing of Law No. 7 in 2006 ratified the 2003 United Nations Convention Against Corruption (UNCAC). Ratification of the UNCAC represents Indonesia's acceptance of the legal provisions of the convention, working toward making these provisions binding in Indonesian law. Five years after ratification, Indonesia became one of the first countries to have its anticorruption policies reviewed by other UNCAC members. In 2010, SBY and the DPR passed Law No. 8, "On the Prevention and Eradication of Money Laundering" (Presiden Republik Indonesia 2010). This law represented another step against corruption by SBY, stressing the international danger of money laundering, stated as a threat to *stabilitas perekonomian*

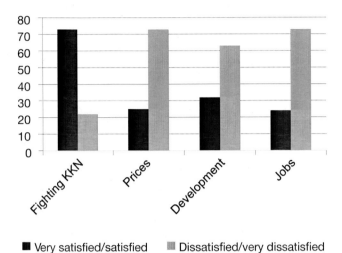

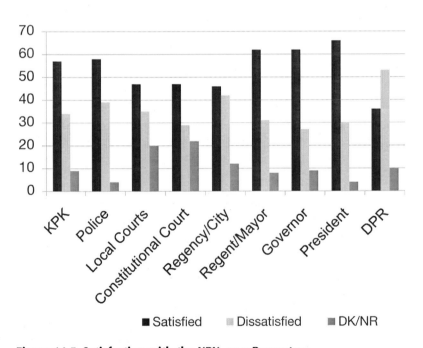

Figure 14.4 Satisfaction with SBY's Administration

Figure 14.5 Satisfaction with the KPK, as a Percentage

(economic stability) and the *sistem keuangan* (financial system), as well as a significant domestic threat to *kehidupan bermasyarakat, berbangsa, dan bernegara* (society, nation, and the state).

Though slightly more Indonesians in 2007 were under the impression that the government's fight against corruption was "ineffective" rather than "effective," it was 2008 that proved to be the perceived high point in the republic's fight against corruption. However, the aggressive turn of the KPK also led to a reaction against it by some members of the

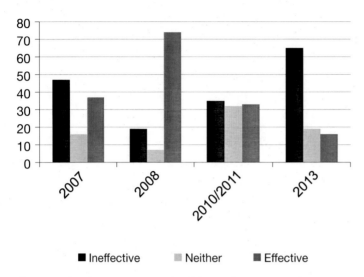

Figure 14.6 The Government's Fight against Corruption

establishment. Between 2008 and 2009, under its new chair Antasari Azhar, the KPK began to investigate some of the "big fishes" it avoided between 2004 and 2007 (Butt 2011: 386).

Almost 75 pecent of respondents thought that the government was effectively fighting corruption in 2008, and in 2009, just after SBY's electoral victory for a second term, an incident occurred that galvanized support for the work being done by the KPK. Susno Duadji, the chief detective for the Indonesian police, incensed that his phone was being tapped during a corruption investigation, menacingly threatened the KPK. The police chief ostentatiously referred to himself and the police force as a *buaya* (crocodile) and the KPK as a meek, little *cicak* (gecko). The gecko versus crocodile narrative had the unexpected effect of resonating with the Indonesian public, fearful of the aggressive and distrusted institutions of the state, such as the police force, who bully the small but hard-working KPK (*Economist* 2009).

The far more serious repercussion of the KPK's aggressiveness was the parliament's passing of Law No. 46 in 2009. This law asserts the right of chairs in regional courts to determine the judges that will comprise the majority on each Tipikor panel. The concern, addressed by Simon Butt (2011), is that the high prosecution rate of KPK cases to Tipikor, 100 percent conviction rate up until 2011, were facilitated by ad hoc judges that were removed from the legal establishment. For Butt, this law grants the regional courts the ability to fill tribunals with choice judges that might not be committed to the fight against corruption (Butt 2011: 389). The even more serious development found in Law No. 46 is an ambiguity on whether the KPK has any formal powers to continue its prosecutions that lead into the Tipikor courts. It has even been suggested that the majority of parliamentarians wanted Law No. 46 to explicitly strip the KPK of prosecutorial powers, and that the ambiguity of the law represented a compromise position.

With Law No. 46 in 2009, this public confidence in the government to effectively fight corruption dropped off in 2010–2011 to where it reached parity with those who thought the fight against corruption was "ineffective" or "neither ineffective or effective." It was 2013, with only a year left for SBY as president, when the public began to feel disillusioned with the fight against corruption, with 65 percent responding that this fight had been "ineffective" (Figure 14.6).

Hoping to earn legitimacy from civil society, the SBY government released its *National Strategy of Corruption Prevention and Eradication: Long Term (2012–2025) and Medium Term (2012–2014)* (known as *Nastra CPE*) in 2012. The stated vision for Indonesia's medium-term future is "a government free of corruption supported by the capacity to prevent and take action against corruption and a system of cultural values with integrity." The long-term strategy is depicted as "a nation free of corruption supported by a system of cultural values with integrity" (Government of Indonesia 2012: 12). The strategy of the government was first to target the public sector, largely the strategy of the KPK, and from there it is hoped that a national consciousness could emerge to eradicate corruption in all other areas of Indonesian economic life. The six strategies to accomplish this formidable goal, outlined in Chapter 2 of the *Nastra CPE*, included: preventive measures; correcting corrupt law enforcement; completing Indonesia's legal harmonization with the UNCAC; encouraging international collaboration on extradition; education and cultural programs; and reporting to the public and international organizations.

The *Nastra CPE* stressed the significance of the Corruption Perceptions Index as one of the key indicators of success in Indonesia's fight against corruption, triumphantly acknowledging that the republic has improved its score more than any other Southeast Asian nation over the last decade and a half. However, Indonesia's score continues to be abysmally low (around 3 out of 10). The document also reported on a 2011 KPK study on public sector integrity. Though the average for the public sector increased from a score of 5.53 in 2007 to 6.31 (Government of Indonesia 2012: 14), it remains a score that does little to boost confidence in the integrity of Indonesia's public sector.

There are two profound concerns expressed in the *Nastra CPE*. The first is at the domestic level and the second is at the transnational. The *Nastra CPE* stated that "the Indonesian public is now more aware of their rights and obligations as citizens" (Government of Indonesia 2012: 12). It acknowledges that citizens of the republic will not tolerate the continuation of corruption, and an efficacious anticorruption strategy is a requirement for Indonesia's "consolidation of democracy" (Government of Indonesia 2012: 6). At the transnational level, corruption is derided in the *Nastra CPE* as "one of the major obstacles in the development of investment and business in Indonesia," discouraging financial inflows and prohibitive of economic life (Government of Indonesia 2012: 13). Though Indonesia is a member of the G20 and projected to become a great power, it remains, and will remain in the coming decades, a less developed country, profoundly shaped by the general *malaise* of poverty.

The Limits of the Eradication of Corruption: Disclosure and Natural Resources as Rents

In a 2012 report, Transparency International identified the rents earned from natural resources as one of the most important factors in Indonesia's corruption (Martini 2012: 1, 3–4, 7–8). Analysis of the investigations (*penyidikan*) of the KPK and its prosecutions (*penuntutan*) reveals a dearth of direct disclosure on cases related to natural resources. The lack of direct references to the natural resource sector is striking because it is believed that the natural resource sector in Indonesia largely conforms to the general trend of corruption and natural

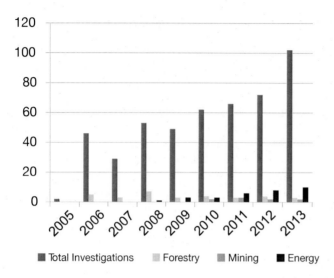

Figure 14.7 Investigations of the KPK

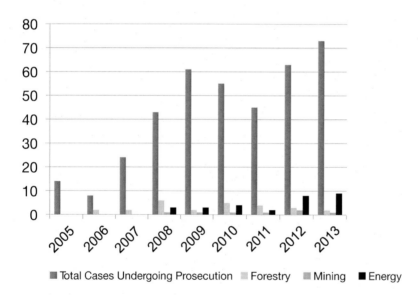

Figure 14.8 Cases under Prosecution

resources, as Indonesian public officials have been known to collect rent from the exports of extractive industries (Martini 2012: 1, 7–8).

Figures 14.7–8 are based on the annual reports released by the KPK from 2005 to 2013. The total number of investigations and prosecutions reported by the KPK are compared against the totals for forestry, mining, and energy (which includes oil, gas, and coal). As each report is released in December of each year, it does not exclusively report on the year of the report. Instead, each report typically includes the first eight months of the stated year and the final four months of the previous year. I have organized annual data as they are reported in the annual reports, so the data presented for 2013 represent the first three-quarters of that year, plus the final quarter of 2012. Because this chapter follows the importance of disclosure in a government's effort to fight corruption, investigations and prosecutions are therefore grouped by the year they are publicly disclosed by the KPK.

There is a clear trend of an increasing number of investigations being pursued by the KPK, as well as prosecutions, without the appearance of an obvious bias against prosecutions in cases pertaining to natural resources. Some of the notable examples from the annual reports on cases where corruption is disclosed in natural resources include the bribery of members of parliament to change the status of protected forests to allow for logging, Pertamina (the state oil company of Indonesia), and money missing from tree plantations. However, the key insight of this study is that it demonstrates that the KPK has been cautious in the disclosure of corruption that exists in the natural resource exports of the republic.

It is important to note that it is simply not possible to assume that these data are infallible. Rather, they are based on what is disclosed in the KPK annual reports to the public. There is a small bias that inflates the data for natural resources, and there is also what this author suspects to be a substantial bias in the reports that deflates the numbers, implying that rents earned from natural resources are a far greater source of corruption than the KPK is disclosing to civil society. First, the numbers in the above figures might be inflated due to the ambiguities in the KPK reports on what sector is being investigated or prosecuted for corruption. There are cases where the report references the Departemen Energi dan Sumber Daya Mineral (the Department of Energy and Mining Resources) without giving any details on whether the case represents corruption going on specifically in either the mining or forestry sector. For these cases, I recorded a tally for both energy and mining. Some cases were even more vague, simply referring to *sumber daya alam* (natural resources). Instead of speculating on which specific sector the case is referring to, I recorded a tally across the board, likely inflating the results.

Second, and what is much more significant, the KPK annual reports are ostensibly under-reporting corruption as it relates to the natural resource sector in Indonesia. The annual reports on investigations and prosecutions are not able to directly disclose the origins of money in the majority of its reported cases to the public. For instance, the annual reports chronicle the bribery of public officials, discernible through public accounting, but it is unable to explain where this money originated from and for what purposes the money was provided. The link between corruption and natural resources seems to be very likely in many of these cases, especially in rural areas that are highly dependent on the natural resources sector such as on Sumatra and East Kalimantan. However, if the reports did not explicitly disclose to the public the fact that bribes or money laundering related to natural resources, I did not include them in the results of this study. The KPK reports similarly chronicle the extensive graft from Regional Assistance Funds for the Outer Islands. Much of this budget is earmarked for the natural resources sector; however, unless natural resources were identified in the reports, they were not included in the results.

Neither the 2004 *National Action Plan for Corruption Prevention and Education, 2004–2009* nor the 2012 *Nastra CPE* directly discuss the natural resources sector; perhaps even more shockingly, neither does the UNCAC. Clearly, the KPK has initiated both investigations and prosecutions as early as 2006 for the forestry sector and 2008 for mining and energy. It is increasing its activities in natural resources, but there is also clearly an inability to move aggressively in this sector or to disclose much information to civil society.

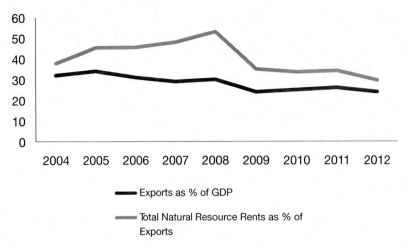

Figure 14.9 Exports as Percentage of GDP and Total Natural Resource Rents as Percentage of Exports

One of the most important reasons behind this is the rent the state accumulates from the sale of natural resources.

Figure 14.9 depicts the total natural resource rents as the sum of the rents collected from the energy sector (oil, natural gas, and coal), minerals, and forestry. First, it shows how important exports are for Indonesia's economic development, hovering between a quarter and a third of the republic's GDP. Second, the figure demonstrates the profound importance of the rents earned from natural resources proportional to the overall exports of the republic, constituting anywhere between 30 and 50 percent of the monetary value of the exports. As noted above, corruption is not wholly a function of the "demand-side" of the curve, public officials. It is also a product of the "supply-side" private and public firms and financial institutions that profit from the advantages of a corrupt system. The importance of the natural resource exports is only going to increase for Indonesia as China rapidly progresses through economic takeoff, hungrily devouring basic commodities and hard commodities and thereby boosting global prices.

What has emerged in the political culture of Indonesia is a growing discontent within the public on the lack of progress in the fight against corruption. This problem is acutely felt in Indonesia on the issue of corruption in natural resource management. The Indonesian press is paying close attention to high-profile corruption cases involving energy, mining, and forestry—especially during the final years of SBY—and linking it to the challenges of economic development in the country. It has been reported that all 47 members of the parliamentary Energy Commission have accepted cash "gifts" of at least US$140,000 from Indonesia's Energy Ministry to "speed up the release of its budget allocation" (LaForge 2014). SBY's son was named by a senior member of the Democratic Party (SBY's party) as involved in a gas field scheme being handed out to an old high school classmate of his (LaForge 2014). Nur Syafriadi, chairman of the provincial legislature for the Riau Islands, told *Tempo* that the bauxite mining companies are largely operating off the books with entire years' worth of trade unaccounted for—using illegal ports for exporting and causing the ruination of the land (Dalle 2014). Another revelation on the mining sector to make headlines was the reported loss of almost US$25 million in state revenue between 2011 and 2012 (Wijaya and Bernadette 2014).

It has not helped that the KPK has become the source of controversy itself. Two deputies of the KPK have been arrested, undermining the activities of the organization and bitterly dividing public opinion in the republic. It was unclear if the arrests demonstrated that the KPK was actually corrupt, or if the arrests were indicative of a corrupt police force that is lashing out at an assertive KPK. The relationship between the SBY Administration and the KPK was equally questioned by the public. Although SBY positioned himself as a leading supporter of the fight against corruption, his actual support for the KPK over his final two years in office became far more tepid than he would have liked to publicly admit. Aulia Pohan (a former executive with Bank of Indonesia and a relation of SBY through marriage) was investigated by the KPK, prosecuted for graft, but then acquitted by career judges at Tipikor. A KPK wiretap that was partially leaked to the public allegedly recorded a high-ranking Indonesian prosecutor boasting about having the support of "RI-1," a reference to the SBY investigation of Antasari Azhar (the former chair of the KPK who was fired after a conviction for murder). Moreover, the other members of the KPK (Bibit and Chandra) were facing criminal charges for allegedly abusing their powers by revoking travel bans given to defendants who were under investigation (Castle 2011: 323). The wiretappings eventually facilitated the release of the KPK deputies save for the former chair, as they strongly suggested that the charges against them were fabricated by the police (Butt 2011: 386–389). While this at first seemed to exonerate the KPK, it also fomented a serious debate in Indonesia on whether the KPK wiretaps were in fact for the public good or if they were unconstitutional—hearkening back to the authoritarian years of the New Order.

Discussion

The KPK has been expanding rapidly and is at something of a crossroads. It is becoming equipped with more robust punitive powers, but it is still challenged. The 2013 Annual Report ushered in the use of two additional methods of deterrence. The first requires convicted felons to pay back all of the money stolen through corruption. The second—and likely to be the far more effective method—is total *pencabutan hak politik* (political disenfranchisement) (KPK 2013: 12). These added powers and enhanced investigative powers have inexorably created tension even for the former anti-KKN president SBY who, at the end of two full presidential terms in office, is no longer held up as the entirely sincere crusader against corruption.

The pervasiveness of corruption in Indonesian public and economic life is daunting. The courts, the career judges, police departments—even the parliament—have come to be derided in Indonesian political culture as the "justice mafia" (*mafia peradilan*). The extent of corruption has made the work of the KPK incredibly challenging. The first few years of the institution represented a period where the KPK attempted to consolidate itself as an institution. Once the KPK began to investigate and prosecute more aggressively, they were met with reactionary forces that challenged its powers, such as the minor but threatening overtures of the "crocodile" and the substantive Law No. 46/2009—which represents a serious threat to the powers of the KPK and the continuation of its fight against corruption. So serious is this fear that the work of the KPK is becoming compromised that Simon Butt (one of the most prolific commentators on the KPK) has begun to question whether the institution is approaching an untimely end.

The paradox of the fight against corruption is that successful investigations of the KPK both give the Indonesian people hope that progress is being made, but demoralize them at the same time. The suspected levels of corruption are all too often found to be an accurate reflection of reality. For the fight against corruption to enjoy continued success—and perhaps even for the continued successful rise of Indonesia as a great power over the next couple of decades—it is imperative that the anti-KKN movement continue to not just push into the natural resource sector, but to also expand the scope of disclosure that is reported to the public. "Regulation by revelation" will not be easy, but its ability to cut through the opaqueness of corruption is too valuable a tool in the fight against corruption to not develop. The trap that Indonesia finds itself in is between the pressure from society to combat KKN and the fear that aggressively investigating the corruption pertaining to the international trade of natural resources will reveal the extent to which the republic is corrupt—eroding the public's confidence in Indonesia's still young democratic institutions.

References

Brown, E. and Cloke, J. (2004) "Neoliberal Reform, Governance and Corruption in the South: Assessing the International Anti-Corruption Crusade," *Antipode: A Radical Journal of Geography*, 36(2): 272–294.

Bukovansky, M. (2006) "The Hollowness of Anti-Corruption Discourse," *Review of International Political Economy*, 13(2): 181–209.

Butt, S. (2011) "Anti-Corruption Reform in Indonesia: An Obituary?" *Bulletin of Indonesian Economic Studies*, 47(3): 381–394.

Castle, J.W. (2011) *Indonesia: Political Pulse, 2009*, Jakarta: Equinox Publishing (Asia).

Dalle, R. (2014) "KPK Urged to Investigate Bauxite Miners on Riau Island," *Tempo*, available at: http://en.tempo.co/read/news/2014/03/10/055560881/KPK-Urged-to-Investigate-Bauxite-Miners-on-Riau-Island (accessed April 3, 2014).

Economist (2009) "Indonesia's Anti-Corruption Commission: The Gecko Bites Back," *The Economist*, available at: www.economist.com/node/14816720 (accessed April 10, 2014).

Elliot, K.A. (1997) "Introduction," in K.A. Elliot (Ed.), *Corruption and the Global Economy*, Washington, DC: Institute for International Economics, pp. 175–233.

Florini, A. (2010) "The National Context for Transparency-Based Global Environmental Governance," *Global Environmental Politics*, 10(3): 120–131.

Government of Indonesia (2012) *National Strategy of Corruption Prevention and Eradication: Long Term (2012–2025) and Medium Term (2012–2014)*, UNODC Indonesia (Trans).

Gupta, A. (2010) "Transparency in Global Environmental Governance: A Coming of Age?" *Global Environmental Politics*, 10(3): 1–9.

Haufler, V. (2010) "Disclosure as Governance: The Extractive Industries Transparency Initiative and Resource Management in the Developing World," *Global Environmental Politics*, 10(3): 53–73.

Heineman, B.W. and Heimann, F. (2006) "The Long War Against Corruption," *Foreign Affairs*, 85(3): 75–86.

IFES (2010) *IFES Indonesia: Electoral Survey 2010*, Jakarta: IFES.

Irland, L.C. (2008) "State Failure, Corruption, and Warfare: Challenges for Forest Policy," *Journal of Sustainable Forestry*, 27(3): 189–223.

Klitgaard, R. (1988) *Controlling Corruption*, Berkeley, CA: University of California Press.

Kolstad, I. and Søreide, T. (2009) "Corruption in Natural Resource Management: Implications for Policy Makers," *Resources Policy*, 34(4): 214–226.

Kolstad, I. and Wiig, A. (2009) "Is Transparency the Key to Reducing Corruption in Resource-Rich Countries?" *World Development*, 37(3): 521–532.

Koyuncu, C. and Yilmaz, R. (2009) "The Impact of Corruption on Deforestation: A Cross-Country Evidence," *The Journal of Developing Areas*, 42(2): 213–222

KPK (2013) *Laporan Tahunan, 2013* [Annual Report, 2013], Jakarta: KPK.

LaForge, G. (2014) "Indonesia: A Legal Plot to Thwart Corruption Fight: Legislators Try to Hobble the Country's Popular Anti-Corruption Body," *The Diplomat*, available at: http://thediplomat.com/2014/03/indonesia-a-legal-plot-to-thwart-corruption-fight/ (accessed April 3, 2014).

Martini, M. (2012) "Causes of Corruption in Indonesia," *Transparency International*, 338: 1–11.

Meagher, P. (2005) "Anti-Corruption Agencies: Rhetoric versus Reality," *The Journal of Policy Reform*, 8(1): 69–103.

Mehlum, H., Moene, K., and Torvik, R. (2006) "Institutions and the Resource Curse," *The Economic Journal*, 116: 1–20.

Pellegrini, L. and Gerlagh, R. (2006) "Corruption, Democracy, and Environmental Policy: An Empirical Contribution to the Debate," *The Journal of Environment and Development*, 15(3): 332–354.

Petermann, A., Guzmán, J.I., and Tilton, J.E. (2007) "Mining and Corruption," *Resources Policy*, 32(3): 91–103.

Presiden Republik Indonesia (2010) *Countermeasure and Eradication of Money Laundering*, available at: www.flevin.com/id/lgso/translations/Laws/Law%20No.%208%20of%202010%20on%20Prevention%20and%20Eradication%20of%20Money%20Laundering%20(MoF).pdf (accessed April 3, 2014).

Robbins, P. (2000) "The Rotten Institution: Corruption in Natural Resource Management," *Political Geography*, 19: 423–443.

Sachs, J.D. and Warner, A.M. (2001) "The Curse of Natural Resources," *European Economic Review*, 45: 827–838.

Setiyono, B. and McLeod, R.H. (2010) "Civil Society Organizations' Contribution to the Anti-Corruption Movement in Indonesia," *Bulletin of Indonesian Economic Studies*, 46(3): 347–370.

Shaxson, N. (2007) "Oil, Corruption and the Resource Curse," *International Affairs*, 83(6): 1123–1140.

Siverson, R.M. and Johnson, R.A.I. (2014) "Politics and Parasites: The Contribution of Corruption to Human Misery," *International Studies Quarterly*, 58: 199–206.

Wang, H. and Rosenau, J.N. (2001) "Transparency International and Corruption as an Issue of Global Governance," *Global Governance*, 7(1): 25–49.

Wijaya, A.S. and Bernadette, C. (2014) "64 Mining Companies Still Owe Royalties," *Tempo*, available at: http://en.tempo.co/read/news/2014/04/29/056574102/64-Mining-Companies-Still-Owe-Royalties (accessed April 20, 2014).

World Bank Group (2003) *Combating Corruption in Indonesia: Enhancing Accountability for Development*, East Asia Poverty Reduction and Economic Management Unit.

Chapter 15

The United Nations and Post-Conflict Zones: Policy Failure in the Afghanistan New Beginnings Programme

Sarah Shoker

Disarmament, demobilization, and reintegration (DDR) are a set of activities that occur during post-conflict stabilization periods. DDR is associated with security sector reform (SSF), a concept that entails the establishment of good governance, development, the rule of law, and the local ownership of security actors (Global Facilitation Network for Security Sector Reform 2008). DDR creates an "enabling environment for political and peace processes by dealing with security problems that arise when ex-combatants are trying to adjust to normal life during the vital transition period from conflict to peace and development" (United Nations Peacekeeping Department 2004). Overseen by the United Nations Development Fund (UNDP), the Afghanistan New Beginnings Programme (ANBP) was a three-year DDR program that lasted from April 2003 to June 2005. Its goal was to reintroduce former combatants into civil society (Ministry of Foreign Affairs of Japan 2004)—although the term "civil society" remains undefined in ANBP documents.

The United Nations has a mandate to encourage the practice of human security among its member states and uses DDR as a way to further this mandate. The UNDP defines human security expansively and the definition includes more than an absence of violent conflict. Security also includes human rights, good governance, access to education, and healthcare (Annan 2000: 4–6). Unlike traditional conceptualizations of security, human security does not prioritize military threats over economic threats. The referent of security is the individual, not the state.

As a participant in the DDR process, the UN acts as a third-party broker designed to facilitate peace processes between parties that "neither trust each other, nor have the capacity to design, plan and implement DDR" (United Nations DDR Resource Centre 2006: 3). The UNDP identifies this lack of state capacity as a problem that prevents the stabilization of the country. The ANBP therefore can be understood as a range of programs designed to increase Afghanistan's institutional capacity that, in turn, would ensure the proper functioning of civil society actors within a stable territorial zone and under the management of a central government. However, as described in the section on trust and international relations, the responsibility for integration remained with ex-combatants and the ANBP did not provide support for civil society groups.

According to the Under-Secretary General for the UN's Peacekeeping Operation, DDR practices are always "changing and evolving" and DDR programs take "different shapes and forms" (United Nations 2010: 5). There is no "one-size-fits-all approach" as all DDR operations involve local militia factions, which have different requests based on the conflict scenario. However, despite the UN handbook on DDR stating that these programs are "people-centered" (United Nations DDR Resource Centre 2006: 7), this approach clashes with statements on the UNDP's website. The UNDP (2010a) states that DDR in Afghanistan exists "to provide demobilized personnel with the ability to become economically independent—the ultimate objective being to reinforce the authority of the government."

As a result of this conceptual murkiness, I argue that though the UN has taken a strong and well-documented position on human security, DDR campaigns are still conducted using a paradigm that defines security through a state-centric perspective. DDR campaigns are used to consolidate power in a centralized government—a strategy that jeopardized the reintegration of Afghan ex-combatants into civil society. This failure resulted for three reasons. First, there was a poor economic understanding of Afghanistan's formal and informal market systems. Second, the ANBP's reintegration program prioritized an incentive structure that treated ex-combatants as primarily self-interested economic individuals. Third, the UNDP chose to measure the ANBP's success using a quantitative method. This process reduced the building of civil society to a project-oriented and technical process (Pouligny 2005: 505) and thus gave a problematic accounting for the success and failure of the ANBP.

The Evolution of DDR

To create a distinction between armed conflict and post-conflict (the latter term often associated with peace) is to wade into a difference that is not apparent in the field. The end of wars do not indicate the presence of peace; in fact, the number of post-conflict deaths created by the spillover effects of war is often comparable to—if not higher than—the number of direct deaths caused during the conflict (Muggah 2005: 439). Due to the volatile conditions in post-conflict zones, the UN views DDR as an integral component to post-conflict rebuilding and development. In a 2000 report to the Security Council, the UN Secretary General argued that DDR was "vital to stability in a post-conflict situation; to reducing the likelihood of renewed violence . . . and to facilitating a society's transition from conflict to normalcy and development" (Muggah 2005: 439). Traditional DDR has the goal of creating a safe political space and contributing to a secure environment (UNDP 2010a: 9). However, despite its endorsement of DDR campaigns, UN peacekeeping operations have usually only overseen disarmament and demobilization campaigns, whereas reintegration efforts were overseen by partners such as the United Nations Development Fund and the World Bank (Durch et al. 2003: 27). DDR funding relies on voluntary donors and it is not accounted for in the initial Peacekeeping Operation's budget. As a result, DDR implementation is often fragmented and underfunded.

Despite these logistical problems, at the most basic level DDR is a set of practices that are replicated across various countries—although the way these practices are implemented vary depending on the conflict. Disarmament is a relatively new phenomenon that gained prominence during the 1990s, when international actors recognized that the development of war-torn communities would be unsuccessful if post-conflict violence continued to exist (Ozerdem 2002: 961). As defined by the UNPD, disarmament and demobilization entail the:

> [C]ollection, documentation, control and disposal of explosives, light, and heavy weapons from combatants and often from the Civilian population . . . Demobilization is the formal and controlled discharge of active combatants from armed force and groups . . . Reintegration is the process by which ex-combatants acquire civilian status and gain suitable income and employment.
>
> (UNPD 2004: 7)

Reintegration is a policy that provides a number of assistance measures to former combatants with the goal of increasing their economic and social reintegration into civil society (Schramek 2003: 7). As a result, DDR integrates economic development with physical security.

Both disarmament and demobilization can be accomplished in a short time period, reintegration being the most complicated and lengthiest part of DDR (Shams 2009: 55). Reintegration is not confined to integrating combatants into society, but is also about ensuring the cooperation of former combatants in the peace process—a central authority cannot function successfully if combatants remobilize and a society cannot have faith that a central authority can provide security if combatants continue to pose a threat (Shams 2009: 62). Depending on the organizing body or scholar measuring "success," DDR programs may be successful if the targeted combatants are formally discharged from their armed forces (demobilization) or if ex-combatants are accepted back into their communities without shame and stigma being attached to their former occupations as non-state soldiers.

Small arms often resurface for the purposes of criminality in urban areas. Police officers and civilians are often "outgunned" by former combatants who have retained their weapons from the conflict, often looted from the country's own arsenal (Shams 2009: 62). Despite regional peace treaties, the rise of post-conflict social violence is common and can spill over neighboring borders and into countries that are deemed "at peace." Perhaps for this reason, the United Nations has now begun referring to peacekeeping operations, under which DDR is housed, as "interim stabilization" rather than "post-conflict stabilization" (United Nations Peacekeeping Department 2004).

Mark Sedra (2003) identifies a number of reasons for reintegrating combatants by using formalized programs, although these programs are situated within a wider body of literature that warns against importing civil society and using a highly technical and mechanistic project-based approach to build civil relationships (Kaldor et al. 2006: 99). Nevertheless, Sedra writes that if combatants cannot see a personal role in a postwar order, then they may turn to banditry or commanders may defect from the peace process. Sedra outlines a number of fairly standardized incentives for attracting ex-combatants to DDR programs and writes that if the benefits of the program prove to be enticing, then self-mobilization can be discouraged by combatants who would stay with the program simply because they do not want to leave their benefits behind. Sedra also argues that former combatants are ill-equipped to navigate the postwar economy and as a result should not be seen returning to their communities empty-handed—as this type of return could damage their reputations and social standing. Finally, Sedra argues that if combatants are not reintegrated, then they may pose a threat to security and stability (Sedra 2003: 7–9).

A successful combatant's reintegration is long term, measured by his or her ability to find viable economic security outside of joining an armed force. In comparison to this goal, the ANBP's short-term measurements of reintegration were problematic (United Nations Peacekeeping Department 2004). Additionally, the ANBP did not assess Afghan civil society's ability to withstand an influx of newly trained professionals. The ANBP had, as part of its mandate, the goal of disrupting the "patriarchal chain of command existing between commanders and their men . . . and . . . diminishing the influence of commanders" (UNDP 2010a). This goal was challenged by the inclusion of Northern Alliance "warlords" in the Bonn Agreement, which, though necessary, ensured the continuation of a patronage system that caused the overrepresentation of certain ethnicities in the ANBP (which continued in the construction of civil society and the state) and disrupted the trust-building among negotiators of the peace process.

The Afghanistan New Beginnings Programme

In December 2001, the Bonn Agreement brought together a number of prominent Afghanistan actors, including militant groups that had assisted the United States and its allies in the fight against the Taliban. These militant groups were from the north of the country and were known collectively as the "Northern Alliance." Several of these warlords are or were loyal to Hamid Karzai, though some continue to fight against each other. Many of these warlords have also been integrated into the Karzai government. Mohammad Qasim Fahim, for example, a prominent Northern Alliance warlord, was appointed as head of the new Ministry of Defence (Schramek 2003: 10). Alliance warlords have also been provided with significant money and weaponry by the United States and the International Security Assistance Force (ISAF) in order to solidify their power and prevent Taliban and neo-Taliban groups from gaining dominance. This funding, however, has had the effect of further entrenching the power of Northern Alliance warlords, but the US and ISAF are hesitant to crack down on human rights abuses and crimes committed by these groups for fear that they would leave the coalition and destabilize the peace process.

Attempts at negotiating peace treaties have centered on including individual combatants and mid-level commanders into rehabilitation and training programs, particularly those who have shown reluctance at being part of a militia but who fear arrest from government authorities or harassment from their own comrades. American and coalition forces, in an attempt to breed goodwill, have released certain prisoners so that they can rejoin their families and communities. In return, community and tribal leaders guarantee that former prisoners will no longer engage in violence (International Crisis Group 2005).

The Bonn Agreement, however, only made vague references to demobilization. More problematically, as only the Northern Alliance and their associates were involved in the treaty negotiation process, the emerging state security apparatus had a clear ethnic bias, giving the impression that certain ethnicities were being privileged by the central government and thus causing an unsteady foundation of distrust among different ethnic groups. Northern Alliance combatants (both commanders and soldiers) were integrated into the new Afghan Military Forces (AMF). The ANBP had, as one of its goals, the decommissioning of AMF units into the new and formalized Afghan National Army (ANA) (by the end of 2004, the AMF became illegal and was replaced by the ANA). Oddly enough, although part of the demobilization agreement included dismantling militia structures and removing the power basis from warlords, only Northern Alliance members and their associates were included in the AMF. Northern Alliance members saw their involvement in the ANA as a reward for assisting US and ISAF forces in the war against the Taliban, and the US and ISAF forces sought to reward Northern Alliance participation. This "reward" meant that only soldiers in the AMF were beneficiaries of the ANBP, resulting in tens of thousands of combatants from other militias being ignored. There was a clear bias that favored the militants from the regional faction that controlled the Ministry of Defense (the milita was called Mazar-i Sharif). Out of the eight regions represented in the ANBP, combatants from Mazar-i-Sharif constituted over 56 percent of the participants (Shams 2009: 60). As a result, there are serious doubts that the patronage system between commanders and their soldiers was disrupted.

The ANBP set a number of benchmarks for success, which changed over the course of the program. In 2002, the UN estimated that there were 750,000 armed people in Afghanistan, with 200,000 of those armed people acting as soldiers in the AMF. The ANBP then set a goal of disarming 100,000 soldiers. This number was later adjusted to 60,000 armed actors when the UNDP realized that Northern Alliance commanders may have inflated the number of armed combatants within their ranks in order to access and receive ANBP benefits (Denny 2005: 2).

According to Christian Denny (2005), attempts at recruiting low- and mid-level commanders in the program failed because there was no package tailored to this population group. In a series of interviews with former combatants, interviewees reported that many of their ex-commanders still retained large arsenals of weaponry and were involved in illicit smuggling activity. This hoarding was also used, according to those interviewed, as a way of retaining their influence, indicating that low- and mid-level commanders felt uneasy with the lack of employment options provided by the ANBP. Low-level commanders reported feeling that they had lost their dignified statures. "One day I'm an officer, an important person, and then I'm a simple shopkeeper," reported a former commander (Zyck 2009: 122).

The ANBP offered different programs for high-level and low- or mid-level commanders. Mid-level and low-level commanders were given the same reintegration package as their soldiers. Mid-level and low-level commanders also had the highest dropout rate from the ANBP. High-level commanders, however, were offered reintegration packages valued at US$1,200 a month, though they were the least in need of assistance because they had the money or connections to garner long-term police, government, or business positions (Denny 2005: 115). Soldiers and low- and mid-level commanders received US$700 a month. Soldiers appreciated the DDR program because it allowed them to avoid conscription and spend more time with their families, but low- and mid-level commanders were left in a policy vacuum.

Norms and Incentives in DDR

Perspectives on post-conflict security have evolved since the Cold War, when the focus was on disarming and demobilizing non-state combatants and securing the dominance of the state's armed forces. These disarmament programs were arranged through bilateral agreements. However, by the late 1980s, the UN became increasingly more active in conflict zones—particularly in sub-Saharan Africa—and recognized a need for a more development-based approach (United Nations Peacekeeping Department). The ANBP conceptual murkiness is a reflection of the tension between these two approaches.

As mentioned above, the United Nations promotes an expansive version of human security in its documents. However, in apparent contradiction to human security, Afghan officials and UNDP personnel saw the DDR process as a method to centralize power in the Karzai government. For example, an Afghan deputy governor was quoted as saying that "disarmament is a top priority—the administrative system can't function as long as people are armed because you have to do what the armed people tell you to do, not what the rules tell you to do" (Shams 2009: 63). Further, the UNDP website explicitly states the ANBP's "ultimate objective [is to] reinforce the authority of the government" (UNDP 2010b).

Practitioners of human security recognize that states are often not the best at providing security for their citizens and that many populations experience more harm from the state than from outside invaders. For this reason, practitioners of human security privilege the individual as the security referent and not the state. Nevertheless, there is an assumption within the ANBP that the state is still the prime guarantor of security. As a result, there is paradigmatic confusion about the purpose of DDR, where UN reports highlight the benefits of development and UNDP policymakers measure success by determining whether or not the state has a monopoly on force. Further complicating the problem is the lack of literature that analyzes the relationships between human security and substate security communities (such as militia groups or community councils).

Consolidating power within a centralized government is, in some ways, understandable, and pointing out that the ANBP faces paradigmatic inconsistencies should not be read as a critique against the very notion of disarmament or demobilization. Afghanistan is a heavily armed country where over a million guns are owned by its citizens, making the country one of the most militarized in the world. The Afghan government has undertaken the disarmament process to increase its administrative power, indicating that the Weberian framing of the state is alive and well. However, these paradigmatic inconsistencies create problems for combatant reintegration, persons that have been recruited into the ANBP under a perception that long-term reintegration into civil and economic sectors are the program's goals, but who are then left in a policy vacuum after the three-year program folds, with no way to ensure that their long-term reintegration efforts are successful.

Instead, the success of the ANBP would be better measured by gauging long-term combatant reintegration, focusing on factors such as whether these combatants are employed in the formal or informal economy, have been accepted by their communities, or have remobilized. Unfortunately, the ANBP lasted for three years, not enough time to ensure whether long-term reintegration has been successful or has contributed to a more secure environment. There are no long-term evaluation mechanisms that have been provided by the ANBP or UNDP.

There were a number of problematic assumptions contained within the ANBP. First, there was the assumption that a legitimate force existed to "fill the security vacuum" and that this force was the appropriate method to lead reintegration efforts. There was the assumption that the majority of the people and the foreign community would "recognize the legitimacy of some central authority." There was also an assumption that the parties to the conflict had reached a consensus on the demobilization process. Finally, there was an assumption that the national economy is capable of "absorbing an influx of new labour" from the armed factions ceasing to employ fighters (Schramek 2003: 10).

The Economic Dimension

Emergency employment programs, usually associated with rebuilding infrastructure and intensive labor in agriculture of manufacturing, have often been funded by the World Bank and have historically operated without actively recruiting ex-combatants to fill these jobs. Supporters of these employment programs argue that they are important for governments that cannot afford the cost of large-scale economic projects. Additionally, these supporters argue that involving ex-combatants in these projects reduces their economic insecurity and provides an incentive to remain within the formal economy as a way of sustaining a livelihood.

There is an erroneous assumption within DDR programs that the country economies are capable of absorbing an influx of new labor. This lesson was learned the hard way by the UNDP several years after the ANBP's completion:

> There appears to be deep-rooted assumptions that in post-conflict settings, economic recovery will occur, providing absorption capacity for former combatants and other war affected people. However, in post-conflict settings, there is often a lack of diversification in the economy and heavy dependence on particular resources.
>
> (UNDP 2010b)

The job training given to former combatants came with significant problems. Often, ex-combatants were pressured to conform to certain job reintegration packages rather than being supported when they had their own visions of reintegration (Hartzell 2011). In some cases, 15 new tailors per village were being trained through the DDR program, thus oversaturating the market (Hartzell 2011). Many involved in the business stream reported finding this particular job path very lonely, due to the companionship they had experienced while working with armed forces. Additionally, because many ex-combatants were trained in business, they also oversaturated a market already filled with entrepreneurs, causing many of them to relocate and the sprouting ill-will between DDR-trained individuals and entrepreneurs who were already established. One business owner epitomized these tensions when he said, "[t]he same men who robbed us and forced our markets to close are now asking to sit side by side with us as if they knew business" (Hartzell 2011).

Similar problems occurred with those trained in agriculture. Ex-combatants who were illiterate or semi-literate reported that they were pressured into joining the agricultural training or animal husbandry program despite the fact that they were interested in another field (Denny 2005: 5). The agricultural packages also only provided a fixed amount of grain to participants, not an increase in land. For those who already owned land, the addition of a different crop did not amount to much increase in income—only to income diversification.

The amount the ex-combatants could harvest, however, remained relatively fixed, as an increase in income required an increase in land ownership. Unfortunately, when a number of combatants chose or were pressured into accepting the same package, the local economy was flooded with an oversupply of the same product. For example, in the provinces of Khoja, Do-Koh, and Jowzjan, exactly 50 percent of ex-combatants chose the livestock package. The "packages" in these areas consisted of goats, with six goats in each package. There were 36 participants, which meant that 216 goats flooded the market. In a good year, six goats would reach a good price. However, the large increase of goats in a localized area can reduce the price per animal, potentially jeopardizing the incomes of these combatants. There were also environmental externalities that were not accounted by the ANBP. Villages in the Khoja Do-Koh region, for example, lie on the edge of the Dashte-Layli desert and the water source is limited. Elders of the governing councils for this region were worried that there was not even enough water or land to raise an influx of 216 goats (Denny 2005: 5–6). Consequently, the ANBP unintentionally jeopardized the economic security of the "civil society" in which it sought to reintegrate its participants.

Stephen Zyck writes that in an effort to win popular support from local actors, the international community has focused development assistance on Afghanistan's least secure provinces—which has the potential of creating a "perverse incentive" and the conditions for the country's further fragmentation. Secure provinces such as Takhar and Sar-i-Pul were scheduled to receive less than a third of the assistance given to insecure provinces such as Kandahar, Uruzgan, and Helmand (which received US$200 of reconstruction assistance per capita). Zyck (2009: 115) notes that "Hazara and other Pashtun officials openly mused that their ethnic kin may wish to begin supporting the Taliban or attacking the government in order to access development assistance." Despite UN attempts at fostering peace between competing factions, the use of financial packages undermined the trust necessary to sustain peaceful relations.

Trust in International Relations

The United Nations holds that trust in the peace process is incredibly important for the successful execution of DDR (UNDP 2010b). DDR is often one of the first provisions to be executed under peace agreements and, consequently, the potential for uncertainty among actors is quite high during this phase. Political will becomes a key factor to the success of DDR, a challenge since many of Afghanistan's elites have been involved in the creation and support of non-state militias. Ironically, though, the economic incentives used to ensure cooperation may have undermined the ANBP's success. Incentive structures can potentially impede relationship-building between factions because trust:

> refers to an attitude involving a willingness to place the fate of one's interests under the control of others. This willingness is based on a belief, for which there is some uncertainty, that potential trustees will avoid using their discretion to harm the interests of the first.
>
> (Hoffman 2003: 376)

While finding a political relationship where actors trust one another unconditionally is unlikely, Aaron Hoffman argues that incentives or mechanisms that force actors to comply are not trusting relationships because these mechanisms make betrayal impossible. Trust is a voluntary action and a belief that "you will not betray my interests, despite your capacity to do so" (Hoffman 2003: 377).

In past iterations of DDR programs, some security practitioners understood that disarmament came with a number of very real risks—but that the elimination of these risks could not come at the expense of overall stability. For example, DDR officials have remarked on how small arms are hoarded, or how obsolete materials are submitted in return for payment. Aldo Ajello, the special UN representative in charge of the DDR operation in Mozambique, stated:

> I know very well that [ex-combatants] will give . . . old and obsolete material, and they will have there and there something hidden. I do not care. What I do is create the political situation in which the use of those guns is not the question. So that they stay where they are.
>
> (Hall 1994: 23)

DDR campaigns cannot look to disarm every combatant of all of his or her small arms arsenal, a goal that policymakers recognize as unrealistic. The strength of disarmament lies in its symbolism; the transition from war to peace is sensitive and disarmament is a means by which to test the commitment of all parties to a peaceful resolution (Paes 2005). However, if symbolism and norm-creation are the more effective reasons justifying disarmament, the ANBP's decision to gauge success by counting the number of SALW returned remains even more perplexing.

Official ANBP documents do not ground disarmament in this fashion, and instead rely on mechanistic incentives that treat ex-combatants as primarily economic actors. Unfortunately, the symbolism of disarmament is lost with the creation of these incentives—which alters the symbolic trust-building component of DDR to a process that assumes all actors are self-interested. The existence of economic incentives does not necessarily undermine the building of trust between actors. For example, Alpaslan Ozerdem (2002) writes that if the combatant is conceived as an impediment to security, then incentives for disarmament are often crafted in a way to ensure that high-risk groups do not further contribute to instability. These incentives resemble bribes. If, however, combatants are viewed as potential contributors to their communities, then incentives are designed to influence their widest possible integration into the country's economic fabric.

In some cases where buy-back programs have existed, combatants will submit weapons and use the money received from this transaction to reinvest in better weapons than those submitted (this exact scenario occurred in Liberia). In situations where the security situation is uncertain, combatants may stockpile higher-quality weapons and become selective about the weapons they return. If there is a lack of capacity to enforce regulations on carrying and using weapons, or if the political and economic climate increases the value of owning a weapon, then disarmament becomes a greater challenge. Consequently, the success of disarmament campaigns is hugely dependent on the development of other sectors (Paes 2003: 263). Recommendations for the development of other sectors were not included in the ANBP. Instead, "civil society" was treated as a static object that would cushion ex-combatants upon return to their communities, despite the fact that the program did not provide assistance to civil society actors or groups—the latter of which would have needed to adjust to the influx of these new community members. And while the ANBP was used as a way to increase the country's institutional capacity to sustain security, the brunt of this capacity-building was carried by individual ex-combatants who were often required to weaken their own social positions in order for the state to gain strength. The ANBP's ex-combatants, therefore, were treated as impediments to security and their weapons were the means by which they would propagate conflict.

Conclusion: The Problem with Quantifying DDR

The United Nations quantified the success of the ANBP program. Though they originally started with a goal of disarming 100,000 combatants and later lowered the number, the UNDP frames the ANBP as a success and lists among its achievements the following:

- 63,380 former officers and soldiers were disarmed;
- 259 units were decommissioned;
- 53,145 ex-combatants selected the reintegration option, and 53,054 completed this process;
- 90 percent are employed; and
- 56,163 weapons were destroyed.

Without any context, these numbers are impressive. However, the 90 percent employment rate is a nebulous number because academics who have searched for former participants of the ANBP cannot locate them, and the program does not have contact information to ensure that these employment numbers remain up to date (Hartzell 2011: 10). Moreover, while over 56,000 weapons were destroyed, this number does not indicate whether these weapons were obsolete, and it certainly does not take into account that the number of weapons destroyed is quite small compared to the country's total civilian gun tally—numbered at over one million. Even using the ANBP's methodology (one that prioritizes quantifiable over qualitative measurements), this number is not impressive.

One of DDR's main benefits is the "strengthening of confidence between former factions and enhancing the momentum towards stability," which is not a goal that requires total disarmament, but is a goal that requires solid relationship-building (Knight and Ozerdem 2004: 503). Despite the acknowledgment by UN actors that trust plays a significant role in the disarmament process, the ANBP's success was determined using quantitative assessments. The ANBP's results were not measured by looking at the trust built between different factions, whether future negotiations were possible, or if the policymaking climate has become chillier from lack of political will. In fact, because the ANBP does not measure "integration" past the three-year program date, there is no indication if "civil society" has altered, welcomed, or rebuked these new community members.

In addition to the ANBP's inability to measure long-term indicators, the program also overcrowded certain regions with monolithic occupations, meaning that ex-combatants may still face a high unemployment rate. The measure of success, therefore, was purely based on disarming, counting, and destroying SALW. The importance of disarmament as a symbolic measure was completely omitted from the analysis of the ANBP's outcomes. These indicators cannot analyze whether or not factions can still rely on one another to maintain a centralized security force.

Although the UN loudly supports the expansion of human security, the lack of long-term measurements indicates a tendency to prioritize state security over human security. Though much of the ANBP's documents cited DDR as a method that would improve economic development and community security, the ultimate goal became the consolidation of power in a centralized government, as indicated by the outcomes the program measured. Unfortunately, this measurement has created a policy vacuum where ex-combatants and alumni of the ANBP are now potentially left with an even worse capacity for integration into civil society and an increased cynicism with respect to the ability and intentions of third-party international actors.

References

Annan, K. (2000) *The Millennium Report of the United Nations' Secretary General*, New York: United Nations, available at: www.gdrc.org/sustdev/husec/Definitions.pdf.

Denny, C. (2005) "Disarmament, Demobilization, and Rearmament? The Effects of Disarmament in Afghanistan," *Japan Afghan NGO Network*, available at: www.ngo-jvc.net/jann/Documents/Disarmament%20demobilization%20rearmament.pdf.

Durch, W. et al. (2003) "The Brahimi Report on the Future of UN Peacekeeping Operations," *The Henry L. Stimson Center*, available at: www.stimson.org/images/uploads/research-pdfs/BR-Complete Version-Dec03.pdf.

Global Facilitation Network for Security Sector Reform (2008) *What Is Security Sector Reform?*, available at: www.ssrnetwork.net/about/what_is_ss.php.

Hall, B. (1994) "Blue Helmets, Empty Guns," *New York Times Sunday Magazine*, January 23.

Hartzell, C. (2011) "Missed Opportunities: The Impact of DDR and SSR on Afghanistan," United States Institute of Peace: Special Report 270, available at: www.usip.org/sites/default/files/SR270-Missed_Opportunities.pdf.

Hoffman, A. (2002) "A Conceptualization of Trust in International Relations," *European Journal of International Relations*, 8(3): 375–401, available at: www.researchgate.net/profile/Aaron_Hoffman/publication/220009537_A_Conceptualization_of_Trust_in_International_Relations/links/0fcfd50fed635a848e000000.pdf.

International Crisis Group (2005) *Getting Afghanistan Back on Track*, available at: www.crisisgroup.org/en/regions/asia/south-asia/afghanistan/B036-afghanistan-getting-disarmament-back-on-track.aspx.

Kaldor, M., Kostovicova, D., and Said, Y. (2006) "War and Peace: The Role of Global Civil Society," *European Journal of International Relations*, 12(1): 371–395.

Knight, M. and Ozerdem, A. (2004) "Guns, Camps, and Cash: Demobilization and Reinsertion of Former Combatants in Transitions from War to Peace," *Journal of Peace Research*, 41(4): 499–516.

Ministry of Foreign Affairs of Japan (2004) *Grant Aid for Afghanistan's New Beginnings Programme*, available at: www.mofa.go.jp/region/middle_e/afghanistan/aid040303.html.

Muggah, R. (2005) "No Magic Bullet: A Critical Perspective on Disarmament, Demobilization and Reintegration (DDR) and Weapons Reduction in Post-Conflict Contexts," *The Round Table: The Commonwealth Journal of International Relations*, 94: 239–252.

Ozerdem, A. (2002) "Disarmament, Demobilization, and Reintegration of Former Combatants in Afghanistan: Lessons Learned from a Cross Cultural Perspective," *Third World Quarterly*, 23(5): 961–975.

Paes, W.C. (2005) "The Challenges of Peacekeeping in Liberia," *International Peacekeeping*, 12(2): 2–53.

Pouligny, B. (2005) "Civil Society and Post-Conflict Peacebuilding: Ambiguities of International Programmes Aimed at Building 'New' Societies," *Security Dialogue*, 36(4): 495–510.

Schramek, M. (2003) "New Remedies for an Emerging Conflict: Toward a New Typology of DDR for Failed and Collapsed States" (Working Paper), Monetary Institute of International Studies, available at: http://sites.miis.edu/sand/files/2011/07/Schramek.DDR-Typology-3.pdf.

Sedra, M. (2003) "New Beginnings or Return to Arms? The Disarmament, Demobilization, and Reintegration Process in Afghanistan," paper presented at ZEF-LSE Workshop in London, May–June.

Shams, S. (2009) "Assessing the Role of DDR in Afghanistan: Internal Security Provision and External Environment," in Y. Uesuji (Ed.), *Toward Bringing Stability in Afghanistan: A Review of the Peacebuilding Strategy*, IPSHU English Report Series No. 24, pp. 55–77.

UNDP (2010a) *Second Generation Disarmament, Demobilization, and Reintegration (DDR): Practices in Peace Operations*, New York: United Nations, available at: www.un.org/en/peacekeeping/documents/2GDDR_ENG_WITH_COVER.pdf.

UNDP (2010b) *Afghanistan's New Beginnings Programme*, available at: www.anbp.af.undp.org/homepage/.

United Nations DDR Resource Centre (2006) *The UN Approach to DDR*, New York: United Nations, available at: http://unddr.org/uploads/documents/IDDRS%202.10%20The%20UN%20Approach%20to%20DDR.pdf.

United Nations Peacekeeping Department (2004) *Disarmament, Demobilization, and Reintegration*, available at: www.un.org/en/peacekeeping/issues/ddr.shtml.

Zyck, S. (2009) "Former Combatant Reintegration and Fragmentation in Contemporary Afghanistan," *Conflict, Security, and Development*, 9(1): 111–131.

Chapter 16

Global Civil Society and UN Anti-Trafficking Agreements

Marguerite Marlin

The phenomenon of trafficking in persons[1] presents an enormous challenge to global govern-ance. As an indication of the scope of the extent of the problem—just the portion that is not obscured by the clandestine nature in which human trafficking operates—UNODC's *Global Report on Trafficking, 2014* statistics alone included data from 40,177 victims of human trafficking from an identified 124 countries. Although states have generally been slow to respond, a turning point for international recognition of and response to trafficking has been the United Nations Convention against Transnational Organized Crime in Palermo, Italy (2000). This provided the first substantial international legislative basis for global action against human trafficking, and was followed by the Protocol to Prevent, Suppress and Punish Trafficking in Persons, especially Women and Children (2003)—which obligated the ratifying states to enact national trafficking legislation and was built upon in 2009 with the International Framework for Action to Implement the Trafficking in Persons Protocol.

As a result of these international agreements, anti-trafficking action has intensified; for example, between 2003 and 2014, the percentage of states covered by UNODC that specifically criminalized most or all forms of human trafficking increased from 19 percent to 84.5 percent. However, an estimated two billion people are still unprotected by such laws, and even in areas where it is criminalized less than half of the countries reported 10 or more convictions annually (UNODC 2014). Criminal groups have made note of this relative impunity for trafficking crimes; it has been observed by Gerard Stoudmann of the Organization for Security and Cooperation in Europe that human trafficking is now widely considered to be a significantly less dangerous business than narcotics trafficking, since the international legal framework to combat it is lacking (Sing 2009: 300). To be sure, there has been tangible progress made in the area of prosecution. Between 2003 and 2008, just under 20,000 traffickers were convicted (Perrin 2010: 118).

However, state approaches to anti-trafficking have generally been characterized by a lack of focus on human rights and victim protection in favor of law enforcement and border control concerns (Haynes 2004: 238). This approach has only intensified in a post-2008 recession climate, where austerity budgets have caused social investment programs such as anti-trafficking initiatives to see a reduction in funding (Hoff 2014). Moreover, amid fears of terrorist threats, politicians and other key state actors have increasingly moved in the direction of viewing migration through a lens of securitization (Bourbeau 2011). In addition, state agencies charged with carrying out anti-trafficking efforts outside of the regular law enforcement capacity are often given this mandate along with many others, such that there is no specific response to the issue made evident. For example, the US Administration for Children and Families (ACF) website states that it "is committed to preventing human trafficking and ensuring that victims of all forms of human trafficking have access to the services they need," but their 2015 budget breakdown does not specify anti-trafficking programs as a specific category (ACF 2015).

For states, the policy area of combating human trafficking presents a conundrum when trying to harmonize and synergize their operations, either under the banner of austerity or as part of a securitization campaign. As will be explained further in this chapter, the tools required to effectively deal with the problem human trafficking are not the same as (and often run counter to) the tools commonly used by states for securitization, migration, and crime policy. This is in addition to the limitations posed by a state's policy initiatives being largely limited at this point in time to operating within its own borders. As a result of this condundrum, globally operating nongovernmental organizations (NGOs) have often found themselves better suited to address the issue on an international level through community-based anti-trafficking programs, and have been largely responsible for progressive strides in the realm of human rights (i.e. particularly milestones in terms of prevention, victim assistance, and repatriation/integration).[2]

From the beginning, the important role of global civil society has been recognized to some degree by the international community of states. At the 2006 Conference of the Parties to the UN Convention against Transnational Organized Crime—specifically devoted to reviewing the implementation of the Trafficking Protocol—25 NGOs were in attendance, as well as 12 intergovernmental organizations (IGOs) and 111 states (Hathaway 2008: 14). This is evidence of a high level of NGO involvement in implementing the Protocol, which has taken shape in the myriad ways described in this chapter.

There are a number of clear advantages to NGO involvement in the implementation of the Protocol. From the outset, NGO groups have more experience than states in anti-trafficking activity. Until the year 2000, much of this type of work was limited the efforts of the nongovernmental sector (Tiuriukanova 2004: 110). Due to the fact that they often operate at the local level, NGOs have also done the most work to address root conditions of trafficking, such as gender inequality and poverty within various communities. Frequently entrenched and connected in local communities, NGOs are aware of the specific and at times complex dynamics that surround them. Members of ethnic minority communities are also reported to trust NGOs more than federal departments and agencies, as they often perceive the latter as distant bureaucratic organizations (Oxman-Martinez et al. 2001: 21). This is a significant indicator given that a sizeable minority of former victims of trafficking in one study (23 percent) escaped and sought assistance from authorities (Laczlo and Gramegna 2003: 189).

It is here posited that because of the effectiveness of NGO activity toward implementing UN legislation and the dynamic of cooperation between IGOs and NGOs to this end, that states should refocus additional efforts to address the international dimension of human trafficking through a securitization lens—such as Canada's changes to human smuggling laws that are now before the Supreme Court over questions about its constitutionality—to provide support to the community-based initiatives led by global civil society. In addition, it is observed that the context of global efforts against human trafficking serve as an iconoclastic example of rigorous IGO–NGO cooperation and NGO involvement in the realization of global governance aims. As anti-trafficking work includes a heightened role for NGOs on many levels, it can be safely argued that this dynamic is noteworthy and of instructional value in the study of how global governance is evolving.

In order to provide a precise picture of NGO involvement in these efforts, this chapter will demonstrate in-depth examples of NGO anti-trafficking activity relating to the following articles of the Protocol and greater Convention Against Transnational Organized Crime:

From the Protocol to Prevent, Suppress, and Punish Trafficking in Persons, Especially Women and Children:
(a)   Article 6: Assistance to and protection of victims of trafficking in persons
(b)   Article 7: Status of victims of trafficking in persons in receiving States
(c)   Article 8: Repatriation of victims of trafficking in persons
(d)   Article 9: Measures against corruption
(e)   Article 10: Information exchange and training

From the United Nations Convention Against Transnational Organized Crime:
(a)   Article 15: Jurisdiction
(b)   Article 20: Special Investigative Techniques
(c)   Article 26: Measures to enhance cooperation with law enforcement authorities
(d)   Article 28: Collection, exchange and analysis of information on the nature of organized crime
(e)   Article 29: Training and Technical Assistance
(f)   Article 31: Prevention

Negotiation of the Convention and Its Protocols

As previously noted, NGOs constituted a large and prevailing voice of input for the crafting of the Protocol. However, not everything advocated by the NGO camp was implemented, and the discrepancies between what was suggested by NGOs and what was adopted serve to shed light on the differing approaches by the various institutions for anti-trafficking efforts. In the negotiation process, NGOs advocated for a provision that trafficked persons would be protected against prosecution for status-related offenses; however, states resisted accepting this provision based on the belief that too many illegal migrants would use trafficking as a false defense (Chuang 2006: 149).

The NGO delegates also pressed for formal recognition of trafficking victims' rights; however, many government delegates allegedly deemed a human rights focus to be inappropriate for the Protocol. As a result, mandatory language such as "state parties shall" is limited to the law enforcement provisions of the Protocol, while more open-ended and ambiguous language is used for the provisions pertaining to protection and assistance (Haynes 2004: 240).

As the Convention does not specify how assets confiscated from traffickers are to be used, the Human Rights Caucus—an NGO network comprised of 11 organizations—issued a proposal in the negotiations that these be used to compensate and reintegrate the victim of the trafficking offense, to fund services to trafficking victims, and fund anti-trafficking programs. However, delegates to the negotiations rejected this proposal (Jordan 2002: 34).

Article 6: Assistance to and Protection of Victims of Trafficking in Persons

The first step in assisting and protecting victims of trafficking in persons is to identify them; to this end, NGOs in destination countries engage actively in outreach work to reach those who may not be aware of support services or are afraid to speak with authorities. This is often done on the streets or through medical services for sex workers, with NGOs frequently employing foreign language-speakers who can translate for those who do not speak the predominant language (Tzvetkova 2002: 63–64).

At the Durbar Mahila Samanwaya Committee (DMSC) in India (an organization for sex workers' rights that protects sex workers from violence and exploitation), volunteers intercept new workers in the red light district of Kolkata. They identify cases of trafficking, often intervening in such cases to repatriate victims of trafficking without the involvement of law enforcement (but often with the involvement of the Ministry of Social Welfare). Between 2000 and 2002, the DMSC recovered 47 trafficking victims in this manner. In Kolkata, the DMSC has also established three local self-regulatory boards to prevent human rights violations within the sex trade and ensure self-determination, with sex trade workers themselves representing 60 percent of the membership (Jana et al. 2002: 75).

After trafficking victims are identified and delivered from their captors, follow-up support and measures to prevent re-victimization are crucial in their recovery. Direct service NGOs provide such care and support. There are many such direct service agencies dealing with indigent populations that have focused some of their efforts on anti-trafficking, though a greater number will be needed as more trafficking victims are identified in the future (Kara 2007: 3–4). NGOs with an explicit faith base have also aligned themselves with the anti-trafficking cause, and many of these have established safe houses for sex trafficking survivors, such as the Salvation Army, Churches Alert to Sex Trafficking across Europe (CHASTE) in the United Kingdom (UK), and nuns from varied congregations located throughout Italy (Pemberton 2006: 399).

In addition to personal care and support, NGOs in destination countries provide legal and administrative support, including assistance with documentation and legal counsel. The effectiveness of this support depends a great deal on national trafficking legislation, particularly whether short-stay permits are granted to survivors, and if these can be obtained with or without testifying against the individual's trafficker. Where residence permits are granted, NGOs will assist in the integration process leveraging social services and language/vocational training (Tzvetkova 2002: 65).

Another unique and emerging area of recovery assistance is counselling with a spiritual element by faith-based NGOs. An advocate for this approach, Pemberton (2006) asserts that instances of traffickers threatening women with curses if they rebel against them have posed a very real obstacle to escaping and recovering from exploitation and abuse. CHASTE works to counteract the effects of such conditioning for those who come from religious backgrounds. Advocates for this type of approach view faith-based organizations as valuable for strengthening the spiritual well-being of trafficking survivors. They assert that in rehabilitation:

> [h]ope that there is some form of future existence, which can be moved towards, that the individual is not abandoned, is profoundly significant. For women who are themselves religious, aspects of religious observance and ritual can facilitate the support of this alternative future.
>
> (Pemberton 2006: 401)

Article 7: Status of Victims of Trafficking in Persons in Receiving States

NGOs have also been active in facilitating the permitting of trafficking victims to remain in a state territory in appropriate cases with consideration to humanitarian and compassionate factors. The Bangkok shelter Bahn Kren Trakarn takes care of foreign victims of trafficking by processing their identity, determining their origins and experiences, providing victims with vocational training for up to six months at the shelter, and then repatriating them into their home country (Arnold and Bertone 2002: 16).

Challenges facing those in the CCPCR network in such matters are substantial. When a brothel is raided, a legal advocate must be on hand to immediately assess the migration and ethnic status of those in the brothel, as well as their age and legal status. Arnold and Bertone (2002: 44) write:

> Even within the same brothel, it may be found that there are a variety of cases and each need to be handled quickly, but with care; therefore, a triage unit is needed. The types of medical, judicial, and social services that are available to Thai citizens are not equally available to hill-tribe girls and illegal migrants. If an illegal migrant is found in Thailand, decisions need to be made about deportation, and prosecution of the victim and/or her trafficker. These decisions must be made carefully between the members of the TRAFCORD network and the police.

Because of the length of time required to deal with trafficking victims' immigration status when pursuing prosecution against their traffickers, members of the NGO Vital Voices assert that such investigations can exacerbate mental and emotional problems suffered as a result of trafficking by victims. Given this, NGOs in the United States (US) pressed for the inclusion of a private right of action against traffickers, enabling them to press lawsuits for damages, which was adopted in the 2003 Trafficking Victims Reauthorization Act (TVPRA) of 2003. Although few lawsuits against traffickers have been litigated thus far, civil action is seen as a potentially effective deterrent to trafficking as it would create a financial disincentive for such activity, lend more control over the case to the victim, and provide more appropriate monetary restitution to the victim than is offered them in criminal cases (Nam 2007: 1662–1667).

Article 8: Repatriation of Victims of Trafficking in Persons

Safely reintegrating a victim of trafficking into their country of origin and facilitating their access to follow-up support is a vital step in the anti-trafficking process. It has been estimated that up to 5 percent of trafficked women who are returned to southeastern European countries are re-trafficked. Where they are assisted, however, the United Nations Children's Fund (UNICEF) has stated that there is an 84 percent reintegration rate for returned trafficked women—a dynamic that is consistent with the IOM's claim that a majority of Moldovan victims of human trafficking who had assisted return and reintegration were still employed in Moldova after a year. The International Organization for Migration (IOM) is a leader in this process, as it monitors the reintegration process after three, six, and 12 months wherever possible (Omelaniuk 2005: 10).

Gender equality in a country plays a large part in the effectiveness of reintegration. In more patriarchal societies existing within states such as Bangladesh and Iran, it has been found to be more difficult for trafficking survivors to reintegrate into society due to lack of professional and personal options (Tzvetkova 2002: 63). In 1999, the IOM established the Counter-Trafficking Module Database (CTM), which facilitates assistance management as well as voluntary return and reintegration activities for victims of trafficking using data from those assisted through IOM counter-trafficking programs. It is a key resource for the creation of IOM policy and project development (IOM 2005: 12–13). Omelaniuk (2005: 11) states that the cases in the databases of IOM and RCP are largely those referred by NGOs and authorities. Though centered in Geneva's IOM headquarters, its content centers around the Balkan region where the IOM first began collecting data for the database. In July 2004, it had data on 2,791 victims from approximately 35 nationalities (Omelaniuk 2005: 11). Laczlo and Gramegna (2003: 187–188) write of the CTM methodology:

> The mission staff carries out in-depth interviews, based on a standardized question-naire, with all trafficked persons assisted by IOM. This interview allows IOM to understand their socio-economic and family background, their experience in migration, their recruitment by traffickers, the route taken, the violence and/or exploitation they suffered, their current condition, and their needs in terms of health, protection, return, and reintegration. The information collected is entered into the mission's database and shared between missions directly involved in the assistance of a trafficked person.

In countries of origin, NGOs often assist trafficking victims to reintegrate into society. Using referral networks, they provide necessities and resources for their physical and mental well-being, and sometimes assist them in reuniting with their families. For example, La Strada-Bulgaria arranges meetings with parents before the trafficked woman returns to explain the situation and provide family members with the resources needed to go and meet her. Reuniting a trafficking survivor with their family is not always the appropriate response; however, there are not many other options for NGOs in countries of origin as the provision of long-term accommodation is rarely available due to lack of resources (Tzvetkova 2002: 61–62).

In Thailand, the staff members of one outfit named Kred Trakarn are responsible for determining whether victims slated for repatriation will be safe and taken care of in their country of origin. If upon contacting shelters in that country they find there is insufficient room for the person in question, they will be permitted to remain in Thailand.

Despite these initiatives, a more comprehensive approach is needed—funded by governments and international donor agencies—as there is a dearth of "effective reintegration programs that address housing, education, health, employment, substance abuse, and trauma" (Omelaniuk 2005: 10). There is also a need for more research on integration or reintegration of human trafficking survivors into the communities in which they live. Supply-side questions have been the focus of many of the current studies, to the detriment of demand-side questions that analyze factors in destination countries that contribute to the existence of trafficking. They also do not analyze the relationship between internal and international trafficking (IOM 2005: 9).

Article 9: Measures Against Corruption

In terms of exposing, combating, and/or preventing corruption related to trafficking in persons, NGOs generally possess the advantage that their personnel are embedded in their communities and have a local presence that is often trusted by the local population. Subsequently, the capacity for NGOs to train state and local law enforcement personnel to focus on human trafficking is thought to be promising, and is strongly recommended for the US, where federal anti-trafficking resources are overtaxed (Kara 2007: 13).

NGO anti-trafficking activism has also been credited with putting pressure on governments, both directly and indirectly (by appealing to state governments to pressure other states to adhere to certain standards of accountability and action) (Arnold and Bertone 2002: 14). Challenges continue to beleaguer NGO efforts in the domain of corruption. For example, though DMSC's anti-trafficking interventions discussed in the section on Article 6 sometimes receive support from local police organizations, they are often resisted by law enforcing authorities who are sometimes entwined in the business of trafficking through corruption. Jana et al. (2002: 76) state:

> In DMSC's experience, the brothel owners who recruit trafficked women have a system worked out by which they can pay a bribe to the remand home authorities in order to have the woman returned to them. They then extract the amount they had invested—often inflating it considerably—from the trafficked woman by making her work without wages . . . At the end of such a process, her already restricted options would be reduced to none whatsoever.

Article 10: Information Exchange and Training

In addition to the IOM's aforementioned CTM database, the ILO has a collection of global data on labor exploitation. The Global Program against Trafficking in Human Beings also has a global database of information taken from international and state organizations, academia, and the media, and the Belgrade Regional Clearing Point (RCP) has a database of information on victims assisted in southeastern European countries (Omelaniuk 2005: 10). The mandate of the RCP—established by the Stability Pact for a South Eastern European Task Force on Trafficking in Human Beings—is to ensure the collection of standardized regional data on victim assistance and protection in terms of effectiveness and continuity. Its implementation is a cooperative effort between the International Catholic Migration Commission (ICMC) and the IOM, and serves as a model for other projects of this type slated to extend to other regions with IOM counter-trafficking programs (Laczlo and Gramegna 2003: 186).

In Thailand, NGOs are currently in the process of disaggregating data from court cases and making this information available to the public. (Arnold and Bertone 2002: 46). There are differing opinions on the value of NGO and IGO intelligence and information exchange regarding trafficking. Tyldum and Brunovskis (2005: 21) assert that outreach organizations and community workers generally do not have adequate registry systems, and cannot be expected to produce better estimates than methodologically trained researchers even in their areas of expertise. Laczlo and Gramegna (2003: 184–185) list methodological differences as a large hurdle to successful gathering of information by NGOs and IGOs, reasoning:

> Some NGOs register first contacts with victims, while others monitor hotline calls or those eligible for temporary residence permits. Finally, some agencies compile data over a one-year period, while others produce statistics covering the duration of a specific project.

Moreover, Laczlo and Gramegna note that valuable information collected by NGO and civil society sources does not always filter into government, one of the reasons for this being that they are mandated to protect the confidentiality of those they are assisting.

Article 15: Jurisdiction

The ability of NGOs to aid in establishing jurisdiction is limited, since by law this is the purview of states. However, NGOs have served as an inspiration for effective governmental agencies, for example in the establishment of an organization called Fight Against Child Exploitation (FACE). The organization was founded for the purpose of rectifying problems of monitoring international pedophiles in Thailand through ECPAT, and to create an exclusive body to monitor cases. In addition to monitoring cases of arrested pedophiles, FACE is responsible for advocacy, campaigning, and raising awareness. Of the organization, Arnold and Bertone (2002: 40) state:

> FACE has been successful because it is providing a service of case monitoring that is indicative of an open democratic space. Sudarat and Wanchai coordinate and encourage law enforcement officers to perform their tasks more actively and effectively, and assist in obtaining evidence, especially from victimized children if necessary. They also may accompany children to court, and act as counselors to the family.

Article 20: Special Investigative Techniques

The ability of the groups and networks to inform and participate in new and innovative types of investigation techniques is deemed by some sources to be quite high; for example, the following figure featured in a report from Tyldum and Burnovski shows that NGOs identify more trafficking victims than law enforcement.

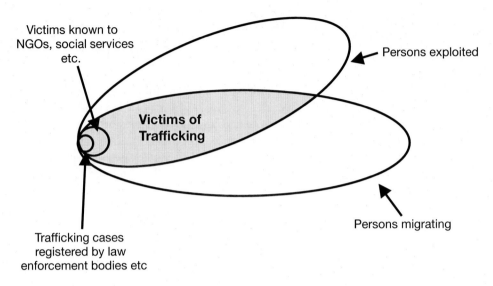

Figure 16.1 Targeting Victims of Trafficking: Subpopulations and Populations Where Victims of Trafficking Constitute Subpopulations

This makes sense when one considers the dynamic that:

> seeking help is a realistic option only for those who have and are aware of an active organization in their community. Thus, areas with many NGOs (or where information about rehabilitation services is well known) are more likely to register victims of trafficking.
>
> (Tyldum and Brunovskis 2005: 25)

This, however, varies from state to state. In Canada, for example, only one trafficking case was referred by an NGO to immigration authorities—a paltry figure compared to countries such as Italy that have a high number of victims identified by NGOs (Perrin 2010: 106). In the US, the Polaris Project operates a 24-hour toll-free hotline for tips on trafficking cases; the hotline receives an average of 400 calls per month, and information is on hand to callers who may be victims of trafficking (Perrin 2010: 209).

In Italy, NGOs work closely with law enforcement and have their own techniques for exposing trafficking. For example, an NGO known as the Transnational AIDS Prevention Among Migrant Prostitutes in Europe Project (TAMPEP) has street units of people of the same nationality as many trafficked women and girls in Italy. These people act as cultural mediators and give them health information, guidance, and establish trust. They also sensitize authorities to the realities and signs of trafficking, and reach out to create networks with victims who might otherwise remain hidden. Since 2006, NGOs and IGOs in Italy have also begun to inspect detention facilities, as well as conduct interviews with migrants in order to identify victims of trafficking (Perrin 2010: 203–204).

Article 26: Measures to Enhance Cooperation with Law Enforcement Authorities

While law enforcement responses to trafficking are in a strict sense the purview of the state, NGOs often play an important role in strengthening capacity of law enforcement authorities in combating trafficking. As NGOs often have profound connections with local communities, their cooperation is often invaluable for successful response by law enforcement authorities. The clearest examples of NGO cooperation with law enforcement are in Thailand, where a Memorandum of Understanding (MoU) was developed between the police and NGOs in response to the 1997 Trafficking Act. This was introduced in order to address problems in dealing with victims of trafficking, all of whom are either migrants or non-Thai. Under the Immigration Act, authorities are mandated to charge all illegal migrants with illegal entry and place them in the International Detention Center (IDC) regardless of whether they are victims of trafficking. Activists such as Sudarat have requested that the police not charge illegal migrants who had been sexually exploited in Thailand. Some law enforcement officers agreed they would use the 1997 Measures in Prevention and Suppression of Trafficking in Women and Children Act before consulting immigration laws, on the condition that there was available space in state shelters for the victims in the Public Welfare Department's shelters. Afterwards, the head of the Royal Thai Police in Bangkok gave a directive that the MoU be enforced seriously, negating the position of police in some regions in Thailand that the Immigration Act needed to be upheld to the letter (Arnold and Bertone 2002: 47).

The MoU has enabled NGOs in Thailand to look at repatriation, locate victims' families abroad, and work with embassies. Most importantly, it states that trafficked persons must be considered victims and given treatment fitting to that status as outlined in the MoU, with foreign children given the same rights as Thai nationals. The Center for the Protection of Children's Rights Foundation (CPCR) in Thailand has also developed a cooperative system to work closely with Thai NGOs and the police to provide a safe living environment for victims of child abuse, forced child labor, and child prostitution. The system of cooperation has been developed in just under 12 years, and is a groundbreaking child welfare agency for children's rights in the country (Arnold and Bertone 2002: 48).

In Bangladesh, the Association of Community Development (ACD) and the 15-member NGO network Action Against Trafficking and Sexual Exploitation work closely with government, law enforcement authorities, and community leaders to ameliorate protection and prosecution initiatives through referral systems, awareness-raising, and monitoring. In turn, states and governments often fund community networking initiatives with an increasingly participatory approach to:

> [e]llicit community-level monitoring of trafficking activity, to encourage private-sector responses, to build the capacity for better-informed professional referral networks, and to initiate new NGOs and to encourage existing NGOs to become more responsive.
> (Samarasinghe and Burton 2007: 57)

In addition to the high-level NGO in processes that may assist in prosecuting traffickers, such as taking evidence or statements from persons, examining objects and sites, and providing information and evidentiary items, service provider NGOs also often pair with advocacy groups for providing legal assistance and shaping anti-trafficking policy (Perkins 2005: 54).

Article 28: Collection, Exchange, and Analysis of Information on the Nature of Organized Crime

Much of NGO anti-trafficking activity has focused on the collection, exchange, and analysis of information related to trafficking. This is a key area of concern for the success of the movement, as experts in the field believe the informational networks of organized crime syndicates to be quite sophisticated, with an international center or "brain" responsible for the organization of a considerable degree of human trafficking activity. This is evidenced by the systematic nature of operations in the trade; for example, in Ukraine, traffickers were found to have used advertising extensively, to pose as tourist agencies and legitimate businesses (such as language schools) and use fake invitation letters and work contracts (i.e. from "ghost" companies abroad to facilitate the trafficking) (Thompson 2000: 48–49, 60).

This type of activity is accelerating in NGOs; for example, in an IOM bibliography of research on human trafficking for which many sources came from NGOs, most of the 260+ titles were published after 2000 (IOM 2005: 7). This shows that there has been a great increase in research on human trafficking after that year. In some cases, NGO reports assume some of the intelligence functions of the state; for example, an NGO in India has established its own Trafficking in Persons report for that country (Omelaniuk 2005: 9).

Research reports produced by NGOs, academic institutions, and the media have also contributed heavily to the Global Program Against Trafficking in Human Beings' (GPAT) global database on trafficking trends. The function of this database is to collect and collate open-source information for comparison between different regions; information from 500 sources had been entered by June 2004 and divided into country reports, profiles, and trafficking routes (Omelaniuk 2005: 9).

Article 29: Training and Technical Assistance

A large part of training and technical assistance for victims of trafficking to reintegrate into their communities is accomplished by NGOs, whereby individuals can receive training in a wide variety of vocations; some shelters, such as the Bahn Kred Trakarn Center in Thailand, sell handicrafts made by those at the shelter at a 20 percent profit (Arnold and Bertone 2002: 40). Certain NGOs, such as one Italian organization known as On the Road, aim to break the cycle of exploitation for victims of trafficking by facilitating internships for them in reputable companies that will use their individual skills as opposed to manual labor or other fields prone to exploitation. Psychologists and tutors assist individuals in building their capacity, and On the Road pays for social security costs and salary during the time of internship. The employment rate of this program currently stands at 90 percent (Perrin 2010: 202–203).

NGOs also serve a training function in terms of instructing professionals in areas related to trafficking to work to combat the problem. For example, an NGO based in Nicaragua named Asociation Mary Barreda educates and nurtures the forming of networks between women working in areas where they may be able to spot young women vulnerable to trafficking (such as bus stations), and to identify and protect them. The women who are trained and comprise this network have reported that their involvement with the Asociation Mary Barreda has had an empowering effect on them. Similarly, the Swedish International Development Agency (SIDA) has worked with NGOs to train religious leaders on how to effectively refer victims of trafficking, and the Polaris Project in the US has launched an "online anti-trafficking database for professionals" and "a law-enforcement toolkit of relevant and regionally responsive information" (Samarasinghe and Burton 2007: 57–58).

Article 31: Prevention

Employing preventative strategies to thwart potential activity in human trafficking is perhaps the area in which NGOs are most active. NGOs have launched education campaigns, hotlines and shelters, and assistance programs that house individuals at risk of trafficking; for example, the New Life Center, Bahn Kred Trakarn, and The Daughters Education Program and Development Center in Thailand house, train and educate at-risk children. Maiti Nepal provides comprehensive services for potential victims of trafficking, including skills training, information on trafficking, and provision of microfinancing. The organization also uses bazaars to mobilize public anti-trafficking rallies and has a series of prevention homes in several high-risk districts in Nepal, which offer volunteer high school students awareness training on the dangers of trafficking, and subsequently send these students to campaign against trafficking in communities that are known to be high-risk (Tzvetkova 2002: 65–66; Samarasinghe and Burton 2007: 56).

Another preventative tactic employed by trafficking victim assistance organizations is to work with the family of the victim to determine whether there may be family-related factors connected to their abuse, in order to prevent abuse to other siblings (Arnold and Bertone 2002: 40–45).

In the Canadian city of Winnipeg, Manitoba, a grassroots initiative called the Grand-mothers Protecting Our Children Council formed in 2007, comprised of Aboriginal clan mothers, elders, and grandmothers. Raising public awareness of sexual abuse of First Nations children in the area, they hold an annual Grandmothers Sacred Walk to "reclaim the streets of Winnipeg from child sexual abuse and exploitation" (Perrin 2010: 179). Raising awareness is a common strategy used for prevention by anti-trafficking NGOs, and is often done through innovative means; for example, La Strada in Eastern Europe educates professional networks and at-risk women about trafficking through multimedia platforms, including cartoon games, CD-ROMs, and school programs (Samarasinghe and Burton 2007: 55).

One strategy used by NGOs for raising awareness is to initiate a one-time media blitz that will have a rapid and profound impact; in Russia, the MiraMed Foundation and the Angel Coalition launched a multiplatform publicity campaign that lasted 100 days and reached 60 million people—the largest anti-trafficking education campaign in the country. As there was a sharp increase in calls to a national trafficking hotline in the days following the campaign, it was considered to have had an immense impact (Samarasinghe and Burton 2007: 57). In the Philippines, a national alliance of women's organizations named Gabriela launched a large-scale public information and education campaign to raise awareness about issues of sex trafficking and mobilize survivors to action called the Purple Rose Campaign (Tzvekova 2002: 65).

Awareness campaigns have also been launched to honor the Palermo Protocol itself. For example, in 2004, CHASTE launched a "not for sale" campaign in for the Palermo Protocol's UK ratification with other NGOs such as Amnesty International, the Women's Institute, and UNICEF. This was successful, as the UK ratified the Palermo Protocol shortly after (Pemberton 2006: 407).

Underlying conditions of gender inequality often contribute to trafficking; for example, in the West African context, girls are sent away by families much more frequently than boys as it is presumed that girls will leave the family upon marrying, and girls are preferred as domestic servants (Dottridge 2002: 42). Recognizing these types of dynamics, NGOs have begun to target this dynamic as a form of prevention, particularly in countries of origin. Tzvetkova (2002: 65) writes:

> An important component of prevention work in origin countries is the tackling of gender stereotypes, and increasing sensitization on themes related to violence against women and women's rights. NGOs in destination countries publish educational materials for migrant women, and provide training, technical, and financial assistance to their partners from the countries of origin.

Some NGOs have also specifically targeted the demand for sexual services and cheap labor, though this is not a consistent approach across nations and regions (Bertone 2004: 19). For example, a group of university students in the Philippines created a film to increase awareness among potential clients of sexual services about trafficking and spread the message that real men do not buy women (Samarasinghe and Burton 2007: 56). One prominent example of this tactic is the United States' Demi and Ashton Foundation, which harnesses celebrity recognition to spread the message that "real men don't buy girls" through high-profile online videos featuring well-known actors and artists.

Problems with NGO Anti-Trafficking Approaches

The top three internal problems of approach facing NGOs in the struggle against trafficking are the following:

1. Division of camps between anti-prostitution and those who look at prostitution as simply another form of labour for which workers should not be exploited.
2. Need to evaluate whether strategies used are effective or wrong-headed.
3. Lack of coherent strategy stemming from different approaches: law and order, socioeconomic and gendered approaches, demand-focused approaches . . .

One of the most oft-cited problems in the anti-trafficking movement is the split between groups: those who see all prostitution as exploitative and endeavor to do away with it using anti-trafficking objectives as impetus to change, and those who see willing prostitution as a legitimate trade but who focus on doing away with forced labor in the sex industry as in any other industry. This division, apparent from the inception of the anti-trafficking protocol and existing to this day, is a roadblock in the successful establishment of anti-trafficking NGO networks necessary for their financial survival and practical effectiveness. The complexity of alliances and rifts resulting from this split is made evident in Samarasinghe and Burton's (2007: 60) description of the anti-trafficking NGO community in Nepal:

> [I]n Nepal the National Network Against Girl Trafficking (NNAGT) is aligned with the Coalition Against Trafficking (CATW), which argues that trafficking and prostitution are a violation of women's rights and their dignity. On the other hand, the

Alliance Against Trafficking in Women and Children in Nepal (AATWIN) is aligned with the Global Alliance Against Trafficking in Women (GAATW), which argue against the abolition and criminalization of prostitution, while upholding the right of adult women to choose to engage in sex work (The Asia Foundation 2001). AATWIN advocates women's right to migrate as a fundamental human right, while NNAGT, adopting an abolitionist perspective on prostitution and viewing migration as a process by which any woman could become a potential recruit to the sex industry, advocates stricter monitoring of female cross-border migration.

Another problem is that scant evaluation of practices and strategies is currently being done, despite indications that such evaluation is of great importance for ensuring effectiveness in anti-trafficking efforts. For example, one such study found that large-scale public awareness campaigns in southeastern Europe were not taken seriously by local populations, which merely viewed them as anti-migration propaganda (Chuang 2006: 158). There are certain questionable practices currently undertaken by NGOs that warrant this kind of evaluation. For example, in Bangladesh, NGOs collaborated with the state to set up booths and interrogate single women attempting to travel across borders, and NGOs providing shelter for trafficked persons have also tested for human immunodeficiency virus (HIV) without the person's consent or knowledge (Jana et al. 2002: 70–74).

As anti-trafficking efforts are intensifying, NGOs and other actors are awakening to a greater plurality of approaches to combat it. More recently, scholars have begun to recognize the role of socioeconomic conditions and trends in contributing to the problem of trafficking. The effects of globalization that widen the gap between rich and poor countries cause the poor to seek migration for their survival. Strict border controls leave these desperate migrants vulnerable to trafficking, a phenomenon considered in this context as a matter of "labor migration gone horribly wrong in our globalized economy" (Chuang 2006: 137).

The limiting of women's employment to informal sectors in many cultural contexts has resulted in women being particularly vulnerable to trafficking, even after they are delivered from their traffickers and repatriated. Women also frequently are motivated to flee based on non-economic gender discrimination such as gender-based violence and lack of access to resources. (Chuang 2006: 141). Because of this, there is also a gendered approach to anti-trafficking espoused by many in the international women's movement, which has helped to draw more global attention to the problem in some cases (Bertone 2004: 14).

The downside of such a plurality of perspectives for this complex issue is that there remains a lack of coherent strategy among states and NGOs to address it. The West African experience in combating child trafficking shows the problems that can arise when different international organizations try to work together: "[e]ach agrees that its general objective is to end trafficking of children, but their strategies for doing so differ and so make contradictory demands on the government and societies involved" (Dottridge 2002: 40).

Similarly, a proliferation of studies and activist projects from various organizations globally on trafficking has caused the movement to become fragmented and politicized, and has caused fierce competition for limited resources. This in turn has resulted in more grassroots organizations missing necessary funding. As the smaller NGOs often address the humanitarian side of anti-trafficking work, Bertone (2004: 15–16) has underscored the importance of keeping these organizations in operation.

Conclusion

The role of NGOs working as human rights advocates has been growing (Omelaniuk 2005: 15), and overall the high level of NGO involvement in relation to implementing the Anti-Trafficking Protocol can be credited with many of the successes of anti-trafficking efforts globally in the past decade. They fulfill a very important role in the fight against trafficking together with IGOs and individual state governments, as they are the most flexible of the three. Because of this, it would be a prudent approach for states to shift discourses and efforts to combat human trafficking away from a securitization lens and toward one that supports global civil society in its work. This is inherently distinct from the "public–private partnerships" that are increasingly gaining traction in the realm of human development, because there is no identifiable opportunity for companies to make profits from these types of community-based efforts (although some recoup the costs of their operations through sale of crafts, these are still importantly nonprofit operations). In the context of further support, a role for states in oversight of these operations would not be inappropriate; however, given the extent and success of IGO–NGO cooperation on this front, IGO oversight may be more conducive to desired objectives.

While the challenges presented by the global trafficking trade remain considerable—with many more resources and much more public momentum needed to properly combat the problem—NGOs have assisted IGOs in all areas of anti-trafficking efforts, and have provided on-the-ground expertise and fast response times to the challenges presented. Arnold summarizes the advantages of NGOs in combating trafficking as follows:

> Better understanding of culture, knowledge of language, capacity to cooperate with police, ability to influence policy. . . . It is to the credit of the local NGOs that they have learned how to communicate their needs clearly to foreign donors in order to be able to best implement the kinds of programs that the local NGOs deem appropriate and feasible given the particular circumstances.
>
> (Arnold and Bertone 2002: 15)

The positive dynamic of NGO and IGO cooperation in the anti-trafficking movement is also instructive for present and future human rights campaigns of global significance. The potential of such partnerships has been remarked upon before; instances are very much demonstrative of how the UN's partnership with civil society networks can serve as a strong foundation for global governance and advocates an even stronger relationship between the two in the future. These groups often possess key strengths that the UN could use to apply their policies, namely: efficiency of operations; on-the-ground expertise; and adequate, relatively reliable funding (Trent 2007).

While the foundation of cooperation is perhaps the strongest in the anti-trafficking realm, this partnership needs to be strengthened further and made more cohesive in order to meet the challenges of upholding human rights on a global level. The challenge that the global trafficking trade presents to global governance by those who would uphold the rights of human beings is substantial, though it is an encouraging sign that perhaps in no other area of global governance is the participation of NGOs more irreplaceable, more vital, and more rigorous.

Notes

1. For this chapter, the definition provided in the Palermo Protocol will be used: "'Trafficking in persons' means the recruitment, transportation, transfer, harboring or receipt of persons, by means of the threat or use of force or other forms of coercion, of abduction, of fraud, of deception, of the abuse of power or of a position of vulnerability or of the giving or receiving of payments or benefits to achieve the consent of a person having control over another person, for the purpose of exploitation. Exploitation shall include, at a minimum, the exploitation of the prostitution of others or other forms of sexual exploitation, forced labor or services, slavery or practices similar to slavery, servitude or the removal of organs" (UNODC 2004: 42).
2. The international organizations in a West African case study were reported to have placed a low priority on addressing questions of victim protection and repatriation upon identification; consequently, in Libreville, one small NGO with very few resources had taken on the burden of addressing this challenge virtually unaided (Dottridge 2002: 4).

References

ACF (2015) "Office on Trafficking in Persons: Frequently Asked Questions," Government of the United States of America, available at: www.acf.hhs.gov/office-on-trafficking-in-persons-frequently-asked-questions (accessed June 4, 2015).

Arnold, C. and Bertone, A.M. (2002) "Addressing the Sex Trade in Thailand: Some Lessons Learned from NGOs Part 1," *Gender Issues*, 20(1): 26–52.

Bertone, A.M. (2004) "Transnational Activism to Combat Trafficking in Persons," *Brown Journal of World Affairs*, 10(11): 9–22.

Bourbeau, P. (2011) *The Securitization of Migration: A Study of Movement and Order*, New York: Routledge.

Chuang, J. (2006) "Beyond a Snapshot: Preventing Human Trafficking in the Global Economy," *Indiana Journal of Global Legal Studies*, 13(1): 137–163.

Dottridge, M. (2002) "Trafficking in Children in West and Central Africa," *Gender and Development*, 10(1): 38–42.

Hathaway, J.C. (2008) "The Human Rights Quagmire of 'Human Trafficking'," *Virginia Journal of International Law*, 49(1): 1–59.

Haynes, D.F. (2004) "Used, Abused, Arrested and Deported: Extending Immigration Benefits to Protect the Victims of Trafficking and to Secure the Prosecution of Traffickers," *Human Rights Quarterly*, 26(2): 221–272.

Hoff, S. (2014) "Where is the Funding for Anti-Trafficking Work? A Look at Donor Funds, Policies and Practices in Europe," *Anti-Trafficking Review*, 3: 109–132.

IOM (2005) *Data and Researching on Trafficking: A Global Survey*, Geneva: IOM.

Jana, S., Bandyopadhyay, N., Dutta, M.K., and Saha, A. (2002) "A Tale of Two Cities: Shifting the Paradigm of Anti-Trafficking Programmes," *Gender and Development*, 10(1): 69–79.

Jordan, A.D. (2002) "Human Rights or Wrongs? The Struggle for a Rights-Based Response to Trafficking in Human Beings," *Gender and Development*, 10(1): 28–37.

Kara, S.I. (2007) "Decentralizing the Fight against Human Trafficking in the United States: The Need for Greater Involvement in Fighting Human Trafficking by State Agencies and Local Non-Governmental Organizations," *Cardozo Journal of Law and Gender*, 13: 657–683.

Laczlo, F. and Gramegna, M.A. (2003) "Developing Better Indicators of Human Trafficking," *Brown Journal of World Affairs*, 10(1): 179–194.

Nam, J.S. (2007)"The Case of the Missing Case: Examining the Civil Right of Action for Human Trafficking Victims," *Columbia Law Review*, 107: 1655–1703.

Omelaniuk, I. (2005) *Trafficking in Human Beings*, New York: UN Expert Group Meeting on International Migration and Development, July 6–8.

Oxman-Martinez, J., Martinez, A., and Hanley, J. (2001) "Human Trafficking: Canadian Government Policy and Practice," *Refuge: New Directions for Refugee Policy*, 19(4): 14–23.

Pemberton, C. (2006) "For God's Sake Not for Sale: Trafficking and the Church in Europe," *Gender and Development*, 14(3): 399–408.

Perkins, W.Y. (2005) "Vital Voices: Advocacy and Service Work of NGOs in the Fight Against Human Trafficking," *UN Chronicle*, 42(1): 54–55.

Perrin, B. (2010) *Invisible Chains: Canada's Underground World of Human Trafficking*, Toronto: Penguin.

Samarasinghe, V. and Burton, B. (2007) "Strategising Prevention: A Critical Review of Local Initiatives to Prevent Female Sex Trafficking," *Development in Practice*, 17(1): 51–64.

Sing, R.S. (2009) *Encyclopaedia on Women and Children Trafficking*, New Delhi: Anmol.

Thompson, D. (Ed.) (2000) *Migrant Trafficking and Human Smuggling in Europe Geneva: International Organization for Migration*, Geneva: IOM.

Tiuriukanova, E. (2004) "Female Labor Migration Trends and Human Trafficking: Policy Recommendations," in S.W. Stoecker and L.I. Shelley (Eds.), *Human Traffic and Transnational Crime: Eurasian and American Perspectives*, New York: Rowman & Littlefield, pp. 91–114.

Trent, J. (2007) *Modernization of the United Nations System: Civil Society's Role in Moving from International Relations to Global Governance*, Opladen, Germany: Barbara Budrich.

Tyldum, G. and Brunovskis, A. (2005) "Describing the Unobserved: Methodological Challenges in Empirical Studies on Human Trafficking," *International Migration*, 43(1/2): 17–34.

Tzvetkova, M. (2002) "NGO Responses to Trafficking in Women," *Gender and Development*, 10(1): 60–68.

UNODC (2004) *United Nations Convention Against Transnational Organized Crime and the Protocols Thereto*, Vienna: Vienna International Centre.

UNODC (2009) *International Framework for Action to Implement the Trafficking in Persons*, New York: UNODC.

UNODC (2014) *United Nations Global Report on Trafficking in Persons*, New York: UNODC.

When Interests Collide: J.H. Merryman's "The Public Interest in Cultural Property" and the Sistine Chapel

Joshua K. Wasylciw

When one references the broad concept of art, many might immediately think of a piece of Renaissance art that they are familiar with; many might also think of Renaissance art of a much more grandiose scale such as the Sistine Chapel. This 530-year-old chapel is considered Michelangelo's crowning achievement and the apex of high Italian Renaissance. Being both significant for its unremitting influence on Western art and being a site of religious importance to the world's 1.2 billion Catholics, it is little wonder why this chapel is so well known. However, questions regarding who has property interests in this great structure surface regularly. It is our intention to demonstrate in this chapter that the elements of a cultural property policy identified by John Henry Merryman, in his "The Public Interest in Cultural Property" are incongruent in their current order of importance with how the Sistine Chapel has been managed for the past 50 years. We set out to accomplish this by first providing a brief summary of Merryman's argument. This will be followed by an exploration of legal ownership of the Sistine Chapel. Lastly, we examine the restoration project that began in the 1960s and the preservation of the chapel that continues today. By combining these three elements, we attempt to demonstrate that the various interests in this specific piece of property have been accommodated by a cultural property policy disparate from that which Merryman outlines.

J.H. Merryman's "The Public Interest in Cultural Property"

Merryman begins his 2012 work "The Public Interest in Cultural Property" with the axiom that generally people care deeply about cultural property, and goes on to ask why this is so. In expressing this view, Merryman endeavors to help define the public interest and thereby assist in formulating a public policy toward cultural property that is responsive to those wishing to experience property—while also balancing the need to preserve property. To accomplish this, he looks at two topics. First, he considers sources of the public interest in cultural property. Second, he takes into account elements of a cultural property policy. While looking at the sources of public interest, Merryman focuses on the expressive values of the property in question and concludes that there are seven types of expressive value in cultural property: truth and certainty, morality, memory, survival, identity, and community. Merryman proceeds to explore the politics of cultural property and shows that political necessity of ownership of a given item sometimes trumps public desire to preserve that item. He applies this line of reasoning to the National Museum of Anthropology in Mexico City. He concludes his examination of the sources of public interest in cultural property by briefly exploring the utility of cultural property.

For the purposes of comparing the policies surrounding the management and the preservation of the Sistine Chapel, Merryman's second topic is of more importance: the elements of a cultural property. After examining the reasons why people bother to care about cultural property previously, Merryman concludes that there are three considerations that should be central to the development of any cultural property policy, and those are—in descending order of importance—preservation, truth, and access. Beginning with preservation, Merryman argues that "the essential ingredient of any cultural property policy is that the object itself be physically preserved. The point is too obvious to need elaboration" (Merryman 2012: 260). Even so, Merryman elaborates this claim by skillfully employing the "Elgin (Parthenon) Marbles." Merryman argues that unless the atmospheric conditions in Athens were to change, or unless the Marbles could be protected from the atmosphere in some manner, that the Marbles should not be returned to Greece. For Merryman, preservation is more important than access to cultural property.

Following preservation, Merryman identifies truth as the secondary consideration when formulating cultural property policy. He uses "'truth' to sum up the shared concerns for accuracy, probity, and validity that, when combined with industry, insight, and imagination, produce good science and good scholarship" (Merryman 2012: 262). The third, and final, consideration that the author suggests should form the basis of any cultural property policy: access. Access, he argues, is of less concern than preservation or truth and should only become a factor in public policy once the previous two concerns are overcome. By again employing the Lord Elgin Marbles, Merryman demonstrates that while accessibility to the Marbles by Greeks has been reduced by their removal and subsequent relocation to London, England, had they not been removed they would have been destroyed—and thus no one would have been able to access them. Merryman concludes his work by dismissing cultural nationalism as a factor to consider when formulating a cultural property policy. He does so by claiming that it is a relic of the nineteenth century that disproportionately influences cultural property policy.

Legal Ownership of the Sistine Chapel

The legal ownership of the Sistine Chapel continues to be a subject of much confusion among art historians and critics of the Catholic Church, among other groups. Although the chapel is located in the center of Rome, ownership of the chapel is vested in the Vatican City state. While many people assume that the Vatican City and the Catholic Church are one and the same, they do so incorrectly. As the last remaining vestige of the Papal States, the Vatican City has remained a sovereign state since the eight century. During the nineteenth century, Italian nationalism necessitated the assimilation of the various states on the Etruscan peninsula. Consequently, the new Italian state enveloped the Papal States following a brief war between the two. Although the Papal States had disappeared, the Lateran Pacts of 1929 re-established the independence and sovereignty of the Vatican City. Signed by both the Kingdom of Italy and the Holy See (the government of the Vatican City state), the Lateran Pacts carved a 108-acre country out of the middle of Rome (Reese 1996). Included within these 108 acres are St. Peter's Basilica,[1] the Lateran Palace,[2] and the Sistine Chapel.

Although the Lateran Pacts had only been signed in 1929, the Papal States and the Vatican City had been functioning as an absolute monarchy since the eighth century. The Pope, continuing to function as absolute monarch today, owns all state property, which includes the buildings, art, and architecture found in the Vatican City (Manhattan 1983). While critics of the Catholic Church have argued that the roughly 18,000 pieces of art owned by the Vatican City should be sold to feed the poor or to house the homeless, the Vatican City has continuously rejected these calls and "[i]n 1986 . . . the Vatican put out a statement saying the artworks and cultural artefacts owned by [Vatican City] constitute 'a treasure for all humanity' and cannot be sold" (Allen 2004: 81). Regardless of one's opinion on whether these pieces should be sold or not, one thing is clear: they are state property belonging to the Vatican City. Claims that the Sistine Chapel belongs to Italy, the Roman Catholic Church, or any other body are simply mistaken.

Restoration and Preservation

Images that make up the Sistine Chapel do not visually depict much in the way of property theory. However, what does illustrate arguments about cultural property policy, which Merryman identifies, is the manner in which the chapel has been *managed* over the past 50 years. Beginning in the 1960s, the Vatican set about on a massive restoration of the Sistine Chapel with the aim of removing 500 years of soot, dust, and grime from the frescoes (Cast 1991, 1995).

Much of the ceiling—including accessories that were added—had accumulated even more grime than the ceiling, which had also revealed cracks as a result of the building's shifting foundations over hundreds of years (Pietrangeli et al. 1986). However, the restoration was not without controversy. Prior to the restoration, the images were dark and gloomy. Following the restorative work, the images were bright and cheerful. Art and art history scholars vigorously debated whether the restoration was appropriate or not, and some tried to prevent it. Art history scholars fought vigorously to stop the restoration as they had spent a lifetime specializing in studying Michelangelo's work, and conventional understandings focused on the painter's dark and gloomy portrayals of subjects (Stokstad 2005). By restoring the chapel, suddenly a mountain of writing on Michelangelo became inaccurate and outdated. However, in the end, the restoration proceeded.

Figure 17.1 Sistine Chapel Frescoes Before and After Restoration

Interestingly, the restorative process seems to have prioritized Merryman's goals of preservation, truth, and access in an inverse order of importance. During the restoration process, a Japanese documentary film company was given exclusive rights to film the transformation of the frescoes (Stokstad 2005). While the art of the chapel was already widely known, a conscious decision was made to film the process in order to increase public access to the pieces, and to the restorative process more generally. The Vatican City expressed its desire for art historians and others with concerns regarding the process to have their trepidation eased by allowing them the opportunity to view every step of the transformation. It was further desirable to film the event because the documentary would increase access to the chapel for people who were unable to travel to the chapel during times when Internet virtual tours were nonexistent.

Of equal—or close to equal—importance regarding access was Merryman's category of truth. While there was no question whether the frescoes in the chapel were original or not,[3] what was of central importance was the truth of the manner in which they were portrayed. The initial idea to cleanse the frescoes stemmed from a desire to return them to the state in which Michelangelo *intended* them to be, and the state in which they were when initially completed (Stokstad 2005). While the frescoes were known as dark and dreary, there was concern that this was an inaccurate depiction of their truth and authenticity. Restoration was initiated as a result of this very concern.

Merryman's third essential element of cultural property policy (preservation) seems to have been of little concern when the decision was made to restore the frescoes. Although there was obviously no intention to *destroy* the frescoes, there was similarly no intention to preserve them in 1960s form. The *raison d'être* of the process was to change what they were—not to preserve. The restorative process not only involved the removal of debris, but also the repainting of areas that had faded, as well as parts of the ceiling, which had been replastered due to (as noted previously) fractures in the original walls and ceiling (Stokstad 2005). While Merryman's preservation argument implies the stopping of the results of time on an object—such as the Lord Elgin Marbles—the Sistine Chapel restoration process involved the undoing of the results of time on the art itself. If one was to undo the results of time on the Lord Elgin Marbles, or on Michelangelo's famous *David*, one would have to repaint them in period style, and this is something Merryman would staunchly disapprove of.[4] Despite Merryman's concern for the authenticity of context, his chief interest remains the preservation of the artifact in its current state (Merryman 2012). The Vatican City disagreed with this element of Merryman's cultural property policy and, to an extent, ignored it when restoring the Sistine Chapel.

Following the completion of the restoration of the Sistine Chapel, the Vatican City since maintained a policy different from that advocated by Merryman. Access to the frescoes continues to be the primary goal of Vatican City. The chapel continues to be one of the most frequented tourist destinations in the Vatican City and in Rome, and despite evidence that the high number of tourists viewing the art is hastening its decay, the Vatican City has not yet curbed the number of visitors admitted to view the images.[5] While some measures have been taken to mitigate the damage caused by the large number of people entering the chapel on a daily basis—such as the installation of dehumidifiers—priority clearly remains *access* over *preservation*.

Conclusion

The Sistine Chapel may be one of the most recognizable works of art in the world and its importance as cultural property cannot seriously be challenged. However, as demonstrated in this chapter, management of this chapel over the past 50 years has occurred in accordance with a policy that is different from what Merryman has identified in "The Public Interest in Cultural Property." While Merryman prioritizes preservation over all other elements and ranks access as least of concern among his three elements of cultural property policy, the owner of the Sistine Chapel—the Vatican City state government—has prioritized access to the frescoes over other elements, and concerns about preservation have gone unheeded. Our intention was to demonstrate that the elements of a cultural property policy that Merryman identified in his "The Public Interest in Cultural Property" are incongruent in their current order of importance with how the Sistine Chapel has been managed for the past 50 years. In order to accomplish this, a brief recitation of Merryman's argument was followed by an exploration of the legal ownership of the Sistine Chapel. Finally, this chapter examined the restoration project that began in the 1960s, the controversy surrounding this restoration, and the preservation efforts that continue to this day. While each of preservation, truth, and access can be seen to factor into the Vatican City's policy of how to manage the cultural property of the Sistine Chapel, they do so in a manner with which Merryman disagrees.

Notes

1. For a detailed history of St. Peter's Basilica, see Scotti (2007).
2. For a detailed history of the Lateran Palace, see Mandel (1994).
3. The frescoes are impossible to move as they were painted into the wet plaster of the walls when the walls were being built and the images thus seeped *into* the wall.
4. Although much of classical sculpture is associated with bare marble, or other stone, research has demonstrated that the vast majority of these pieces were painted to resemble lifelike people, objects, or landscapes.

5. Resulting damage is not intentional vandalism. The damage is largely caused by high levels of humidity in the atmosphere of the room, which in turn is caused by such a large number of people breathing in such a small space on a daily basis.

References

Allen, J.L. (2004) *All the Pope's Men: The Inside Story of How the Vatican Really Thinks*, New York: Doubleday.

Banks, M. (2013) "Join in 'Mediation' with Greece over Elgin Marbles, UNESCO Urges Britain," *The Telegraph*, October 15, available at: www.telegraph.co.uk/news/worldnews/europe/greece/10381163/Join-in-mediation-with-Greece-over-Elgin-Marbles-Unesco-urges-Britain.html. Accessed November 1, 2013.

Cast, D. (1991) "Finishing the Sistine," *Art Bulletin*, 73: 669–684.

Cast, D. (1995) "Finishing the Sistine," in W.E. Wallace (Ed.), *Michelangelo: Selected Scholarship in English*, Hamden: Garland, pp. 447–462.

Duggan, B. (2013) "Did the Vatican Ruin the Sistine Chapel Frescoes?" *Big Think*, January 24, available at: http://bigthink.com/Picture-This/did-the-vatican-ruin-the-sistine-chapel-frescoes. Accessed November 1, 2013.

Mandel, C. (1994) *Sixtus V and the Lateran Palace*, Milan: Istituto poligrafico e Zecca dello Stato, Libreria dello Stato.

Manhattan, A. (1983) *The Vatican Billions*, Ontario: Chick Publications.

Merryman, J.H. (2012) "The Public Interest in Cultural Property," in G.S. Alexander and H. Dagan (Eds.), *Properties of Property*, New York: Wolters Kluwer Law & Business, pp. 256–264.

Pietrangeli, A., Shearman, J., O'Malley, J.W., de Vecchi, P., Hirst, M., Mancinelli, F., Colalucci, G., and Bernabei, F. (1986) *The Sistine Chapel: The Art, The History, The Restoration*, New York: Harmony Books.

Reese, T.J. (1996) *Inside the Vatican*, Cambridge, MA: Harvard University Press.

Rutkowski, S. (2011) "Nov. 1: All Saints' Day; Day of the Innocents; Sistine Chapel's Public Debut," *ABC News*, November 1, available at: http://abcnews.go.com/blogs/extras/2011/11/01/nov-1-all-saints-day-day-of-the-innocents-sistine-chapels-public-debut/. Accessed November 1, 2013.

Scotti, R.A. (2007) *Basilica: The Splendor and the Scandal: Building St. Peter's*, New York: Plume.

Stokstad, M. (2005) *Art History*, Upper Saddle River, NJ: Pearson Education.

Chapter 18

ASEAN: The Intersection of Democracy, Civil Society, and Human Rights

Benoît Masset

Regionalism is one of the most famous contemporary concepts in political science. This phenomenon is described as "a process through which geographical regions become significant political and/or economic units, serving as the basis for cooperation and possibly identity" (Heywood 2011: 481). It tends to emulate through out the world. At the same time, human rights—a long-standing concept in the field—appeared to be more than ever intertwined with regionalism. The primary research question posed in this chapter can be stated as such: *Does the ASEAN as a regional organization trigger human rights' improvements within Myanmar?* This chapter, as the title implies, also focuses on the issue of human rights, which can be thought of as a series of rights that are *universal* and *natural* to all human beings.

In an attempt to respond to the aforesaid question, this chapter proposes a theoretical framework with the aim of defining the main two concepts, which are *regionalism* and *human rights*. Greater emphasis was placed on the concept, with the eventual emergence of the concept of *new regionalism*, during the second wave of regional organizations. It is characterized by a less institutional regional integration process and a greater emphasis on the economy (Wunderlich 2007: 29). The later section applies the hypothesis to a specific case study. One should observe if the positive impact of a regional organization (in this case, the Association of Southeast Asian Nations [ASEAN]) over human rights in a specific country (Myanmar) holds true. This chapter briefly looks at ASEAN as a regional organization since its creation vis-à-vis the 1967 Bangkok Treaty through to its later/current developments. This presentation is made in the light of ASEAN's more general evolution, but particularly its development into a more prominent actor in terms of human rights in Southsast Asia (SEA). Two recent ASEAN tools are given special attention: (1) the ASEAN Intergovernmental Commission on Human Rights (AICHR); and (2) the ASEAN declaration of human rights (ASEAN Secretariat 2012). The final part of the section analyses the veracity of the hypothesis by scrutinizing any improvements in the Myanmar case (Burma) thanks to several reports of Human Rights Watch (HRW) and Amnesty International (AI).

Theoretical Framework

Before analyzing the possible positive correlation between regionalism and human rights, this chapter proposes to clarify the main two concepts developed for a better understanding of the case study. Regionalism is one of the most appealing contemporary phenomena in political science. During the last half-century, one should observe that the world order was greatly challenged by the emergence of multilevel governance. Indeed, in different parts of the world, different nations chose to integrate. Heywood (2011: 481–482) describes regionalism as the coordination in social, economic, political field of a same geographical region, and a "process of cooperation or integration between countries in the same region of the world."

Regionalism began in Europe with the European Union (EU) as the model of the first wave of regional integration. Best and Christiansen (2011) entails that the process, which gave birth to regional organisations, had several dynamics. For them, regionalism is characterized by three dynamics: (1) management of independence; (2) management of interdependence; and (3) management of internationalization. First, they reason that states choose to pursue regional integration because they need to manage their independence—"the settling down by newly independent states in their relations between themselves, with the former colonial power, and other powers" (Best and Christiansen 2011: 431). Second, another dynamic that pushes states toward regionalism is the management of interdependence as "this partly refers to economic and social interaction but also issues of peace and security. Regional organization can foster security communities" (Best and Christiansen 2011: 431). Third, management of internationalization refers to "the interrelationship between regional arrangements and the rest of the world" (Best and Christiansen 2011: 431).

After dynamics stimulating states to group or integrate together through regional organization, one should seek to understand the different characteristics of regionalism. Heywood (2011: 482) stresses that regionalism is "a practice of coordinating social, economic or political activities within a geographical region comprising a number of states." He highlights three main characteristics, which might differ slightly within the various forms of regional organization. Institutionally, regionalism "involve[s], the growth of norms, rules and formal structures through which coordination happens" (Heywood 2011: 482). On the other hand, on the affective level, "it implies a realignment of political identities and loyalties from state to the region" (Heywood 2011: 482). Though, regionalism can be achieved through two main modes of integration: *supranationalism* or *intergovernmentalism*. Supranationalism is the strongest form of regional integration, whereby states "surrender" some of their sovereignty to central institutions. The other mode refers to intergovernmentalism, whereby states remain the one according to which regional integration is fostered.

Moreover, regionalism does not correspond to a one-size-fits-all recipe. Thus, different forms of regionalism exist throughout the world. Economic regionalism is the first type. It is defined as "the creation of greater economic opportunities through cooperation among states in the same geographical region" (Heywood 2011: 482). More specifically, economic regionalism induces the creation of trade blocs and the creation of free trade areas, customs unions, and/or common market in between the members. The second form is security regionalism, where emphasis is placed on cooperation to assure protection between the members from their common enemies. Lastly, political regionalism "refers to attempts by states in the same area to strengthen or protect shared values, thereby enhancing their image and reputation and gaining a more powerful diplomatic voice" (Heywood 2011: 482). Arguably, regionalism cannot be analyzed with a single-minded view. Though, even if these three forms tend to present a divided definition or conceptualization of regionalism, one should be aware that regionalism is actually composed of all three forms. The subsequent case study of ASEAN is a very meaningful example of it.

Regionalism, moreover, is a constant evolutionary process. It is recognized that the general framework explained above is still valid for recent cases of regional integration. Nevertheless, the second wave of regionalism that started after the Cold War and gave birth to the case study presented in this chapter entails different specificities. This revolutionized form is commonly known as new regionalism.

Wunderlich (2007: 29) argues that "the period from the late 1980s has witnessed a renewed interest in regionalism theory. Partly responsible for this is a renaissance in regionalisms around the world in form of new regional projects and the revival of old ones." New regionalism emerged in a rather different world context than during the first wave of development of regionalism as "the end of the Cold War unleashed a worldwide structural transformation process. The unipolar moment the US is enjoying, and the acceleration of neoliberal globalization, are re-defining the structural and agentive relations between national, regional and global contexts" (Wunderlich 2007: 30). Wunderlich (2007: 35) also highlights that new regionalism was animated by "the promotion of export growth strategies has advanced the reality of increased economic regionalization." The process of globalization pushed the nations considerably to participate in the world economy be means of increased political, economic, and social interaction and even dependence.

Hettne and Inotai (1994: 3) conceptualizes new regionalism as a process that "presupposes the growth of a regional civil society opting for regional solutions to local and national problems. The implication of this is that not only economic, but also social and cultural networks are developing more quickly than the formal political cooperation at the regional level." Therefore, new regionalism is a novel variance of the traditional form as it mostly embraces "an economic character, and it largely takes the form of the creation of regional trade blocs" (Heywood 2011: 488).

Moreover, new regionalism took into account the downsides of the first wave of regionalism, more precisely the EU. It is not surprising to observe that to avoid blockages that can be observed in the European example, most second wave regional organizations did not take the form of highly supranational institutionalization. They have remained on an intergovernmental level. According to Hettne (1994: 2):

> whereas the old regionalism was created from outside and from above, the new is a more spontaneous process from within and from below (in the sense that the constituent states themselves are main actors" and "whereas the old regionalism was specific with regard to objectives, the new is more comprehensive, multidimensional process.

Even if human rights are broadly discussed around the globe, one should see that its definition is not that well known or is still debated in various parts of the world. This section proposes to clarify what this chapter means when referring to the concept and practice of human rights. It presents an important theory related to human rights.

Donnelly (2011: 496) expresses the idea that human rights are linked to a global regime, which "is based on a strong and widely accepted principles and norms but very weak mechanisms of international implementation." Therefore, one should not be surprised that the best definition is proposed by the United Nations (UN) Office of the High Commissioner of Human Rights (OHCHR 2012):

> Human Rights are rights inherent to all human beings, whatever our nationality, place of residence, sex, national or ethnic origin, color, religion, language or any other status. We are all equally entitled to our human rights without discriminations. These are rights all interrelated, interdependent and indivisible.

Nevertheless, the concept of human rights is always changing. Throughout history, it has changed for the better. Human rights appeared under the influence of Cyrus the Great who freed his slaves and declared that religion should not be enforced on the people. The next major evolution was during ancient Rome, when academics realized that "people tended to follow certain unwritten laws in the course of life, and Roman law was based on rational ideas derived from the nature of things" (United for Human Rights 2014). Clapham (2007: 7) highlights the idea that after recognition of the natural aspect of human rights, a major quantitative improvement occurred when human rights was recognized as belonging to everyone and no longer to a select group of people. Though, it is only with the French Revolution in 1789 that rights were fully recognized as *natural*. Finally, after the widespread and systematic atrocities that were committed during the course of the Second World War, under the influence of the UN, these *natural* rights were recognized as *human rights*.

Indeed, the very concept of human rights has traveled a long and turbulent path, with many different opinions about human rights having emerged. For the purpose of this chapter, the idea of human rights is taken as that which is enshrined in the Universal Declaration of Human Rights, adopted in 1948. The declaration is a general framework for 30 different types of rights. Most of the time, as Donnelly (2011) states, they are categorized under two main categories: (1) civil and political rights; and (2) economic, social, and cultural rights. The category induces "legal protections against abuse by state and seek to ensure political participation for all citizens. They include rights such as equality before the law, protection against arbitrary arrest and detention and political participation" (Donnelly 2011: 496). The second category of rights presented in the declaration is supposed to "guarantee individuals access to essential goods and services and seek to ensure equal social and cultural participation" (Donnelly 2011: 496).

The Human Rights Declaration recognizes three main principles that should be attached to the 30 different rights forming the concept of human rights. These are the principles of *interdependence* and *indivisibility*, *equality* and *nondiscrimination*, and the principle of *rights obligation*. The first principle is understood as:

> all human rights are indivisible, whether they are civil and political rights such as the right to life before the law and freedom of expression . . . are indivisible, interrelated and interdependent. The improvement of one right facilitates advancement of the others. Likewise, the deprivation of one right adversely affects the others.
>
> (UN 2012)

The second principle refers to equality and non-discrimination, which functions as "the principle applies to everyone in relation to all human rights and freedoms and it prohibits discrimination on the basis of a list of non-exhaustive categories such as sex, race, color and so on" (UN 2012). The last principle stipulates that:

> human rights entail both rights and obligations. States assume obligations and duties under international law to respect, to protect and to fulfill human rights ... at the individual level, while we are entitled our human rights, we should respect the human rights of others.
>
> (UN 2012)

Nevertheless, even if the Universal Declaration of Human Rights is considered to be the universal basic framework of rights, one should observe that in South East Asia, it has not ever always been understood in such a way. Some countries tried to develop a parallel doctine. This was not always the case, even in the recent past. They tried to develop a parallel doctrine. During the 1990s, opposition toward human rights as conceived by the West emerged in Asia. One should refer to it as *Asian values*, which are characterized as "while not rejecting the idea of universal human rights, Asian values drew attention to supposed differences between western and Asian value system as part of an argument in favor of taking culture difference into account in formulating human rights" (Heywood 2011: 195).

Eldridge (2002: 36) develops on this concept, so advocated by Mahatir Mohamad and Lee Juan Yew—two former primer ministers of ASEAN's founding countries Malaysia and Singapore. Asian values toward human rights include such elements as "Confucian style values, patron-client relations, personalized authority, dominant political party and strong state" (Eldridge 2002: 36). Asian values were also supposed to correct, in an Asian "way," human rights as "individualism had been emphasized over the interests of the community; rights had been given preferences over duties and civic and political freedoms had been extolled above socio-economic well-being" (Heywood 2011: 195).

Vincent (2010: 138) suggests that clash between Asian values and human rights happened because "South East Asian states were more concerned with social cohesion, community, and solidarist cultural values. Further, Asian states seen the need for social and economic development before any civil or political rights can be established." Nevertheless, Asian values did not prevail in terms of popularity, as they were considered by some responsible for the Asian financial crisis during the late 1990s. Moreover, even if one can understand that human rights is a sensible issue within SEA, the following section makes the link between regionalism and human rights by observing the effects of ASEAN and its policies toward human rights improvement.

ASEAN and Myanmar (Burma)

This section observes if regionalism represented by ASEAN has improved the overall condition of human rights over the past several decades. Particular attention is given to Myanmar (Burma)—an ASEAN member state that has a turbulent human rights record.

ASEAN: A Brief Overview

Before analyzing the possible human rights improvement that one could attribute to regionalism, it is necessary to highlight the main characteristic of regionalism in SEA. Thus, a brief overview of ASEAN is required. ASEAN is composed of 10 member states with a secretariat based in Jakarta, Indonesia. ASEAN was officially created in 1967 when Indonesia, Malaysia, the Philippines, Singapore, and Thailand signed the Bangkok Declaration. The Bangkok Declaration is considered the founding document (of the association) that declared cooperation in common interest areas as its main objective" (Kuhnhardt 2011: 160). The seven objectives laid out by the Bangkok Declaration are still valid today and still aim to:

> accelerate the economic growth, social progress, and cultural development in the region through joint endeavors in the spirit of equality and partnership . . . to promote regional peace and stability through abiding respect for justice and the rule of law in the relationship among countries of the region and adherence to the principles of the United Nations charter . . . to promote active collaboration and mutual assistance . . . to provide assistance to each other in the form of training and research facilities . . . to collaborate more effectively for the greater utilization of agriculture and industries, the expansion of trade . . . to promote Southeast Asian studies . . . [and] to maintain close and beneficial cooperation with existing international and regional organizations.
>
> (Than 2005: 15)

The founding document did not hint at the creation of an institutional framework to be developed for the ASEAN as "having recently achieved independence, nationalism was not discredited in the region" (Wunderlich 2007: 82). Best and Christiansen (2011: 436) state that "regional cooperation was to be built by ASEAN way based on consultation, consensual decision-making and flexibility." Subsequently, Heywood (2011: 489) notes that "ASEAN was a product of the cold war period, its initial interests focusing mainly on security matters, especially those linked to settling intra-regional disputes and resisting superpower influence."

ASEAN received its legal framework during the first Heads of State meeting held in 1976. During the Bali Summit that was also held that same year, the heads of states "signed: the ASEAN Concord and the Treaty of Amenity and Cooperation in Southeast Asia (TAC)" (Wunderlich 2007: 82). Both documents embraced, once again, the principles "of mutual respect, non interference, and peaceful settlement of differences" (Heywood 2011: 489). As Wunderlich (2007: 84) puts it, "while the first document was mainly concerned with the broader norms and principles to be adopted by the signing parties, the ASEAN Concord specifies the details of how to achieve enhanced regional cooperation."

From the 1990s onward, integration was marked by a new impetus as "the member states agreed to create an ASEAN security community, an ASEAN economic community, and an ASEAN socio-cultural Community by 2020" (Heywood 2011: 490). Though, Kuhnhardt (2011: 161) stresses that "so far the structures of ASEAN have remained weak and intergovernmental. ASEAN remains a bureaucratic operation, its visibility largely a function of political summit." Thus, one can understand that ASEAN is a slow-moving boat according to some but one that is certainly gaining momentum and is likely to gain momentum further still in the coming years. With rising optimism over the future of integration and the association, Indonesia, Malaysia, the Philippines, Singapore, Thailand, Brunei, Vietnam, Laos, Myanmar, and Cambodia signed a new charter in 2007.

The new charter was instrumental in bringing a strong human rights policy to ASEAN. During the 2005 Heads of State Summit in Kuala Lumpur, leading political figures of ASEAN urged the creation of an ASEAN Charter. According to their hopes at that time, the charter was supposed to "codify ASEAN norms, rules and values and reaffirm the ASEAN agreements signed and other instruments adopted before the establishment of the ASEAN Charter" (Kuhnhardt 2011: 172). One can compare the ASEAN Charter as a process equivalent in its aims to the European Constitutional Treaty. Few, if any, real challenges stood in the way of the charter entering force, which occurred as recently as 2008.

Interestingly, the charter "provides the legal status and the institutional framework for ASEAN. The Charter codifies ASEAN norms, rules and values, presents accountability and compliance and sets clear targets for ASEAN" (ASEAN Secretariat 2012: 3). After the charter came into force, more traditional ASEAN perspectives regarding the matter of non-interference began to fade considerably, and "ASEAN's movement toward the signing of the ASEAN Charter echoed an incremental and successful experience with the dialectics of deepening and widening ties" (Kuhnhardt 2011: 163). The ASEAN Charter further pledges the creation of a mechanism or mechanisms to foster the improvement of human rights within its member states—creation of the ASEAN Intergovernmental Commission on Human Rights (AICHR) and the drafting of an ASEAN Human Rights Declaration.

ASEAN Policies and Human Rights

Human rights issues have always been controversial for states situated in SEA. As a consequence, ASEAN's position toward human rights has been rather ambiguous in the past. Even if the ASEAN Secretariat engages in self-praise when it says that human rights have always been present through the elaboration of ASEAN, especially since the 1993 Vienna Declaration and program of action whereby ASEAN agreed enthusiastically to promote human rights, one should be aware that in terms of ASEAN's *real* action toward human rights, two key moments can be identified (ASEAN Secretariat 2012: 5).

Human rights development and promotion throughout ASEAN have always been subjected to the "ASEAN way." *What does this mean?* Eldridge (2002: 60) argues that "the consensus principle, which lies at the core of ASEAN's ethos and practice, requires countries to avoid interference in each others' internal affairs and to cooperate in resisting outside intervention." The principle of noninterference, which has been at the core of the regional integration process, allowing ASEAN to overcome its diverse challenges and various crises, did not really allow ASEAN to push a real agenda upon its member states about real action toward human rights. In fact, despite the progress that was made through the formulation and implementation of an ASEAN charter, the association found that diffusing the principles contained within the charter through the various member states did not come without its challenges. Hsien-Li (2011: xii) recognizes that:

for a long time, human rights institutionalization in ASEAN did not seem possible. Even when state-civil society engagement on human rights began in the 1990s, the setting up of a regional mechanism to promote and protect human rights appeared to be several generations away in the future.

ASEAN confined itself to acknowledging the validity of human rights; however, it was unable to enforce them due to the actual debate over them when some of its members were full-fledged democracies and others were still under partial dictatorial/communist ruling or completely authoritarian. Myanmar is one such member state that is located on the dictatorial/authoritarian side of the political ledger (Hsien-Li 2011: 9).

Nevertheless, the ASEAN charter finally gave legal ground to ASEAN to become more proactive in the promotion of human rights within various domains of its member states. Article 14 of the charter declares that "in conformity with the purposes and principles of the ASEAN charter relating to the promotion and protection of human rights and fundamental freedoms, ASEAN shall establish an ASEAN human rights body" (ASEAN Secretariat 2008: 19). This article of the charter induces the creation of AICHR, which became a reality in July 2009. One should perceive AICHR as the main actor within the ASEAN framework with the capacity to improve human rights within the regions. The Secretariat states, "AICHR is ASEAN's commitment to pursue forward looking strategies to strengthen regional cooperation on human rights" (ASEAN Secretariat 2012: 10).

More practically, the AICHR is made of a governing board composed of one representative nominated by its member state. The work realized by the AICHR should respect the principles of consultation and consensus. One could note that the AIHR in the light of the poor Human Rights history of the region is qualitative progress. Nevertheless, in term of international standards for the protection of Human Rights, the AIHR appears to be a weak. It possesses 14 mandates:

The AICHR did not lose any time providing ASEAN member states a declaration of human rights biding on all of them. The Phnom Penh Summit in Cambodia was an ideal occasion for presenting the ASEAN Human Rights Declaration (AHRD). The AICHR wanted "to create a document that met the standards of the United Nation Declaration of Human Rights (UDHR), and also contained an added value for Southeast Asia" (Renshaw 2013: 559). The AHRD possesses similarities with the UDHR such as Articles 3 and 5 "concerning the right to recognition before the law and the right to an enforceable remedy" (Renshaw 2013: 560). ASEAN member states agreed to respect the principles established by the declaration as:

> reaffirming our adherence to the purpose and principles of ASEAN as enshrined in the ASEAN charter, in particular the respect for and promotion and protection of human rights and fundamental freedoms as well as the principles of democracy, the rule of law and good governance.
>
> (ASEAN Secretariat 2012)

The declaration is subdivided into six main parts. One should observe that these main parts are used for categorizing the various rights recognized by the member states. The first part is about general principles such as the principle that "all persons are born free and equal in dignity and rights" (Renshaw 2012). The second part of the declaration presents the civil and political rights to which the citizens of ASEAN are entitled. It is followed by economic, social, and cultural rights and right to development. The last two sections present the articles and their connection with the right to peace and cooperation in the promotion and protection of human rights (Renshaw 2013: 45). Waves of criticism have come up against what has been referred to as an "imperfect" declaration. However, Renshaw (2013: 579) explains that

Table 18.1 The AICHR's 14 Mandates

(1) To develop strategies for the promotion and protection of human rights and fundamental freedoms.	(2) To develop an ASEAN Human Rights Declaration with a view to establishing a framework for human rights cooperation.
(3) To enhance public awareness of human rights among the peoples of ASEAN.	(4) To promote capacity-building for the effective implementation of international standards.
(5) To encourage ASEAN member states to consider acceding to and ratifying international conventions.	(6) To promote the full implementation of ASEAN instruments related to human rights.
(7) To provide advisory services and technical assistance on human rights matters.	(8) To engage in dialogue and consultation with other ASEAN bodies and entities associated with ASEAN.
(9) To consult, as may be appropriate, with other national, regional, and international institutions and entities.	(10) To obtain information from ASEAN member states on the promotion and protection of human rights.
(11) To develop common approaches and positions on human rights matters of interests to ASEAN.	(12) To prepare studies on thematic issues of human rights in ASEAN.
(13) To submit annual report on its activities.	(14) To perform any other tasks as may be assigned to it by the ASEAN foreign ministers.

Source: ASEAN Secretariat (2012: 14–15)

"the great strength of the instrument is that which emanates from the region itself: no Southeast Asian government will ever again be able to deflect criticism on the basis that human rights are an external imposition."

Analyzing Myanmar's Situation

Here, I turn to Myanmar. In doing so, the aim is to determine whether or not regionalism, principally through ASEAN and its human rights policy, allows for the development and strengthening of human rights conditions in this authoritarian state. Bunyanunda (2002: 118) presents the historical path that Myanmar followed under the rule of the military junta (Tatmadaw) "from the 1960s to late 1980s Burma was one of the most closed societies in the world, akin North Korea today" and the country went from authoritarian ruling to another as in 1988, "the Burmese military or Tatmadaw crushed the pro-democratic protests—ushering in a new era of repression under the State Law and Order Restoration (SLORC)" (Bunyanunda 2002: 118). The SLORC is not currently in place, yet represents one of the first major changes that has occurred in Myanmar in terms of human rights since the country's ASEAN accession.

As stated previously but stressed once again by Hsien-Li (2011: 146), "human rights were never originally professed to be a fundamental ASEAN concern, schemes for such protection have for a long time been omitted from ASEAN documents." ASEAN members, even before Myanmar's 1997 accession, have always been interested in cooperating with this dictatorial country. ASEAN, according to its ASEAN way doctrine, invented the principle of constructive engagement. Constructive engagement is defined as "one of its ostensible objectives a liberalization of the human rights situation through close cooperation between Burma and its ASEAN neighbors on a wide range of issues" (Bunyanunda 2002: 119). At a time when Myanmar was considered a pariah state, ASEAN states believed that it was through cooperation that human rights could be improved.

ASEAN's influence over Myanmar has been conceptualized through the principle of constructive engagement, which lasted from 1991 until its ultimate failure was recognized by Thailand. Constructive engagement was perceived by the ASEAN member states as the best way to handle the Myanmar problem and its human rights record, "constructive engagement aimed at creating better relations with potentially hostile and unstable countries, with the ultimate goal of enhancing regional security through socializing aspect of active political and economic cooperation" (Wunderlich 2007: 121). One should understand this principle as an outgrowth from the long-standing ASEAN way or the noninterference principle. The goal was "to encourage the Burmese junta into realizing the benefits of integrating their country into the region and into the mainstream of international community" (Bunyanunda 2002: 118). Constructive engagement allows, according to its supporters, for the improvement of human rights thanks to an economic motivating carrot rather than stick.

The same logic pushed the ASEAN member states to include Myanmar as a full member state of the ASEAN, as highlighted by Wunderlich (2007: 121):

> despite the serious misgivings of Europe and the US. The speed with which Myanmar was integrated into the ASEAN framework is worthy of note. Myanmar signed the Bali Treaty in 1996 and gained observer status the same year. A year later it became full member of ASEAN.

Nevertheless, Myanmar expected that its membership to ASEAN would not force it undertake major reforms thanks to the principle of noninterference, but it quickly realized that the inverse was the case.

One year after Myanmar's accession, Thailand (diplomatically exasperated by the non-progression of its neighbors and being the first side effect of the SLORC internal policies) "proposed flexible engagement, instead of ASEAN's policy of constructive engagement towards Myanmar" and "as the majority of ASEAN members agreed with Myanmar's argument, the concept of flexible engagement was shelved" (Than 2005: 92). Nevertheless, it revealed that several member states were ready to go further in terms of handling ASEAN business. This movement from the member states toward more pro-activism will result in a strong emphasis toward human rights development and strengthening in the ASEAN Charter of 2007, the creation of the AICHR in 2009, and the ASEAN Declaration in 2012.

ASEAN's influence over Myanmar, and more precisely the ruling junta, has been increasing over time. If one looks to Myanmar since the promulgation of the ASEAN charter in 2007, major improvements in term of human rights are clear. The SLORC or, under its new name since the new millennium, the State Peace and Development Council (SPDC), has been replaced by an "officially" elected government, as HRW observes in its 2011 report "Burma in 2010 Held Long Planned Elections. These took place in an atmosphere of intimidation, coercion and widespread corruption, with laws and regulations strongly favoring military controlled parties" (Human Rights Watch 2011). The HRW report in 2012 takes note of "some significant moves by the government, which formed in late March following November 2010 elections" and "freedoms of expression, association, and assembly remain severely curtailed. Although, some media restrictions were relaxed" (Human Rights Watch 2012). The same year, the new Myanmar government freed more than 316 political opponents.

In 2012, the same year as the promulgation of the ASEAN human rights declaration, Myanmar increased the pace of its stride toward a better, more "friendly" human rights state, though the situation remains far from ideal. Amnesty International (2013) highlight that "[i]n April, Myanmar held by elections, which international observers determined to be largely free and fair. The opposition party, the National League for Democracy (NLD), won 43 of the 44 seats it contested and were allowed to take their seats in parliament." Moreover, the former political prisoner Daw Aung San Suu Kyi, who was previously released from house arrest and allowed to travel the previous year, obtained a notable role in the parliamentary committee. The same year, under the effort of ASEAN and due to an apparent will to reform, most international restrictions imposed on Myanmar were actually lifted. Therefore, "although, Myanmar authorities would most probably deny that such acts were the results of Myanmar's membership in ASEAN, there are evidently some grounds to believe that the timing is not entirely coincidental" (Than 2005: 109).

Despite the progress made toward human rights, particularly political and civil rights attained by Myanmar, further improvement is needed as a whole to consider Myanmar as a state truly upholding and respecting human rights. As a consequence, the ASEAN Declaration of Human Rights and Human Rights Watch reports continuously point out "serious problems continuing throughout the country. Basic freedoms of assembly and association improved by laws were enforced inconsistently and in several instances peaceful demonstrators still faced arrest" (Human Rights Watch 2014). Amnesty International (2013) stress that "security forces and other state agents continued to commit human rights violations, including unlawful killings, excessive use of force, arbitrary arrests, torture and other ill-treatment and unlawful confiscation or destruction of property and livelihood."

Conclusion

This chapter examined two major concepts within the field of political science: *regionalism* and *human rights*. In doing so, the following question was posed: *Does ASEAN as a regional organization trigger human rights improvements within Myanmar?* The theoretical component within this chapter stresses that human rights are globally accepted according to the principles laid out in the United Nations Human Rights Declaration (Donnelly 2011). It is recognized that ASEAN has had a significantly positive impact on the human rights of one of its member states—Myanmar. Nevertheless, it also recognizes that the hypothesis from the case study might not be applicable in other situations. Thus, it is limited in the scope of research due to ASEAN's recent more proactive policy toward human rights.

To be sure, the concept of human rights have been debated to a great extent within the political realms of ASEAN member states and have certainly affected the daily lives of many, if not all, of its member states—including those that are currently classified as dictatorial/authoritarian states. They have been debated as well in light of the "Asian values" debate in which human rights have been largely perceived as Western ideals that have inherently failed to take Asian cultural and social factors into account (Eldridge 2002). Subsequently, the chapter stresses the importance for further research to continue the investigation in the years to come with the aim of determining whether or not the changes undertaken by Myanmar are lasting—and if ASEAN will become even more proactive toward human rights promotion and protection.

References

Amnesty International (2013) *Annual Report 2013: The State of the World's Human Rights*, London: Amnesty International.

ASEAN Secretariat (2008) *ASEAN Charter*, Jakarta: ASEAN.

ASEAN Secretariat (2012) *AICHR: What You Need to Know*, Jakarta: ASEAN.

Best, E. and Christiansen, T. (2011) "Regionalism in International Affairs," in J. Baylis (Ed.), *The Globalization of World Politics: An Introduction to International Relations*, Oxford: Oxford University Press, pp. 434–449.

Bunyanunda, M. (2002) "Burma, ASEAN, and Human Rights: The Decade of Constructive Engagement, 1991–2001," *Stanford Journal of East Asian Affairs*, 2: 118–135.

Clapham, A. (2007) *Human Rights: A Very Short Introduction*, Oxford: Oxford University Press.

Donnelly, J. (2011) "Human Rights," In J. Baylis (Ed.), *The Globalization of World Politics: An Introduction to International Relations*, Oxford: Oxford University Press, pp. 506–521.

Eldridge, P. (2002) *The Politics of Human Rights in Southeast Asia*, London: Routledge.

Hettne, B. and Inotai, A. (1994) *The New Regionalism: Implications for Global Development and International Security*, Helsinski: UNU World Institute for Development Economics Research.

Heywood, A. (2011) *Global Politics*, Basingstoke: Palgrave Macmillan.

Hsien-Li, T. (2011) *The ASEAN Inter-Governmental Commission on Human Rights: Institutionalizing Human Rights in South East Asia*, Cambridge: Cambridge University Press.

Human Rights Watch (2011) *World Report 2011: Burma*, New York: HRW.

Human Rights Watch (2012) *World Report 2012: Burma*, New York: HRW.

Human Rights Watch (2014) *World Report 2014: Burma*, New York: HRW.

Kuhnhardt, L. (2011) *Region-Building*, New York: Berghahn.

OHCHR (2012) *What Are Human Rights?* Geneva: OHCHR.

Renshaw, C. (2013) "The ASEAN Human Rights Declaration," *Human Rights Law Review*, 13(3): 557–579.

Than, M. (2005) *Myanmar in ASEAN: Regional Cooperation Experience*, Singapore: Institute of South East Asian Studies.

UN (2012) *What are human rights?* Available at: http://www.ohchr.org/en/issues/pages/whatarehuman rights.aspx

United for Human Rights (2014) *A Brief History of Human Rights*, Los Angeles, CA: United for Human Rights.

Vincent, A. (2010) *The Politics of Human Rights*, Oxford: Oxford University Press.

Wunderlich, J-U. (2007) *Regionalism, Globalization, and International Order: Europe and Southeast Asia*, Farnham: Ashgate.

Index